THE FUTURE OF JOURNALISM IN THE ADVANCED DEMOCRACIES

The Future of Journalism in the Advanced Democracies

Edited by
PETER J. ANDERSON
and
GEOFF WARD
University of Central Lancashire, UK

ASHGATE

Published by
Ashgate Publishing Limited
Gower House
Croft Road
Aldershot
Hampshire GU11 3HR
England

Ashgate Publishing Company
Suite 420
101 Cherry Street
Burlington, VT 05401-4405
USA

Ashgate website: http://www.ashgate.com

British Library Cataloguing in Publication Data
The future of journalism in the advanced democracies
   1. Journalism - Social aspects
   I. Anderson, Peter J., 1954- II.Ward, Geoff
   302.2'3

Library of Congress Cataloging-in-Publication Data
The future of journalism in the advanced democracies / edited by Peter J. Anderson and Geoff Ward
      p. cm.
   Includes bibliographical references and index.
   ISBN-13: 978-0-7546-4404-0
   ISBN-10: 0-7546-4404-9
   ISBN-13: 978-0-7546-4405-7
   ISBN-10: 0-7546-4405-7
  1. Journalism--Great Britain--History--21st century. 2. Journalism--Developed countries--History--21st century. 3. Press and politics--Great Britain--History--21st century. 4. Press and politics--Developed countries--History--21st century. I. Anderson, Peter J., 1954- II. Ward, Geoff, 1954-

   PN5119.F88 2006
   072'.0905--dc22

               2006020605
ISBN-13: 978-07546-4404-0
ISBN-13: 978-0-7546-4405-7

Printed and bound in Great Britain by TJ International Ltd, Padstow, Cornwall.

Contents

Part 3: Comparative Perspectives from Other Large Advanced Democracies

Preface

Omissions, Commissions and Thanks

Every book of this nature invites questions as to the inclusion and exclusion of content. We would like briefly to explain our approach here.

This multinational project focuses on the news media of the world's most powerful advanced democracies, currently six in all. It does so because this is a group of states, from Europe, the Americas and Asia, that ticks several useful boxes from a comparative point of view – their advanced status economically and technologically, their political power and the fact that they are all liberal democracies. The US has unparalleled global reach, both economically and politically. Japan still rivals it in terms of economic influence. The UK, Germany, France and Italy are the key powers at the heart of the EU. Arguably, such power is always in need of healthy journalism. It is required to keep the peoples of such states informed as to what is done in their name and, some would say, their governments in check.

The six countries that we examine offer fascinating and in some cases disturbing insights on the ways in which journalism is changing in the twenty-first century. The reasons for the core focus on the UK are explained in detail in the introductory chapter.

We are aware also of the way the world is changing. In the view of many, for example, India will be among the large economically and technologically advanced democracies within the next half-century or less and would then be included automatically in a book of this nature.

We would have liked to include two other things of importance, the first of which would have been a larger study of the current and developing situation regarding diversity in journalism employment. We commissioned two people to provide this for us but the pressure of their other commitments prevented either from delivering by the deadline. The material that we have included, most particularly in Chapter 4, does a useful job concisely, nevertheless. Second, we had hoped for more chapters from women contributors. Four women originally were involved with the project but pressure of work forced three to withdraw before the end.

On the other hand, as some people left, other excellent writers joined and the project has benefited enormously from their presence. We are particularly pleased to have tempted Anthony Weymouth out of retirement to join the project. Besides co-authoring Chapter 2, he stepped in to edit four chapters when one of the editors' international commitments sent him flying around the globe at crucial moments. He has performed also an enormously valuable role both with regard to some of the project's administration and with regard to the identification of areas that needed to be covered in addition to the original agenda for the book.

We would like to thank the Faculty for providing a six-month sabbatical for one of the editors and for meeting some of the project's costs; also Mike Green, for supplying the paperback cover photograph and sorting out troublesome software gremlins that struck, with immaculate timing, right on the deadline. We owe another debt of gratitude to Cathy Darby and Delwyn Swingewood for their valuable assistance during the proof-reading stage. Finally, we appreciate greatly the patience, support and courtesy throughout of the editors at Ashgate.

Peter J. Anderson
Geoff Ward
Department of Journalism, University of Central Lancashire

March 2006

Notes on Editors and Contributors

Editors

Peter J. Anderson is the Journalism Research Coordinator at the University of Central Lancashire. He has published a variety of books, articles and book chapters on both communication and politics, including (with Anthony Weymouth) (1999), *Insulting the Public? The British Press and the European Union* (Harlow: Longman); (with Christopher Williams and Georg Wiessala, eds) (2000), *New Europe in Transition* (London: Continuum); and (1996) *The Global Politics of Power, Justice and Death* (London: Routledge). He taught previously at the universities of Lancaster and Southampton and runs a small consultancy on the EU, the news media and the citizenry.

Geoff Ward currently is Principal Lecturer in Journalism at one of the UK's two oldest journalism schools, now part of the University of Central Lancashire, and is responsible for the university's international journalism programmes. He was a journalist for 25 years before joining the lecturing staff at Preston in 1992. He was a senior news sub-editor at the *Daily Mail* in Manchester for 12 years, a reporter for an independent news agency and has worked for a number of regional daily newspapers. He has also edited a group of weekly newspapers.

Project Consultant

Anthony Weymouth was a Principal Lecturer at the University of Central Lancashire until 1997 and has many years of experience teaching and writing about the news media. Latterly a freelance writer and consultant on the media, he has written a variety of books, articles and papers including (with Bernard Lamizet, eds) (1996), *Markets and Myths: Forces for Change in the European Media* (Harlow: Longman); (with Peter J. Anderson) (1999), *Insulting the Public? The British Press and the European Union* (Harlow: Longman); (with Stanley Henig, eds.) (2001), *The Kosovo Crisis* (Harlow: Reuters).

Contributors

Robert Beers is a Senior Lecturer in Journalism at the University of Central Lancashire. He is the winner of many US national and regional awards, including two Gold Medals at the New York International Film Festival and an Emmy. He has been news manager of WTVJ/CBS Miami. After being hired by CBS News as a reporter to run their Miami Bureau, he covered Central and South America. He covered the conflicts in El Salvador and Nicaragua for CBS News in the 1980s. Subsequently he went to BSP Americas and did work for Knight-Ridder, CBS and the National Education Association, among many others.

Heinz Brandenburg (PhD, Trinity College Dublin) is a Lecturer in Politics at the University of Aberdeen. His teaching and research focuses on the field of political communication. His interests include the application of quantitative methods to the study of electoral campaigns and political rhetoric, the relationship between the military and the media, and the alleged value of online media for political deliberation. His recent work has been published in journals such as the *Harvard International Journal of Press/Politics*, *Irish Political Studies* and the *Journal of Elections, Public Opinion and Parties*.

John Drury has had a long and distinguished career as a journalist and television executive. He has won many plaudits, including a British Press Award (as a newspaper journalist with *The Sunday Times*), the Sony Best Documentary award (twice), a Royal Television Society award for Best Documentary and has been a BAFTA runner-up for Best Factual Drama. His wide experience includes periods as a Head of Factual Programmes at Granada International and the BBC, as well as a spell as Commercial Director of the BBC's Manchester Network Centre. Currently he is CEO of Top Notch Productions and Acrobat Ltd and also works part-time at the University of Central Lancashire, where he contributes to its broadcasting teaching programmes.

Paul Egglestone is a Senior Lecturer in Television at the University of Central Lancashire, leading an International Documentary MA and teaching television at undergraduate and postgraduate levels. He also teaches online journalism. He still makes programmes and writes music. A former independent producer working for BBC, ITV and Sky on regional and national programming, he now focuses on international documentary and digital content generation for broadband and mobile dissemination.

Julie Freer is Course Leader of the BA (Hons) Journalism programme at the University of Central Lancashire. She graduated in history and politics from Warwick University in 1980. She worked in UK regional newspapers for 20 years before moving into teaching. She has taught previously at Salford University and is a member of the Higher Education Academy.

Knut Hickethier is Professor of Media Studies in the Institute for Media and Communications Studies at the University of Hamburg. His work focuses on film theory, television theory and the history of broadcasting and television in Germany and Europe. His publications include: (1998), *Geschichte des deutschen Fernsehens in Deutschland* (Stuttgart: Metzler); (2003), *Einführung in die Medienwissenschaft*

(Stuttgart: Metzler); (ed.) (2005), *Kriminalfilm* (Stuttgart: Reclam); (ed.) (2006), *Komiker, Komödianten, Komödiendarsteller* (Remscheid: Gardez Verlag).

Guy Hodgson is a Senior Lecturer in Journalism at the University of Central Lancashire and continues to write on a regular basis about international and Premiership football for the *Independent on Sunday*. He has been a journalist for more than 30 years, during which time he has worked for the BBC, *The Independent* and the *Independent on Sunday*. He was golf and tennis correspondent for the *Independent on Sunday* and northern sports correspondent for *The Independent*, during which time he also reported on two Olympic Games.

Raymond Kuhn is Professor of Politics at Queen Mary, University of London. He has written widely on the French media and on political communication in France and Britain. His 1995 monograph, *The Media in France* (London: Routledge), is the standard work in English on the subject. In 2002 he co-edited with Erik Neveu a book entitled *Political Journalism: New Challenges, New Practices* (London: Routledge).

Paolo Mancini is full Professor at the Dipartimento Istituzioni e Soceità, Università di Perugia. His major publications in English include: (with David Swanson) (1996), *Politics, Media and Modern Democracy* (New York: Praeger); and (with Dan Hallin) (2004), *Comparing Media Systems* (Cambridge: Cambridge University Press). With this book Hallin and Mancini won the 2005 Goldsmith Award from Harvard University.

François Nel has been a Senior Lecturer in the Journalism Department at the University of Central Lancashire since 2000 and currently is the Course Leader for the Journalism Leaders programme. He gained experience in radio, television and newspapers, before emigrating from Zimbabwe to South Africa in 1991. He has been a head of department at the Cape Peninsula University of Technology in Cape Town. He remains an active freelance journalist. He has authored two books for Oxford University Press: *Writing for the Media in Southern Africa* (3rd edition in 2005) and *The South African Style Guide*, a usage and reference dictionary for media writers. He holds fellowships from the Poynter Institute in the US, and from the Media Institute of Southern Africa, Namibia. His other awards include the South African Specialist Press Association's top award for magazine journalism.

Alan Rawlinson is Course Leader for the MA in Online Journalism at the University of Central Lancashire. He is a former print reporter, columnist and sub-editor with the Weekly News Group on Merseyside (Swale Press), the *Altrincham and Sale Guardian*, the *Evening Leader* (North Wales Newspapers) and the *Shropshire Star*. He has also worked as a freelance page designer and sub-editor across North and Mid-Wales and the north-west Midlands. He became a university lecturer in 1996 and in 2000/1 was also employed as a writer by <about.com>, the New York web publisher.

Mike Ward is Head of the Department of Journalism at the University of Central Lancashire. A former BBC journalist, Mike writes, broadcasts and provides consultancy on digital and online journalism. His widely selling book *Journalism Online* was published by Focal Press in 2002. He was recently instrumental in bringing the Johnston Press Chair in Digital Journalism to the department.

Yoshikazu Yada has worked as a journalist for the *Asahi Shimbun* for around 20 years. He has been an economic correspondent covering the car, machinery and electronic manufacturing industries in Japan. He also covered macro economic policy during the Koizumi Cabinet. In addition, he has worked for the weekly magazine *AERA*, published by the *Asahi*, as a staff writer and as an editor. In connection with this he launched the magazine *AERA English*, which was intended to be a new bilingual news magazine in Japanese and English. Currently he works as an editor for the Saturday edition, *be*.

Part 1
The Key Issues Facing Journalism in the Advanced Democracies

Chapter 1

Introduction

Peter J. Anderson (with Geoff Ward)

Introduction

Much of the debate about journalism is conducted within two largely separate camps, those of academics and journalists. Even then, the discussion is a lopsided one, with academics debating the key issues much more than journalists seem inclined to do. This is a book which attempts to rectify the imbalance and stimulate exchanges of ideas and opinions within the professional world of journalists that are at least as wide and as vigorous as those within the media-observing community of academics. This work sets out to bring the two groups together, both in terms of the people who write it and the common 'language' in which it is written, one which will avoid unnecessary jargon without any sacrifice of intellectual rigour.

Journalism is a much maligned profession. Politicians in the UK and elsewhere frequently accuse the media of sensationalism, trivialisation, narrowness of focus and straightforward factual inaccuracy. However, the same politicians employ 'spin doctors' to try to generate favourable publicity, submit themselves to media training in order to learn how to communicate effectively on radio and television, sometimes announce new initiatives to the media before parliaments have been informed, are not reluctant to schedule major announcements to fit in with the agendas of prime time news programmes and frequently are hungry for media appearances when they have a view or a policy to sell.

Indeed, journalists and the news media for which they work are the main point of contact between politicians and the people whom they are supposed to represent. The truth of this assertion could not be better illustrated than by the furious altercation between the UK government and the BBC in 2004 over allegations that the Blair government 'sexed up' a key document which it used to sell the idea of the war against Iraq to the British electorate. The general population does not tend to read political manifestos or look at the details of the speeches delivered by politicians throughout the year. Such activities are still the preserve of a minority within electorates and most people retain their reliance on the reports and interpretations produced by journalists when trying to keep abreast of political events. Equally, as government becomes ever more complex and time-consuming, politicians do not, for the most part, have very much opportunity to communicate directly with significant numbers of the electorate and rely on the media to provide a channel through which they can contact potentially thousands or millions of the voting public.

In addition, the following facts should be considered: firstly, the news media overall employ still significant numbers of journalists to report on those activities of politicians deemed newsworthy; secondly, even with decreasing circulations, the populations of democracies such as the UK still buy newspapers in their millions; and thirdly, the television and radio audiences for major political events such as the Iraqi or Afghan wars, or the attempted impeachment of former US President Bill Clinton, encompass millions around the globe. It can therefore be stated with confidence that journalism sits at the heart of the political process. It is expected to carry on its shoulders some of the most crucial responsibilities of the democratic societies.

However, when referring to the political process, it is important to note that we do not see political journalism as pertaining solely to the reporting of parliamentary news, for example. Throughout, the term political journalism will refer to reporting and commentary on politics in its widest sense, whereby the latter:

> ... can be defined as the processes by which decisions are made which regulate people's freedoms, rights, obligations and access to resources within local, national and global society. It determines everything from the way in which people are allowed to treat animals, to the amount of income they are allowed to earn, to their right to engage in religious worship, to their chances of being killed by acts of terrorism and war, or tortured or executed by the state. It is therefore the most fundamental concern of everyone's daily lives and is ignored at their peril (Anderson, 2003).

The heterogeneous development of the media in the post-1945 period is such that there is not simply one type of journalism that occupies the position within the political process referred to above. The higher end of the market (that represented by *The Guardian* or *The Times* in the UK, or *The Washington Post* and *The New York Times* in the US, for example) is supposedly in the business of providing predominantly news and comment that is sufficiently serious and detailed to allow 'news consumers' to make informed, objective judgements about political/economic/social issues and events. It is generally the rule that the more newspapers or broadcast programmes adopt popular tabloid-type news agendas and methods of presentation, then the more difficult it becomes to distinguish much of their news reporting and comment writing from entertainment, or 'infotainment'. It would therefore be easy to dismiss popular tabloid-style news media as non-serious players in the political process.[1] But the scandal, sex and celebrity-focused UK *Sun*, for example, makes claims for the influence of its usually very limited amounts of political reporting and comment that would be less surprising were they to come from a newspaper at the quality end of the market. Those claims are backed up by widely leaked information from inside the Westminster village that one of the key factors shaping Prime Minister Blair's caution about joining the EU's single currency has been his fear of *The Sun*'s

---

1   However, it should be realised that, while there are very distinct examples of popular and quality news providers, there are also some who inhabit a middle ground between the two. Britain's *Daily Mail* newspaper or *News at Ten* TV programme are examples of the latter.

opposition and its alleged ability to shape the voting intentions of millions of people. Equally, increasingly the UK quality newspapers are accused of adopting styles of presentation, news values and story contents that have been imported from the popular press.

There is therefore clearly a crossover 'zone' where both the popular and the quality press and their broadcast equivalents engage in reporting and commentary on matters of a serious political, economic or social nature. While this zone is one that, in countries like the UK, is much more substantially inhabited by the quality newspapers and BBC news programmes like *Newsnight*, if the claims of *The Sun*'s influential former chief political correspondent, Trevor Kavanagh, are to be believed, then it is not the proportion of a paper or programme that is devoted to serious news that matters in terms of political influence but the size and nature of its readership/ audience. In short, in terms of its impacts upon political events, it could be argued that popular journalism can be even more significant than the so-called 'quality' or 'highbrow' journalism and needs therefore to be treated just as seriously.

But as technologies become ever more numerous and sophisticated, traditional print and broadcast media are no longer the only conveyers of serious news. The Internet is now heavily populated by news websites run by anyone from dedicated amateurs through to news organisations of high professional status like the BBC. While, as later chapters will show, electronic journalism is still in its relative infancy, it does provide entirely new ways of accessing recent and breaking news 24 hours a day. Potentially it could be argued that the Internet provides a channel through which news provision can be truly democratised. Despite his enormous power and influence within the print and broadcast media, for example, Rupert Murdoch's newspapers and television stations can find their view of the news world challenged and contradicted by anti-capitalist news sites on the web that people all over the world are able to view whenever they want and without charge. As will be shown later, such sites have not as yet achieved sufficient trust or status to enable them to attract viewers in the numbers that would be required for them to provide an electorally significant alternative to the existing primary news media. But clearly the potential for electronic journalism is enormous. Even at its currently relatively low levels of take-up it provides an extra string to journalism's bow and supplies it with the means by which it can reach those news consumers whose clear preference is for computer-based news provision.

So, having demonstrated something of the range and current importance of journalism, it would be useful to explain the precise nature of the concerns that lie at the heart of our analysis of this most crucial profession.

The Aims and Scope of the Book

This book is being written when the world of communication is undergoing a period of rapid and often quite fundamental change. The technological developments of the last ten to fifteen years – perhaps symbolised most dramatically by former Russian President Boris Yeltsin's use of satellite news link-ups during the Moscowled resistance to the attempted coup by Communist hardliners in 1991, the dramatic growth of the Internet and the highly competitive news environment created by the advent of digital multichannel broadcasting – have both accelerated greatly the speed at which news can be transmitted and affected significantly the range of issues that can be covered. At the same time, the organisational structures within which news is gathered, selected and distributed have been undergoing fundamental changes, with the growth of conglomeration and cross-media ownership, which have been seen as serious cause for concern from the point of view of the media's role within democratic societies. Politically, the US has become even more of a dominant global force after the massacres of its citizens in September 2001 than it was during the previous 'American century'. Its increasingly interventionist policies mean that it is more important than ever before that the American public has available to it a balanced and effective news media that can enable it to make informed electoral judgements on what its President does in its name. The evidence suggests that such a facility is missing, as a later chapter will show. The increasingly complex range and nature of issues that confront the world's citizens as a result of scientific and technological progress – from cloning to the rights and wrongs of the genetic modification of foodstuffs – place an ever more demanding requirement on journalists to be able to mediate and explain adequately the key issues to their readers, viewers and listeners.

This book is a response to the challenges that all of this change presents. For example, one of the accusations frequently made against the advent of multichannel television in the US is that the increased competition that it has produced has helped reduce the resources available to the traditional quality terrestrial news broadcast programmes and helped push the news agenda of television in an ever more populist direction. One of the core questions that we will ask, therefore, is: *to what extent is traditional hard news losing ground to soft news[2] across the media of the advanced world and what can be done to reverse this trend if this is a serious problem?*

Rightly or wrongly, conglomeration and cross-media ownership have been accused of being likely to reduce the range of issues covered. Equally the charge is heard that multichannel television makes it too easy to flip channels whenever a complex issue is discussed on a news programme and that this knowledge acts as a pressure to reduce the depth of coverage of such issues in a competitive multichannel media environment. The second core question we will ask, therefore, is: *to what extent is the range and depth of coverage of news issues within the advanced democracies adequate for the purpose of ensuring that electorates are adequately informed about the world around them?*

---

2   What is meant by hard news and soft news will be explained in detail shortly. For the moment it is sufficient to note that the former term is used here to refer to news that has a significant political, economic or social impact on people's daily lives and well-being, while the latter refers to coverage of sport, celebrity, music, and so on. The term 'hard news' is used interchangeably with 'news journalism' throughout the book.

Equally, it has been argued that the increasing concentration of media ownership raises serious questions about the extent to which it is possible for viewers, readers and listeners to have access to a diverse and balanced presentation of the news. In the UK, for example, it is possible already for a reader of the Murdoch newspapers *The Sun* or *The Times* to switch on their televisions and rely on the Murdoch television channel Sky for their broadcast news, thereby seeing the world entirely through the eyes of Murdoch-owned news producers. Under former Prime Minister Berlusconi the problem was far more acute for consumers of the Italian media. The third core question that we will ask, therefore, is: *to what extent is it possible to access balanced presentations of the news within the various advanced democracies within this study?*

However, in addressing this last question the chapter concerned with the US will confront the arguments for balance head-on with the counter-arguments of those who believe that there is a strong case for what might be termed 'benevolent bias'.

It is of course possible to argue that there are other questions about journalism of at least equal importance that should be asked in a book like this. However, given the range and depth of material that will be covered in the chapters in which the three core questions will be addressed, a firm limit has to be set on the overall number of questions to be asked. Why we believe that these are the most important questions will become apparent in the next section. Many of the additional questions have already been discussed in some depth in the US (see McChesney, 2000, for example) and in the UK (see Lloyd, 2004, for example).

In addressing the three questions we will be looking at everything from local newspapers and local radio stations through to global media players such as the BBC or News Corporation. We will do this first of all within the UK and will then move out into a comparative focus. This will bring in the very different media markets of countries like Italy, where Berlusconi's democratically problematic role and influence during his period as Prime Minister will be examined, together with those of Germany and the US. As will be seen later on, currently there are some particularly worrying trends affecting journalism within the latter.

Where we find that there are deficiencies in the media in respect of the answers provided to each of the above three questions, at the end of the book we will attempt to provide a means of resolving the problems that those deficiencies create.

Before we proceed any further, however, it is necessary to define precisely what it is that we mean by journalism within this study.

Defining Journalism

Past studies have provided a range of answers to the question of how journalism should be defined and clearly the discussion so far has implied some very specific understandings of the term. We have defined already what we understand to be involved within a specific *variety* of journalism, namely *political* journalism. We now wish to look a little more at the root idea of journalism itself, from which the varieties spring. At its most *basic*, journalism can be defined simply as the practice of news gathering and presentation. Precisely because this definition is basic, it is also unsatisfactory, telling us little about the sophistication of much modern-day journalism. The interesting questions about any form of journalism relate to issues concerning the *types* of news gathered, the *range* of events and issues covered and the *manner* in which news is presented in terms of its *interpretation, analysis and context.* The focus here, for the most part, is upon journalism of the most important kind in terms of its subject matter and potential consequences. For the initial purposes of our discussion here we shall refer to this kind of reporting as hard news journalism. By this we mean journalism that covers the political/economic/social issues *that affect significantly people's lives* at a global, regional, national or local level within one or several parts of the world. For now it is perhaps sufficient to say that it is journalism that can be recognised as having the primary intent *to inform and encourage reflection, debate and action* on political, social and economic issues.

The huge swathes of journalism that fall outside our definition (as represented by much of the journalism pertaining to periodicals, sport, music, popular culture in general, and so on – often referred to as the coverage of 'soft' news) are not unimportant. Nor are they necessarily irrelevant to many of the themes and issues pursued in this book. Indeed, for reasons that will be examined in that chapter, we have included a piece on sports journalism which looks very specifically at its relevance, among other things, to helping provide the very financial foundation upon which hard news journalism depends. In other words, we are not adopting some elitist, or paternalistic, viewpoint that would deny audiences the possibilities of engagement in the worlds of, for instance, entertainment, celebrity, gossip and the off-beat. We acknowledge also that the important can, and should, be made interesting and that the interesting can be often important. Ultimately, however, it is necessary to get down to basics. It is a simple truth that the amount of *freedom* available for the pursuit of activities such as sport, art and popular culture is determined by the key political, social and economic decisions, ideas and movements that govern societies. This was usefully demonstrated by the discrimination against black athletes during the apartheid period in South Africa, or the difficulties involved in trying to stage theatrical productions seriously criticising the Soviet Union for most of its existence. The journalism that covers these types of issues must be regarded as being the most important for people's daily lives, even if this is not appreciated currently by many of (particularly) the younger readers, listeners and viewers.

This said, we have some problems with the term 'hard news'. It is taken often as denoting what many teens and twenties see as a staid and stodgy form of news communication, where the subject matter is dull and the style of presentation rather formal and uninspiring. Hard news, as we define it, might be perceived by middle-class under-thirties as the type of news that they would expect to find in whatever quality newspaper many of their parents would buy. Many are much more inspired by the 'now', informalised journalism of *Heat* in the UK or its overseas equivalents, where the focus is on accessible language, vibrant formats and a mishmash of (appropriately) hot topics centred around celebrity, lifestyle, music, and so on. In addition, it is notable how some of the key ideas that have developed and been debated within the broad spectrum of postmodernism have been filtering down to the young via film-makers (*The Matrix* is an obvious case in point) and others who feed into the media-led dimensions of youth culture. This contemporary philosophical mode of thought seems to have spawned new, often globally linked (via the Internet and other evolving technologies) protest movements against globalisation, environmental abuse, and so on, which have in common a cultural contempt for traditional sources of social organisation and power, combined with a rather hazy view of what should replace them. This creates additional problems for the communication of 'hard' news in so far as the young often equate it precisely with these, as they see it, discredited power sources and structures.

The Problems of the Present and Looking to the Future

Bearing in mind these problems, in thinking of the journalism of the future, one of the ideas that needs debating is how far it is possible to reinvigorate the language and presentational formats of traditional 'hard news' journalism (which we will refer to also as *news journalism* in common with practice elsewhere) in order to attract a wider audience for its subject matter without debasing the core quality of the fact and informed opinion dimensions at its heart. One of the things that could be investigated is the idea that it is possible to weave the styles that characterise news journalism and soft news styles and even content together (in a rather more successful manner than that attempted by, for example, *The Daily Mirror* in the UK in the wake of the 9/11 attacks in the US) in such a way as to convey successfully the core concerns raised by 'traditional' news journalism stories to a much wider and inclusive audience than previously has been possible. It would be useful also to look at ways of communicating the kinds of stories news journalism traditionally selects that provide for their conversion into a form where their importance can be seen and noted by younger (as well as older) audiences, instead of their minds being instantly turned off on the grounds that political news, for example, equals just the irrelevant ramblings of a discredited establishment.

What we are talking about here is only 'dumbing down' if it is done badly. At its best this is a very sophisticated and extremely demanding form of the journalist's art that balances delicately the measured use of soft news techniques with the need to get across to readers, viewers or listeners the most crucial issues that arise within the sphere of news journalism. To a degree it is being experimented with already – from the use of the visually and linguistically highly expressive, 'put it in a nutshell' journalism of former BBC political editor Andrew Marr and his successor Nick Robinson, to some of the visually arresting, semi-popular tabloid formats used to convey hard news on the front pages of the UK quality newspaper *The Independent*, for example, during and after the 2003 war against Iraq. The need is to think through the furthest extremes to which this technique can be taken before cracking and collapsing into what is frequently derided as 'dumbing down'.

We will be suggesting in the final chapter of the book a means by which all of this could be debated in a better resourced and potentially more effective manner than has been the case so far.

The focus needs to be very precisely on how to make serious news more accessible without compromising it in terms of its range of chosen subject matter, or the presentation of its complexity and context. The concern is the most crucial conundrum at the heart of contemporary journalism, that of how to begin to reverse what critics of the media have argued to be a distinct trend that increasingly is diluting the quantity of news journalism within even its historically most committed providers, such as the quality print press.

The fact that traditional news journalism has been losing ground to what frequently has been referred to as its soft news counterpart is worrying, but not entirely unexpected. In addition to the influences of popular youth culture (Hobsbawm, 1995) and the diluted and often misunderstood posturings of postmodernism, it is a frequently observed phenomenon that freedom is something that is easily taken for granted and even squandered by those who have not had to fight for it or experienced its loss. Equally, it could be argued that the growth of Western prosperity during the last decades of the twentieth century (that paradoxically was won by a more politically aware generation than the present) has taken much of the 'sting' and interest out of politics for the beneficiaries. The convergence of political parties around the centre in countries like Britain has exacerbated this phenomenon. Nevertheless these disparate and deep-rooted problems should not be seen as causes for despair but rather measures of the heights which journalism has to scale if it is both to preserve then reclaim and expand its audience for serious news. This is the fundamental challenge. This book attempts to point the way towards some of the solutions.

Turning to the second of our core questions outlined at the beginning, the alleged problem of the inadequate *breadth and depth* of the serious news agenda that is set across the media's different arms will be examined. The question of the numbers and types of issues which touch ordinary people's daily lives that are *not* covered within one or more of the several branches of journalism that make a claim to covering serious news is of course an interesting one. That which the media leave out of their news agendas within advanced democracies frequently tells us much about the underlying ideologies and commercial pressures that shape currently dominant news values (and the chapter about the US will provide a useful case study in this regard). Those values in turn obviously are crucial because they shape the version of 'the world and its problems' that is communicated to the man and woman on the street. If things are being left out that are important to people, we both need to know why and how.

Obviously, it should be expected that there will be variations between the different countries and cultures that the book will examine in terms both of the ideologies and the commercial pressures shaping dominant news values. One of the book's functions will be to note and analyse these variations.

However, it is not enough simply to look at the range and depth of issues that are presented to audiences. Turning to the third of our core questions addressed at the beginning of the chapter, it is possible, obviously, for there to be an extremely wide range of in-depth news coverage within a newspaper, or other news medium, which is cast in such a biased manner that the reader might well have been better off being left completely uninformed for all the similarity to the 'real world' that the reports might bear. Inevitably, therefore, we are brought face to face with the problem of objectivity. Much as the highly opinionated journalism of *The Sun*, the *Daily Mail* and *The Daily Mirror* might be disliked by many, British notions of free speech mean that it would be unreasonable to insist that they aimed for the kind of balance that the BBC is required to pursue within its overall coverage. The traditional way of dealing with the bias of particular news providers has been to argue that as long as there is a diversity of newspapers and other news media available, then the requirements of democracy are met because citizens can check off one set of reports and views against another and make up their own minds. However, the problem with this approach is that many news 'consumers' simply buy the newspaper that fits their views and do not bother to cross-check what they read with accounts provided by other news providers. There is, in addition, the previously mentioned problem of the multi-ownership of news providers with regard to people like Rupert Murdoch and Silvio Berlusconi.

As pointed out at the beginning of the chapter, therefore, our concern will be to establish the extent to which balance is lacking across the advanced democracies that we discuss and, where appropriate, to propose remedies to deal with any deficiencies.

Together, we see our three questions as deriving from the most fundamental requirements for the media dimension of the *public sphere*, Habermas' compelling view of what democracies need at their heart if they are to provide a satisfactory means for the public fully to participate in the governance of their societies (Habermas, 2002). This is why they are put forward here as the potential core of the book. The analysis that occurs during the course of Chapters 2, 3 and 4 will confirm the extent to which that potential is realised as an important by-product of the main discussion. The content of the three chapters is explained below.

Setting the Background Context for the Case Study Chapters

Chapters 2, 3 and 4 will provide the background context for the case study chapters that follow them, as well as evaluating in more detail than here the appropriateness of focusing on the three questions already outlined. The three chapters will provide an analysis of the range and significance of the changes that journalism has been undergoing in recent years and will assess the extent to which they provide normative challenges for the profession. Should it be decided ultimately that the three questions are indeed appropriate as the core of the study, then the background context that the next three chapters provide will feed directly into their consideration within each case study chapter.

Chapter 2 will examine the key issues facing journalism in the twenty-first century. Initially, we will analyse the nature and impact of the various changes to which the world of journalism is subject. The increasing pace of that change can be illustrated by an examination of the telescoping histories of today's main news platforms – newspapers (340 years), radio (75 years), television (60 years) and the Internet (12 years, as at the time of writing). Our focus will be relevant political, economic, technological and cultural changes and developments and the ways these have impacted on journalism in advanced democracies. The neoliberal political and economic environments will be shown to have had inevitable consequences for the commodification of journalism and increasingly conglomerated and transnational patterns of ownership. We will assess the ways in which these factors, and allied technological developments, have altered the world journalists report on and the world they inhabit at work. New patterns of gathering, reporting and selecting/processing news will be examined and related to the wider social and cultural environments and, specifically, to the audiences who complete the 'production circuit'. An important element of these considerations will be the changing nature of the 'knowable' in a world of increasing complexity and media saturation.

Having explored some of the main determinants that explain *why* journalism is the way it is, the next chapter moves on to consider normative views of *what* journalism should be. This begins with a brief analysis of traditional journalism norms, from the fourth estate to the public sphere and the US public journalism movement. The main thrust is an evaluation of the applicability and utility of different normative perspectives in relation to the current social and cultural changes identified in the preceding chapter. This analysis leads to the reinforcement and consolidation of the key perspective that will underpin discussion in the book – that journalism's public function is (as explained above) democratic and its role (broadly) political. The chapter will discuss also the relationship between journalism and different types of liberal democracy and provide the reader with a means of gauging the extent to which democracy is present in a meaningful sense in each of the countries studied.

Drawing on the groundwork of the previous chapters, attention in Chapter 4 turns to detailed consideration of the consequences of change and the possible resolution of gaps between the existing and the ideal. Issues relating to institutional arrangements and journalism production, texts and reception are drawn together into *challenges* facing journalism now and in the future. These are discussed predominantly in terms of the *economic* and *technological* pressures and opportunities that journalism currently faces, together with the *political* and *regulatory* forces that affect them.

The precise nature of the challenges to journalism that are presented under the above headings will be explained, in detail. As stated previously, wherever they are relevant they will then feed into the answers that are sought to the book's central questions. This chapter will end by confirming the appropriateness of the three core questions put forward in Chapter 1.

The UK as a Case Study

Having laid the necessary foundations, the book then moves into a series of detailed UK case studies, which in turn lead into a broader but still substantial discussion of the current problems of journalism and their possible remedies in a contrasting selection of additional advanced democracies. The UK is chosen as the 'base focus' from which everything else pans out for two main reasons. First and most obviously, it forms the core area of expertise of the team responsible for the book's first two sections. Second, the London-based parliamentary system is one of the oldest and least interrupted amongst all of the advanced democracies. Indeed, as noted above, Habermas identifies it as the first home of what might be termed a public sphere (Habermas, 2002). Its political communication problems and experience might therefore be expected to have the deepest roots and to provide one of the most fertile breeding grounds for potential solutions. The history of the BBC as the prototype and still most respected state broadcaster is one of the most vivid illustrators of the usefulness of this approach.

The UK section focuses primarily on the media that cover the largest number of British citizens – the newspapers, television channels, radio stations and Internet news sites that are based in England. Not everyone outside the UK is aware that Scotland, Wales and (depending upon the political situation at particular times) Northern Ireland all have their own parliamentary assemblies and executives with varying degrees of power. Currently, the Scottish Executive exercises the greatest power of all of the devolved governmental bodies and Scotland has its own national press. While, ideally, it would be useful to look at the latter, there is not the space within a book of this size to examine all of the different characteristics of the media within the various countries within the Union. It is for this simple, practical reason that it has been decided to focus on the English media as that covering the largest section of the population. However, the Scottish, Welsh and Northern Ireland media will be referred to at points where they have a unique significance.

The English media are covered in six chapters, five of which concentrate in turn on the national print media, the local and regional print media, the key terrestrial, satellite and cable television broadcasters, the national and local radio broadcasters and the online media. An additional chapter on sports journalism within the UK is included for the reasons mentioned earlier. Each chapter will adopt a common structure to facilitate comparative analysis (although this will be less true of the necessarily distinctive sports journalism chapter and, for reasons that will be explained within it, the online journalism chapter). Looking, for example, at the television industry, key aspects of its historical development will be explained first in order to provide the background context that is necessary to understand why the structures and regulations of the present have their specific shape. Next, the key challenges facing the television industry will be identified and explained. The ways in which the normative debate outlined in the opening chapters applies to the industry will then be analysed. The three core questions will sit at the heart of the chapter in a form that is adapted to consideration of its specific subject matter, namely:

• To what extent is traditional news journalism losing ground to soft news within the UK television industry?

- To what extent is the range and depth of coverage of news issues within the UK television industry adequate for the purpose of ensuring that the electorate is adequately informed about the world around them?
- To what extent is it possible to access balanced presentations of the news within the UK television industry?

The answers that are found to these questions will be used to assess the extent to which the industry is meeting the requirements of the news dimension of the public sphere as defined by ourselves. Where deficiencies are found, then possible remedies will be suggested.

The conclusions from each of these chapters will then be brought together at the end of the book and compared with those from the chapters on a selection of other advanced democracies in an attempt to assess the current state of *the news media as a whole* across the case study states. The book's three core questions will sit at the heart of this process.

The International Comparative Studies

Part 3 introduces five additional players in the shape of the US, France, Germany, Italy and Japan. One of the key reasons for the selection of these states is explained in the preface and it is not proposed to duplicate it here. It is possible to criticise any such selection as being inadequate for a variety of reasons – for not including small states, for not including enough Pacific states, for not including enough states with particular common problems, and so on. To all such criticism we plead guilty and admit that certain logistical factors – time, the range of available expertise and the book's word limit – have imposed upon us, as they do upon journalists themselves, the need for selection. So rather than wilting under the vices of the selection made here, our intention is to concentrate on its virtues. Subsequent studies, in journals or similarly themed books, can fill many of the gaps that we are forced to leave for very practical reasons.

First, Italy selects itself. At the time of writing the Italian public is waking up to the deficiencies of a political system that allowed former Prime Minister Silvio Berlusconi to achieve direct and indirect near-monopoly control of its terrestrial television broadcasters, together with significant influence within its print media. That such a situation could occur within a member state of the EU, especially given its memories of media control under the Fascists, is seen as a fundamental affront to the principles of democracy both by many within Italy and certainly by many outside it. For some, the challenges that the Italian media face are perhaps the most serious and the most worrying of all the advanced democracies. Our contributor, however, sees something positive that has come out of all of this as well, as his chapter will show.

The US also is an inevitable presence within the book. Given its massive and all-pervasive military, economic and political power and influence and its current role as 'the new Rome' in world politics, the extent to which the US media are able to inform and educate their domestic public about the issues in which their country chooses to become involved around the globe is crucial. Arguably, the American public is potentially the most effective counterbalance to the power and ambitions of a presidency that neither the United Nations nor the EU is able to resist effectively on many issues. If that public is so woefully uninformed about global politics, leaving aside its own politics, as a result of deficiencies in the performance of its media, then the whole world has serious cause for concern.

Germany equally selects itself. While currently neither the German Chancellor nor the German electorate is willing to take on the leading international role that their country is capable of, it is undoubtedly both the most powerful state within the EU and potentially capable of exerting real influence on the shape of global politics. It is only because Germany chooses for the moment not to take on such a role that Britain is able still to put itself forward as the major global player within the EU. What Germany says and does matters and as an advanced democracy it is important that its voters are adequately informed about the world outside as well as internal politics. The role of the German media is therefore crucial.

France is interesting on several grounds, but one of the most influential considerations in choosing to include it within the book was the contrast which its print media provides in terms of its range of political perspectives, the quality of analysis of its best papers and the range of issues which it addresses, when compared to other advanced democracies, not least its British neighbour.

Finally, Japan was chosen both because of its role as the second most powerful Pacific democracy and because of its significance as an example of how Asian societies can adopt similar forms to Western democracies but operate them in very different ways. It will be interesting to see how these impact upon the way that the Japanese news media operate and the extent to which their problems correspond with, or are distinctive from, those of the European and American democracies.

To facilitate the most effective comparison with the UK chapters, each international chapter will adopt roughly the same structure as was outlined above for each UK chapter, with the partial exceptions of the sports journalism and online journalism chapters. While, again, it would be ideal to be able to look at each of the additional countries' media industries in the same depth as the UK, practicality in the form of a lack of space makes this impossible. Nevertheless, the overview that each chapter will present will still be of great value, given that it is produced on the basis of expert, in-depth knowledge. It will allow for the *key* challenges facing the media of each society to be identified definitively, and equally will provide sufficient detail for the book's three core questions to be addressed. It should allow for a broad picture of the current state of the media across the chosen advanced democracies to be painted and for an initial evaluation to be made of the extent to which any crucial failures in media performance can be rectified. It will also allow conclusions to be drawn concerning the degree to which different cultural, economic and political contexts shape the practicalities of what might be aspired to in terms of a media role as a key player within the advanced democracies.

In short, while the core concerns of the book – what journalism currently is about in the UK and other advanced democracies, what it should be about and how to get there – might initially seem clear-cut and simple, the comparative perspective of Part 3 will make it clear just how difficult and complex a subject matter for study all of this really is. In the overall conclusion the book will suggest a means of finding solutions to the problems that it identifies, but it will emphasise that this will not be easy to implement.

References

Anderson, P.J. (2003), *Defining Politics and Political Journalism*, part of the intranet resource base provided for journalism students at the University of Central Lancashire.

Habermas, J. (2002), *The Structural Transformation of the Public Sphere* (Cambridge: Polity).

Hobsbawm, E. (1995), *The Age of Extremes* (London: Abacus).

Lloyd, J. (2004), *What the Media are Doing to our Politics* (London: Constable and Robinson).

McChesney, R. (2000), *Rich Media, Poor Democracy: Communication Politics in Dubious Times* (New York: New Press).

Chapter 2

The Changing World of Journalism

Peter J. Anderson and Anthony Weymouth
(with Geoff Ward)

Introduction

The traditional news media in pluralistic societies have often made great claims about being at the heart of democracy. As most of the quality news media continue to lose readers and audiences and new forms of communicating news outside of the control of the media companies, such as blogging, gain popularity amongst younger people, one thing is clear. Whatever importance they ascribe to themselves, the traditional news media have no God-given right to retain their position at the communicative core of the democratic process. Indeed, as Barbie Zelizer noted in her excellent 2004 survey of the state of journalism research (Zelizer, 2004: 204), there have been four studies in recent years which have taken 'the end of journalism' as their title.

There can be no doubt that, in the face of all of this, journalism is currently undergoing an identity crisis the reasons for which are well enough documented. Over the last two decades in particular, socio-economic, socio-cultural changes and technological development have combined to impose change upon the profession and to oblige its practitioners to re-examine their roles as journalists in the context of these rapid developments at the beginning of the new century (see, for example, Lloyd, 2004). These changes are due to two principal factors. Firstly, there has been an 'information explosion', fuelled mostly by the Internet, whereby the manner in which the public receive and consume information has reduced the input by professional journalists. While the impact of this in terms of the gaining of new Internet audiences for political news remains modest overall (Van Dijk, 2005: 118–119), there are serious worries that this reduction is a process that will gather momentum during the next decade. Secondly, for reasons rooted in socio-economic development, society's perceived needs have evolved to a point where the traditional 'interpretative' functions of journalism are deemed in some quarters to be no longer necessary. These are serious developments that have implications for journalism throughout the advanced democracies, more serious in some than in others but all consistently pointing in the same direction of significant change. While this transition period brings with it great democratic potential, it can also be argued that the role of journalism is evolving in a way wherein its traditional functions and its relationship to the democratic process in reality are being redefined in a manner that is frequently not in the public interest. A key question therefore, for journalists, proprietors, politicians and the public, is 'how can this change be managed (if indeed it can be managed at all)?' in the best interest of the profession itself and of democracy that, until recently at least, it was assumed to serve.

In the course of this chapter we shall examine the past and present journalistic practice, the way that it has been affected by the changes that have transformed its market from being 'supplier-driven' to 'consumer-driven', as well as speculate upon its future directions. First of all, let us look again at the assumed context within which the media operates in the advanced democracies.

Some Basic Principles

When we speak of advanced democracies, we assume *at least* five basic underlying principles that characterise them:

- universal suffrage;
- regular and frequent elections;
- accurate and honest voting returns;
- freedom of speech;
- freedom of movement.

These five principles are always set within a wider context of a national/international legal framework and overarching legislative assembly. The first three principles are always enshrined in the law of the country and applied in the form of strictly defined procedures governing eligibility to vote, the intervals between elections and the manner in which elections are to be conducted. Serious violations of these principles are comparatively rare in the advanced democracies because in the main they are part of a verifiable and transparent process. For reasons that we hope will become clear, both in this chapter and throughout this book, the fourth principle, the need for freedom of speech, is an issue of far greater contention for media observers than any of the others. The constraints and conditions that impinge upon journalists and determine the manner in which they represent events of primary importance to people's lives are of central interest to all those who believe in the democratic process. But unlike the first three principles listed above, the fourth – freedom of speech – is a concept open to interpretation and in consequence also open to abuse. For this reason, the manner in which the fourth condition is implemented in the countries that form the objects of our study will occupy the considerable attention of the contributors to this book. In a similar way the fifth principle, that of freedom of movement, is also a domain where the necessity, the degree of provision and manner of its implementation are frequently contested. The focus of our attention, however, necessarily is on the fourth principle: freedom of speech.

Freedom of speech is such a self-evident precondition of the democratic process that it would seem unnecessary to pursue it further. In reality, such an assumption is not merely unfounded but dangerous. The way in which information is currently managed and the media representation of a given society's interests, its ethical and moral attitudes that govern its reaction to events, from the highest echelons of our institutions to the individual citizen, are phenomena that should occupy constant interest and, we would argue, never more so than in this period of change of the early twenty-first century. A critical understanding of these things has clear implications for journalistic practice both in the present and future. We begin by examining the importance of the latter in exposing and helping control one of the great weaknesses which lies at the heart of democracies, as indeed it does within other systems of governance.

The Trouble with Democracy and its Need of Good Journalism

It is both a justifiable and commonplace view at the beginning of the twenty-first century to regard its predecessor as a time of ideological, political and social upheaval. Such a view, in the light of events that saw the rise and fall of two massively destructive forces – communism and fascism – and the loss of over 60 million lives in the process, is beyond dispute. It has been wryly suggested that, all things considered, democracy may have emerged as the least worst form of governance in modern times. If such a view has any credence, then it follows, since it is associated with democracy, that liberal orthodox economics, or 'capitalism', could be the least worst form of economic system by which society generates the wealth needed to sustain its citizens in gainful, fulfilling and liberating lives. There is more than a grain of truth in this too. But such generalisations should be treated with caution. We do not, as Voltaire's Dr Pangloss would have us believe, live in the 'best of all possible worlds'. Far from it. Any study of democracies, past and present, and their associated economic systems, consistently throws up several common factors, of which one of the most striking features, beyond the variable presence of the five principles already mentioned, is the presence of high-level corruption among some of their politicians, civil servants and business leaders (although it should be said that this weakness is hardly limited to democracies). An important function of the media, and of journalists in particular, has been and remains the exposure of corruption in all its manifold forms and it is one that is crucial to the fair and effective working of democracy.

It is tempting to characterise corruption within democracies by reference to the nature of its country of origin or particular culture and the way in which it is perceived by others. However, it is very clear that there are corrupt practices that all democracies have in common. In this respect we need hardly look very far. In recent times clouds of scandal (political, financial and other) have hovered over the heads of many elected representatives internationally, including Chancellor Kohl, Presidents Nixon, Clinton, Mitterrand, Chirac and Prime Minister Berlusconi. There have been also the well publicised transgressions of Lord Jeffrey Archer, Dame Shirley Porter and the former government minister Jonathan Aitken in the UK.

In addition to political chicanery, the marketplace too has had its share of scandals. Unelected but supposedly upstanding people and institutions are constantly failing to live up to the trust that we are encouraged to place in them. Enron, one of the most powerful and respected of US corporations, was involved in fraudulent practices on a massive scale, defrauding its shareholders of millions of dollars, just a few years ago. Very recently, Shell, in the UK, was admonished by the City for exaggerating its crude oil assets 'in the ground' in order to boost its share values. Appropriately enough, the writing of this chapter also coincides with a new transatlantic scandal in which the former owner of *The Daily Telegraph*, the recently ennobled Conrad Black, has been accused of financial irregularities involving excessive compensation, unapproved bonuses, loans and personal expenses amounting to $400 million in his dealings with the American company Hollinger.

But this corruption in the democracies is not limited to politics or to big business. Our spiritual leaders have also been found wanting. In the US and in Ireland the faithful have been shocked at the allegations of sexual abuse of children made against a minority of the Catholic clergy. As this page is being composed a British judge has been sentenced to months of community service for downloading pornographic pictures of children. And so it goes. But lest ordinary citizens of democracies become too indignant at the corrupt behaviour of the great and the good, they should take note of the behaviour of some of their fellow citizens who have been engaging in various forms of corrupt behaviour of their own. Any contemporary review of the role of the media in advanced democracies must therefore examine not only political and institutional phenomena but also social behaviour at all levels of society.

None of the misdeeds mentioned above necessarily indicates that the advanced democracies are in some kind of unprecedented moral free fall. It is more likely that it was ever thus. We may know about such practices more through changes in social attitudes – a willingness to speak out and higher standards of accountability – coupled with new forms of transparency, facilitated by advances in communication technology, than from a real decline in public morality. But the fact remains that such events, coming to light on a regular basis as they do, indicate the permanent and significant presence of corruption within our democracies and the need for strong and socially aware journalism to expose it where otherwise it would remain hidden.

The Forces Shaping Journalism and its Ability to Perform its Various Roles Within Democracies

The exposure of corruption is, of course, only one of the several jobs that it has been argued that journalism should undertake within democracies. As well as being a watchdog, it has been seen as a crucial provider of the information necessary for effective democratic participation and, within some perspectives, as an educator and enabler of the citizenry. A frequent accusation in recent years has been that increasingly it is being reduced to the role of entertainer (Franklin, 1997). The extent to which it is able and willing to undertake any of these roles is influenced by a variety of factors that have significantly impacted upon the advanced democracies, their media and journalism over the last two decades. They include the following:

- the achievement of global dominance by liberal orthodox free market economics and the way, for example, that this has created the conditions necessary for the emergence of media concentration and national and transnational cross-media conglomerates, such as News Corporation;
- associated with this, the deregulation of markets and the advance of market values into the public sphere;
- social fragmentation and the decline of 'traditional' social and professional institutions, including the journalism unions, whose creation, amongst other things, was intended to guarantee the maintenance of professional standards and independence in the news media;
- a significant reduction in interest in politics in key Western societies as a result of the compression of the gap between left- and right-wing politics, in both public life and the media, following the collapse of communism in the former Soviet Union and Eastern Europe;
- increased wealth, leading to Galbraith's 'culture of contentment' (Galbraith, 1992), and less visible interest on the part of many of the beneficiaries in their societies' ills, injustices and corruptions;
- increased leisure and the negative impact that the consequent growth in competitive entertainment provision, 'shopping opportunities', and so on, has had on the sales of the news media, such as Sunday newspapers;
- important technological advances in communications, in particular the Internet, which has offered unlimited access to news providers outside of the journalism profession, and multichannel television, which has fragmented viewing habits and reduced the audiences for news of the highest quality;
- new methods of information gathering, resulting in the growing requirement for journalists to be multi-skilled and multimedia and the consequent pressures on crucial practices such as fact checking and background research, especially when it is accompanied also by 'downsizing'.

The role and relevance of a selection of these factors will be examined shortly.

Media observers of the late twentieth century severely criticised certain sectors of the Western media for their perceived shortfalls in delivering information of central interest to their various audiences that implied the violation of free speech. Most if not all of this criticism can be linked to the points listed above. Information and the unhampered spreading of news and the freedom to express opinions are regarded as part of the bedrock upon which democracy, through the resultant capacity of the people to make informed decisions at the ballot box, is founded. The alleged failure of the democratic media is perceived to express itself in many ways, of which the most often quoted are:

- a lack of balance (either deliberate or through lack of professional competence);
- the omission of important information;
- the frequent incorporation of PR material in 'news reports' due to declining resources for independent reporting;
- trivialisation (that is, diversions from significant events and lack of focus on context);
- sensationalism (distortion in the interest of sales);
- commercialisation (sales practices targeting readers/audiences as consumers rather than information seekers);
- the precedence given to market values over professional journalistic ethics and public service practice;
- the packaging of news as selected information and *opinions* for targeted audiences instead of as part of an area for debate;
- the decline in popular satisfaction with the services provided by journalists to the extent that, with the availability now of alternative access to news, sometimes from dubious sources, via the Internet, they are starting to be sidelined.

These alleged weaknesses are both serious and often vindicated. They do not speak well for the past and future mediation and functioning of democratic government, although it could be argued, on the basis of the study of some of the national media sectors covered within this book, that some democracies may, in the future, fare better than others.

It is not possible in an introductory chapter, which is necessarily something of a 'broad-brush' survey of the major changes that have affected journalistic practice over the last 50 years, to explain in detail how all of the above factors interact or have acquired the importance that they now have. However, some brief elaborations can be offered here which will be expanded on in much greater detail in later chapters within the book. It is, for example, crucial to understand the importance of conglomeration for both the quality and quantity of news journalism now available. It has been mentioned above how the growth of conglomerates like News Corporation was facilitated by the increasing dominance of deregulatory free market economics during the 1980s (and beyond), symbolised most aptly by the triumph of the Reaganites and the Thatcherites in the two most prominent Anglo-Saxon powers (McChesney, 2000). This has been further facilitated by the shrinking audience for any one news product that has been occasioned by such above-mentioned factors as: the increasing competition that news has faced from the growth in leisure-time products; the reduced interest in politics occasioned by the end of the cold war and the move towards the centre-right in many democratic societies; and the fragmentation of media audiences that has resulted from both the advent of multichannel television and the Internet. This audience shrinkage often has resulted also in the shrinkage of advertising revenues for any one news product, which in turn has made it difficult or at least unattractive for smaller media operations to remain independent. In consequence, huge chains of local newspapers have replaced the old independents in the US, UK and elsewhere, previously independent national newspapers have become part of larger media groups, television companies have merged and, most significantly, giant transnational media corporations have emerged which own news products across all of the media platforms currently available around the world. This in turn has reduced diversity.

Another significant result of these pressures, facilitated by rapid progress in the field of digital technology, has been convergence. Digitisation and economies of scale mean that convergence results in the reprocessing of *single* pieces of news into *scattered multi-platform/format news*. Thus convergence, while bolstering the finances of news producers, works against plurality and diversity as far as audiences are concerned. So, as commentators have not been slow to point out, the plurality of media outlets does not necessarily equate to the plurality/diversity of views. Alternative views may be represented in the small media or on the Web, but as will be seen in the section on the Internet, the number of people accessing the Web for hard news remains relatively small, while available evidence suggests that many of those who do use it for this purpose only do so in a fairly superficial way (Van Dijk, 2005).

The economic pressures that newsrooms are under in the face of the increased competition for shrinking audiences leads also to a growing dependency on agency and other swap agreement products and more 'saleable' news focusing on lifestyles and celebrities. As pointed out in the bullet points above, rather than forming an area for debate (public sphere) increasing amounts of news are packaged as selected information and *opinions* for targeted audiences. Facilitating all of these changes are the declining influence of news producers on corporate decision making (journalism/news departments represent a shrinking proportion of corporate personnel and corporate decision-making structures), and their consequent disappearing ability to fight effectively declining corporate investment in news production. On top of this, as already mentioned above, there has been a decline in professionalism and socially responsible journalism following on from the breaking of the power of the journalism unions. This has further reduced the ability of those trying to preserve good-quality journalism to prevent the growing 'softening' of the product.

It is not hard to see, therefore, how these fierce economic pressures, having resulted in down-sized and increasingly 'converged' newsrooms, have led in turn to reductions in both the breadth and depth of news coverage by many commercial producers (particularly in the US, where public service provision is only marginal), an increasing reliance on public relations handouts which have not even been adequately checked out, and accusations of trivialisation and sensationalism.

The full extent and role of these various trends and problems will be brought out in the chapters that follow and should be kept in mind as background during the next section.

Fifty Years Back: Fifty Years Forward

How best can we understand the changes that have taken place in the media over the last 50 years and the new direction that the media and journalism in particular may be taking in the first half of the twenty-first century? The answer to this question is obviously located in the history of the media over the last half century and must take account of the significant political, economic and socio-cultural factors, both national and international, in which the media developed. We make no apologies for taking this historical approach and expanding on some of the themes raised within the previous section. In our view, only if we understand these forces and how they have developed over time can we fully understand the significance of current trends and the future direction in which journalism and the information industry generally is likely to move in the early twenty-first century.

At the outset, we need to take note of the fact that an essential difference between the media of 50 years ago and that of today is one of supply and emphasis. When we speak of supply we mean that the media, in the post-World War II period, was very much a suppliers' market in the sense that there were far fewer media outlets and these outlets were highly sought after by a 'mass' public hungry for news. All across Europe and beyond, the people clamoured for information concerning how the Great Powers (the US, the UK, France and the then Soviet Union) were dividing up the world in ways that would change their lives for ever. Today things could hardly be more different, although the need for 'quality' information is as urgent today as it was then.

The media landscape of the twenty-first century would indeed be unrecognisable in both form and function to the practitioners of 50 years ago. Firstly, it has been transformed from a *supplier* to a *consumer* market where providers of information jostle, often ferociously, for the attentions of a public that, far from seeking information, is suffering from 'information overload', and some would claim 'interpretive deficit'. Secondly, this overload is available to the consumer in myriad forms. We no longer get our news from the newspapers, radio and television alone. Instead, information is received and absorbed from cyberspace via the astonishing variety of websites that have set themselves up, free of national regulation, ranging from well-known and ethically motivated news sites and passing through others targeting, for example, surfers, Hell's Angels and Christian fundamentalists, to the lone 'blogger' regaling us with his views on world news, his love life and obsession with hunting rifles, from a bedroom somewhere in South Carolina. Moreover, this information is available not only online through our computers but also via the latest generation of iPods and mobile phones, from which incidentally we can, and often do, send informative pictures of our personal world back to friends, family and even to the professional media themselves. It may be argued that the access to these individualised forms of information, particularly on the part of young people, some aged still in single figures, holds out the possibility of a new kind of journalism undreamed of even a decade ago.

In the light of these extraordinary circumstances, it is small wonder that the journalism profession perceives the need to adapt itself radically in order to fulfil its traditional democratic functions in this century. It would be useful to provide an initial overview of how these various developments have impacted on the individual sectors of the media. The broader, briefer overview presented in the previous section should be borne in mind throughout. Even so, restriction of space here means that it will not be possible to raise all of the themes mentioned there *and* provide an adequate portrait of sectoral media development. However, themes raised previously that are not covered or covered adequately below will be mentioned briefly again in the conclusion and will be covered fully in other chapters within the book.

The Newspaper Sectors

In the absence of any of the kinds of facilitating technology mentioned above, and with significantly less leisure time and wealth available, it may not be surprising to learn that the 1950s have often been called the 'Golden Age' of the newspaper industry among the Western democracies and, indeed, in Japan too, since that country was undergoing one of the most fundamental social and political changes in its entire history under post-war American control.

The newspaper sector in the UK, for example, reached record circulation figures as a war-weary but expectant people turned to them for news of the great social reforms in social security, health, education, transport and the major industries that the Labour government began implementing in the immediate post-war period. Not only were there many more titles in 1955 but the circulation figures of that time are sufficient to make modern editors contemplate their falling readerships and bite their lips in envy of the former 'Golden Age' (Weymouth and Lamizet, 1996).

Comparatively speaking, the newspaper sector in the UK remains among the strongest and most dynamic among the Western democracies. Nevertheless, as with the press sectors of the latter, the British press has succumbed to a decline in readership both in the daily and Sunday editions, and particularly the latter. In hard figures this decline starts from the maximum circulation of around 16.3 million in 1955 to 12.1 million in 2004 (Weymouth and Lamizet, 1996; Alden, 2005). But, this decline of over four million conceals both quantitative and qualitative issues: firstly, the fall in circulations has accelerated more rapidly in the ten years 1995–2005 than over the earlier period 1955–1995; secondly, in this earlier period there was a gradual ideological realignment towards the political right/centre-right and loss of quality journalism, following the disappearance of left-of-centre papers such as the *Daily Herald* and the *News Chronicle* on one hand, and the arrival, on the other, of what some would see as the sulphurous tabloids, *The Sun* and the *Daily Star*.

The most marked decline of the UK press sector is among the Sunday editions, which have been hit particularly badly by the inroads that have been made into their sports journalism market since the advent of Sky Television (Weymouth and

Lamizet, 1996; Alden, 2005) and the increase in competing leisure products that has occurred in recent years.

The picture in the mid-1950s of an expanding and commercially healthy press sector is true for France, Italy, Germany, the US and many other countries emerging from the dark days of World War II into the post-war period of reconstruction and optimism. In the case of countries that had been occupied by Nazi Germany, their media had been dismantled, purged of their fascist toxins and reconstructed by the Allies in the immediate post-war era.

The subsequent decline of the written press in the UK at least can be located as starting around the early 1960s (Weymouth and Lamizet, 1996). But the picture across Europe and the US is more or less the same in terms of the general decline in the circulation of newspapers (Weymouth and Lamizet, 1996; McChesney, 2000). The reasons for this decline are fairly clear and include the fact that, from the second half of the twentieth century onwards, there has been a clear shift away from the written word to the image, driven for the most part by television technology. The majority of the public now get their news primarily from the small screen. The reasons for this change are several. The developments in sport and its coverage that will be explained in Guy Hodgson's chapter, for example, have led people increasingly to turn to television rather than newspapers for sports news. Amongst these are the growth of saturation coverage of live sporting events on television following the emergence of new, commercially aggressive broadcasters, such as Rupert Murdoch's Sky and his introduction also of 24-hour television news coverage. This has made it almost impossible for newspapers to be first with the news of big sporting or political events. Other factors causing newspaper decline include such simple developments as changes in commuting habits. The move away from buses and trains to cars in many areas as wealth has increased has led to people switching from newspapers to their car radios for news. The emergence of new technologies such as the Internet have made further inroads into the market for the traditional printed word and indeed have caused newspapers to set up Web versions of their paper editions on a mixed subscription/advertising basis.

This last point illustrates neatly how the companies owning newspapers are beginning to adapt to the increasingly fierce news environment. They are looking at new outlets which can be used to disseminate the news produced by their print operations and ways in which that news can be best adapted to suit the new media. These include everything from mobile phones to iPods. In the UK, for example, they have also been thinking increasingly about new ways of presenting their existing printed news products. This has resulted in relaunches of several quality broadsheets, with *The Times* and *The Independent* switching to the more reader-friendly tabloid format, while *The Guardian* switched to the Berliner format in October 2005. Along with changes in size have come changes in content and design. *The Guardian*, for example, has eliminated black and white photographs, illustrations and cartoons and gone for an all-colour edition. The whole look of the paper has been changed by means of new story layouts, fonts and picture usage in order to create the impression of a busier, more concise and readable product.

Other changes in content have been established for far longer. The tabloids, for example, for some years have been increasing their coverage of television celebrities and scandals at the expense of hard news as a way of responding to the increasing allure of the small screen.

As mentioned earlier, media companies have also started to move increasingly towards the multi-skilling of journalists, so that any one reporter is able to produce news for a variety of media formats, thereby making more efficient use of news resources. How this might affect the quality of the news coming out at the end is an issue that will be investigated in later chapters. As will be seen, there are concerns that such developments, in conjunction with 'downsizing' in newsrooms, are increasing the pressure on journalists' ability to fact-check, reducing yet further the time they have to get out of the newsroom and do the 'legwork' that in the past would often uncover the details that the telephone could not and the time that they have in order to do the background research necessary for the adequate provision of context in stories.

The other, and perhaps most obvious, consequence of increasingly fierce competition is the decline in the number of independents and the increasing concentration of ownership, as explained in an earlier section.

The Broadcasting Sectors

If the newspaper was the principal mediator of early modernist thinking that shifted power from one social stratum to another in the late eighteenth and nineteenth centuries, then it may be argued with some force that the radio was a massive shaper of cultural and political attitudes in the twentieth. Comparatively speaking, the arrival of the 'wireless' as a universal medium of communication in the first half of the twentieth century was as significant in effect as the subsequent impact of television and the Internet in the second. Its impact was life-changing and the cultural potential of the radio was grasped early in its introduction in the 1920s, principally by John Reith, whose vision of what came to be called public service broadcasting set ethical standards and an international cultural mission for radio and television broadcasting that has lasted into the new century (see below).

The essential difference between radio broadcasting in the mid-twentieth century and broadcasting in its current form rests upon assumptions made about audiences in these different times as well as upon the available broadcasting technology itself. The 1950s was a time of massive worldwide post-war reconstruction. It was the time of the so-called 'cold war', where simultaneously the Western European democracies were implementing massive social reforms in health, education and labour, and, in alliance with the US, ideologically and militarily confronting the Soviet Union in a nuclear stand-off that was to last almost to the end of the century. There was a perceived need to inform the masses in the West of both these huge tasks, the first of which was designed to immeasurably improve their lives by redistribution of wealth and improved living standards, while the second risked quite literally blowing it all away in a nuclear holocaust.

In Europe certainly, the assumptions and styles of broadcasting in the mid-twentieth century were those of authoritative voices of the educated classes addressing the people en masse. In those times of *mass media*, the big messages and controlled media outlets, little thought was given by journalists to the audience differentiation (other than social class) – along the lines of gender, age, sex, income, ethnic group and leisure – that characterises and determines styles of broadcasting in the twenty-first century. By the 1970s national broadcasting systems (outside the US) were still characterised by two or three terrestrial television channels and a centralised radio network, again with two or three stations, with perhaps, as in the case of the UK, an additional single commercial TV channel and a degree of regional broadcasting in both radio and TV. But by the early 1980s rapid changes were being set in motion.

The changes that have taken place across the globe since the 1980s via the use of satellite, digital and computer technology have, in association with the changes in economic ideology mentioned in an earlier part of the chapter, transformed broadcasting systems from regulated, national, terrestrial transmission to transnational, satellite and digital broadcasting, of which a significant part is unregulated directly by a national government. Within national systems there has been a sharp rise in the number of television channels available and an even sharper increase in the number of radio stations. As frequently happens in developments of this kind, the social patterns that were emerging in the late twentieth century, those of social fragmentation driven by increased wealth and the above-mentioned shift in economic ideology, which has increased concern for individual interests at the expense of key aspects of traditional notions of society, coincided with the kinds of new technologies best able to serve the break-up of the former mass social and institutional groupings of the earlier period. With fragmentation came different voices too. The authoritative tones of the media establishment have conceded significant space on the airwaves to the more demotic and regional dialects, to women, to minority groups, to the voices of the young, the poor and otherwise dispossessed and until recently, the unheard or unheeded sections of society.

In the light of these extraordinary developments it would be foolish and short-sighted not to appreciate their potential for rolling back the boundaries of communication and information; always, however, with the proviso that they are in the right hands and that they function to reinforce and promote democratic values rather than control or subvert them. It must be added that in some areas of media activity the manner in which information is being presented gives real cause for concern. We shall return to these later in this chapter and throughout this book.

Radio (UK)

The arrival of the radio in the 1920s provoked mixed responses among the established, dominant classes across the world that are of interest to us today, if only for the ways in which some of these were repeated with the advent of television and information technology at later times in the century. In the UK not everyone shared John Reith's vision of cultural enrichment derived from the almost limitless potential of a medium that could theoretically put voices, music and information into every front room in the land at the turn of a switch. Reith well understood the cultural and political implications of a medium such as radio that was able to entertain, inform and educate the masses for an affordable licence fee. Under Reith's directorship of the newly formed BBC, the concept of public service broadcasting was born, a concept which to this day has not only survived in the UK, principally within the BBC, but elements of which have also been incorporated into every broadcasting system in the advanced democracies.

It was said by some that the radio would be a corrupter of morals by the broadcasting of popular music, jazz in particular, and the enticing of the public away from indigenous forms of creativity. It was also said that the radio would supersede the book and lead to lower levels of literacy. Both doom-laden prophecies were found subsequently to be groundless. Similar fears were expressed with the coming of television, with regard to the forecast end of radio and decline of reading. Yet radio in the twenty-first century is one of the extraordinary success stories of modern times. The doom-merchants had overlooked the fact that it is a moveable feast of infinite variety that can be consumed and digested while doing something else – in particular, driving a motor car or working at a computer. In addition the economic and technological changes mentioned in the previous section added significant numbers of commercial stations to those provided by the traditional broadcasters from the 1980s onwards.

All of this means that radio remains both attractive and convenient to modern audiences. That attractiveness, it is argued, is being greatly increased by the advent of digital radio, which allows for the opening up of many newer stations able, if they so wish, to specialise in and serve well the niche audiences that previously enjoyed much less coverage of their interests. Digital radio also can be received at greater convenience on more platforms. Digital television viewers, for example, can switch to the radio by simply pressing a button on their television remote handsets.

However, the proliferation of a medium is not necessarily beneficial for its news output. At its best, on BBC Radio 4, for example, much of the radio news still remains a high-quality product that, not being reliant on the distraction of pictures, can spend more time than its television counterpart going into the issues behind the reports that are being presented. BBC Radio also remains free of the pressures of advertising reliance. At its worst, on many commercial news stations, news is something that has been downgraded radically, with only skeleton staffs, little reporting and much material simply imported from elsewhere. One of the problems that radio news has is that while the medium itself prospers, commercial pressures increasingly have pushed towards the simple maximisation of listening figures and advertising revenue. When this view of things moves towards the absolute then anything that does not 'pull its weight' in driving these economic objectives forwards is an automatic candidate for radical cutbacks. Given the perception that younger audiences are not much interested in politics, or traditional 'hard news' in general, it is the stations serving them in particular that are most notable in the declining commitment towards news. Even on a public service broadcaster such as the BBC, the brevity of the news broadcasts on its national youth-orientated station, Radio 1, is notable. These are issues that will be returned to in more depth in later chapters.

Television

Although some countries such as the US and the UK did have television before World War II, the medium only became established in Europe in the 1950s. In the UK the coronation of Queen Elizabeth II in 1953 is often cited as a landmark for television acquisition by the masses, and indeed the sales for that year support the opinion that 1953 was the year when television viewing became a widespread public activity.

The importance of both radio and television as media of information and their potential political and social impact upon the public was well understood by governments the world over. In consequence broadcasters were carefully regulated by laws that gave governments control over the granting of broadcasting licences and the allocation of transmission frequencies. Such power in the hands of governments raised questions related to the issue of the freedom and independence of the broadcasters that have echoed down the years from the beginning of radio and television transmissions to the present day and which have profound implications for journalists in broadcasting. The most recent example of this controversial relationship between the state and public service broadcaster occurred in 2004 in the UK. This was in relation to a story put out by the BBC at a time of great international tension over Iraq; it resulted in the resignations of the Director General of the Corporation, the Chairman of the Board of Governors, the journalist concerned (Andrew Gilligan) and the suicide of the journalist's main source, Dr David Kelly.

If there was a politically convenient case for governments keeping a close watch on the broadcasters in the period up to the late 1970s in the interests of maintaining a fair and unsaturated use of transmission frequencies, it was seriously undermined in the last 20 years of the twentieth century by extraordinary advances in transmission technology. The advent of fibre optics, broadband, satellite and digital technology swept away broadcasting barriers between nations and created possibilities for the emergence of literally hundreds of new stations and channels. These advances coincided with the previously mentioned period of growing privatisation and deregulation, a time when public service broadcasting was going through its most difficult reassessment by governments who, pressed by the private sector for a place in the market, made very significant concessions to commercial radio and television.

The result of these political reassessments and technological changes, set against a background of social fragmentation, increasing wealth and the rightward shift of economic ideology and consequently greater demand for a diversity of television production, was a significant increase in the number of channels in the private sector. Operators led by Rupert Murdoch's Sky in the UK, and Silvio Berlusconi in Italy, using new legislation, and the new satellite, cable and digital 'platforms' to great advantage, established an irreversible position *vis-à-vis* the public service broadcasters. Goaded by this competition from the private operators, the public sector broadcasters, and the BBC in particular, fought back to expand and consolidate their own activities in digital and online communication.

The impact upon journalism and the quality of information output as the result of deregulation and the massive increase in private sector involvement in broadcasting since the 1980s are the subjects of an ongoing debate among media practitioners and media observers (Curran, 2002: 216–36; Hoggart, 2004: 108–39; Calabrese; 2000: 43–62; Harvey, 2004: 194–210; Franklin, 1997; McChesney, 2000). From a news point of view, many critics have argued that the downside outweighs the socio-cultural advantages. As far as simple deregulation is concerned, as Heinz Brandenburg will show in his chapter, the US has often been seen as the most worrying example of what can go wrong. In combination with the growth of multichannel television, many critics argue that deregulation has led to the quality of television news being forced radically downmarket.

In the UK, on the one hand, the advent of a second terrestrial commercial broadcaster during the 1980s (Channel 4) provided an additional extended quality evening news bulletin which largely has held onto its standards, while Rupert Murdoch's Sky satellite broadcaster introduced also the first 24-hour quality dedicated news station. On the other hand, the fragmentation and increased pressure for audiences that has followed the introduction of digital and satellite television has been accused of forcing the quality of news coverage downwards. It is possible to hop from one commercial digital or satellite channel to another, for example, without ever encountering any quality news output. Equally, it is now almost inconceivable that ITV, the main commercial terrestrial broadcaster, could be persuaded permanently to restore its main evening news slot to the long-abandoned 10 p.m. This is due to its perceived need to run programmes, films particularly, continuously through the evening peak time in order to keep hold of its audience and advertisers in the face of today's fierce competition. Neither is it likely to restore the much-cut funding of ITV news to the levels of fifteen years ago. Equally, the BBC's digital Channel 3 station was allowed in October 2005 to abandon completely its commitment to anything other than short news bulletins on the grounds that it needed to build up its audience and the younger people who watched it were not interested in its longer bulletin and were channel-hopping elsewhere (there were alleged additional grounds, which will be explained in Chapter 4).

In short, deregulation and the unleashing of fierce market forces have been argued to have damaged much of television news qualitatively in terms of both its breadth and depth. Consequent cutbacks in news resources have made such damage inevitable, it is said. An assessment of the extent to which these accusations are true will follow in later chapters.

The Opening of the Floodgates? The Coming of the Internet

It is only in recent years that the Internet has become a significant platform for news providers. Sparks notes that it was not until late 1994 onwards that it began to take off, with hundreds of newspapers flooding online from then onwards (Sparks, 2000: 270). The attractions of low costs, easy access and (potentially) global reach have made the Net an option that is attractive to many and impossible to ignore for others. But it has not proved quite as attractive as some first thought would be the case as far as those traditional news providers who have expanded into an online presence are concerned. Newspapers, for example, have found it difficult to charge for their basic services when provided online. This has made the impact of the costs of specialist news teams, necessary to work in tune with the distinctive news rhythms of the Net, and of the designers needed for the separate requirements of online pages, more difficult to offset (although converged newsrooms are now cutting costs). Sparks notes that *The Washington Post*, for example, was spending around ten per cent of its group revenues on its electronic initiatives during the late 1990s (Sparks, 2000: 276–7).

He contends also that online developments offer some serious challenges to the business model of offline newspapers and, by extension, to their democratic role as far from perfect, but nevertheless crucial members of the Fourth Estate. He argues that they do this through intense competition that, as far as an online presence is concerned, makes smaller newspapers compete on the same platform as larger ones and larger ones on the same platform as, for example, broadcaster-owned online sites, like that of the BBC. They also undermine the traditional commercial news providers' role as the main carriers of substantial amounts of advertising by giving advertisers the opportunity to reach large numbers of people by other means than, for example, newspapers, via the Net. In addition, he sees a real danger that, as newspapers relatively become less important as providers of serious news as a result of the intensified competition online, they will turn to less serious matters, such as community interactive and participation ventures in place of the coverage of politics. Furthermore, he believes that there is a risk that these pressures will lead to yet further concentration of news providers in the hands of an unaccountable few (Sparks, 2000: 288–9).

For others, however, such dangers are much less of a problem. An independent US report noted in July 2006, for example, that, 'newspapers, which have seen their audience decline in recent decades, are now stemming further losses with the help of their online editions' (Pew Research Center for the People and the Press, 2006). Others believe that dangers such as the above are compensated for by the fact that the low cost of setting up news blogs and additional forms of alternative news provision on the Internet opens up a wide range of independent news sources to the online user. Allen notes that one of the obvious advantages is that users no longer have to allow themselves to be spoon-fed news by traditional providers, but can carry out in-depth research on specific issues, if they so choose, by following web links, going to primary sources online, or whatever. He notes also that online news sites can provide users with a level of interactivity that is not possible on the traditional platforms (Allen, 2005: 67–81).

However, there are serious doubts as to just how many people within the advanced democracies are likely to use the Internet in such a sophisticated way or even use it for following hard news at all. Citing data published within the US in 2002, Van Dijk notes that only 36.8 per cent of American males overall were using the Internet to seek news about politics (a figure that a 2005 report showed has not increased greatly since – Pew Internet and American Life Project, 2005) and that, at the less educated levels of Internet usage, the figure for both men and women dropped to around 25 per cent (Van Dijk, 2005: 119). He also paints a picture, which he sees as being close to the reality, in which between a quarter and a third of the populations of the most advanced societies do not access the Internet for any purpose (Van Dijk, 2005: 178–9). Figures released in the US in 2005 back up this view in that they show that around a third of the American population remained offline (Pew Internet and American Life Project, 2005). In July 2006 a report noted that while one in three Americans now regularly access news online, the growth of the online news audience has markedly slowed since 2000, with 'virtually no growth in the percentage of 18-24 year olds' stating that they regularly access online news. Twenty-nine per cent did so in 2000 and by 2006 this figure had shown only a 1 per cent increase (Pew Research Center for the People and the Press, 2006). In the UK, polls show that even during the 2005 General Election, an event which automatically brings politics to the attention of the electorate, only around a third of young voters turned to the Internet as their primary source of political news and information (BBC News Online, 2006).

The 2006 Pew report noted also that:

> For the most part, online news has evolved as a supplemental source that is used along with traditional news media outlets. It is valued more for headlines and convenience, not detailed, in-depth reporting.
>
> The audience for online news is fairly broad, but not particularly deep. Those who use the web for news still spend more time getting news from other sources than they do getting news online. And while nearly half of Americans (48%) spend at least 30 minutes getting news on television, just 9% spend that long getting news online (Pew Research Center for the People and the Press, 2006).

The implications of all of this will be considered within later chapters, particularly in the conclusion. However, it can be noted here that the development of the Internet as a source of alternative information and content raises some interesting questions about the extent to which the different types of 'alternative news' can be regarded as being on a par with that available through traditional news providers. Lone bloggers, for example, have in some cases provided the only first-hand news that is available in troubled locations like Baghdad, where anti-occupation sentiment has made it impossible for most Western journalists to go into many areas without unacceptable risk of kidnap or death. Where, over time, alternative news sites appear, in the judgement of relevant experts such as specialist academics and serious journalists, to be publishing credible, insightful and competently enough produced reports, they can acquire several professionally respected news roles – as well-regarded news sites in their own right, as regular or ad hoc presences within mainstream news sites, or simply as sources quoted in the reports produced by authoritative others. But the three basic criteria of credibility, insightfulness and competent writing or broadcasting mentioned here have to be seen as the entry-level criteria which it is necessary for a site to meet before it can be regarded as having any weight as a provider of serious news.

The next level of judgement that needs to be applied is that relating to the *range* of issues over which a news site can be regarded as a quality provider. The fewer the people producing it and the more limited the number of first-hand sources available to them outside of their own specialist area(s), then the more limited will be the range of issues on which they are able to supply news with authority. Sites that overstretch themselves, a temptation that can be dangerous after a little initial success has been achieved, run the risk of quickly losing their initial credibility.

However, it is not necessary for individual alternative sites to cover a range of news issues that is comparable to that covered by mainstream sites for them to rival or, theoretically, even replace their more traditional competitors. What is necessary instead is for the news audience to start using, *on a truly significant scale*, sites that meet the above entrance criteria, and which *collectively* cover a wide range of issues, and to use them regularly for hard news as well as, or instead of, traditional news providers. Providing enough sites could become available that meet the necessary criteria, then this would start to become feasible.

Having said all of the above, it is important not to over-estimate the importance of phenomena like blogging from a news journalism point of view. For example, a 2006 national survey of American bloggers found most to be focused on recounting 'their personal experiences to a relatively small audience of readers and that only a small proportion focus their coverage on politics, media, government or technology...' (Pew Internet and American Life Project, 2006). Another report in the same year found that in terms of 'what journalists would call reporting', among blogs only 5 per cent of postings matched the criteria (Project for Excellence in Journalism, 2006). Figures cited within the report containing the bloggers survey results suggest that only 9 per cent of all US Internet users get their news from a blog (Pew Internet and American Life Project, 2006). With regard to the UK, in concluding that '[t]he Internet played no more significant role in the 2005 General Election than it did in 2001', Deacon et al. noted that blogging was found to have had minimal impact on election coverage: 'The significance of blogging was hyped in the UK before the election but proved to be of little importance during the election campaign' (Deacon et al., 2005).

So to summarise the discussion so far, the advent of the Internet as a news platform has intensified competition for traditional news providers (many of which have also become owners of online news sites) and simultaneously opened a potentially global audience to new, independent news providers who previously at best might have been restricted to a small-circulation localised newspaper or alternative radio station. While in theory being good for the news 'consumer', as is the case with the traditional media, there is a need for evaluative criteria to be in place in order for judgements to be made regarding their accuracy and trustworthiness. Equally, the future importance of online news will be determined ultimately both by how many people come to use it and the extent to which they use it. At the moment, the data suggests that hard news usage remains relatively low. Accordingly, while the Internet obviously has tremendous potential, as far as news is concerned estimates of its importance need to be kept in proportion to that usage.

Diversity in the Newsroom

As this topic will be covered in some detail in another of the introductory chapters, we need only mention it briefly here. Diversity, and often the lack of it, and its impact upon journalism has been a serious concern in a number of advanced democracies. In the UK, for example, while much progress has been made in terms of the increasing employment of women in newsrooms, there remains a glass ceiling at the more senior levels of news providers. There are few women in senior editorial positions on newspapers, for instance (Ross, 2005). Equally, while there is a small but noticeable television presence of reporters and news presenters from among the ethnic minorities, the situation remains one of considerable under-representation across the news media as a whole (Society of Editors, 2004). The problem is perhaps most visible at the level of the leading journalism schools, where, while women now make up around 50 per cent of annual intakes, ethnic minority students are few and far between. Given that progress towards diversity remains so limited, there are continuing concerns for the possible negative effects upon the breadth and nature of the news agenda in the UK. The extent to which this phenomenon applies to the UK and to other democracies will be examined in Chapter 4.

Conclusion

It will have become apparent already, from all of the foregoing, that a number of key factors are having an impact on news journalism across *all* of the above sectors. It is clear that, overall, people within the advanced democracies are spending less of their time accessing news than was the case during, for example, the late 1940s and the 1950s, or even the 1960s. There is a much wider range of alternatives available to people now for the spending of their leisure time and, as has been seen, the ending of the cold war and its tensions has had an impact also. It has reduced popular concern with a global political environment that affects them directly much less (occasional terrorist incidents excepted), while simultaneously the movement towards the middle in politics and the rise in economic living standards for many has taken much of the interest out of domestic politics. With the advent of multichannel broadcasting and the Internet, the choice of news providers and the opportunities for avoiding news programmes altogether have increased dramatically.

The result of all of this has been that there are ever-shrinking audiences for many news products. This has accelerated the move towards conglomeration and convergence, which threaten the diversity and plurality of the news supply and have occasioned a whole variety of other damaging consequences for serious news, including the downsizing of newsrooms and the decreasing influence of news gatherers over company policies, increased reliance on unchecked public relations briefs, reduced coverage and analysis of important political and social issues and, at the most worrying end of the spectrum, an increasing trivialisation and sensationalisation of news.

As later chapters will show, unsurprisingly, all of the above are serious concerns for the future of journalism.

References

Alden, C. (ed.) (2004), *The Guardian Media Directory 2005* (London: Guardian Books).

Alden, C. (ed.) (2005), *The Guardian Media Directory 2006* (London: Guardian Books).

Allen, S. (ed.) (2005), *Journalism: Critical Issues* (Maidenhead: Open University Press).

BBC News Online (2006), 'Campbell says he never used Net', 21 February.

Calabrese, A. (2000), 'Global Debates over Media Standards', in Sparks, C. and Tulloch, J. (eds), *Tabloid Tales – Global Debates over Media Standards* (Lanham MD: Rowman and Littlefield).

Curran, J. (2002), *Media and Power* (London: Routledge).

Deacon, D., Wring, D., Billig, M., Downey, J., Golding P. and Davidson, S. (2005), 'Reporting the 2005 U.K. General Election, Introduction and Executive Summary', The Electoral Commission. Available at <http://www.electoralcommision.org.uk/files/dmst-160805Final19222-14/61_E_N_S_W_.pdf> (Accessed 31 January 2006).

Franklin, B. (1997), *Newszak and News Media* (London: Arnold).

Galbraith, J.K. (1992), *The Culture of Contentment* (London: Sinclair-Stevenson).

Harvey, S. (2004), 'Living with Monsters – Can Broadcasting Regulation make a Difference?', in Calabrese, A. and Sparks, C. (eds), *Toward a Political Economy of Culture* (Lanham MD: Rowman and Littlefield).

Hoggart, R. (2004), *Mass Media in a Mass Society: Myth and Reality* (London: Continuum).

Lloyd, J. (2004), *What the Media are Doing to our Politics* (London: Constable and Robinson).

McChesney, R. (2000), *Rich Media, Poor Democracy: Communication Politics in Dubious Times* (New York: New Press).

Pew Internet and American Life Project (2005), 'How Women and Men Use the Internet', Pew Research Center. Available at <http://www.pewinternet.org.pdfs/

PIP_Women_and_Men_online.pdf>.

Pew Internet and American Life Project (2006), 'Bloggers: A portrait of the Internet's new storytellers', Pew Research Center. Available at: <http://www.internet.org/PPF/r/186_display.asp>.

Pew Research Center for the People and the Press (2006), 'Online Papers Modestly Boost Newspaper Readership', Pew Research Center. Available at <http://www.pewresearch.org/reports/?ReportID=38>.

Project for Excellence in Journalism (2006), 'State of the News Media: Tough Times for Print Journalism – and In-depth Reporting', Pew Research Center. Available at <http://pewresearch.org/reports/?ReportID=13>.

Ross, K. (2005), 'Women in the Boyzone: Gender, News and *Her*story', in Allen, S. (ed.), *Journalism: Critical Issues* (Maidenhead: Open University Press).

Society of Editors (Cole, P.) (2004), 'Diversity in the newsroom: employment of minority ethnic journalists in newspapers'. Available at <http://test1.nepsecure.co.uk/s/Societyofeditors-cmoS2/uploads/documents/84132/Diversity%20in%20the%20Newsroom%20Report%20>.

Sparks, C. (2000), 'From Dead Trees to Live Wires: The Internet's Challenge to the Traditional Newspaper', in Curran, J. and Gurevitch, M. (eds), *Mass Media and Society*, 3rd edition (London: Arnold).

Van Dijk, J. (2005), *The Deepening Divide: Inequality in the Information Society* (London: Sage).

Weymouth, A. and Lamizet, B. (1996), *Markets and Myths* (Harlow: Longman).

Zelizer, B. (2004), *Taking Journalism Seriously* (London: Sage).

Chapter 3

Competing Models of Journalism and Democracy

Peter J. Anderson

Introduction

Opinions relating to the role of the news media in a democracy vary between two extremes. At one end there is what may be called the pragmatic, market view which claims to give the people the news that they want, in forms that are constantly changing, and which go hand-in-hand with commercial viability. This is the dominant 'market' model and it represents in effect the rationalisation of the status quo in the advanced liberal democracies.

At the other end, there is the more theoretical view, that claims a more rational, idealistic function for the news media as a vital force for the participation and empowerment of the people in the democratic process. This view is more prescriptive, more detached and less susceptible to the profit motive that underpins the laissez-faire, market model. In the UK a good example of the market model of news presentation is *The Sun* newspaper; an example of the more idealistic and socially responsible model of news dissemination is the BBC. It will be seen that, in their own ways and with varying degrees of emphasis, the news media of all the democracies that figure in this book operate between these two parameters. Between these two extremes, there are also intermediate models that take on the attributes of both.

It would seem to us that the most important of these various models suggest directly, or by implication, that the news media should:

1. Provide the information necessary for the meaningful[1] functioning of

---

1   There are many 'democracies' where the degree of information flowing to the majority of voters (who, as research by Van Dijk (2005) and others shows, do not use the huge resources of the Internet to access hard news regularly) is so restricted by the traditionally used news media or other factors that it is not possible to say that the electorate is adequately informed. For this reason we would question whether the 'democracy' that occurs in them is 'meaningful'. The US is now a case in point. We further refine our discussion of democracy as the chapter progresses, looking in particular at the provocative analysis of Stromback (2005).

democracies either as:

a) individual presenters of balanced news agendas that attempt to include everything that is *practically* possible and of importance to the interests and welfare of their target audience, or

b) presenters of news within a competitive media environment where the continuous presence and high-quality presentation of competing opinions and ideologies is guaranteed by means of state intervention in the form, if necessary, of legislation or disinterested subsidies, and so on, or

c) presenters of news within a competitive media environment where there is legally guaranteed freedom of expression but the variety of opinions expressed at any one time is left to market forces to decide, or

d) presenters of news in a generally competitive media market that provides a mixture of opinions and ideologies, but which exists in the presence of a substantial news provider that is required to be impartial across the broad range of its coverage in the manner of the BBC;

2. Undertake the role of the Fourth Estate and act as a watchdog and, when necessary, as a counterbalance to those in society who would abuse their power;

3. Act as advocates for actions, policies and laws believed to be in the public interest and show their audience how to help achieve these measures.

Some of the models above go beyond or undermine traditional notions of the public sphere (Habermas, 2002; Calhoun, 1992), which is 'independent of governmental and commercial interests and in which rational critical debate can take place' (Polat, 2005), while others obviously facilitate it. It is not our intention here to re-rehearse the arguments critiquing the notion of the public sphere of Curran (1997; 2002), Dahlgren (1997) and others. While useful in some respects, the concept is problematic in others (even after Habermas' revisions), and too central a focus on it would distract from the main purposes of the book. Rather, it is suggested that the simple but important notion of 'meaningful democracy' is a more potent and easily applicable tool to use for the analysis that follows. The use of this term will permit useful conclusions to be drawn in the final chapters without becoming unnecessarily embroiled in the more abstruse dimensions of media theory debates. It will be combined ultimately with the ideas of competitive democracy and participatory democracy to provide a refined yet easily applied research device.

The Informational Role and the Question of Overlaps

It is of course possible for one or more of the models outlined above to overlap. Some of the newspapers that could be described as helping to provide the information necessary for the meaningful functioning of democracies, for instance, could be argued to be doing so for the same reasons as less serious newspapers provide a mix of celebrity news and gossip, sexual scandal and very limited hard news coverage for their readers. In the case of the upmarket *Times* and the downmarket *Sun*, for example, two daily UK newspapers owned by News Corporation which fit this profile of motives, both are in the business of attracting readers and advertisers in order to make a profit for the parent company. It just so happens that, in order to attract the sophisticated readers whose loyalty will persuade advertisers to part with substantial sums to gain access to their spending power, *The Times* knows that it needs to cover hard news in both breadth and depth. Both newspapers are responding to the market demands of their different audiences and of their common shareholders, but one does so in a manner that enables it to portray itself as being more towards the 'virtuous' public service end of the news provider spectrum.

In the eyes of the most economically liberal media interests and thinkers within democracies there is nothing wrong with the news media's role being driven by the market first and any notion of 'public service' second. All that matters is that freedom of speech should be guaranteed within the constitutions of democracies.[2] How what is said within parliament, business or other arenas is *disseminated* is a separate question and where costs are involved as a result of the need to employ journalists, and so on, then automatically it is an *economic* matter. Those who report, interpret and distribute the news in liberal democracies have the right to expect an economic return for their efforts and equally a right not to cover those things for which there is insufficient demand. Shareholders will not be sympathetic generally to news organisations that go for lower profits when higher ones are known to be available. So, decisions about what types of news (to cover) and how much of it to cover are economic ones for media organisations that adopt this viewpoint and perfectly justifiable as such. They are not stifling democracy in omitting issues for which they do not feel there is a 'consumer demand'. Rather, it can be argued, it is up to those with 'unmarketable' issues that they want to see covered by news organisations to come up with ways of 'repackaging' them into a more marketable format.

These economic considerations, it can also be argued, help to explain why the first of the above models (1a) is not a popular option in a world in which everything has a cost in its production. One problem is that much that is of *importance* to news audiences is deemed not likely to be of *interest* to many of them by shareholder-driven, profit-oriented news organisations. The coverage of parliamentary debates within the UK within quality newspapers, for example, has declined considerably in quantitative terms since the 1960s, as has the coverage of local government. Equally, as the chapter on the American media notes, US television coverage of hard news issues has seriously declined in recent years. In the UK, extracts from the day in Parliament can be found in the pre-midnight graveyard slot on the quality BBC Radio 4 station and there is digital access to a parliament television channel showing debates from the Houses of Parliament, but such detailed coverage is left very much to the public service sector. If economic criteria alone determine whether or not this type of coverage should be offered, then the small audiences for it automatically

---

2   See, for example, McChesney's (2000) extensive discussion of the US media.

provide a negative answer. If, however, public service criteria are used, then the argument becomes one of the need to make the coverage available, in order to provide sufficient information for 'meaningful' democracy to operate. It is up to the public to decide whether or not they wish to access it. The important underlying principle of this approach is that if something of potential importance to the public occurs in parliament, or in other arenas of power, then some outlets at least within the news media should be prepared to present and, where necessary, interpret it for those who are interested. If the public choose not to be interested then that is their right, but at least the information flow necessary for meaningful democracy will have been provided.

However, even where this public service view is adopted, the issue of what it is practicable to cover remains a serious constraint. Even the best quality newspapers have a limited amount of print space, broadcasters have equally obvious limitations upon the amount of time that they can expect to hold a news audience (and consequently the size of the slots that are available to cover each news item) and while online news sites, theoretically, are unconstrained in the number of pages and items that they can run, all news producers are of course limited by the numbers of staff that they can afford to employ to report and edit the news. A BBC-style model would attempt to resolve this problem by prioritising among the range of possible news events and issues on a 'need to know basis' and allocating resources to cover stories that fit within these parameters wherever possible. It would also, as we have emphasised above, do this in a manner which is impartial across the broad range of its coverage.

If we switch to model 1b outlined above, wherein state subsidies, for example, guarantee the continuous presence and high-quality presentation of competing opinions and ideologies within a competitive media market, then we are presented with a credible alternative to the public sector model in meeting adequately the information needs of the citizens within democracies. Indeed, subsidies to Swedish newspapers have been seen as an example of how such a model could work successfully, helping protect hard news content against strong commercial pressures for increasing soft news coverage. However, the downside of the argument can be seen in France, where in the past government subsidies to the French press have been seen as the cause of omission or under-coverage of some important issues which might produce an unfavourable reaction from the subsidy provider. This model is considered in more detail later in the chapter.

The Fourth Estate – Myth, Mask or Media Ideal?

In addition to the various possible informational roles of the media within democracies, there is also the long-running debate over the notion of the news media as the Fourth Estate. This model provides for news media going beyond the role of crucial information provider, within the public sphere, to take up the mantle of guardians of democracy. This concept suggests that the news media have an important role in exposing and counterbalancing the centres of political power whenever they start to abuse that power. The most penetrating and occasionally spectacular way in which they can do this is via investigative journalism of serious political and constitutional issues. The yardstick of all such exposés remains the work of Woodward and Bernstein in bringing to light the Watergate scandal and the abuse of power of the Nixon presidency in the US during the early 1970s, a piece of journalism ultimately that contributed directly to the fall of the President. However, as is pointed out frequently, the Woodward and Bernstein episode was unique. As is explained elsewhere within the book, as profit-driven journalism has become ever more cost-conscious, the expense of investigative journalism of a *serious* political nature has meant that it has all but been extinguished as a characterising mark of the modern democratic news journalism. Investigative journalism, where it does exist, is subjected to the fiercest scrutiny and any loopholes in its reporting are relentlessly exposed by the powerful bodies or individuals it seeks to expose. The enormous political and legal ramifications that can arise when journalists are perceived to cut corners in their fact-checking, or make simple errors in investigations that penetrate through to the centres of power, were emphasised to the whole world when the full weight of the UK government descended on the BBC following the report by Andrew Gilligan resulting from his investigation of Iraq-related issues. Gilligan, the Director General of the BBC and its Chair of the Board of Governors were all forced to fall on their swords on what many regarded as a black day for both democracy and the news media.

However, whatever the rights and wrongs of this affair, tragic at many levels, there is also the question of the legitimacy of the news media's claims to act as 'guardians' of democracy. News providers are not elected and generally are run by conglomerates whose first duty is to their shareholders, who frequently are globally distributed, rather than to the citizens of the states in which their news products are made and sold. It is perhaps only those organisations that have a properly regulated requirement to be impartial that can claim any credible legitimacy as guardians of the public interest, but, as the Gilligan affair illustrated, even this status is open to the accusation of abuse. Claims to legitimacy by those claiming to be members of the Fourth Estate in the sense defined above must therefore be made with care and examined with equal care by those judging them.

There is another way in which some producers of the news interpret the idea of the Fourth Estate and that is as an additional source of power for self-interested individuals or groups within the body politic. This view sees the power and influence accrued by some news organisations as being usable to (try to) persuade governments to follow directions preferred by the proprietors or editors of the news outlets concerned. News Corporation, for example, is an organisation that has often been alleged to be well versed in the arts of behind-the-scenes lobbying and charm offensives aimed at governments and legislators (see, for example, BBC, 2006) and direct threats issued via its newspaper subsidiaries. The UK's New Labour government has more than once been reminded on the front page of *The Sun* that Rupert Murdoch's pre-1997 understanding with it, which led to *The Sun*'s 'wolfhound' political journalists being called off the party's trail, would be revoked if it strayed too far from policies of which he approved. This interpretation of the term 'Fourth Estate' is subversive of democracy rather than protective of it.

The Media as Advocates and Facilitators of Actions, Policies and Laws Believed to be in the Public Interest

There is a view, represented by strands of the public journalism school within US media thinking, that sees the presentation of balanced, objective news reports of complex issues as leaving much of the electorate perplexed as to how best to interpret and act on issues that affect directly their interests and welfare. This, it is argued, is one of the reasons why many American voters no longer participate in elections, because they have been left feeling confused and powerless (Merritt, 1999). From this point of view, far from strengthening democracy, the traditional American objective approach towards journalism actually serves to weaken it.

What is needed, according to some, is an alternative approach in which well-informed journalists help their readers to interpret the world around them and offer them guidance as to how they might best try to deal with its challenges. This 'hearts on sleeves' (informed but partial) kind of journalism, it is argued, is the best way of bringing voters back as active participants in the political system and of recreating a vigorous and meaningful democracy.

Criticisms of this point of view note that this is an approach which, however well intended, has the effect of removing independent thought and participation from those voters who follow it through an inability to formulate alternative viewpoints. It is far better, it is argued, to provide the news audience with balanced news in which alternative viewpoints are so effectively explained that they are able to understand them well enough to make up their own minds, rather than depend on the opinions of others. It is, in other words, the quality of the explanation in an objective approach to journalism that is the true servant of meaningful democracy.

The Measure of Democracy

The debates surrounding many of the above models are both well established and long-running and it would be an act of pointless duplication to rehearse them here in greater detail than above. The purpose rather in this chapter is to establish which of the above models most fits in with and facilitates the concept of meaningful democracy as outlined earlier. The results of our findings – after having been refined by a discussion of Stromback's study (2005) shortly – will then provide a rough measure to be used in the concluding chapter against the findings from the various country chapters. It will help the editors arrive at an overall judgement on the question of whether current trends in journalism are likely to undermine or strengthen democracy in the future.

In this regard, of the models listed at the beginning of this chapter, only 1c, which refers to the belief that news providers should act as *presenters of news within a competitive media environment where there is legally guaranteed freedom of expression but the variety of opinions expressed at any one time is left to the market to decide*, is automatically disqualified as a means of facilitating meaningful democracy. As was seen earlier, the market is simply too fickle and unpredictable a mechanism to be trusted with the making of decisions as to which information and opinions should be disseminated within societies and which should not. There is too great a danger that it will leave untold stories whose telling is in the interests of particularly the less privileged.

As far as the other three models listed in the same paragraph are concerned, some of the problems with 1a, which refers to the belief that media organisations should act as *individual presenters of balanced news agendas that attempt to include everything that is* practically *possible and of importance to the interests and welfare of their target audience*, have been discussed already. The goal of comprehensiveness central to this model is difficult to achieve for even the most conscientious of profit-driven commercial news providers, given that the importance of news and mass audience interest, that is, ratings, are often perceived not to overlap. It is much more the type of goal that can be adopted by public service corporations like the BBC, which have a large measure of established independence, both financially and editorially, and which are not beholden to the market for their survival. But the goal of providing the widest practicable coverage requires also an organisation of considerable size and resources and again we would have to look to the BBC as an example of the scale of operation that would be needed. Its national and international networks of reporters and correspondents give it potentially a range of coverage that few can rival.

Again, in the brief preceding discussion of 1b (which refers to *presenters of news within a competitive media environment where the continuous presence and high-quality presentation of competing opinions and ideologies is guaranteed by means of state intervention in the form, if necessary, of legislation or disinterested subsidies, and so on*), a major problem has been identified already. It has two dimensions. First, there is always the danger that, behind the scenes, governments providing subsidies might subtly or otherwise threaten the recipients with cuts or withdrawal if they cross forbidden lines in their reporting. Second, there is the problem of self-censorship where, without being directly asked, news organisations might tread over-carefully concerning issues that the providers of subsidies would find sensitive. Where the atmosphere and attitudes of a democracy's political environment are sophisticated enough to preclude such problems, then state interventions such as subsidies can be a valuable protector of hard news content against the increasing encroachment of soft news. But if it is to be guaranteed that the above problems do not arise then the provision of assistance, such as subsidies and inflation-linked periodic increases in these, must be placed within a protective legal framework that precludes government mischief. There is a potential downside even to this 'protected' approach, however, that needs to be borne in mind from a democratic point of view. Subsidies may encourage complacency that blunts the appetite in the newsroom for creative effort and energised reporting. In France, for example, where, in the past, in the opinion of some, subsidies have made some newspapers complacent by cushioning them against the 'real world' and encouraging them to stick with 'stodgy' formats and reporting styles that have lost them readers. Where this is the case, then it could be argued that subsidies actually operate against the democratic interest through the consequent loss of readers that can occur.

If we move on to look at the Fourth Estate model we find that there exist complications with the idea that this might be a facilitator of meaningful democracy. Questions of legitimacy and of whether or not a news organisation is able to adopt a disinterested, unbiased stance are paramount. It is of course impossible to remove all bias from any human perspective on an issue, as the literature on *framing* within journalism ably demonstrates (Fairclough, 2001: 83–4, 99–100), but it *is* possible to remove a significant amount. Within the constraints of the real world, this relative freedom from bias is the most that can be expected. As long as a news organisation credibly aims to achieve this relative freedom, it then can claim legitimacy.

In practice, as pointed out previously, it is difficult for any news organisation, other than those that have a properly regulated requirement to be impartial, to claim any credible legitimacy as guardians of the public interest. In the UK, for example, the commercial or ideological motives that can interfere with the journalism or editorials of news providers such as the *Daily Mail, The Daily Telegraph, The Guardian, The Daily Mirror, The Sun, The Times*, to name but a few, must always raise the suspicion that Fourth Estate postures that purport to be in the interests of meaningful democracy are contaminated. The same suspicions are markedly less visible with regard to the journalism of the BBC.

With regard to the final model, referring to the idea that the news media should act as advocates for actions, policies and laws believed to be in the public interest and show their audience how to help achieve these measures, it is clearly possible for this perspective to be compatible with meaningful democracy. For this to be the case, it is necessary that there exists a competitive media environment in which alternative viewpoints are freely available and that a news organisation of the scale and nature of the role of the BBC be present also. The greater the number of these prerequisites then the more compatible with democratic advocacy journalism becomes. It is for the significant reason already explained in the discussion of this form of journalism above that problems begin to arise when the presence of these prerequisites is inadequate or they are missing.

Refining the Analysis – Four Models of Democracy and their Implications for the Types of Information that Journalism Should Provide

While it is useful to speak of meaningful democracy being dependent upon adequate flows of high-quality information, as we propose here, we should bear in mind, as Stromback (2005) points out, that there are different models of *democracy* and different *types of information* that might flow within them. If the intention is to produce journalism that will strengthen democracy, then the problem is that some characteristics of journalism will strengthen some models of democracy but weaken others. To develop his point, Stromback identifies four different key models of democracy within the literature – procedural democracy, competitive democracy, participatory democracy and deliberative democracy – and distinguishes between the different demands that each places upon journalism.

Procedural democracy focuses centrally on free and fair elections as the primary mechanism for securing the common good and requires of the citizenry at minimum that they respect democratic procedures. It requires of journalism that it acts as a watchdog or a burglar alarm (Zaller, 2003), exposing wrongdoings.

Competitive democracy focuses on the competing records and the competing platforms of political parties. It requires of journalism the following: it should act as a watchdog or burglar alarm; it should provide information on the record of officeholders that is adequate for voters to make an informed judgement on their performance; it should provide sufficient information for voters to judge both the platforms of political candidates and the political actors themselves. Finally, it sees the voters as reactive rather than proactive.

Participatory democracy is very much concerned with citizen participation in public life within political parties and outside them as well. It requires that journalism should mobilise the citizens' interest and participation in public life and help them set the agenda. Unlike the competitive model's tendency to portray politics as a strategic game played by elites which, outside of elections, the voters merely watch, participatory democracy requires journalism to frame politics as a process open for the active participation of everyone. In order to show that this can be a positive endeavour, it requires also that journalism focuses on the solving of problems and not just the problems themselves.

The final model, *deliberative democracy*, moves a little too far into the theoretical world and away from the reality of everyday life to be considered as a practical alternative here. It assumes a degree of rationality, impartiality and deliberative discussions among all sections of the public and their representatives that is unlikely to be realised in an imperfect world. Despite its impracticalities, however, it is worth noting in passing that some of its requirements of journalism fit neatly the ideal of those who favour the BBC-style news provision, namely the fostering 'of public discussions characterized by rationality, impartiality, intellectual honesty and equality' (Stromback, 2005: 337 and 341).

What Type of Democracy and What Type of Journalism is Relevant Here?

It seems to us that if the democratic empowerment of citizens is the core concern of news provision, then, while competitive democracy is essential in order to provide for the removal or voting into power of governments, the encouragement of participatory democracy is essential also if those representing the electors are to be kept fully in touch with citizen interests between elections. Governments faced with electorates that are, to a noticeable and potentially 'irritating' degree, proactive as well as reactive, have much more of an incentive to keep listening to those who elected them between elections. From a practical point of view, if Stromback's summary analysis is taken as a useful guide, then the *types of information* that journalism provides should be a combination of those meeting the requirements outlined above under the headings of competitive democracy and participatory democracy. It is proposed that these be adopted for the purposes of this book, while accepting simultaneously that the extent to which they can be provided is dependent upon the resources available to news organisations and the time and space available to them for presenting news information.

Audiences and Reception

Before drawing the chapter to a close it is important to emphasise once again a point made near the beginning, namely that while those forms of journalism that most facilitate meaningful democracy do so by maximising the availability of high-quality information about the issues that most affect the electorate, *ultimately it is up to the electorate as to whether they access it or not*. It is perfectly possible that significant numbers of voters will choose to ignore much of the information presented to them. This is not necessarily because of idleness or disinterest, but can be the result of the pressures of their long working hours, for example, or the switch to radio in place of the broader compass of quality newspapers as a result of people deciding to commute by car instead of public transport. All that can be attempted is the establishment of the best news media provision that practicality allows in line with the above suggestions. There is no perfect democracy in which everyone will make use of such a facility.

Conclusion

In this chapter we have set out a selection of models relating to the role of the news media in the advanced democracies. Whether contributors refer explicitly or not to them in their chapters, various of these models will be revealed as operating within the countries that they examine. The identification of their presence will help the reader determine the extent to which meaningful democracy is operating within each of these states. We have noted also how, following Stromback's terminology, meaningful democracy can be profitably further refined into the concepts of competitive democracy and participatory democracy.

It is now possible to move on to our final discussion in Part 1, that relating to the challenges facing the journalism of the future.

References

BBC (2006), *Newsnight*, 28 July.

Calhoun, C. (1992), *Habermas and the Public Sphere* (Cambridge MA: MIT Press).

Curran, J. (1997), 'Rethinking the Media as a Public Sphere', in Dahlgren, P. and Sparks, C. (eds), *Communication and Citizenship: Journalism and the Public Sphere* (London: Routledge).

Curran, J. (2002), *Media and Power* (London: Routledge).

Dahlgren, P. (1997), 'Introduction', in Dahlgren, P. and Sparks, C. (eds), *Communication and Citizenship: Journalism and the Public Sphere* (London: Routledge).

Fairclough, N. (2001), *Media Discourse* (London: Arnold).

Habermas, J. (2002), *The Structural Transformation of the Public Sphere* (Cambridge: Polity Press).

McChesney, R. (2000), *Rich Media, Poor Democracy: Communication Politics in Dubious Times* (New York: New Press).

Merritt, D. (1999), 'Public Life: Why Telling the News is Not Enough', (excerpt) in Tumber, H. (ed.), *News: A Reader* (New York: Oxford University Press).

Polat, R.K. (2005), 'The Internet and political participation: exploring the explanatory links', *European Journal of Communication* 20 (4), 435–59.

Stromback, J. (2005), 'In search of a standard: four models of democracy and their normative implications for journalism', *Journalism Studies* 6 (5), 331–45.

Van Dijk, J. (2005), *The Deepening Divide: Inequality in the Information Society* (London: Sage).

Zaller, J. (2003), 'A new standard of news quality: burglar alarms for the monitorial citizen', *Political Communication* 20 (2), 109–30.

Chapter 4

Challenges for Journalism

Peter J. Anderson

Introduction

One of the tasks undertaken by our contributors to the country-specific chapters is to identify both negative and positive aspects of the various new developments in journalism that are happening already, about to happen or may possibly occur in the future. The focus in this chapter is entirely on the challenges, those issues that journalism will need to respond to if it is to retain the high levels of quality that are available still at the top end of the media spectrum, and at the very least improve the situation amongst the less quality-conscious news providers.

Of the book's three core questions, as set out in Chapter 1,[1] the first will be addressed most directly in the section on media economics, while the second will be examined most closely in the section on technology. The third is an obvious consideration in the discussion on diversity. The questions will be raised at the points that they are most relevant here, sometimes indirectly. Because the debates and themes that they provoke will arise throughout the book, overall conclusions relating to them will be reserved for the final chapters.

It is in the nature of most developments affecting professional activity that they can be double-edged swords. Those most enthusiastic about digital journalism, for example, often serve as missionaries for all of its many possibilities. However, those with a more cynical eye tend to point to the temptation to cut staffing and other costs that it provides and argue that ultimately, in the hands of profit-led conglomerates, for whom news provision is but one of their myriad business activities, it will damage rather than enhance news quality. It is arguments such as the latter that will be examined critically here.

The main danger for journalism now and for the immediate future is one of being caught in a pincer movement from which there is no easy escape. It is faced with what might be termed the 'ec-tech' squeeze – simultaneous and increasing pressures

---

1   That is, (1) to what extent is traditional hard news losing ground to soft news across the media of the advanced world and what can be done to reverse this trend if this is a serious problem? (2) to what extent is the range and depth of coverage of news issues within the advanced democracies adequate for the purpose of ensuring that electorates are adequately informed about the world around them? (3) to what extent is it possible to access balanced presentations of the news within the various advanced democracies within this study?

from both economic forces and the accelerating pace of technological change. Chapter 2 outlined some of the key ways in which this is happening and subsequent chapters will provide more detailed examples with regard to specific segments of UK journalism and across a selection of the other advanced democracies. What we can note here is that the pace of technological developments affecting the news media is now so rapid that parts of this book inevitably will be outdated, or on their way to becoming so, by the time it is published. However, it is likely that this problem will affect mostly specific technologies, not the issues surrounding them, which tend to be inherent in the underlying process of continuous innovation and development itself.

It is proposed firstly here to look at the nature of the technological challenge and possible responses to it and then subsequently to do the same with the economic challenges. Finally, an additional significant issue, that of diversity and its related challenges, will be examined and some overall conclusions drawn.

The Pressures Driving Media Technology Forwards and Some of Their Consequences

The accelerating rate of development of technologies relevant to journalism has been fuelled by several factors, which include among others:

- huge amounts of military spending in the US, focused on keeping in the vanguard of weapons technology, a phenomenon that has resulted in a variety of crucial spin-offs, from advances in chip technology to crucial developments facilitating the birth of the Internet;
- the growth of global markets for consumer goods and services (including those relating to the media) and the technologies needed to produce them (most recently and most massively in China);
- the growth of global corporations determined to exploit the expanding markets and able also to invest vast sums in research and development, enabling them competitively to drive technology forwards towards increasingly sophisticated and attractive products/services and take full advantage of the new market opportunities.

One of the powerhouses at the heart of the liberal orthodox free market economics that is fuelling the surge in the development of communication technologies is the popular desire for wealth and the prestige accruing from the use of the latest products. In turn, free market economics encourages such desires through mass advertising, lifestyle magazines, internationally marketed aspirational television programmes and the celebrity soft news culture that has grown up around and because of it. These factors in turn have been reinforced in their effect by the political shift towards the centre and centre-right that has occurred across many of the advanced democracies (see Chapter 2), and the ideological assurance that has helped justify this from the time of Thatcher and Reagan onwards; namely, the old liberal argument that the pursuit of individual wealth is desirable because it drives economic growth upwards. This, allegedly, is to the benefit of all. It is not within the remit of this book either to challenge or accept this economic rationale, but rather to note both its existence and the powerful role which it plays in helping drive technological advance forwards for media-related products such as multichannel television receivers, digital radios, Internet-connected computers, mobile phones that can receive television and/or radio programmes, view/listen-on-demand equipment, and so on. The development and sales of all of these can have an impact not only on the range of platforms on which news is provided, but also on the way in which it is provided. A most obvious example of this impact upon news presentation, which followed the growth of the Internet as a popular resource and of increasing sales of equipment able to access it, results from the decision of various mainstream traditional news providers to set up online news sites. They did this in order to retain/increase news audiences in the face of the distractions occasioned by this growing new technology. Very soon after doing so *The Washington Post*, *The Guardian* and the BBC were all obliged to provide their news in a different format from that offered on their traditional platforms. This was because, among other things, of the different way in which people read online news from print news and the difference in the time that people frequently spend accessing online news as compared to broadcast news. New, specialist staff were required also to make this possible. Now that portable electronic books are almost upon us it will not be long before their newspaper equivalents appear. The impact of the latter could be enormous, not only allowing for video footage, regular updating of stories and interactivity to be included within a handheld daily newspaper but also cutting both production costs and jobs, given the likely decline in demand for the traditional paper versions with their need of transport and distribution and other labour-intensive services.

Equally, as a result of the process of continuing technological development producing new, cost-effective digital/multichannel transmission routes, the growth in the number of television channels and radio stations has prompted broadcast-relevant software and hardware manufacturers to invest in product development that will help to meet competitively the needs of this expanded sector of the media industry. The potency of the resulting new developments in, for example, camera technologies, editing technologies and computer technologies has been enhanced by another of the factors mentioned in Chapter 2, namely the shrinking channel/station audiences for individual news products caused by the massively increased competition for reader/ audience attention. This has made even more attractive the technologies that news organisations believe will give them a competitive edge. Technologies that facilitate news production using fewer people have become increasingly appealing to profit-driven media companies, for example. One of the consequences of the resulting downsizing has been that the quality of news products has been perceived as falling, as we saw in Chapter 2.

As digital broadband technologies increase in popularity and capability, they will make it increasingly likely that traditional newspaper and television companies will be reconfigured by their owners (in most cases conglomerates) as multimedia content providers. Broadband users could become travellers across a seamless web of news, information and entertainment, switching from traditional television news, for example, to online news sites owned by the same provider offering more information, interactivity and search and research facilities with links to the sites of the group's various newspapers, then on to digital radio. The ability of companies to offer desirable content across all of these formats and more would give them a much better chance of holding on to these 'travellers' as they move from one type of content to another. As the online journalism chapter shows, there is a possibility that individual content providers will move towards Danish-style converged newsrooms to ensure that stories are handled effectively on every available platform, from mobile phones to e-newspapers, print newspapers, and so on. Such a move would maximise both audiences and income. While the news and information possibilities of this type of development are in theory very attractive, critics have again pointed to the temptation to downsize and to the resulting loss of quality journalism that such a cost-saving policy would bring about.

The point of setting all of this down here is to illustrate both the power of the forces behind the phenomenon of accelerating technological development and the likelihood of it remaining as both a problem and an opportunity for news journalism for the foreseeable future.

The Heart of the Matter: What Kinds of Responses to these Technological Challenges are Required?

All of this debate so far leads neatly into the heart of the matter as far as the implications of technological development for news journalism are concerned. In short, new technologies, or more advanced forms of existing ones, can both enhance or detract from the quality of news journalism. When decisions on whether or how to use them are left solely to particular forms of economic logic and/or simple judgements as to whether they are an improvement technically on existing tools used in the news production process, the positive or negative effects on the quality of news journalism[2] are random rather than intended. Clearly, if the quality of news journalism is the central concern (which, in practice, as other chapters in the book show, is often no longer the case in conglomerate-owned news operations), then the likely impact on it of new technological developments needs to be thought through carefully prior to their introduction. However, because all news operations need to make at least enough money to stay in business, it may be the case that some new developments potentially damaging to the quality of the journalism will have to be adopted anyway to supply the cost-efficiencies or general competitiveness necessary to survive. But at least if the implications have been thought through thoroughly then measures can be taken to try to minimise or compensate for the damage.

---

2   That is, the effects on the quality of analysis, background research, and so on, as opposed to the quality of, for example, television pictures or newspaper illustrations.

Unfortunately, examples abound of cases where new technologies and the possibilities that they open up have been implemented without proper concern for their impact on news journalism, and without ways of compensating for any consequent damage. Lack of space prevents us from covering the situation in every country in a single chapter, so the examples used here are taken mainly from the UK. However, as such diverse authors as Mancini (1997), McChesney (2000) and Brandenburg (in this book) have emphasised, it is important to bear in mind that different democracies work in different ways and that not all of the principles and ideas offered by our examples below would be relevant to all of the countries examined in this book. What follows, therefore, must be regarded as illustrative rather than definitive of ways in which to represent specific key technology-related media problems and their possible solutions.

Multichannel Problems

Prominent among examples of the introduction of a new technology without adequate consideration of the consequences for news journalism was the introduction of multichannel television following on from developments in cable and satellite technology. Chapter 2 explained how the channel-hopping freedom opened up by the significantly increased competition has not only made it possible now for audiences to avoid completely the quality news programmes provided by the BBC, Channel 4 and, to a lesser extent, ITV (or indeed, *any* news programmes) in the UK, but also has caused even respected news producers to downgrade, in some cases radically, the amount or prominence of their news coverage, for example BBC3. The fragmentation of audiences occasioned by multichannel has made it increasingly difficult for those wishing to hold the line on the quality and quantity of hard news in commercial companies. It was notable also that ITV's rolling news channel received the death sentence at the end of 2005 following the fragmented market's failure to sustain three operations competing for the same audience (BBC Online, 2005a).

Equally, hard news documentaries, once seen as vital opportunities to pursue key news items in greater depth or even make the news, have gone into massive decline in countries like the UK, where they were once a prominent part of television schedules. The BBC's *Panorama*, for example, suffered a significant decline in its audience after being moved to the near-graveyard slot of 10.15 on Sunday evenings. Respected ITV1 counterparts such as *World in Action* and *This Week* have long disappeared. In the eyes of many programmers with a brief to maximise audience share, programmes like these have become too much of a liability and a lost 'audience opportunity' in an age of competing multichannel and multi-entertainment platforms.

Yet, despite all the evidence for these adverse trends, the UK government has continued to try to forge ahead with the switch-over from analogue to digital television with a minimum of regulatory conditions relating to the quality of news journalism. It has pressured the BBC into leading the march towards what will become multichannel for all, whether people want it or not. The lack of thought at government level as to how this might impinge on the quality of news operations was evidenced when, after insisting that BBC3 should have a respectable news provision prior to its launch in 2003, the Culture Secretary, Tessa Jowell, changed tack in October 2005. She did this when presented with evidence that her requirement was simply losing channel-hoppers in a market that was already so fragmented that the struggling channel was experiencing real difficulty in attracting a large enough audience to justify its existence to licence payers (see, for example, BBC Online, 2003). She defended her action by citing the Barwood Report's observation (BBC Online, 2005b) that BBC3's target audience accessed their news in other ways. The result was the ending of the half-hourly 7 p.m. news programme in December 2005. BBC3 news now consists solely of hourly 60-second bulletins.

In short, joined-up thinking at either government or industry level, or in some cases, both levels, has been noticeable by its absence where the impact of promoting multichannel television in the UK has been concerned. There does not seem to have been any proper thinking through of the impact on the quality of news provision and news journalism that this new development might have. Admittedly, this lack of forethought was masked at the beginning when Rupert Murdoch was careful to ensure, via his 24-hour television news operation, that he could claim that the advent of multichannel added to, rather than subtracted from, the overall range and quality of broadcast news provision. But as channels have continued to proliferate, this argument no longer holds, and what is missing from official (and a lot of industry) thinking on digital and multichannel broadcasting in general is how mechanisms can be introduced to compensate for some of the damage already done to news provision, and, indeed, to news accessing by potential audiences. Even were this situation to change, the possibilities of what can be done in the commercial sector certainly are limited by the very consequences of the audience fragmentation produced already by multichannel. Limited audiences mean, by definition, limited resources for quality news production.

It could be argued that, if multichannel television and radio *are to meet the information and understanding needs of a democracy* as laid down in Chapter 3, governments should introduce a requirement that all channels, except shopping-only and pornography channels and other such special interest exotica, carry substantial news bulletins produced to specified minimum quality criteria during breakfast, lunchtime and evening peak-time viewing. The quality criteria could be adjusted in line with audience profiles. Where programme providers are unable to run news operations of sufficient quality to meet these criteria, they could be required to air news programmes run by providers who can, such as the BBC or Sky. In order to counter the problem of channel-hopping during news programmes, the requirement could be that news provision should be in the same slots across all channels. (The problems created for all of this by the advent of multi-platform broadband and view/ listen-on-demand will be discussed below.) However, realistically, it must be said that the liberal free market, minimum regulation preferences of both of the main political parties in the UK at the moment make such a bold step as this unlikely.

If they defied all expectations and did so, the most fervent free market broadcasters would portray the idea of universal news slots on multichannel television/digital radio as an infringement of people's right to choose and a temptation for viewers (and listeners) to stop watching or listening to TV-sourced digital radio during such slots and simply to partake of one of the myriad alternative distractions that computers (through which digital television also can be viewed) and other modern technology make possible. The answers to these specific complaints are that choice in the sense used by the marketeers conceals the loss of a much greater freedom. It results in a situation where people can end up in such a state of information poverty about the world around them that they lose the ability to make informed choices about the politics and economics that affect their lives. It is not sufficient to argue that the 'information-poor' can pick up what they need to know from newspapers, on which many of them already choose not to spend their money and the most popular of which in any case contain little hard news, or from the Internet, which available figures suggest is most often used for purposes other than the accessing of high-quality hard news (Van Dijk, 2005). Television and radio have the advantage, between them, of still being the most commonly accessed media for long periods of people's leisure time every day. In Europe, for example, 95 per cent of the population watches television for an average of around three and a half hours per day (Wallström, 2005) and in the UK the average citizen spends 26 hours per week doing the same (Mason, 2006). While those households that access broadband Internet services within the UK spend an average of 16 hours per week online, this figure is still far short of the television viewing figures. Indeed, convergence will mean that in future television viewing should become an increasing part of people's time online. A survey by the O_2 mobile phone company showed that a sample of 400 people provided with mobile phones capable of accessing television programmes used their handsets for an average of three hours per day for television viewing, extending yet further the platforms on which television can be an attractive leisure pursuit (BBC, 2006). If there is any one medium through which democracies can most effectively try to ensure that their citizens get the information that they need to be informed participants in society, then arguably television is it. The addition of radio as a still prospering, albeit less accessed, medium would be a bonus.

The answer to the second complaint relating to audience defection from news broadcasts, in the circumstances proposed above, is that a degree of audience switch-off is predictable and will need to be built into company budgets if minimum news provision obligations are accepted as a condition of transmission in democracies that are likely to malfunction without it. But if people choose to avoid the news necessary for them to understand their world then that is their right, foolish though it may be to exercise it. But they should at least have the choice. From a democratic perspective, the key concern is that the means of securing access to the information provided by good-quality journalism should be as easily accessible as possible. In the light of what we know about the use of leisure time it is clear that television and radio are the media that most completely meet that requirement.

However, television is only going to continue to meet this requirement if, across its range of provision (excluding for the moment 'view-on-demand' programmes), there is sufficient quality programming of the kind that the various major segments of the audience desire, *when* they desire to see it. In this regard, the increased programme competition provided via multichannel television, together with the increased competition for advertising from other multichannel providers and the Internet, presents commercial companies with a serious problem. This combination of factors has made it increasingly difficult for them to find the money necessary for the expensive, high-quality programmes that those sectors of their audiences most attractive to the advertisers may require for purposes connected more with their need as citizens than as consumers.

Problems Raised by View-On-Demand and Listen-On-Demand Technologies

A further problem derives from the possibilities opened up by the new developing view-on-demand and listen-on-demand technologies. These have serious implications for news in so far as they enable viewers of television programmes and also radio listeners to construct their own daily schedules. McNair has observed that, 'From the offices of News Corp to the boardrooms of the BBC, the age of top-down, elite-controlled media is passing ...' (McNair, 2006). Whereas, for example, television news programmes that appear regularly in traditional channel slots have the potential to grab the attention of the marginal viewer through skilfully constructed 'hooks', simple programme listings do not have the same 'hooking' power. It is possible, therefore, that viewing and listening on demand will decrease significantly the audience for television and radio news. This would obviously be the case if it is taken up by large numbers of marginal news accessors choosing simply to omit news from their personal schedules in the absence of the audio-visual hooks normally needed to grab their attention.

So, in a situation where democracies allow technological advance to be, in effect, the key deciding factor (that is, not their citizens or their legislators) of the extent to which the news that is necessary to inform electorates is likely to be accessed, there is an uncomfortable truth to be endured. *Even if universal news slots were introduced on multichannel television, their compensating effect for uncontrolled and still-advancing technology would be limited.* The only answer to this is to try to boost the attractiveness of news programming before viewing and listening on demand really takes off in the hope that this will increase and retain its audience, even if many of those who receive it choose to switch largely to the new interactive technology. This may well be a pious hope rather than a real prospect.

The way in which viewing and listening on demand could blow apart the kind of illustrative regulatory arrangement discussed above is a neat illustration of how, currently, media technologies are dictating the information formats and flow patterns in democracies rather than the other way around. Opinions differ: on the one hand there is what seems to be an accepted view that whatever can be done in the field of consumer media technology should be done in accordance with the dictates of the market. On the other there is the view that modern democracies must take as one of their core concerns the need to ensure the presence of *high-quality, independent and **as near universally received as possible*** channels of political/economic/social information and analysis, with the resulting democratic empowerment that such channels bring.

To go back to an earlier argument: from a democratic standpoint, those new technological developments that provoke the concerns expressed in the second of the above views need to be considered carefully in terms of their implications for the quality of news journalism. It may be that all new communication-related technologies should be subject to a licensing process and given greater scrutiny with regard to their potential effects on information flow before their use is sanctioned. Where such scrutiny determines that they could damage seriously either news journalism or the accessing of news provision by the public, then both industry and private individuals could be invited to suggest means by which any damage done could be credibly compensated for. Where no credible means emerge, then the licence could be refused.

To suggest such a regime is, of course, to invite ridicule in societies where democracy has very much become subordinated to the market and incessant demands for consumer goods that are 'the latest' or the most pleasure-giving, or both. However, such a proposal does nevertheless perform two useful functions. First, it shows something of what the requirements now are if the communicative needs and obligations of advanced democracies are to be taken seriously in the face of unprecedented and consistently challenging rates of technological development. Second, it demonstrates just how far from being true democracies many societies that describe themselves as such have become. While the editors do not agree with all of the ideas and analysis in Robert W. McChesney's *Rich Media, Poor Democracy*, it is worth looking at his recommendations for reforming the US news media for cross-cultural comparative purposes (McChesney, 2000: 317) here. If democracies are to recover the credentials that they have lost, then there has to be a sea change in their thinking about such matters. The challenge, for those who wish to move them towards such a revolution, is in how to present them with incentives that are sufficient to bring this about. This is indeed tricky, particularly when the economic muscle of some of the media industry operators, whose interests and instincts lead them automatically to oppose any such ideas, is considered. It is economic matters that we now turn to.

The Challenges from Economic Forces

Economic and technological pressures on news journalism do, of course, overlap, as the above section has demonstrated, not least because currently they are both being driven forwards by a particular economic ideology. If liberal orthodox free market economics is the principal engine that is driving technological change forwards, and is likely to continue to do so for the foreseeable future, it is driving also a variety of other changes that are challenging the standards of news journalism. One of the purposes of this section is to examine a selection of the most important of those changes and the challenges that they present.

A number of these issues were mentioned in Chapter 2. They include: the process of conglomeration and the power of owners that results from it; the commodification of news; the trivialisation of news; declining diversity in news provision; and the fragmentation of the audience, with some of the consequences mentioned in the previous section, as a result of massively increased competition.

Much has been written about these various phenomena elsewhere (Franklin, 1997; McChesney, 2000; Bagdikian, 2004) and while they will be examined to the extent that space and relevance permits, it is not proposed here to duplicate debates that have occurred already in other chapters. The priority aim here is to unpick crucial parts of the economic logic underpinning some of the key processes that are challenging the quality standards of news journalism and to do this in layperson's terms. An accessible dissection of the logic is essential for an understanding of a large part of the current pressures on news journalism. We intend subsequently to look at the implications of our findings for news journalism and the steps that need to be taken to protect or at least partially restore its highest standards.

The starting point is the frequent tendency of competition to be a self-reducing process, whether within a media market or any other. After all, at its most basic, it could be seen as a Darwinian process involving the survival of the fittest. It is, for example, possible to start with a market in which there are many competing television production companies, both within a particular country and across the globe. By definition, initially those companies that produce the largest number of financially profitable programmes for their home market will begin to dominate that market and it will become increasingly tempting for less successful companies to merge with, or be taken over by, them. Investors tend to flock to success and away from under-performers, so it becomes harder for the latter to catch up once they have fallen significantly behind. In a business as expensive as television production, it becomes more and more difficult for new market entrants to challenge the market leaders once their position has become established. Equally, where companies with the benefit of huge domestic markets from which to earn the profits and investment necessary for large-scale television production are successful and combine that success with an ability to produce programmes with international appeal (as has been the case with the largest American companies), they can gradually narrow down the competition elsewhere. For example, even the larger domestic companies in smaller markets like the UK can appear too small to raise the finance necessary to compete with the giants, either at home or overseas. This is one of the reasons why Carlton and Granada, already under pressure from falling advertising revenues, merged within the UK in 2004. Unless regulation prohibits it, the temptation to create super-large domestic players, via mergers or takeovers, can become irresistible to company boards and to shareholders. The argument that the size of a company is a key factor in determining whether it can compete successfully in both domestic and international markets tends to become crucial to their thinking.

This tendency towards concentration may seem to be contradicted by the huge growth of competitive multichannel television in countries like the UK or the US, but in reality the major channels are offshoots of the existing big players.

In other words, within liberal orthodox free market economic systems with minimal regulation, competition ultimately has a tendency to become transformed into concentration. This is manifested in its most extreme form in huge multimedia entities such as Rupert Murdoch's News Corporation, the scale and range of whose media assets is monumental (McChesney, 2000: 98–9).

However, while all such comment as this provides a useful if crude *introductory* analysis of the way media economics works, the logic leading towards the concentration of media production within such companies as News Corporation is a little more complicated in the real world. As is shown elsewhere in the book, it can include:

- the need of newspaper companies to become part of larger groups, within which costs can be reduced by using common in-house advertising sales operations or printing operations, *as profitability and markets decline in specific newspaper sectors*;
- the related desire in more successful companies, potentially greatly facilitated by the advent of Danish-style converged newsrooms,[3] to cut costs and *maximise existing profits* via the economies of scale gained through being bigger and more integrated;
- the simple desire of profit-seeking companies to increase their profits by acquiring, at a suitable price, (1) other profit-generating media companies, such as successful local and/or regional newspaper groups, or television companies, or (2) overseas broadcast rights for their existing subsidiaries;
- and relatedly, the desire of large profit-seeking companies to reduce competition by purchasing those providing it, thus hopefully attracting more advertising, investment and profit to their own operation.

Unsurprisingly, the economic logic driving concentration has consequences. A variety of things, some beneficial, some quite damaging, potentially can happen to news operations as they become swallowed up within the conglomerates that now dominate the national and international markets across the advanced democracies. At the most basic level, for example, whereas local newspapers that were owned by small, dedicated news production companies in the 1950s and 1960s[4] knew that the interests of their proprietors would be focused solely on them, those same newspapers that

---

3 See the online journalism chapter.

4 The *Southport Visiter* in the UK, for example, grew to become a large player amongst a small number of Lancashire/Merseyside local newspapers within the Stephenson Newspapers company, which itself remained independent until 1957 (<www.ketupa.net>, 2006). It is now

have survived down to the present and become but one part of media conglomerates with widespread interests have no such comforting reassurance. As was stated in Chapter 2, it is becoming increasingly difficult for editors and journalists to be heard within the decision-making circles of the giant media companies, a number of which have far wider interests than news journalism. Within such corporate frameworks it is all too easy for news to cease to be seen in any sense as a public good with relevance to the well-being of democratic societies. Instead it is viewed simply as one more item on a company's list of products or services that shows up as a profit or a loss in the accounts.

It is at this point that the definition of news itself comes under most pressure. When news is seen *simply* as a product then the kind of news that emerges ceases to include that which is relevant to people's well-being but does not, naturally, pull in large audiences. Instead it becomes simply 'the news that sells' and the news that sells the most newspaper copies currently, for example, is soft news. One of the most noticeable points to emerge from the country-based chapters is the extent to which soft news is becoming an increasing presence within newspapers and television in nearly every country, from Japan to the US to the UK. Chapter 5 (on the UK national newspaper sector) and Chapter 10 (the sports journalism chapter) both illustrate the extent to which soft news is creeping right across most of the UK quality newspaper agenda. In such a corporate environment the 'news that sells' in turn is complemented by 'the news that is cheapest to produce' in order to keep costs down and maximise profits. This means that the jewel in the crown of hard news journalism, for example, in the form of investigative journalism of serious issues of public concern relating to politics, business corruption, and so on, is now an extreme rarity because of its cost and a prevailing view that no one is interested anyway. Even the proper research and investigation of normal stories is becoming worryingly compromised as numbers of journalists are reduced in the interest of cost savings and reporters become more and more tied to their desks. The convergence of platforms is also increasingly likely to mean that the pressures on the research, fact-checking and thinking time of journalists are made worse. This is a consequence of journalists being expected to be more and more 'time-and-cost-efficient' and to multitask in order to produce stories in different forms for the various platforms that their companies operate.

As soft news takes up more space on the news agenda there is, by definition, less space for the explanation of the complexity and context that underlie hard news issues. Equally, the chances of key issues being covered, those of importance to both the electorates of the advanced democracies and the people that they could help around the world (via poverty relief, and so on), are further reduced. Following on from this, those many people who still use the news as their main source of information will have a shrinking picture of the world that affects them, and which they in turn affect, as the space for hard news comes under further pressure. Increasingly, many

---

merely a very small part of the huge Trinity Mirror empire, with its once local printing and advertising operations handled elsewhere.

hard news journalists simply are not being provided with the opportunity to do the job that most of them feel is fundamentally what they are about.

Another consequence of increasing conglomeration is declining diversity in the news agenda. Even though the UK's *The Sun* and *The Times* newspapers are aimed at very different markets, with the inclusion of differing ranges of political views (for example), News Corporation insists on a single news policy for both publications on some issues, the question of whether or not the UK should join the European Monetary Union being one example (Harding, 2002). This is the result not so much of the economic forces at work in any direct sense, but rather of the increased powers that conglomeration gives to owners to impose their political views on their publications at the expense of the diversity of views that their more sophisticated readers might hope for.

What all of the above suggests – and it is only part of the picture – is an irresistible force meeting an all too moveable object. The huge lobbying power of, for example, Murdoch in Washington and London has been the product of his accumulation of news-producing companies, together with politicians' perceptions that some of these in particular are potentially of enormous electoral significance. It has been noted frequently that electoral sensitivities can make some very strange bedfellows, not least Murdoch and the British Labour Party. The power and influence of such media barons as Murdoch has helped significantly in creating the (increasingly) free marketeer/liberal orthodox media market in the so-called Anglo-Saxon democracies referred to in Chapter 2. Such markets offer little defence against the kinds of deterioration in the quality of the news journalism environment and of the journalism itself, referred to above. Even the BBC has been affected by these free market forces, as, for example, the earlier reference to news on BBC3 demonstrates.

Can the Challenges be Addressed Effectively?

What should or should not be done about the cost side of the costs/benefits equation relating to this 'market phenomenon' is again dependent on the view taken by the societies whose news journalism is being affected negatively. If many people within audiences do not have the educational background, analytical skills or simply the leisure and 'thinking' time to appreciate that the quality of news journalism that they are receiving is declining, for example, then, by definition, deterioration can occur without them noticing. This is particularly the case if changes occur gradually, instead of in the form of a rapid and noticeable downgrading of quality.

A second and related point is that people have *to care* about decline in the quality of news services. As the UK national newspapers chapter will show, editorial staff at the two mass circulation 'red tops' are confident that, far from losing them readers, the replacement of much hard news content by soft news within their pages during the last 20 to 30 years has helped to keep them afloat economically. Their readers have not been writing to them in droves asking for less on celebrity lifestyle issues and more on the inner workings of the British Houses of Parliament. Similarly, as the chapter about the US shows, far from being angered by the 'dumbing down' of television news in their country, many American viewers actually trust the 'dumbed down' version more than they do quality news products. Indeed, some newspaper groups in the UK are becoming so concerned by the difficulty of getting people to pay for hard news or, in some cases, read it, even if it is given away in 'free', entirely advertising-supported newspapers, that they are producing 'lite' editions. The emphasis in these is very much on the soft news end of the spectrum. London's *Evening Standard* was a pioneer in this new trend.

Third, even if people both notice a deterioration in the quality of news journalism and care enough to want to do something about it, they have *to know how to act effectively*. It is not difficult to find people from the World War II generation of UK citizens who will complain in detail about the poor quality of much of the news programming that they receive currently. Nevertheless, ITV was able to get away with both the significant reductions in the budget for ITV news that have occurred over the past decade or so and the abandonment of the fixed, weekday 10 p.m. half-hour news slot with only some slight moderation of the latter decision as a result of pressure from the ITC, the regulator at the time (Curran, 2002). The fact that the great majority of ITV's viewers live with the changes without any effective, organised indications of mass complaint has persuaded ITV that it made the right decision. It clearly feels that it need take only minimal notice of minority complaints, even if they originate in the nation's legislature (as some did). Indeed, the fact that there was no great public outcry seemed in itself to undermine parliamentarians' case for the restoration of the 10 p.m. news slot. However, appearance and reality often diverge and it is likely that many who feel deprived by what they see as a deterioration in the quality and quantity of ITV's news output simply do not know how to complain in an effective and coordinated fashion.

In such circumstances as the above, there are several responses to what those who believe in the importance of the media as a key ingredient of a vibrant public sphere would see as a problematic decline in the quality of news journalism. Of these responses we can usefully examine three.

First, it is possible to take a market approach and argue that a lightly regulated market will always provide a quality of news that corresponds to the demand and that, if the public is not demanding that news provision should be protected from decline, then so be it. To put it even more bluntly, if there is no demand for high-quality news from the public in any significant numbers then there is no justification in supplying it to the market. Where low levels of demand do exist, runs the argument, then specialist niche programmes or publications will be produced to meet it, providing it is attractive enough to the advertisers.

Second, from the point of view of those professionals involved in news production who care enough about the business to want to preserve and indeed increase high-quality news output, it could be argued that if the audience currently is not showing sufficient interest in hard news then new ways must be found of attracting them to it. For all its faults, the BBC still remains a benchmark of quality in news production, and has been keen to try to address this issue of quality news. To this end it has recruited and deployed several correspondents with crucial skills in communication and explanation that enable them to report, often on complex issues, without loss of the essential meaning and implications for their audiences of the events in question. The BBC1 6 p.m. and 10 p.m. half-hour television news programmes, for example, have used first the considerable writing, oral and visual skills of Andrew Marr and currently those of Nick Robinson to turn Westminster politics into something that comes across as both comprehensible and lively. Equally, they have used Evan Davis to the same effect, giving him the freedom to turn the dry complexities of economics and economic policy into something that comes across as accessible yet significant in its impact on the daily lives of viewers. Under Helen Boaden[5] the BBC has been trying also to improve simultaneously the accessibility, breadth and depth of its coverage of the EU on all of its major news platforms. The appointment of another effective communicator, Mark Mardell, to the main EU correspondent's job was a major plank in the new policy. Attempts to add both interactivity and further information to stories through, in particular, BBC Online, where all four of the above journalists have been used highly effectively, has been another aspect of this policy.

However, whilst the temptation to do so is great, it is not the function of the present chapter to examine the issue of how news journalism can be made more interesting in depth. The concluding chapter will point towards means that might be able to address this task.

The third possible response to concerns about quality could take as its starting point the belief that there has to be an agreed gold standard of news provision in every democracy and measures taken to ensure that it is present and available to all. Without such standards, it could be argued, the claim that a society is truly democratic is just a sham. The means chosen to impose such a standard is that of top-down regulation. This argument espouses an ideological view relating to the nature of democracy itself; namely that high-quality, independent news journalism which provides accurate and thoughtful information and analysis about current events is crucial to the creation of an enlightened citizenry that is able to participate meaningfully in society and politics. Just how crucial it can be argued to be is well demonstrated by authors such as John Lloyd (2004).

The first section of this chapter on technological advances outlined one significant way in which such high-quality provision could be made with regard to multichannel television, together with the problems that would accompany any attempt to introduce it. It will be also interesting to see what the individual country-based chapters have to say on regulation. For the present, however, we shall refrain from further discussion, reserving judgement on this issue for the concluding chapter. What can be said here though, on the basis of the foregoing analysis, is that any system of regulation that might be introduced in one or more democratic states could never be seen as being permanent for very long. It would need to be reassessed and reshaped constantly in the face of the pressures of continuous technological development that are fuelled by liberal free market economic systems.

---

5   The Head of BBC News and Current Affairs (at the time of writing).

Diversity

The final challenge that confronts news journalism in the advanced democracies, that of diversity in terms of career paths for women and ethnic minorities, is both serious and complex. In the UK, for example, there is a variety of problems. On the one hand, the recruitment of women students to some of its top journalism schools is now running at around 50 per cent, while on the other, practising women journalists feel that, apart from a few exceptions like *The Sun*'s Rebekah Wade or the BBC's Helen Boaden, there is still very much a 'glass ceiling' in operation as far as the top editorial positions are concerned (Ross, 2005). In the UK Islam is now the second religion, as indeed it is within other European countries, yet there are very few journalists who come from an Islamic background working in the mainstream UK news media. The same picture is reproduced in other advanced democracies across Europe, where non-white ethnic groups are seriously under-represented in the news media of their home countries. Kuhn, for example, shows this to be the case in his chapter on France. The limited and initial exploratory investigations conducted by this author on the subject in the UK suggest that the problem is twofold. First, some (although not all – the BBC is an obvious exception) of news media employers seem to look less favourably on ethnic minority candidates, no matter what their equal opportunities policies might state to the contrary. Second, many ethnic minority citizens rule out journalism as an university subject or a career choice because of a perception that prejudice of the above nature is widespread. A third explanation is offered by research which shows that journalism is a low-status career option in the eyes of some ethnic minority communities (BJR, 2004).

In the US, the latest available figures on the 2006 ASNE website are both outdated and unpromising:

> Newsrooms at U.S. daily newspapers collectively improved their diversity by nearly a half of one percentage point in 2003, but the growth to 12.94 percent lagged behind the 31.7 percent minorities in the U.S. population (American Society of Newspaper Editors, 2006).

But amongst all groups of potential recruitment there are problems as well. In the UK the very low starting salaries paid to journalists by some of the conglomerates effectively exclude working-class novices who cannot afford to live on them. In effect, they largely limit the entry positions in the profession to the children of middle-class families who are unfazed by the current debt culture, or whose parents are in a position to help them out financially until they become established.

The major consequences of these various types of under-representation, it could be argued are as follows:

- the loss of specific socially and culturally informed and culturally tuned perspectives on key news issues; and
- the perpetuation of narrow news agendas in a world that is being brought ever closer together by globalisation (see, for example, Runnymede Trust, 2005).

The challenge to journalism is how to universalise a diversity agenda that is reflective of the social mixes within individual democracies. We do not claim to have the answer to this problem, but would emphasise the importance of solutions being found if news agendas are to be perceived to reflect the broad interests of the societies within which they are set.

At the same time, it is important to emphasise that there are no wholly effective solutions to these issues. Ethnic minority viewpoints in cultural 'melting pots' like the UK or the US are so diverse that it is impossible to represent all of them fairly. Equally, boosting the number of women in top jobs is all very well, but what if the majority of the successful candidates are white middle-class, with the resultant under-representation of the views of other social groupings? Furthermore, views on free speech within some religious and cultural communities diverge considerably from those of the advanced democracies within which they live. Such divergences of belief provide yet another challenge to those determined to increase the representativeness of the news media.

What is clear is that the ethnic/cultural/gender-based imbalances of the current employment situation within the news media (American Society of Newspaper Editors, 2006; Society of Editors, 2004; Mahtani, 2005; Ross, 2005) have to be addressed *because of the centrality of the role of communication within advanced democracies.* But the manner in which they are tackled is very much a matter for detailed and honest debate and negotiation between media employers, regulators and the various other relevant groups that constitute the media industry. Unfortunately, we see little chance of this happening within the cultural context of several of the advanced democracies examined within this book. We are nonetheless willing always to be surprised by future developments.

Conclusion

So, overall, even a necessarily brief analysis as the foregoing demonstrates that twenty-first-century news journalism is subject to a number of serious challenges that threaten the quality of its service as a provider of hard news and thereby its usefulness within democracies. Where journalistic trends in the UK are concerned, the answers to our first two core questions are shaped significantly by the impact of technological and economic developments and are not encouraging. Hard news is losing ground in the news agenda to soft news on many fronts, even within the quality newspapers, and it is increasingly unlikely in our opinion that much of the future news provision in the UK will meet the informational needs of a democracy in the face of the 'ec-tech' squeeze. There is no hard evidence as yet that Internet-based 'citizen journalism' (in the form of independent blogs, and so on) will be able to provide a sufficiently credible, substantial and authoritative option to persuade enough 'news consumers' to access it to enable it to fill the gaps that are likely to appear increasingly in mainstream news provision. Furthermore, the significant under-representation of ethnic minorities within the news media as a whole raises doubts about the possibility of accessing balanced presentations of issues like immigration, asylum seekers and terrorism, most particularly within the written press. The evidence provided by the highly negative coverage of these issues by popular tabloids such as *The Sun*, the *Daily Express* or the *Daily Mail* during the past three years would seem to confirm this point.

A variety of ways in which it is possible to try to remedy the perceived information deficit caused by the 'ec-tech' squeeze have been suggested in this chapter. It will be interesting to see the extent to which the authors in the country sections of the book agree with our views or offer radically different perspectives. An assessment of the implications of what they have to say will be included within the overall conclusions. The main purpose here has been to sketch out some of the major problems of the moment and, crucially, *to provide an understanding of the forces that are driving them.*

Whatever our overall conclusions on these matters might be, one thing always needs to be remembered and it is that there is no perfect news agenda. The world is too populous, too complex and too geographically large for anything but a small proportion of important daily events within it to be reported by even the largest and richest news organisations. By definition, reality always has to be mediated and edited in less than ideal ways. The issue for journalism, and indeed the nub of the matter, is to try to do this in a manner which, over the course of an average working year, manages to make its audience aware of the key matters of health, wealth, life and death affecting not only itself but a representative selection of the rest of the planet's peoples in a manner that is informative, responsible and interesting – all very worthy objectives but ones which, in the light of our experience in liberal democracies, are extremely difficult to obtain. Even so, our concern at the end of the book will be to present for consideration a route via which this might be made possible, despite all the challenges and pressures currently besieging the profession.

References

American Society of Newspaper Editors (2006), 'Newsroom employment drops again: diversity gains'. Available at <http://www.asne.org/index/cfm?id=5145>
Bagdikian, B.H. (2004), *The New Media Monopoly* (Boston MA: Beacon Press).
BBC (2006), Radio 4 11 a.m. *News*, 17 January.
BBC Online (2003), 'BBC Three denies ratings "failure" ', 23 April.
BBC Online (2005a), 'ITV's News Channel to close down', 14 December.
BBC Online (2005b), 'BBC Three drops nightly news show', 21 October.
BJR (Editorial) (2004), 'Faces of the future', *British Journalism Review* 15 (4), 3–5.
Curran, J. (2002), *Media and Power* (London: Routledge).
Franklin , B. (1997), *Newszak and News Media* (London: Arnold).
Harding, J. (2002), 'Media king warms to his subjects', *Financial Times*, 11 June, 30.
Lloyd, J. (2004), *What the Media are Doing to our Politics* (London: Constable and

Robinson).

McChesney, R. (2000), *Rich Media, Poor Democracy: Communication Politics in Dubious Times* (New York: New Press).

McNair, B. (2006), 'The culture of chaos', *The Guardian*, 'Media Guardian' section, 1 May, 1.

Mahtani, M. (2005), 'Gendered News Practices: Examining Experiences of Women Journalists in Different National Contexts', in Allen, S. (ed.), *Journalism: Critical Issues* (Maidenhead: Open University Press).

Mancini, P. (1997), 'The Public Sphere and the Use of News in a "Coalition" System of Government', in Dahlgren, P. and Sparks, C. (eds), *Communication and Citizenship: Journalism and the Public Sphere* (London: Routledge).

Mason, P. (2006), 'Rolling news RIP', *The Guardian*, 'Media Guardian' section, 16 January, 1–2.

Ross, K. (2005), 'Women in the Boyzone: Gender, News and *Her*story', in Allen, S. (ed.), *Journalism: Critical Issues* (Maidenhead: Open University Press).

Runnymede Trust (2005), 'What is the role of the media in promoting race, equality and community cohesion?', *Runnymede's Quarterly Bulletin*, March. Available at <http://www.runnymedetrust.org/projects/SocialCapital/MediaSession.pdf>

Society of Editors (Cole, P.) (2004), 'Diversity in the newsroom: employment of minority ethnic journalists in newspapers'. Available at <http://test1.nepsecure. co.uk/s/Societyofeditors-cmoS2/uploads/documents/84132/Diversity%20in%20t he%Newsroom%20Report%20>

Van Dijk, J. (2005), *The Deepening Divide: Inequality in the Information Society* (London: Sage).

Wallström, M. (2005), 'Opening address at the Plenary Session of the Committee of the Regions, 17 November', Brussels: Commission of the European Communities SPEECH/05/387. Available at <http://europa.eu.int/rapid/pressReleasesAction. do?reference=SPEECH/05/701&format>

<www.ketupa.net/trinity2/htm>, accessed 31 July 2006.

Part 2
UK Case Studies

Chapter 5

UK National Newspapers

Geoff Ward

Introduction

The early years of the new millennium have not been kind to the UK national newspaper industry as it has battled to slow the ebb of readers and advertisers to new and fragmented news sources. This historically fiercely competitive industry at times is seen as being like a group of shipwrecked sailors clinging to a life raft wondering who will be the first to slip off, with the guilty knowledge that the loss of one will delay the death of those remaining.

So, is this chapter merely an advanced obituary for the dinosaurs of journalism? No. Rather we see a highly influential news sector, with a large repository of journalism skills struggling, not always successfully, to cope with fast-changing production and audience environments. At an internal level change is driven by the will to survive, which often overshadows any desire to perform a social role. The external drivers that have placed the national press in this predicament include a complex web of social, political, economic and technological changes that have irreversibly altered the needs and consumer patterns of news audiences and challenged journalism to question traditional practices and values.

This chapter considers the nature of, and responses to, these challenges in relation to the core themes of this book, which emphasise the democratic, social, political and emancipatory potential of news media.

For those who consider that the health of this highly political sector is important to a vigorous and fully functioning democracy, there is plenty of cause for concern. But it is worth remembering that the death knell has been sounding for newspapers for many years, notably since TV established a firm hold on the leisure and information habits of the nation some 50 years ago. So, it is worth repeating the concluding paragraph of a highly respected study of newspapers published just over ten years ago by Jeremy Tunstall:

> The leading newspapers in Britain (and probably in most comparable countries) will continue to be extremely powerful both within the media and across the broad range of public policy and public life. On some measures the newspapers will continue their industrial decline. But the newspapers are likely to remain the most politically interested, most politically focused, most partisan, and most potent of the mass media (1996: 427).

This chapter continues by laying out a brief overview of the situation of national newspapers in late 2005 and relates this to some key historical factors. It then summarises the main challenges faced by the press and considers how these have presently been met in the journalism used by nearly 30 million readers each day (NRS, 2005).

Contexts and Histories: The Industry

For the purposes of this chapter national papers are defined as the mainstream general-purpose daily and weekly newspapers with headquarters in London, that seek sales across the whole of the UK. It is appreciated that Scots and Welsh regard papers such as *The Scotsman* and *The Herald* or *The Western Mail* as their national papers; however, the global scope of this book, and the need for comparability, necessitated adopting a 'British' perspective.

Therefore this chapter concentrates on ten daily newspapers and ten associated Sunday equivalents. They are commonly considered as being clustered in three market sectors and are identified here with their associated Sundays in brackets after daily equivalents:

- downmarket: *The Sun (News of the World), The Daily Mirror (Sunday Mirror, The Sunday People), Daily Star (Daily Star Sunday)*;
- midmarket: *Daily Mail (Mail on Sunday), Daily Express (Sunday Express)*;
- upmarket: *The Daily Telegraph (Sunday Telegraph), The Times (The Sunday Times), The Guardian (The Observer), The Independent (Independent on Sunday).*

Absentees from this list include the *Financial Times* and *The Business*, regarded as specialist rather than 'mainstream', and the *Daily Sport* and its Sunday edition, viewed as having insufficient public affairs content to be regarded as newspapers.

The majority of these titles have a history stretching back to the earliest part of the last century, or beyond. The flurry of newspaper activity that marked the growth of the industrial press from the 1850s settled down at the end of the first quarter of the twentieth century to show a fairly stable number of nationals from 1921 to the present. The most notable recent launches are *The Star* in 1978 and *The Independent*, in 1986.

In 2005, the nationals considered here were owned by seven different companies. This pattern of overall diversity of ownership is fairly typical over the last 100 years. But it masks some significant issues. Firstly, and this has historical parallels, one group has a dominant position in the UK marketplace: Rupert Murdoch's News International, commanding nearly 40 per cent of all national sales through *The Sun, News of the World, The Sunday Times* and *The Times*. Further, the top three groups, News International, Daily Mail and General Trust (*Daily Mail, Mail on Sunday*) and Trinity Mirror (*The Daily Mirror, Sunday Mirror, The Sunday People*) control three quarters of total national circulations.[1] Whilst troubling for the present, this has a worrying potential towards declining diversity in the future if financial uncertainties lead to the collapse of titles or mergers. Secondly, there has been considerable change in the ownership of many established papers, with *The Sun*, *Daily Express*, *The Times*, *The Daily Mirror* and *The Daily Telegraph* having a particularly chequered history of corporate change. Only the *Daily Mail* and *The Guardian* have remained in stable ownership.

The market sectors outlined above clearly reflect sharp divisions based on social class. As Tunstall (1996: 8) has observed, class segregation in newspaper readership is common internationally, but usually in confining readerships to the middle classes. The UK is unusual in extending readership to large numbers of the lower strata of social classes who make up about 40 per cent of newspaper readers. These divisions are usually identified by using the fairly blurred market research designations that place professional and skilled workers in ABC1 categories and the less skilled and unemployed in C2DE categories. These show that about two thirds of downmarket newspapers' readers come from the C2DE groups whilst ABC1 readers make up two thirds of midmarket readerships. The upmarket sector is more clearly defined, with nearly 90 per cent of readers coming from ABC1 groups.

Looking at these figures from the perspective of the class backgrounds of the overall pool of readers, it is seen that ABC1s make up just over half the total and this group is evenly divided in choosing to read papers from each of the market sectors. The slightly smaller C2DE group is much more segregated with nearly three quarters reading downmarket papers.[2]

The distinctive nature of the three market sectors began to be established more than 100 years ago when Alfred Harmsworth recognised the potential to create mass audiences from the expanding lower-middle classes. He launched the *Daily Mail* in 1896 to serve up a diet of populist but conservative and tasteful material (by the standards of the preceding 'penny dreadfuls'). The periods between the two world wars were marked by the fierce battle, eventually won by the *Daily Express*, for domination of this lower-middle-class market that formed the basis of mass audiences. It was only after World War II that the mass market switched towards the manual end of the labour market, an audience that benefited from post-war prosperity and needed, and expected, a voice that recognised their wartime roles. *The Daily Mirror* scooped up this new market and through the late 1950s and 1960s produced a unique blend of traditional sentiment and entertainment, balanced by social concern, to achieve regular sales above five million. It appears generally accepted that it then

---

1   The data is calculated from monthly circulation figures compiled by the Audit Bureau of Circulations. Available from Guardian Unlimited at http://media.guardian.co.uk/ pressandpublishing (accessed 29 December 2005.)

2   This data is calculated from readership figures for July 2004–June 2005 compiled by National Readership Surveys. See http://www.nrs.co.uk/open_access/open_topline/ newspapers/index.cfm (accessed 14 December 2005).

lost track of its working-class roots and the social changes that were altering the needs and expectations of its readers.

As *The Daily Mirror* watched its audiences drift away Rupert Murdoch gratefully took off the hands of its proprietors the ailing liberal *Sun*, a paper that they saw as an embarrassing and unwanted addition to their portfolio. In 1969 Murdoch re-launched *The Sun* in a manner that appreciated new social and cultural realities and redefined the popular market in the way we see it today in an increasing absorption of sexualised discourses, consumerism, celebrity and entertainment – issues returned to later in this chapter. *The Sun*'s success in applying this formula saw its sales rise in less than ten years from one to four million, whilst a slower, but still spectacular, decline set in at *The Daily Mirror*.

A key theme of this chapter is the impact falling circulations have had on the increasingly competitive environment for national newspaper journalism. Tunstall (1996: 31) noted that a 'newspaper crisis' was being talked of in Fleet Street as far back as 1965. However, he also pointed to exaggerated concerns over sales drops which had levelled out in the 1960s, with total circulations staying stable at around 14 million from 1969 to the mid-1990s (1996: 33). Unfortunately, a slow but consistent slide in sales started soon afterwards, with total daily circulations down to 12.9 million by 1998 and slumping to 11.5 million by 2005. Moreover, this misery was shared across all three sectors, which each recorded drops of about 7 per cent from 2001–2005. A similar trend is apparent also for Sunday papers, which ended up with total sales of 12.2 million in 2005, although with more variable declines in the three sectors. *The Sun*, with a circulation of just over three million in 2005, has been the UK's biggest selling newspaper for the last 25 years, only outstripped by its Sunday stablemate, the *News of the World*, which sells about half a million more copies. The once-dominant *Daily Mirror* ended 2005 with a circulation of just 1.7 million. Even more worryingly for its management, it has seen the *Daily Mail* easily outstrip it in the new century, ending 2005 with a circulation of 2.3 million.

Whilst the upmarket sector is the largest in numbers of titles, it has the smallest sales. At the end of 2005 *The Daily Telegraph* was maintaining its traditional lead in the sector with a circulation of just under 0.9 million, with *The Independent* at the bottom of the league table with 0.25 million. The Sundays tend to have fairly similar circulations to their daily equivalents, except for *The Sunday Times*, which dominates the upmarket sector with sales of about 1.3 million.[3]

The causes of declining circulations are complex and considered later in this chapter. For the industry, solutions seem hard to find and the mood of weary resignation is illustrated by the return at the end of 2005 to promotional 'giveaways' – now DVDs – and price-cutting, the strategies of the previous decade. Fortunately, technological advances that in some ways threaten newspapers' futures have also contributed to their survival. Cost savings in production and distribution continue

---

3   The data is calculated from monthly circulation figures compiled by the Audit Bureau of Circulations. Available from Guardian Unlimited, http://media.guardian.co.uk/ pressandpublishing (accessed 29 December 2005.)

to flow from computerised news and print technologies and are also the reason for the one clear area of growth – the astonishing increases in the total number of pages and content.

This 'bulking up' trend was led by *The Sunday Times* which, from a position of market strength in the 1980s, bought heavily into the philosophy that 'biggest is best'. The increase in the size of newspapers has been dramatic when compared to figures for 1987 produced by Seymour-Ure (1996: 149) and adjusted to express all pages as tabloid equivalents. *The Sun* rose from 32 pages to 76 on a typical 2005 weekday and, with supplements, rises to 144 on Saturdays. The *Daily Mail* increased from 41 pages in 1987 to 88 on a weekday in 2005 and 216 (with supplements) on Saturdays. The same 'bulking up' trend is equally apparent in the already bulkier upmarket sector. For instance, *The Daily Telegraph* managed an average of 74 pages in 1987. By 2005 this had soared to 144 on weekdays and 374 on Saturdays (again, including supplements). The traditionally larger Sunday editions also grew and in 2005 a typical *Sunday Times* had a massive 508 pages, *Mail on Sunday* 276, and the *News of the World* 150.[4]

Obviously newspapers are competing amongst themselves, and with other media, for both audiences and advertisers. It is worth emphasising the fact that applying conventional market models to newspapers ignores a distinctive economic aspect of the industry. As Croteau and Hoynes (2001: 26) note, the media industries are unique in operating in a 'dual product' market. Newspapers are first a product designed to be sold to audiences. This creates a second product – an audience – which is then sold to advertisers. Since the rearrangement of advertising allocations that occurred with the arrival of commercial television, the nationals have successfully held on to a substantial proportion of the total spend. By 2004 this represented £1,973 million, which at 10.7 per cent represented the fourth largest share of advertising expenditure across media sectors. By the end of 2005, it appeared that income from this source would show a small rise (Advertising Association, 2005). However, there is a dark cloud on the horizon. Whilst journalists have been concerning themselves with challenges from the speed, accessibility and 'cost-free' usages of Internet news, their advertising colleagues have been worrying about the Internet threat to lucrative recruitment classifieds, a particularly significant revenue stream for the upmarket sector. Those who questioned the economic sanity of newspaper organisations investing (and losing) heavily in their own websites can now appreciate the logic of these actions which are being reinforced by 'buying up' Internet recruitment sites. Such diversification is important in a media sector that includes some loss-making enterprises. It is generally accepted that only *The Sun*, *News of the World*, *The Sunday Times* and the *Daily Mail* are likely to be substantially profitable.

---

4   The 1987 figures draw on data presented by Seymour-Ure (1996: 149) which he warns give a 'rough indication' of increase in size. The 2005 figures represent a 'snapshot' of pagination, including all supplements, in a small sample of newspapers in early to mid-December. These figures should be treated with caution and are produced merely to illustrate trends.

Contexts and Histories: The 'Free Press'

So far, this chapter has concentrated on 'industry' aspects of national newspapers. However, it is broadly accepted that news media, unlike most other industries, are expected also to perform a public role and are a key democratic component in the functional arrangements of mass politics. This indicates obvious tensions – if not conflicts or contradictions – between private ownership and public good, or the favouring of shareholder values over social values. It is therefore instructive to look briefly at the history and present-day perspectives on the place and role of the so-called 'free press' in a long-established liberal democracy, such as the UK.

The first 'newspapers', actually newsbooks, which aimed for continuous publication, appeared in the UK from 1622 onwards. Present-day critics of 'dumbing down' will find they are treading a well-worn path when it is considered that these early newspapers were composed of 'a rough blend of fact, conjecture and transparent sensationalism' (Herd, 1952: 14). These tendencies have never been entirely absent from the history of the UK press, although this fact should not obscure their role in challenging royal power, supporting Parliament and mass enfranchisement, confronting social inequalities and uncovering corruption. Up to the late nineteenth century, when the *Manchester Guardian* editor, C.P. Scott, came up with his famous dictum that 'comment is free but facts are sacred', there is little to indicate any great belief in what is now regarded as 'objective' journalism. Scott's ideas were not original; the editor of the forerunner of today's nationals, the *Daily Courant*, declared in the first edition in 1702 that he would not 'give any comments or conjectures of his own, but will relate only matters of fact; supposing other people to have sense enough to make reflections for themselves' (Herd, 1952: 39). However, the popularity of the dry and factual format of the *Courant* may be judged by its fairly rapid closure in 1735.

To further understand the political and social place given to the press today and its placement in private hands, with relatively little state control, it is necessary to skip forwards to the middle of the nineteenth century and the ending of the final attempts at direct state control of the press through a 'stamp duty' on sales prices and other taxes. Liberal historians (for example, Herd, 1952; Williams, 1957; Koss, 1981) view the repeal of what became known as 'taxes on knowledge' as the beginnings of a 'free press' in the UK. It certainly heralded expansion in newspapers, the industrialisation of production, increased readership, more advertising revenue and the rise of the popular press. More critical commentators see the tax reforms differently. Curran and Seaton (2003: 20) say: 'The driving force behind the campaign were liberal industrialist MPs who saw in the repeal of press taxation a means of propagating the principles of free trade and competitive capitalism.' This viewpoint, shared by others (such as Louw, 2005), can be briefly summarised as the triumph of emergent liberal forces in gaining control of the political, economic and communicative systems.

Whilst debates will continue to rage over the instrumentalist or 'conspiracy theory' nature of such latter views, it can be accepted that belief in the infallible correctness of a privately owned press, broadly free from state control, is now so deeply embedded in the political and public psyche that fundamental challenges to it are unlikely in the foreseeable future. Indeed academics, such as Schudson, point to the fact that there is plenty of evidence that the absence of commercial news media, or their domination by the state, 'is the worst case scenario' (2000: 179).

In practice liberal perspectives have been used successfully to ward off occasional political threats of statutory control by establishing a system of self-regulation, starting in 1953 with a voluntary Press Council, which was replaced in 1991 by the Press Complaints Commission. This sees itself as an independent organisation, as the majority of members come from outside the print industries, although their adjudications, mainly on issues related to accuracy, refer to a code of conduct drawn up by senior figures in the print media. A point of interest for the general themes of this book is that this code is a set of ethical standards broadly concerning accuracy, privacy, intrusion and payments to witnesses and criminals. It does not lay out public duties or roles that journalists might be expected to perform, although a statement of the public interest is referred to as offering exceptions to the standards. However, this is limited to defining the public interest as including, but not confined to, detecting or exposing crime or serious impropriety, protecting public health and safety, preventing the public from being misled and an acknowledgement that there is a public interest in freedom of expression itself (PCC, 2005).

The freedom from state interferences discussed above has traditionally been interpreted as including the freedom to be politically partisan. Historically, the majority of the nationals sided with the right and supported the Conservative Party at elections (Seymour-Ure, 1996: 216). The so-called 'end of ideology' – combined with a weak Conservative Party – in the latter part of the twentieth century may have been influential in a reversal of this trend which has led, since 1997, to most of the national press swinging to Labour. Despite changes in approaches to public affairs reporting, national newspapers continue to be highly political and politicised media with extensive journalism and political expertise. A particularly significant part of their power is in the ability to set agendas for public debate by highlighting some events or issues (and ignoring others) and, through news treatments, commentary and analysis, defining 'attributes', or understandings, of them. As McCombs (2005: 544) puts it: 'The media not only can be successful in telling us *what to think about*, they can also be successful in telling us *how to think about it*.'

Perhaps of equal importance is the nationals' influence on the agendas of other news media. Here their freedom to be partisan is likely to be as influential as their high status amongst other journalists which causes them to '... routinely look over their shoulders to validate their sense of news by observing the work of others, especially the work of elite members of the press ...' (McCombs, 2005: 549).

Challenges for Journalism

The key challenges to national newspapers can be most clearly seen in falling circulations, an increasingly competitive environment and associated trends towards a more 'corporate' view of performance. These economic factors reflect technologically driven expansion in news outlets with a resulting fragmentation of audiences and wider social and cultural changes.

National newspapers have always existed in a fiercely competitive marketplace, but by the mid-1990s Tunstall (1996) was noting the start of an era of 'super-competition'. Since then this trend has accelerated to a point where we are left grasping for suitable adjectives. For some in the industry it is not so much a fight for marketplace advantage as a fight for survival. It is an accepted principle of free market economics that competition leads to higher quality and lower prices. However, many have noted that, in media marketplaces, increased competition generally leads to more homogeneity around products with mass appeal rather than intellectual quality (for example, McManus, 1994). In national newspapers this is evident in entertainment-driven news agendas with proven audience appeal. Such 'bottom line journalism' is further sanctified by managements increasingly aware of the power of investors and shareholders. This has shifted the role of senior journalists towards business and management areas and prompted the rise of 'entrepreneurial editors' (Tunstall, 1996). The rising power of shareholders was seen in 2004 when American investors were influential in the sacking of Piers Morgan as editor of the *Mirror* (Morgan, 2005: 10) after his paper was hoaxed into publishing faked pictures of British troops apparently abusing Iraqi civilians.

The national press has faced competition from other media platforms from early in the twentieth century and has generally met these challenges by adopting strategies of coexistence. These could be relatively easily formulated when, as was the case in the early days of TV, the threat came from a limited number of alternative outlets. However, the establishment of satellite TV in the early 1990s heralded a rapid expansion in multichannel viewing opportunities and rolling 24-hour news programmes. At about the same time Internet growth presented audiences with additional news sources that were available on demand and, importantly, free. The comfort zone provided by 'knowing your enemy' disappeared in an era of uncertainty.

The final major challenge comes from changes in the social and cultural environments in which newspapers exist, and also influence. A useful starting point may be the rise of a highly commercialised 'youth culture' (Hobsbawm, 2001: 324–34) in the late 1950s and early 1960s which placed a high value on individual gratification. Add to this broadly expanding social wealth, often bought at the expense of longer work hours, and the increased involvement of women in the workplace, technologically enabled expansion of leisure distractions, and the gradual movement towards the political centre of all the major political parties after the end of the cold war, and we end up with a rough and ready appreciation of the situation in 2005. Politically the shift to the middle ground was a troubling development for newspapers that had flourished on political conflict. With wide areas of ideological consensus it was unsurprising that political reporting switched to superficial judgements of processes and presentation.

The upmarket sector has not been immune from social change. Sparks (2000: 33) points to the rising numbers of people with higher levels of education as potentially providing more readers for serious newspapers, or serious news in other papers. He goes on to identify two trends that militate against this and which have thrown news markets 'into such chaos'. Firstly, an increasing number of these educated people are women, who have also entered the employment market in increasing numbers. However, women are traditionally reluctant newspaper readers. Secondly, graduates take jobs with a lower social status than would have once reflected their education. As they do not command positions of economic and social power they have little use for the traditional newspaper material that would serve them in those roles. Sparks concludes: 'This group of what we might term "educated subalterns", and in particular its female members, are the least likely to be the readers of newspapers, whether they are the traditionally serious or the traditional tabloid titles ...' (Sparks, 2000: 34).

Journalism in the Twenty-First Century

So far, this chapter has mainly concerned itself with the key economic, social and cultural challenges to the national newspaper *industries* and *business* and *commercial* trends. Within these terms, it is possible to go on to talk about journalism as the *commodities* or *products* of these industries. In relation to national newspapers the key concern is whether processes of *commodification*, prompted by challenges outlined earlier, have driven out journalism of social value and replaced it with editorial content of primarily economic value. The overwhelming view from commentators and academics (for instance, Sampson, 1999; Franklin, 1997; Rooney, 2000; Hackett, 2005) is that a diminution of serious content is readily apparent across all sectors in a process variously dubbed as 'dumbing down', 'tabloidisation', 'infotainment' and 'newszac'. As Sparks (2000: 2) warns, this is a '... heated, and often ill-informed debate ...'. Nevertheless, attention needs to be paid to frequently identified trends within journalism, including: sensationalism; obsession with celebrities and a linked orientation to personalising issues and policy matters; trivialised news agendas; an avoidance of policy and issues; overemphasis of 'human interest'; an increasing focus on consumer, entertainment, leisure and lifestyle matters; an increasing shift from facts to opinions; and the impact all of this has had on replacing or downgrading 'serious' social and political information and analysis.

Some evidence of the presence of such trends within newspaper journalism emerged from research on coverage of the UK general election in 2005, which noted low levels of coverage across all news media and the displacement of political news by other events and celebrity gossip. Even when election events were covered, policy issues represented only between 22 and 24 per cent of reporting across all the national newspaper sectors (Deacon et al., 2005: 30).

A brief review of newspapers carried out for this study in December 2005 indicated that a substantial proportion of the increased pagination, referred to earlier, was devoted to areas such as sport, television, entertainment, lifestyle and leisure. The indications were (see Seymour-Ure, 1996: 150 for an analysis of contents from 1947–75) that the quantity of 'serious' news – current events, public affairs and business – increased. However, the one-sided, simplified and personalised nature of this reporting in the downmarket and midmarket papers was striking and there was an observable trend away from coverage of events and towards commentary and analysis in many upmarket papers.

Downmarket papers have always treated 'serious' political news with some disdain, although at their best they have been capable of presenting a refreshing challenge to elite and establishment views by pricking pomposity and speaking up for the less advantaged. Remnants of this remain, but increasingly downmarket newspapers are presented as primarily entertainment media – entertaining in themselves and bringing information and gossip from other areas of entertainment. There is a strong agenda of drawing on, and trading off, the popularity of TV game shows and soaps, typically through explorations of the private, or semi-private, activities of celebrities, and if this can be combined with a traditional interest in sex and scandal, so much the better. An extensive further area of interest is the off-pitch activities of footballers. Even cursory examination shows that pictures of semi-clothed women are popular features, although less extravagantly portrayed in *The Daily Mirror*, so it is not surprising that most readers are male. Crime stories get what the industry would term a 'good show', but appear to be judged to have less reader impact than in the past.

It could be thought, as Rooney does (2000: 101), that papers such as *The Sun* and *The Daily Mirror* have abandoned the public sphere and there are indications of this in their minimal routine and regular coverage of social and public affairs. However, when events and opportunities occur that match the need for drama and competitive advantage, the sector's strong skills base can still produce the goods. As this chapter was being edited in early 2006 the *News of the World* revealed allegations of abuse of Iraqis by British troops. It may be that 'scandal' in its many forms continues to be judged as a 'seller' but something of importance was put into the public domain. Whilst this may be a 'winner' there is clear evidence that long-term concentration on policy issues is a 'loser', shown by the *Mirror*'s anti-Iraq war stance that cost it substantial numbers of readers and which has ended any immediate possibility of a return to the campaigning agendas that were once its hallmark.

A journalism executive on a downmarket paper interviewed for this chapter commented that he had 'no great pride or enthusiasm' for entertainment-driven agendas but recognised a market rationale:

> Our main job, about 10:1, is to entertain, rather than educate. Our policy is to 'editorialise' – we don't do the bald presentation of objective facts, everything is slanted and opinionated. We are less and less interested in party policy – we are more moving towards what readers want. This is a cut-throat business and we are in a fight for survival (Anon A, 2005).

Like many in the industry he was realistic, but relaxed, about the future.

It's impossible to predict but we don't feel that threatened by the Internet. We will thrive because of our content skills, someone's got to edit all that [web] stuff down. Maybe in 50 years' time we will be an Internet paper but that will just mean doing what we do best in some sort of electronic format (Anon A, 2005).

Whilst the downmarket papers are brash and obvious in their intentions, the midmarket sector is more subtle, aiming to be popular without being obviously populist or sensationalist. Readers are seen as socially and politically conservative. Under the editorships of Sir David English, and later Paul Dacre, the *Daily Mail* has been hugely successful in pulling off this 'popular with a hint of gravitas' balancing act. Further, it has done all this whilst uniquely winning a majority of women readers, to some extent correcting the male bias elsewhere in the sector. It is a complex formula and it resists summation, especially in its appeal to women that resides essentially in an old-fashioned view of their roles as 'home makers' and carers that is at apparent odds with their readers' careers and work aspirations. The secret of its commercial success appears to lie in constructing and appealing to a romantic myth of an assured, secure and homely 'middle-England' perspective on life. The strength of this appeal can be illustrated from the author's own experiences as part of a 100-plus *Daily Mail* journalism team in Manchester in the 1970s and 1980s, producing the paper with a more gritty and realistic edge judged to be necessary for northern English and Scottish readers. When new electronic technology sounded the death knell of the large Manchester operation, the author and most of his redundant colleagues sat back to watch their 'gritty' northern readers desert in droves as their paper more obviously reflected 'soft southern' lifestyles and aspirations. They did not. Instead they appear to have bought into the myth and within months northern circulations were increasing.

The once-dominant *Daily Express* treads an uncertain path in the shadow of its more successful rival. The news and political agendas are generally similar, although a little more downmarket. Given the vast imbalance in resources it is unsurprising that it often lacks the *Daily Mail*'s professional gloss. Celebrity forms an important part of the content, as its owner Richard Desmond draws on material and access created by his gossip and celebrity magazine, *OK!*

Three trends stand out in the upmarket sector. Firstly there is the growth of 'added value' supplements designed to attract advertisers. Some represent various employment and social sectors whilst others reflect the lifestyle and leisure opportunities open to free-spending readers.

Secondly, *The Independent* and then *The Times* decided to give the dumbing down critics the 'brush off' by actually going tabloid in size, or as they sometimes like to term it 'compact'. The decision largely reflected the increasing number of readers who had switched to public transport and needed a smaller and more 'user-friendly' paper. *The Guardian* (and shortly afterwards *The Observer*) took the expensive option of investing in new presses and printing in a continental European size that they choose to call the 'Berliner', roughly halfway between tabloid and broadsheet in overall dimensions. These exercises in repackaging, and allied editorial changes, prompted significant short-term circulation gains, although the impact seems to fade with time. *The Daily Telegraph* and the *Financial Times*, so far, show a disdain for sizing down. The bulky *Sunday Times*, which in all-tabloid format would come out at a whopping 500-plus pages, probably has no choice in the matter.

Thirdly, in a trend most obviously seen in *The Independent* and *The Guardian*, there has been a switch from factual news to commentary and analysis. *The Independent*, probably because it has least to lose at the bottom end of the circulation league, had led the way in converting to tabloid format and was most up-front in recognising the inherent inability of newspapers to challenge TV, radio or the Internet as immediate sources of news. The editor-in-chief, Simon Kelner, declared it was no longer a *news*paper but a *views*paper (Kelner, 2005). This is most apparent in the way the front page has generally ceased to present the most important news *event* of the day in favour of an *issue* for the day. Whilst initially refreshing, this has become wearisome in the daily repetition of 'shock issues' that run the danger of losing the ability to shock, or even interest, readers.

The Guardian's editor, Alan Rusbridger, may have had this in mind when he declared the new approach for the Berliner format would be 'slightly more measured' (Preston, 2005). However, in keeping with the paper's tradition, the new look was radical, especially for its recognition of coexistence with electronic sources of news. The use of colour on every page and the overall layout was selected to attempt to imitate the main features of a web page. The way readers get immediate news of key events from TV and Internet sites was recognised by merely briefly recording much of this 'old news' in small modular chunks. The space this freed up was then used for in-depth coverage and analysis of major current issues, taking up a whole page or more.

It is interesting that these changes are most apparent in the left-leaning, and smaller circulation, papers with younger readers, whilst *The Daily Telegraph* follows a more traditional approach, perhaps recognising the conservative nature of its readership who continue to expect comprehensive coverage of UK and world news. *The Times* has flirted with a more midmarket agenda but analysis shows that it continues to substantially follow a hard news agenda.

The retreat from traditional news agendas was recognised by an executive in the upmarket sector: 'We are not the primary bearers of news ... we should be a forum for ideas and take a more pro-active role in commentary, analysis, campaigns and investigations.' There was a recognition of the danger that in doing this media were 'increasingly feeding off themselves' and that journalists were spending less time 'on the road' meeting the public, which was 'partly to do with cost'. He believed political coverage had to change to match, 'the shutdown of old-fashioned parliamentary democracy and the move towards the executive'. However, this was followed by a comment often heard from journalists, perhaps aware of the unelected nature of their role: 'Politicians have an exaggerated view of the importance of newspapers' (Anon B, 2005).

At this end of the sector there is a sharpened appreciation that its middle-class and affluent readers are heavy users of the Internet:

In the long run that is probably the future. What matters is the journalism, not the platform. Young people appear to have no intention whatsoever of buying a paper. It could be that in 30 years' time newspapers will be an adjunct, in paper form, of an entire journalistic structure on the Web (Anon B, 2005).

Conclusions

It is readily apparent that in the early twenty-first century national newspapers exist in an environment of extreme competition, resulting from technological, social and cultural changes. It is equally apparent that industry responses have mainly centred on an increasing concentration on entertainment, leisure and lifestyle content presented in appealing and user-friendly packages. Such trends clearly show the application of well-established marketing principles. The adoption of such practices is unsurprising, given that national newspapers are an industry and, like other commercial organisations, must produce goods which appeal to consumers.

The problem that arises from this is that consumers are also citizens. The opening chapters of this book have sought to demonstrate that, within mass democracies, news media play a vital and central role in providing knowledge and understanding of public issues, the rational formation of public opinion and the means to feed this back to the political establishment and policy makers. Traditionally, and often controversially, national newspapers have been a highly influential part of this process. The fear is that if journalism is treated as a mere marketplace commodity it retreats from its public roles and leaves a vacuum in the political system. The assumption that underlies the most fervent market-driven approaches, that readers are uninterested in political and social affairs, is at odds with everyday experience of life. These private consumers are the public, the people whose spending, security, education and welfare opportunities are enabled or constrained by political decisions whose potential impact they need to know about.

So, how far do national newspapers go to meeting this public need? Are they responding to increasing political apathy or encouraging it? With the exception of the *Daily Star*, news of a broadly public nature continues to be presented. However, the content and style of this 'serious' news increasingly reflect the entertainment approach which dominates the majority of downmarket newspapers. Political actors are presented as celebrities and complex issues simplified and reduced to dogmatic certainty around a single viewpoint. There are clear signs that this type of approach is spreading up the market spectrum. It is likely that one consequence is to increase public disengagement by placing audiences as mere spectators.

An additional concern arises from the way all national newspapers are devoting increased space to entertainment, leisure and lifestyle matters. Even a cursory examination of front pages, from downmarket to upmarket, shows that these are dominated by promotional displays for this type of material. In other words, they are being presented not as newspapers, but as magazines. This alters readers' expectations and lowers the status of the minority of journalists still producing news of public importance.

Such pessimism needs to be balanced. As has been noted, *The Guardian* and *The Independent* especially are repositioning themselves – not always successfully – in a fragmented marketplace by redefining themselves as commentators and analysts. Not even the *Daily Star* has totally abandoned the idea of covering news and political matters, although there must be doubts about the type and scale of social knowledge provided for readers, especially in the downmarket and midmarket sectors. It is entirely possible that at some point readers and producers will appreciate a need to reinvent *news*papers, maybe in a non-traditional form, but in a way that re-engages audiences in the public arenas where decisions about their lives are made. As yet, however, there is little sign of this happening.

References

Advertising Association (2005), 'Key statistics for 2004' and 'UK advertising expenditure forecast to grow 2.3% in 2005'. Available at <http://www.adsoc.org.uk> (accessed 27 January 2006).

Anon A (2005), Anonymous subject's interview with author, conducted 26 January 2006.

Anon B (2005), Anonymous subject's interview with author, conducted 4 January 2006.

Corner, J. and Pels, D. (2003), *Media and the Restyling of Politics* (London: Sage).

Croteau, D. and Hoynes, W. (2001), *The Business of Media: Corporate Media and the Public Interest* (Thousand Oaks CA: Pine Forge Press).

Curran, J. and Seaton, J. (2003), *Power Without Responsibility* (London: Routledge).

Deacon, D., Wring, D., Billig, M., Downey, J., Golding, P. and Davidson, S. (2005), 'Reporting the 2005 UK General Election'. Available at <http://www.electoralcommission.org.uk/files/dmst-160808final_19222-14161_e_n_s_w_.pdf> (accessed 3 January 2006).

Franklin, B. (1997), *Newszac and News Media* (London: Arnold).

Hackett, R.A. (2005), 'Is There a Democratic Deficit in US and UK journalism?', in Allan, S. (ed.), *Journalism: Critical Issues* (Maidenhead: Open University Press).

Herd, H. (1952), *The March of Journalism* (London: George Allen and Unwin).

Hobsbawm, E. (2001), *Age of Extremes. The Short Twentieth Century 1914–1991* (London: Abacus).

Kelner, S. (2005), Lecture at University of Central Lancashire, Preston, delivered 8 February 2005.

Koss, S. (1981), *The Rise and Fall of the Political Press in Britain* (London: Hamish Hamilton).

Louw, E. (2005), *The Media and Political Process* (London: Sage).

McCombs, M. (2005), 'A look at agenda-setting: past, present and future', *Journalism Studies* 6 (4), 543–57.

McManus, J. (1994), *Market-Driven Journalism* (London: Sage).

Morgan, P. (2005), *The Insider: The Private Diaries of a Scandalous Decade* (London: Ebury Press).

NRS (National Readership Surveys) (2005), 'NRS (National Readership Surveys) estimates of average readership of last 12- and 6-month periods, ending June 2005'. Available at <http://image.guardian.co.uk/sys-files/media/documents/2005/09/19Readershipsurvery.pdf> (accessed 21 October 2005).

PCC (Press Complaints Commission) (2005), 'Press Complaints Commission Code of Conduct'. Available at <http://www.pcc.org.uk/cop/cop.asp> (accessed 20 February 2006).

Preston, P. (2005), 'A new face looking in another direction', *The Observer*, 'Observer Media' section, 11 September, 8 (London).

Rooney, D. (2000), 'Thirty Years of Competition in the British Tabloid Press: The *Mirror* and the *Sun* 1968–1998', in Sparks, C. and Tulloch, J., *Tabloid Tales* (Lanham MD: Rowman and Littlefield).

Sampson, A. (1999), 'The Crisis at the Heart of Our Media', in *News. A Reader* (Oxford: Oxford University Press).

Schudson, M. (2000), 'The Sociology of News Production Revisited (Again)', in Curran, J. and Gurevitch, M., *Mass Media and Society* (London: Arnold).

Seymour-Ure, C. (1996), *The British Press and Broadcasting since 1945* (Oxford: Blackwell).

Sparks, C. (2000), 'Introduction: The Panic over Tabloid News', in Sparks, C. and Tulloch, J., *Tabloid Tales* (Lanham MD: Rowman and Littlefield).

Tunstall, J. (1996), *Newspaper Power: The New National Press in Britain* (Oxford: Oxford University Press).

Williams, F. (1957), *Dangerous Estate* (London: Longmans, Green and Co.).

Williams, K. (1998), *Get Me a Murder a Day! A History of Mass Communication in Britain* (London: Arnold).

Chapter 6

UK Regional and Local Newspapers

Julie Freer

Introduction

The regional and local newspaper industries are where journalism connects with the everyday lives of readers. They give information and answer questions of direct and immediate concern to readers. Why have the bins not been emptied? What caused that traffic jam? How can children secure a place at the best secondary school? And they provide a forum where the electorate can tell those in authority precisely what it thinks about the decisions they make.

If, as this book suggests, the primary intent of journalism should be to inform, encourage reflection, debate and action on political, social and economic issues, the local press has the ability to put this into action. Politicians in the town hall know that they must read the comments of citizens and take the time and trouble to draft a direct reply. Politicians, both local and national, seeking re-election ignore the local newspaper at their peril. Former Foreign Secretary Jack Straw's tongue was not too firmly in his cheek when he was reported to have called Bill Jacobs, political correspondent of the *Lancashire Evening Telegraph*, 'the most important journalist in the world'. His 7 a.m. call was a vital part of Straw's daily routine because this was his main connection with his Blackburn constituents (Straw, 2003: 32).

However, this chapter will show that the local press is an increasingly complex industry which is at something of a crossroads as editorial teams struggle to redefine local news in changing social and cultural environments. It is complex because it is a highly competitive industry which, like most newspaper sectors, is facing circulation falls. Yet it is highly profitable and substantially operates with local monopolies. While many of the UK's national newspapers (see Chapter 5) fight for survival, in this sector the talk is of 'managing decline', which is seen in cost-cutting to protect profits and the extending of local trading monopolies into Internet arenas. Local journalists face pressures from these internal organisational imperatives as well as external challenges presented by changes in the ethnic and social make-up of towns and cities, increasingly secretive political structures and slick town hall PR machines.

This chapter continues by presenting a picture of the local press today and relates this to the historical background. In terms of the book's key social themes, it goes on to consider the challenges to grassroots journalism and the responses that have come from this sector, before identifying key concerns for the present and the future.

Changing Times

There are 1,299 daily and weekly, paid-for and free, local newspaper titles in the UK. Around 1,200 of these titles are weekly papers. There are 19 paid-for and eight free morning papers, 75 evening papers and 21 Sunday papers. There are 531 paid-for weekly titles and 645 free weekly papers (Newspaper Society, 2006). However, in addition to the traditional forms of regional newspapers, there are now 300 magazine and niche publications, more than 600 websites, 23 radio stations and three television stations (Newspaper Society, 2005). The Newspaper Society, the organisation that represents local publishers, says in its 2004–5 annual report that: 'Publishers are layering their local markets to give readers a choice of channels to access local news and information and advertisers extra opportunities to target local communities.' The industry employs around 45,000 people, of which 12,000 are editorial staff (Newspaper Society, 2006).

The origins of the UK regional newspaper industry can be traced back to the end of the seventeenth century. There is some debate over which is the oldest newspaper in continuous production – *Berrow's Worcester Journal*, *The Rutland and Stamford Mercury* and the Belfast *News Letter* compete for this title.

Established in 1690, *Berrow's Worcester Journal* claims to be the world's oldest, although publication was irregular until 1703. However, it has reported on the Battle of Culloden, the death of Nelson and the American War of Independence. Editor Stewart Gilbert (2005) believes the aims of the paper have remained unchanged. He states they are: 'To serve the community – to inform, educate and entertain – it is as much a cornerstone in publishing today as it was all those years ago. On paper or through electronic information technology, the message is still the same; it is one of public service.' Yet this historic piece of 'olde' England is now owned by US multimedia giant Gannett through its UK-based Newsquest, the third largest UK regional newspaper group. *Berrow's Worcester Journal* can now count *USA Today* as one of its sister papers.

In many ways, the tale of *Berrow's Worcester Journal* is a microcosm of the most dramatic development in the industry since the mid-1990s – the concentration of ownership. More than £6.8 billion has been spent on regional press acquisitions since October 1995. This has led to further concentration of ownership and reinforced monopolies in many areas. The top 20 publishers now account for 89 per cent of all local newspaper titles in the UK and 95 per cent of the total weekly circulation. Although there are 986 regional publishers, 40 of these produce just one title (Newspaper Society, 2006).

Trinity Mirror is the largest, with 230 titles and a weekly circulation of 14.36 million readers. Johnston Press became the second largest when figures were released in January 2006, with 283 titles and a total weekly circulation of 10.195 million readers. Newsquest's 216 titles have 10.15 million readers, Northcliffe's 113 titles have 8.7 million readers (Newspaper Society, 2006). The top four publishers now own 842 of the regional newspaper titles – the top six own 951 titles.

Despite an overall market decline in sales, the major players report substantial profits which largely reflect the strength of local advertising, which in 2004 represented a £3,132 million spend, making regional papers the second largest advertising sector in the UK, beaten only by television (Advertising Association, 2005).

Trinity Mirror group's operating profit for 2004 was £253.1 million, with regional papers accounting for £150.6 million (Holdthefrontpage, 2005). In their regional sector, advertising accounted for 77 per cent of turnover (Trinity Mirror, 2005). Holdthefrontpage (2005) reported in March 2005 that Johnston's profits had risen by 18 per cent to £150.6 million. Johnston's shares have increased more than fivefold in the past decade, rising from about 100p in 1994 to a high of 570p.

To further understand the industry in the twenty-first century it is helpful to consider the history and rapid evolution from the 1970s of the local and regional press sectors.

Marr (2004: 27) describes how the expansion of local newspapers was driven by industrialisation in the nineteenth and early twentieth centuries. 'The vast growth of the press saw weeklies, evening dailies and then daily morning papers spring up across Britain, not only in the great merchant and industrial cities – but in hundreds of dormitory towns and suburbs whose sense of themselves was based around a local paper.' In big cities, there were often up to three competing papers, staffed by articulate and ambitious journalists drawn from the roots of communities. It was an industry that gave a 'bright, glittering opening to sharp, literate working-class boys trying to avoid a lifetime as a clerk or shop assistant' (Marr, 2004: 27).

The 'golden age' of the regional press, particularly the dailies in the large urban conurbations, peaked in the period of post-World War II prosperity. From the early 1960s the industry began to contract. For instance, Manchester had two evening papers until, in 1964, the *Manchester Evening Chronicle* closed despite sales of around 250,000, leaving the *Manchester Evening News* with a near-monopoly in the city (Franklin and Murphy, 1998: 7). As Catlow (2005) explained: 'Evening newspaper circulation was built up around a world where workers left a factory and bought a paper to read while they caught the bus or tram home. Now, of course, people get in a car and they don't always stop to pick up a paper.'

In a sharp contrast to today's highly corporatised industry, ownership was often in the hands of small family businesses with journalists rubbing shoulders with the boss. Marcus Tillotson was grandson of the founder of the *Bolton Evening News* and went on to became chairman of the company. When he died in 2005, former editor Les Gent (2005) recalled that he had known him for more than 50 years and described him as 'dignified, shy and caring'. News gathering was a standard diet of courts, councils and inquests combined with ultra-local community news. Late afternoon deadlines for the regional evenings gave reporters the time to build up local contacts as they gathered news for the same day's newspapers. Crime reporters would stroll over to the police station early in the morning for a chat and a cup of tea with the local police chief. No job was too small or too detailed for the local newspaper reporter. Many went so far as taking down the names of mourners at funerals. Wedding reports in many local papers were expected to carry every last detail of the event, down to the flowers in the bouquet and the material the bridesmaids' dresses were made from. Courts and council meetings were reported in meticulous detail. Meetings of the Women's Institutes, clubs for the over-60s, scouts and guides events, school sports days, clubs and societies were all part of the diet of local news.

However, as John Sergeant, later ITN's political editor, recalled about his early experiences at the *Liverpool Daily Post* and *Liverpool Echo* in the 1960s, newsrooms were predominantly male with a distinctly 'blokey' atmosphere. His wife Mary was axed after only six weeks as a trainee despite arriving on the paper as a Cambridge graduate. 'Miniskirts were not mentioned, but they were certainly a factor. Far more important, it seemed, was that the small herd of trainees had to be culled' (2001: 95).

Sergeant himself feared that, as a graduate, he too struggled to fit in. 'I was all too well aware how much I had to learn and how the other trainees seemed to fit more easily into the matey, sporty, non-intellectual world of Liverpool journalism.'

The status quo in the regional press began to be challenged in the 1970s by the rise of free newspapers (Franklin and Murphy, 1998: 8). As McNair (1999: 200) pointed out, free newspapers received only 1.4 per cent of advertising revenue in the regional press in 1970. However, by 1990, the figure had risen to 35 per cent. In 1975, there were 185 'frees' publishing in the UK compared to 1,140 paid-for papers. By 1986, the balance was 842 frees to 867 paid-fors. The 'free-sheet' was delivered to every house and advertisers believed this could give them unrivalled access to the local market. In the early days, many journalists felt that it was demeaning to work for papers with what Franklin and Murphy (1998: 245) would term such strong 'advertorial' content. However, as the market became more successful economically, the journalism in some titles became of a better quality. In 2004, just two years after it was launched, the independently owned *Kent on Sunday* became the first free title to win newspaper of the year in the *Press Gazette* Regional Press Awards.

The launch of the *Metro*s, aimed at the commuter in the major cities of the UK, was perhaps the point at which the free-sheet became mainstream. Associated Newspapers launched the first *Metro* in London in 1999, aimed at 'a generation too busy to read newspapers', and it was an instant success. It made a profit 11 months after its launch and did not appear to damage sales at Associated's *Evening Standard*. There are now *Metro*s in Newcastle, Manchester, Birmingham, Glasgow, Edinburgh, Leeds, Sheffield and the East Midlands. More than one million copies a day are now picked up.

The news content is a mix of national, international and local information written in a concise way that can be immediately digested. The *Metro*'s website claims that its papers are read by a young affluent audience with 65 per cent of the readership in the ABC1 social category and 77 per cent in the 15–44 age group (Metro, 2003). Doug Read, executive director of *Metro*, said:

> *Metro* has brought new readers to newspapers who didn't read a paper before. Around half of our readers didn't read anything before we launched. … Our young, white-collar workers are the ones a lot of advertising wants to target. But they were supposed to be

the electronic generation who don't read newspapers. We have found a lost generation (Read, 2003).

The 1970s and 1980s were also decades of technological change brought about by computerised typesetting. The watershed of this revolution, which brought huge economic benefits to managements throughout the newspaper industry, was at Eddy Shah's *Warrington Messenger* in 1983. Huge cost savings resulted from the manner in which words were presented ready for typesetting by journalists, resulting in the loss of jobs of compositors and the ending of the power of the print unions.

The previous decades had prepared the industry for the next step on the journey to the highly concentrated and profitable sector seen today. In the early 1990s acquisitions, mergers and swap arrangements gathered pace to restructure the sector around ownership in the hands of a few major corporations with increased monopolies in many areas of the UK.

Franklin and Murphy (1998: 18) detail the way the process happened in two phases. First, larger groups such as Thomson and Reed restructured their organisations and swapped titles to gain control of circulations in individual areas. Reed acquired the *Lancashire Evening Telegraph* in Blackburn to protect their Lancashire base while in return Thomson acquired Reed's free newspapers in the north-east.

The second phase involved owners such as Reed and Thomson moving out of regional newspapers and a spate of buying and selling papers began. Trinity became the largest regional publisher in the UK when it bought a group of daily and weekly newspapers from Thomson. In 1997, Mirror Group acquired Midland Independent Newspapers, publishers of the *Birmingham Evening Mail*, *The Birmingham Post* and *Sunday Mercury* for £305 million. In the same year, Mirror Group acquired a licence to publish the *Racing Post*, and Trinity bought the Dublin-based *Sunday Business Post*. In September 1999, Trinity and Mirror Group merged to become the biggest newspaper publisher in the UK (Trinity Mirror, 2005).

Newsquest was formed in 1995 from a management buy-out, backed by private equity funds, of Reed Regional Newspapers. The company effectively doubled in size in December 1996 when it acquired Westminster Press. Newsquest floated on the Stock Exchange in October 1997. The company was acquired by US-based media giant Gannett in July 1999 for £1.03 billion (Newsquest, 2005).

Another new major player, Johnston Press, had around 50 local newspapers, including its 1767 founding title, the *Falkirk Herald*, in the early 1990s. Now, the group owns 283 titles. It bought Portsmouth and Sunderland Newspapers in 1999 and Regional Independent Media, publisher of titles including the *Yorkshire Post*, in 2002. It has also recently bought Score Press in Ireland, its first acquisition outside mainland Britain. Operating margins have been at least 30 per cent (Armistead, 2005). Chief executive Tim Bowdler said in an interview in *The Sunday Times*: 'We don't own local papers for the celebrity status, we own them because they are good businesses' (Armistead, 2005). But they were still looking for new opportunities:

> We have only 15 per cent of the market at the moment. We have launched 30 new publications and we are setting up websites that could carry television and audio news

in a few years. … We are also expanding the very regional press – doing news sheets for small communities – which is a great gap in the market.

On the face of it, this growth in corporate power and profits is at odds with clear evidence of declining circulations and readerships. These sales trends are examined before offering an explanation for the apparent contradictions.

In *Press Gazette*, Ponsford (2004) described some of the ABC circulation figures for the big regional dailies in 2004 as 'cataclysmic'. The evening *Leicester Mercury* was down 9.5 per cent, the *Yorkshire Evening Post* lost 11.7 per cent, the *Belfast Telegraph* dropped 12.9 per cent and *The Southern Daily Echo* declined by 11.6 per cent. This is an industry where minus figures far outweigh pluses and where a fall of anything less than five per cent is considered a success story.

Birmingham's two daily titles are seen in the industry as perhaps the biggest challenge in terms of halting a circulation decline that dates back more than 30 years. The city's fluid population and large ethnic communities presented particular problems. Two successive falls in circulation of more than 10 per cent were recorded for the evening *Birmingham Mail* in 2004/2005. The morning *Birmingham Post* was down 23.4 per cent. The *Sunday Mercury* declined by 12.7 per cent and the nearby *Coventry Evening Telegraph* by 12.2 per cent. Despite a £1 million relaunch in October 2005, the *Birmingham Mail* reported an 11.9 per cent fall for the second half of 2005 (Langan, 2006). The ABC figures for the second half of 2005 showed that only one of the UK's evening papers increased sales – the *Belfast Telegraph* which was up 2.5 per cent after also launching a morning edition.

Weekly newspapers have traditionally performed better in circulation ratings, with more than half the titles celebrating sales successes in 2004 (Langan, 2004). According to figures released by the Newspaper Society (2005) readership of paid-for weeklies had grown by more than 15 per cent over the last ten years. However, ABC figures for the second half of 2005 (*Press Gazette*, 2006) showed many weeklies had joined their daily brethren on the circulation slide. While 105 weekly titles increased their circulation, some 313 titles went down. The *Worksop Guardian* was up 17.4 per cent to 18,124 and the Norfolk-based *Beccles and Bungay Journal* was up 9.1 per cent to 7,445. However, only one of the top 20 biggest circulation weeklies put on sales – the *Rotherham and South Yorkshire Advertiser* (0.9 per cent). The *Surrey Advertiser* series dropped 6 per cent and the *Kent Messenger* series, which has the biggest weekly circulation, dropped 4.1 per cent to 55,109 copies.

In contrast, the largest free weekly newspapers now reach a vastly larger audience. The *Manchester Metro News* series is distributed to 309,516 homes, the *Nottingham and Long Eaton Topper* to 210,023 homes and the *Nottingham Recorder* to 149,675 homes. All of the top ten free weeklies go to more than 100,000 homes (*Press Gazette*, 2006).

Challenges and Responses

At a business level it is clear that this is an industry that has, so far, been highly successful in dealing with circulation decline and maintaining, or increasing, profitability. The secret of this success would appear to lie in new corporate structures that have enabled an effective defence of local advertising markets and brought about efficiencies of scale reinforced by the stringent pursuit of cost savings. These internal responses have taken place within a period of rapid social change in the structures and diversity of local populations and the manner in which they are governed at the local level. In addition to this complex mix of economic, social and political factors, local newspapers have also had to respond to technological innovations that have offered both challenges and opportunities. For the industry, the Internet especially presented a threat to local advertising monopolies and the responses have been robust in integrating this new medium into business planning. For journalism, online platforms have challenged traditional practices as well as offering new ways to connect to citizens. The following sections discuss these aspects and draw on industry viewpoints acquired in a series of interviews conducted by the author and from published sources.

When Barrie Williams took early retirement as editor of *The Western Morning News*, he reflected that in the 1980s, when he was asked to join the board of the *Nottingham Evening Post*, that he was told 'don't mention profits in front of the chairman, he doesn't like to talk about profits'. Slattery (2005) commented: 'What a contrast to the regional press today, when the pursuit of higher profit margins is seen by some as the major force shaping the industry.' However, the chief executives and directors know that such profits, and even the forces that have led to the increased concentration of corporate ownership, have an uncertain future. Corporate imperatives seem to have taken an increasing toll on editors. At Northcliffe in 2005 Mike Lowe left the *Bristol Evening Post*, David Gledhill departed from *The Bath Chronicle* and Barrie Williams left *The Western Morning News* to be followed by *Western Daily Press* editor Terry Manners, who resigned on the same day as job-cut plans were announced. Sean Dooley retired as editor of *The Sentinel* in Stoke at the end of the year.

Circulation figures appear to be the key to judgements on editors' performances. Chris Walker, managing editor of Trinity Mirror in the north-west, said that 'managing the decline' in circulation is now part of the management of a regional newspaper company (Walker, 2005). In public, the industry is upbeat about sales trends. The Newspaper Society (2005) boasted of being 'an industry in renaissance'. However, Keith Sutton (2005), editorial director of Cumbrian Newspapers Group and editor of the *Evening News and Star* in Carlisle until his retirement in 2005, has warned that falls in circulation of more than 10 per cent year on year cannot go on forever – there comes a point where the decline can no longer be managed, titles fold and advertisers go elsewhere.

The downward trend is not new and can be attributed to a number of factors. The Internet in particular has increased the range of sources for local, community and sports news. Social changes include population mobility, ethnic diversity, work and commuting habits, 'time poverty' and more individualistic, consumerist and lifestyle orientations. The combined effect of these has had more impact on daily papers than weeklies. Chris Walker commented: 'People are now more picky about the way they buy the newspaper. They tend to buy for two or three nights rather than order a copy every night' (Walker, 2005).

Such change, and responses to them, have brought almost apocalyptic responses from some academics. Back in 1997 Franklin and Murphy commented: 'Local and regional newspapers are in serious and probably irretrievable decline' (1997: 214). At that time the technological threat was seen as coming mainly from TV but some of their other concerns are familiar in 2006.

> New technology such as cable television, combined with marketing and transnational ownership, projects a future which is increasingly unstable and in which the prospect for the local press as investigators and informers of the public in the process of local democracy looks even bleaker than that for the democratic process itself (Franklin and Murphy, 1998: 22).

The nature of the local journalist is also changing. The steady supply of bright young journalism graduates wanting their first break into the industry has allowed employers to resist the wage demands of established staff and has gradually allowed reporters with years of knowledge and experience to drift away from newsrooms. Barrie Williams reflected on how the days when a bright lad like himself from a council estate could enter the industry at 16 and work his way up the ladder have gone (Slattery, 2005). Richard Catlow, editorial director of Greater Manchester Newspapers, also commented that increasingly applications were coming in for reporting jobs from graduates living in the city's leafier suburbs (Catlow, 2005).

This is often attributed to low wages in the industry. As Tony Harcup (2005) asked, will wealth, not talent, dictate who enters journalism? Dominic Ponsford (2004) compared journalists' pay to the average starting pay for a graduate of £21,000. He cited the Association of Graduate Recruiters as saying trainee pay for the 'big five' regional newspaper companies ranged from £12,000 to £15,000 a year. While the average UK salary was £22,776, a local reporter after ten years could expect to earn between £13,000 and £20,000 a year. Discontent amongst journalists can be summarised as 'overworked and underpaid', and in 2003 there was the first significant outbreak of industrial unrest among journalists since the 1980s, with strikes at Bolton and Bradford. In May 2005, strikes were threatened at two evening papers – the Trinity Mirror-owned *Coventry Evening Telegraph* and the Newsquest-owned *Southern Daily Echo*. As Joanna Leapman (2004) predicted, 'trouble is brewing for skinflint newspapers.'

Staffing levels, which many journalists complain are already minimal, face further cuts. *Press Gazette* reported, in October 2005, that Trinity Mirror journalists had been told that jobs were at risk. There was also a story in the same edition that 47 jobs were under threat at Northcliffe's West Country titles.

Within this atmosphere of industrial discontent, journalists find themselves in the frontline of varied responses to declining circulations. One view is that local papers have moved downmarket to meet the demands of advertisers and the needs of a time-poor readership and slimmed-down newsrooms with overworked journalists relying heavily on press release material, rather than having the time and resources to carry out proper investigative journalism. Franklin and Murphy (1998: 17) said:

> The 'tabloiding' of local newspapers has resulted in a 'dumbing down' of the local press. The publication of shorter, brighter, 'frothier' stories and the increasing reliance on stories about entertainment, consumer items and 'human interest' stories, are the infallible hallmarks of the tabloid genre.

However, interviews with industry professionals for this chapter present a much more complex picture. While some editorial teams believe that newspapers need to move away from the standard diet of community news and change their content to meet the needs of a new time-poor readership, others are going 'back to basics' with a belief in reporting community news combined with strong, campaigning journalism.

Simon Bradshaw, when he was editor of *The Argus* in Brighton, felt that local news values needed to reflect the changes in society, particularly in a cosmopolitan city such as Brighton with a high-earning commuter population. He explained (Bradshaw, 2003) that he was planning to 'think the unthinkable' and ditch traditional community news. He said: 'Is the woman who is working in London, living in a plush seafront apartment, really interested in Mrs Miggins and her whist drive? It is possible that we are not engaging people any more – particularly busy people with a short attention span.'

In January 2004, *The Argus* was relaunched along the lines that Bradshaw outlined. However, by March 2005 circulation had dropped by 9.7 per cent compared with the previous year. Simon Bradshaw left. His replacement, Michael Beard (2005), said that there would be more community news in the paper in future.

This is the 'back to basics' formula successfully employed by Steve Dyson when he was editor of the *Teesside Evening Gazette*, one of the few papers to chalk up a circulation rise in 2005. Now the editor of the *Birmingham Mail*, Dyson is adopting this approach in an attempt to halt a 30-year circulation decline. He said in an interview for this chapter a few days before taking up his new appointment that he believed in the 'one of us' factor in determining news values.

> The reader in every street should know what is going on around them because the local newspaper tells them. In Teesside, every single reporter has a community news network. Whether it is a coffee morning or a meeting to complain about ASBOs, we will cover it. We make it very clear to our readers that it is their newspaper and we will report about the things they are passionate about (Dyson, 2005).

He also believes that strong campaigning journalism has a significant part to play, even if it is not popular with all readers. Although there was strong reaction to plans to set up a children's home in a well-heeled part of town, he decided that the paper would take the line that these were disadvantaged children who needed to live somewhere in a safe environment. The *Gazette*'s 'Let the Boats Come In' campaign also provoked a strong reaction. It was the only paper in 2004 to campaign for a so-called 'toxic ghost fleet' of 13 World War II ships to be allowed across the Atlantic to be recycled in neighbouring Hartlepool.

There is universal agreement that major local hard news stories will always boost circulations. Keith Sutton (2005) said that 'big, bad news' still sells. 'Does anyone remember any other ship that set sail in 1912 apart from the Titanic?' The *Evening News and Star* circulation in Carlisle rose from 25,000 to 65,000 during the floods in January 2005. However, the emphasis is on the local. Richard Catlow (2005) summed up the traditional news values of local papers when he talked about the *Rochdale Observer*, one of the papers in his group:

> If someone dropped an atomic bomb on Bury, we would want to know which way the wind was blowing. If it was in the west, the story would be about radiation fallout in Rochdale. If it was in the east, the story would be about anyone from Rochdale who was shopping in Bury.

As with national newspapers, sport is increasingly finding its way onto the front pages of regional newspapers in addition to the back. Sport, and in particular football, is a major selling point for the regional press. It can also lead to a strained relationship with the ever-powerful football clubs seeking to allow papers access to interviews and pictures on their own terms. The club's website or its own TV station tends to be where breaking news is placed rather than an exclusive for a local reporter.

Local newspapers need to appeal to a changing readership that may not have its roots in the town. With ever more fluid population trends, many readers may have no traditional links with the community. Richard Catlow (2005) explained that they aim to attract such a readership through focusing on two areas of news content that all residents will care about – their children and their environment.

There are also concerns that journalists and journalism are failing to connect with substantial ethnic and cultural minorities. A report entitled 'Diversity in the newsroom' (Cole, 2004) found that many newspapers have few or no journalists from these communities working for them. This has played a major part in distancing journalism from ethnic minorities and rendering them 'invisible' as 'vast chunks of the media remain unable to tell the whole of our national story', in the words of Trevor Phillips, chair of the Commission for Racial Equality (Phillips, 2005).

In June 2004, Newsquest announced its intention to recruit more journalists from ethnic minorities. One of its titles, Bradford's *Telegraph and Argus*, has organised training in the community and staged a seminar to encourage ethnic minority recruits. Then, in October 2005, the National Council for the Training of Journalists launched a Journalism Diversity fund to support the training of journalists from ethnically and socially diverse backgrounds.

Whilst issues of disconnection from ethnic minorities are obviously important, others have identified problems over the role media plays in the local political environment. Franklin and Murphy (1998: 13) pointed to the influence of advertisers in moving coverage away from public affairs. 'Bowing to these pressures, the content of local press began to shift from its previous emphasis on the municipal and the political towards the provision of information about consumption.' There is no doubt that the days of routine coverage of council committees and meetings have largely ended. In slimmed-down newsrooms, the temptation for a hard-pressed reporter to churn out a press release is obvious. However, Chris Walker (2005), who described himself as a 'political anorak', admitted that if democracy is to function effectively, newspapers must do more than simply 'pay lip service' to major political events such as elections.

But Richard Catlow emphasised the necessity of covering local politics in a way that appeals to readers. 'When I started in journalism, it was like Hansard – reporting everything that was said. Now we look for the story.'

Indeed, rather than the regional press being politically powerless compared to their national counterparts, strong campaigning regional journalism can be at the forefront of a shift in how newspapers are influential in local politics in its widest sense. Keith Sutton (2005) argued:

> Newspapers are part of the local power structure. You cannot take on a big, nasty brute locally if you are an individual. We have the structure to make a real difference. We can challenge big important money people and we can beat them. There will always be a need for a nucleus of journalists to take on other power structures.

Whilst some may wonder how commonly such challenges occur across the sector, or about the emphasis, expertise and priority that is assigned to them, care needs to be taken in assuming that the local press has abandoned its watchdog role or fails to serve communities in new and relevant ways. The *Lincolnshire Echo*'s campaign about mismanagement in Lincolnshire County Council led to the jailing of the council leader and the resignation of his successor and the full cabinet of the council. In 2005, the paper won the *Press Gazette* regional newspaper of the year award.

At a time when voter turnout for local elections is low, the response to regional parliaments lukewarm and there are accusations of more town hall secrecy, it is likely that local newspapers have a more important role than ever to play in informing readers of what is really going on in their towns and cities. The introduction of 'cabinet-style' local government in 2000 was meant to modernise local councils by placing important decisions in the hands of a cabinet of leading councillors. It brought immediate responses from editors that decisions would be made in secret and many local journalists believe this is happening. Similarly, the creation of hospital trusts in the 1990s meant that reports on the running of hospitals were no longer presented to health authorities where journalists had open access.

The final part of this section turns to the important influence new technology has had on the industry. While editors interviewed for this chapter immediately referred to the decline in circulation when asked what they saw as the biggest challenge the industry faces over the next decade, Tim Bowdler, chief executive of Johnston Press, had a different answer. 'Undoubtedly the biggest challenge facing the industry is the changing means of distribution of news' (Bowdler, 2005). He added:

The regional press uses news and content to give advertisers access to local markets. The content will be delivered in different ways and different forms. The relationship between the provider and the consumer will change – there will be more interactivity. We are still feeling our way with this. Journalism has been essentially print-based and we have been uploading material on to the Internet. However, I can well see a time when video journalism and moving pictures will be a part of this.

The impact of this on journalism and, especially, how this may, or may not, reinvigorate the 'political' roles of journalism at a local level are still uncertain. Presently, opinions seem to be divided between a 'business as usual' perspective, albeit delivered in new ways on new platforms, and more radical visions of 'cyber citizenship'. What is not disputed is that local newspaper journalism will no longer be confined to newsprint alone.[1]

Catlow (2005) explained how 'convergence' was interpreted in his group. Journalists no longer simply produce copy for their weekly paper – instead they will provide material for editions of their sister papers, the *Manchester Evening News* (both main and Lite editions), for the Greater Manchester weekly, *Metro*, for the group's website and for Channel M, a local TV station. 'I think what won't change is that people will still be interested in local news and there will be a need for journalists to give it them.'

Walker (2005) had a similar view. 'There is no evidence that people have any less interest in the local news, but what is changing is how they access it and how often.'

However, 'blogging' and citizen journalism have added another dimension to local news coverage. Industry expert Vin Crosby (2005) told a newspaper conference that small circulation papers in America had seen page views double with the introduction of popular daily blogs. He told an audience of editors and circulation bosses how advertising was now being sold on the back of blogging. He proposed a challenge to journalists: 'This is the idea that journalism is not to be handled only by specially-trained individuals.'

Freelance journalist Sean Dodson predicted that the next generation of local papers could look like 'a print version of eBay' (Dodson, 2004). He added: 'Imagine a newspaper without any real reporters where the news agenda rested on the whims of its readers, and sub-editors are a thing of the past.'

However, even editors like Keith Sutton, who have embraced blogging on their websites, express a need for caution. While the traditional readers' letters column has always had the potential for libel actions, blogs are harder to control and have potential for greater danger. 'Local journalism is known for tradition, trust and objectivity – but the anarchic blogger doesn't care about that' (Sutton, 2005).

---

1   Johnston Press and the Department of Journalism at the University of Central Lancashire in Preston have joined forces in a three-year £200,000 collaboration that aims to exploit the benefits of digital technology and involves the establishment of the Johnston Press Chair in Digital Journalism.

On the horizon is another challenge to local newspapers from print's traditional rival, TV. The BBC has announced plans to start tightly targeted pilot local news broadcasting. *Yorkshire Evening Post* editor Neil Hodgkinson said there were good reasons to be worried. He questioned how such services will find stories. 'The suspicion is that it will lead to even more lifting of local press stories' (Hodgkinson, 2005). Sutton believed it was a threat to the regional press. 'The biggest challenge to local newspapers is the power of the BBC to access the licence fee and invest the money in distributing channels – it is distorted and unfair.'

Conclusions

Overwhelmingly, this review has established that, presently, this is a highly profitable industry that is increasingly concentrated around a handful of key corporate players who have business skills in exploiting possibilities of cost-effectiveness, adaptability to new technology and an acute awareness of local advertising markets.

On the face of it none of this bodes well from the perspective of critical communication and journalism studies that emphasise the manner in which commodification threatens involvement in public affairs and raises doubts about journalism that is consumer-orientated. Even at a corporate level there are questions. Former *Guardian* editor Peter Preston (2005) asked:

> For years, there have always been buyers. The great newspaper chains of Britain and America – Gannett, Trinity Mirror, Johnston Press, Knight-Ridder – have all grown by buying small family groups. But what happens when the music of easy acquisition stops? What happens, indeed, if buy turns to sell?

He suggested that there are already signs of a slowing down of the economy on both sides of the Atlantic that is leading to falls in advertising revenue. 'The regional newspaper industry, which for so long seemed slump-proof, is producing a great many grey faces.'

Indeed, the Daily Mail and General Trust called off the sale of its regional Northcliffe Newspapers in February 2006 which was expected to raise £1.5 billion.

The *Press Gazette* (Slattery, Ponsford and Langan, 2006) reported that, in a statement to the Stock Exchange, the offers for the group did not 'fully reflect the long-term value of the business'. Northcliffe said the offers 'reflected the recent downturn in trading in the regional newspaper sector caused by the weakening of the broader UK economy'.

However, the local and regional press has always been close to its public, which is defined in this sector as local people. Whilst this audience might be heterogeneous in social, cultural and party political terms, it is homogenous in terms of shared and immediate concerns, from the quality of refuse collection and piles of dog waste to health issues in local hospitals and the chances of children in the education system. In this way audiences respond as local citizens. As local consumers they have an interest in the goods advertised so extensively in their newspapers. In this way 'localness' can serve to unite citizen and consumer. It can be said that no local or regional newspaper would have survived until the present day without recognising this.

The questions, therefore, could be said to revolve around how effectively local news journalism *has acted* on this recognition and how much new technology (in the shape of the Internet) threatens its ability to continue to do this (with its emphasis on advertising markets) or enables it. If it does threaten it, then how much does it hand over traditional expectations of journalism to a new and possibly 'anarchic' citizen power? And how will this new local citizen power impact on established structures of local democratic arrangements?

These are big questions. They reflect on debates about what the character of local news should be and the various ways of addressing this that have been illustrated. As the industry and its journalists confront these debates driven by declining circulations, they are faced with a confusing, and in some ways distracting, complex mix of economic, social and technological change. The answers would appear to lie in how effectively new needs are recognised, new technology encompassed and converged possibilities for social engagement exploited. Given the chance, local journalists who are part of their local community could, for example, turn some of the new technologies into tools that improve their ability to report and fact-check good, informative stories that their audience would want to read and from which local democracy would benefit. The question is whether, in an increasingly commodified environment, they would be allowed to do so.

References

Advertising Association (2005), 'Key statistics for 2004' and 'UK advertising expenditure forecast to grow 2.3% in 2005'. Available at <http://www.adsoc.org.uk> (accessed 27 January 2006).

Armistead, L. (2005), 'Interview with Tim Bowdler', *The Sunday Times Business Section*, 4 September, 7.

Beard, M. (2005), *Press Gazette*, 9 September, 14.

Bowdler, T. (2005), interview with the author, 31 October.

Bradshaw, S. (2003), interview with the author, 26 August.

Catlow, R. (2005), interview with the author, 25 May.

Cole, P. (2004), 'Diversity in the newsroom', reported in Ponsford, D., 'Regional press fails the diversity test', *Press Gazette*, 29 October.

Crosby, V. (2005), <www.holdthefrontpage.co.uk/behind/analysis/05.04.05> (accessed 10 June 2005).

Dodson, S. (2004), *Press Gazette*, 22 October, 12.

Dyson, S. (2005), interview with the author, 7 July.

Franklin, B. and Murphy, D. (1997), 'The Local Rag in Tatters?', in Bromley, M. and O'Malley, T., *A Journalism Reader* (London: Routledge).

Franklin, B. and Murphy, D. (1998), *Making the Local News* (London: Routledge).

Gent, L. (2005), *Bolton Evening News*, 16 August.

Gilbert, S. (2005), website for *Berrow's Worcester Journal* at <www.berrowsjournal. co.uk/editor/index> (accessed 16 August 2005).

Harcup, T. (2005), *Press Gazette*, 27 June, 19.

Hodgkinson, N. (2005), interview in *Press Gazette*, 9 September, 18.

Holdthefrontpage (2005), www.holdthefrontpage.co.uk/behind/analysis/, 17 March, (accessed 10 June 2005).

Langan, S. (2004), *Press Gazette*, 3 March, 11.

Langan, S. (2006), 'Belfast Bucks the Trend', *Press Gazette*, 10 March. Available at <www.pressgazette.co.uk/090306 belfast_bucks_the_trend>.

Leapman, J. (2004), *Press Gazette*, 18 June.

McNair, B. (1999), *News and Journalism in the UK* (London: Routledge).

Marr, A. (2004), *My Trade* (London: Macmillan).

Metro (2003), source <www.advertising.metro.co.uk/audience/ouraud> (accessed 12 August 2003).

Newsquest (2005), company website at <www.newsquest.co.uk/history>.

Newspaper Society (2005), 'Annual Report 2004/05', 4. Available at <www. newspapersoc.org> (accessed 16 August 2005).

Newspaper Society (2006), source <www.newspapersoc.org> (accessed 4 March 2006).

Phillips, T. (2005), *The Independent*, 17 October.

Ponsford, D. (2004), *Press Gazette*, 6 February, 18.

Ponsford, D. (2006), *Press Gazette*, 9 March. Available at <www.pressgazette.co.uk/ article/090306/editorial_investment_seen_as_the_key>.

Ponsford, D. and Langan, S. (2005), *Press Gazette*, 21 October, 1.

Preston, P. (2005), *Observer*, 26 June. Available at <www.guardian.co.uk/columnists> (accessed 25 September 2005).

Read, D. (2003), *Press Gazette*, 28 February, 16.

Sergeant, J. (2001), *Give Me Ten Seconds* (London: Macmillan).

Slattery, J. (2005), interview with Barrie Williams, *Press Gazette*, 30 September, 18.

Slattery, J., Ponsford, D. and Langan, S. (2006), *Press Gazette*, 24 February, 10.

Straw, J. (2003), quoted in *Press Gazette*, 4 April.

Sutton, K. (2005), Forum at the University of Central Lancashire, Preston, 12 October 2005.

Trinity Mirror (2005), company website at <www.trinitymirror.com> (accessed 26 October 2005).

Walker, C. (2005), interviews with the author, 30 June 2004 and 29 June 2005.

Chapter 7

UK Radio Journalism

John Drury

Introduction

The main purpose of this chapter is to assess whether or not radio news journalism can survive in the face of the 'ec-tech' squeeze outlined in Chapter 4. Linked in to this throughout will be an evaluation of the extent to which the changing face of radio can remain compatible with the needs of 'meaningful' democracy as defined in Chapter 3. The book's three core questions will be explicitly or implicitly present throughout this part of the discussion. Because of increasing convergence within the media industry it is inevitable that radio will have to be discussed in relation to some of the new and emerging platforms that complement it, or threaten to replace it. The chapter includes also something of the history of radio, in so far as it is a prerequisite for understanding both the present and the future of journalism in this field. But given the complex detail needed for the core discussion, it does not duplicate the historical material already covered in Chapter 2. We begin with what seemed like 'the beginning of the end' for talk radio in the era when broadcasting became opened to the economic pressures of Reaganism and Thatcherism.

The Decline of Commercial Radio Journalism

When MTV was launched a minute after midnight on 1 August 1981 the first music track it transmitted was 'Video Killed the Radio Star' by the unlikely named Buggles. Never mind the hubris – it all seemed so easy and inevitable. The 'tanks were on the lawn' – a media coup launched from the twin towers of pop music and dynamic video images threatened the long-term existence of music-based radio shows and therefore also put a question mark over the future viability of radio as a mainstream technology for the delivery of content in the commercial sector at least. Without a stranglehold on pop music, what price the business model that had sustained commercial radio for almost ten years? The logical response to the MTV revolution was for commercial radio to abandon all superfluous speech content and fight back with almost wall-to-wall music shows.

Twain-like, the demise of commercial radio was somewhat exaggerated, but the MTV revolution gathered pace as Napster and the iPod appeared as visions in young techno-enthusiasts' dreams. Commercial radio's underlying *raison d'être* as a 'plugger' for a record industry that was itself under threat looked vulnerable. The Cassandras predicted that its means of support as a lucrative source for advertising revenues would be downloaded into the history books by the new, non-linear forms of self-scheduling content delivery, followed in time by radio itself as the BBC struggled to keep the medium alive with its emphasis on speech and a restricted diet of music, even on its most popular station, Radio 1.

By the early 1990s the video (and CD) revolution had pushed the commercial radio sector further towards a 'music-only' zone. The alarm bells began to ring, warning of a serious threat to the range and extent of news and current affairs coverage on the radio and, by extension, a threat to democracy itself.

As early as 1998 Peter Barnard wrote about this emerging situation in the commercial sector:

> Whereas no commercial applicant for a licence would have dreamed of leaving out a commitment to news bulletins a few years ago, now the signs are that news is more or less an *option*. The Radio Authority has even allowed some existing stations to drop or reduce their news bulletins.
>
> This ought to be worrying someone and one of the people it ought to be worrying is Tony Blair. The Prime Minister expressed concern about low turnout in the recent council elections. If young people in the 16–25 age group, who predominantly listen to music stations, cease to be exposed to any of the issues in the news, who can expect them to visit polling stations when the time comes? (Barnard, 1998).

Barnard went on to comment:

> Commercial broadcasters claim that, in surveys, their listeners report irritation when news bulletins interrupt music. But it would be interesting, and I suspect highly informative, to chart how these responses vary depending on when the survey is undertaken: there are few signs that anyone was 'irritated' by coverage of Dunblane or the death of Princess Diana of Wales. [These older stories could be replaced by those of terrorist events in London in 2005.]

He continued:

> Stations that are dropping news bulletins would do better to take a lesson from those that are adapting their bulletins to the audience. Many stations with AM and FM outlets now produce a more traditional bulletin for older listeners on AM with a much more tabloid approach on FM. The latter is less abstract, more likely to be conveyed via an interview between a studio presenter and a reporter on the beat. Some frown on this approach to news, but if it works it should be welcomed. *No news is the real bad news* (Barnard, 1998).

Whilst there are always notable exceptions to general rules and trends it is broadly the case that in struggling to maintain its audience share under such conditions, commercial radio gradually eschewed the structured speech elements in its schedule – with the interesting exception of 'phone-ins' (to which we shall return) – and largely left the talking up to its main, celebrity presenters. Some stations had 'seamless' music shows where all traces of live, human activity were limited to the continuity announcements between shows and extremely short, sharp news bulletins and travel and weather information. Perhaps more significantly for the role of the media in facilitating the democratic process, commercial radio reduced its commitment to current affairs and 'built' speech programming. In many eyes, by doing so, it had abandoned much of the pretence to partner the BBC in a public service broadcasting (PSB) role.

Fast-forwarding, recent events suggest an intervention from TV broadcaster Channel 4 may bring about a small but meaningful reverse in this trend as they explore the viability of broadcasting radio programmes under a PSB flag. To these surprising events we shall return, but even if Channel 4's plans materialise, there can be little argument that the BBC carries almost all the weight and responsibility of preserving serious, long-form speech programming and analysis, discussion and debate of current affairs on its shoulders. For this reason the present chapter concentrates on the role of the BBC in this regard.

It is less clear with news coverage. Issues of style, content, duration and volume sometimes obscure the real intent and commitment of commercial and public service broadcasters alike. For example, changes in presentation style, the reduction in length of news items (or bulletins), altered priorities for subject matter may all be positive signs of editors seeking to engage disaffected audiences and to corral new listeners, particularly younger ones. Commercial radio may, despite apparent reduction in the volume of news coverage, still have a robust case for claiming a significant reach in the UK as a result of its syndicated news output.

Therefore, it is not the intention of this chapter to discount entirely the role of the commercial radio sector in determining the future of news coverage and radio journalism (although it would be harder to find it a significant place when it comes to current affairs), but realistically the key driver of response and reaction to changes in the public service broadcasting environment will be successive hierarchies at the BBC. The defining and most important measures – editorial and economic – for maintaining the link between broadcasting and the democratic process will not be taken by the senior managers within commercial radio.

Before we examine how the BBC is reacting to technological developments and changes in the marketplace, it may be useful to draw the latest regulatory landscape fashioned by the 2003 Communications Act and bring into present context the position of commercial radio.

The 2003 Communications Act

In theory, at least, regulation of the media is designed to safeguard the public interest and tends to cover two broad areas: the rules governing media ownership and the regulation of the content – that is, the products which the media industry creates.

There is nothing new in such regulation, nor in its function as a response to the development of new media configurations. A number of measures have been enacted over the last 80 years to establish various watchdogs and monitoring systems mostly designed to serve the public interest. In the spirit of the new millennium, in December 2000 the government introduced a White Paper addressing the UK's convergent electronic media and telecommunications which, it claimed, would be 'flexible enough … to respond to rapid changes in technologies, services or public expectations' (DTI/DCMS, 2000).

This resulted in the setting-up of Ofcom, a new single 'converged' media regulator to replace the pre-existing Independent Television Commission, Radio Authority and Broadcasting Standards Commission. It proposed the introduction of new rules for content regulation of public service and non-public service broadcasters. It also flagged up a relaxation of the rules on media ownership. The aim was clear – to balance the interests of media owners and those of media consumers.

The context was also relatively easy to grasp. Radical developments in so-called 'new media', by which technology released extraordinary potential for new ways of delivering content, had provoked fierce commercial competition with major media companies competing for the best options to diversify onto these new delivery platforms. Such changes offered up a whole new range of products and services which could be cross-promoted across traditional media, the Internet and mobile phones. These developments have already begun to produce an irrevocable and dramatic effect upon the structure, ownership and regulation of the media industry in the UK. Media companies, the regulators and consumers are being propelled forward by the 'First Law of Technology', a phrase coined by Roy Amara of the Institute for the Future, who identified:

> A consistent pattern in our response to new technologies …. we simultaneously *overestimate* the short-term impact and *underestimate* the long-term impact (Hanson, 2003).

Many who think along these lines have argued that the accelerating rate of adoption of new media technologies by both audiences and broadcasters is evidence that they are becoming more optimistic about their uses and potential and that radical changes in the way that information is used and received will result. The question emerges as to whether this transformation can be in the interest of all – consumers, citizens, journalism, the public interest and media owners – or whether there must be winners *and* losers as a result of these revolutionary events.

In December 2003, the new media watchdog, Ofcom, inherited all of the regulatory activities previously supervised separately for commercial television, radio and communications, whilst the BBC retained its own, exclusive system of governance through its Board of Governors, *although* it is accountable to Ofcom on certain issues, such as meeting general standards and independent production quotas.

Ofcom presents a persuasive *raison d'être*. It exists, in its own words, 'to further the interests of citizen-consumers as the communications industries enter the digital age'. And the scope of its ambition does not end there. It also aims to:

- balance the promotion of choice and competition with the duty to foster plurality, encourage informed citizenship, protect viewers, listeners and customers and promote cultural diversity;
- support the need for innovators, creators and investors to flourish within markets driven by full and fair competition between all providers.

(Because the BBC stands on the fringes of Ofcom's radar, its regulations and exhortations have a limited impact and influence upon the direction of the Corporation's activities in striking the type of fundamental balances that the watchdog has in its sights. But as a template for scrutinising the performance of the BBC in relation to its PSB obligations, it might be argued that Ofcom's 'mission statement' provides a useful measure of success.)

With regard to content regulation, the Communications Act created different *tiers* or levels of regulation for public service broadcasters like the BBC, ITV, C4 and C5, which would continue to provide programmes of range and quality in accordance with the terms of their broadcast licences, and for non-public service broadcasters like Sky and other satellite and cable channels, which would only be bound by general rules like those on taste and decency.

But perhaps the most controversial aspects of the new legislation were proposed changes to rules on media ownership which, in the case of radio, would allow for greater consolidation in the commercial radio sector. Waiting in the wings, commercial radio interests emerged with an early challenge to Ofcom's stated ambition of balancing the interests of owners and consumers.

The Problem of Mergers

Since its launch in the UK in 1973, commercial radio had become a powerful and profitable force in British broadcasting. Up until 2004, 70 separate companies owned the 270-odd local and regional commercial radio stations in the UK. Of these only about 20 companies were of any significant size, and just three – Capital Radio, Emap and GWR – owned nearly half of all commercial radio broadcasting licences between them.

Then there were two.

Perhaps surprisingly, a disproportionate amount of the controversy and debate during the 'nuts and bolts' stages of the Communications Bill centred on the future of radio. Fears were angrily and openly expressed that if ownership of the UK's commercial radio network became *even more* concentrated, listeners might find themselves with *even less* choice as stations began to 'file share' programmes. In the wake of the 2003 Communications Act, the odds on a merger between two of the big companies, Capital and GWR, shortened considerably until in October 2004 the companies announced a £711 million merger to form a single company to control 150 stations, and capture the attention of a formidable 38 per cent of the UK commercial radio audience. Capital and GWR bent over backwards to tell anybody who would listen (which was after all what they did best) that there would be no rampant homogenisation of the output and no loss of regional nuance or diversity as a result of the merger, although they were rather more reticent about any plans for cost-cutting.

Another concern raised by the Communications Act had been the potential for a foreign takeover of the UK's commercial radio network, since this was now permitted under the revised media ownership rules (the favourites being the US-based media company Clear Channel). But the defensive bulk provided by the Capital and GWR merger raised the stakes and the price of such a foreign invasion to what appears to have been a prohibitive level. However, the possibility of such aggrandisement remains, as do the fears of what this might mean for commercial radio's remaining coverage of news and 'serious' speech programming.

Meanwhile, the familiar but still timely debate continues as to the costs and benefits of such mergers. Supporters of such moves argue that they lead to the creation of major media players whose consolidated resources can achieve greater dividends for their shareholders whilst still ploughing a significant proportion of profits into programme resources – including the capture of major presentation talent that drives ratings and advertising revenues – as well, of course, as producing more entertaining and popular programming.

From a purely economic standpoint it is also argued that such consolidation creates greater efficiency by cutting down the wasteful duplication of resources. Another important argument is that alliances such as these between relatively cash-rich companies release money for and encourage investment at a time when 'opportunities' abound for diversification within the electronic media industry.

The pessimists insist that the GWR/Capital merger is an unhealthy development for the future of radio. Again the arguments are familiar: it concentrates too much power and influence in too few hands; it works against local and regional sensibilities and encourages the consolidation of content across the commercial network for economic reasons, whilst diminishing the opportunities for creative competition over content because it reduces the alternative outlets for such endeavours.

Furthermore, the critics add that if ever commercial radio had any lingering sense of a public service remit (and it can certainly point to an impressive past in producing ground-breaking journalism), then this merger did nothing to maintain the remnants of this 'mindset'. Inevitably, they argue, the abandonment of the public service ethos leads to a decline in programme standards.

It also increases the burden on the shoulders of the BBC to save and protect the soul of public service broadcasting within the radio sector.

The BBC's role in preserving public service broadcasting should not be confused with protecting the Corporation's radio services. Indeed it has been argued on a number of occasions that music-based channels such as Radio 1 and Radio 3 should be hived off to the private sector and no longer financed by the licence payer. If it can be delivered with a commercial business model then why should the British public pay a tax in order to listen to such content?

Radio as But One of Several Audio Means to the Same End

In any event, it is not the survival of radio technology *per se* that matters, but that there exists a significant and diverse means of production and delivery of high-quality speech-only content that helps play the central role in preserving *democracy* that was suggested for the news media in the early chapters of this book.

Ofcom's Ed Richards expressed the same value when he coined the phrase the 'citizen rationale', which links the broadcaster directly to the democratic process itself: '[Public service broadcasting] can support a society which understands different points of view, it can contribute to an effective, healthy democracy ... through news, information and analysis of current events and ideas' (Richards, 2004).

It is patently obvious that not all (and maybe none) of the BBC's audio services currently supplied via radio, including its output of music, drama, sport and live event programming – as well as news and current affairs – will necessarily depend in the future on the survival of radio as a broadcasting object or technique. The unique properties of radio – cheapness, portability and 360-degree surround-sound – can now, for example, be replicated with self-scheduling, 'listen again' services delivered through the Internet onto laptops and 'podcasting' through MP3 players, which are also invading radio's erstwhile sanctuary – the motor car.

On a broader front, Helen Boaden, former Controller of BBC Radio 4 and now Director of News and Current Affairs at the BBC, concedes there may be circumstances that could hole radio, as a medium, below the waterline. She says:

> ... you could speculate about audiences that have grown up mostly with television and playstations suddenly being able to get pictures conveniently on hand-held devices and in the end being incredibly seduced by that. That portability factor which you've never had with pictures. But there's always going to be a problem with pictures because, however good the hand-held device, it's always going to be little, the picture is going to be little, plus I suspect the wiring of some people will always find sound more engaging than image, although we know that human beings are always drawn by image first, but I don't think that's going to disappear. And there's always going to be an audience that will just want depth. The other thing is ... you can't watch pictures when you are driving a car. At least not safely. You know there are certain things that you do where audio will prevail. Look we thought books would disappear but people still read books (Boaden, 2006).

The central issue is about production, *not* delivery. It is not about technological determinism. Consumers are being offered and will accept plenty of new and different ways to listen without necessarily changing their preferences for content or indeed without necessarily abandoning old and habitual forms of reception. The issue is a cultural one, whether consumers choose to engage with particular kinds of content irrespective of changes or greater variety in the means of delivery. This is something that cannot be predicted with any precision.

The Robustness of News and Current Affairs Journalism

First, then, we must examine the robustness of news and current affairs as a discrete type of content. There is no evidence for a reduction in the volume of such content. Indeed, with digitisation the reverse has been true not only in terms of basic numbers but also in terms of the depth and diversity of news output, if not current affairs. Niche news – whether it be political, financial, ethnic-based, the weather or sport, has gathered pace.

Rightly or wrongly, there is a belief amongst some of the key decision makers in the quality broadcast news media that the uncertainties of a post-September 11 world have increased the demand for accurate, authoritative journalism. This belief suggests that hard news coverage, at least, can pay its way in ratings terms and produce quality brands that target important demographics for advertisers and opinion formers. In other words, responding to competitive pressures and concern for the health of this key element of British public service broadcasting need not be mutually incompatible.

In the period of writing this chapter Channel 4 announced that it intends to further its stake in radio. It has ambitious plans to launch a series of speech and music radio stations to take on the BBC, using its television talent and programme brands to attract listeners. The broadcaster announced plans to bid for the national digital radio licence due to be advertised by the media watchdog Ofcom in 2006 (sales of digital radios have surged during 2005 to over three million), giving it enough capacity for up to eight new radio stations plus interactive services, such as mobile television.

Channel 4's chief executive, Andy Duncan, said that if it wins the licence it will launch a mixture of public service and commercial stations to take on the BBC, which has a 56 per cent share of radio listening. Channel 4 had already taken a 51 per cent stake in the digital radio station One Word. Simon Cole, chief executive of One Word's other shareholder, UBC, said: 'It will compete head to head with anything Radio 4 can do.' He added: 'Our aim is to contribute something new to the radio mix by offering a public service alternative to the BBC in news, current affairs, entertainment, lifestyle, comedy and music.'

Channel 4 says it has plans to originate programmes ahead of bidding for the digital licence and which will be podcast. Interestingly, the first off the line is a current affairs show, to be hosted by Channel 4 news presenter Jon Snow, examining the controversy over the link between cannabis use and mental health problems.

The BBC's Director of News and Current Affairs welcomed the news: 'It's incredibly important that you have a multiplicity of outlets. It's like newspapers, you need many voices, you need many stances, you need the public to have a lot of choice' (Boaden, 2006).

Overall, audiences for speech radio have also been growing. Despite the rampant growth of digital TV and 'new media' services, people still tune in to radio for news as well as entertainment and music. Also, the traditional 'phone-in' and drive-time shows have prospered and provided an important support for the idea of a 'citizen rationale'. However, despite this overall growth, and despite the previously mentioned optimism of some news producers, the picture specifically with regard to broadcast coverage of politics and current affairs is less comforting. For example, a report by the Independent Television Commission showed that 70 per cent of the public had little or no interest in the television coverage during the 2001 general election (ITC, 2001) – compared with 56 per cent in 1997 (ITC, 1997). In 2005 the ITC survey was replaced by an Ofcom poll of viewers and voters. Although it used a different methodology the survey reported 50 per cent of voters as having 'little interest' in coverage of the 2005 election (Ofcom, 2005).

It was noted at the beginning of the chapter also how news and current affairs has been slipping off the radar of much of commercial radio for some years as a result of a perceived lack of audience demand.

The early harbingers of doom had already predicted negative consequences arising for democracy in the age of new technology. In 1996, Andrew Kohut, director of the Pew Center, said: 'The ultimate irony is that the Information Age has spawned such an uninformed and uninvolved population.' Since then, record low turnouts at the polls, increasingly poor recognition counts on political issues and general disaffection with politicians and politics suggest he may not have been totally wide of the mark. 'After a steady series of breakthroughs in information technology,' wrote David Shenk in his 1997 book *Data Smog*, 'we are left with a citizenry that is certainly no more interested or capable of supporting a healthy representative democracy than it was 50 years ago, and may well be less capable' (Shenk, 1997).

But if there is truth in these observations, to what extent is that truth the result of any failure in the efficiency of the specific link between the media and our democratic processes? Poor parenting and poor schooling are just as likely contenders for blame as may be what many regard as a frothy and dysfunctional 'mass culture'. The content of the mass media is decided partially in a transaction between the consumer and our media institutions via the check-out counter and the remote control which provides the means to by-pass public service offerings.

Current affairs programming is perhaps the hardest testing ground for the public service broadcasting model. As the Director of News and Current Affairs at the BBC, Helen Boaden, concedes, it is unlikely that television will be the key to its survival: 'The BBC won't give up on television, serious television that's aimed at giving the citizen that knowledge … but if you look across the piece, radio and online could well be the two sources of the most information and the most in-depth information' (Boaden, 2006).

On these platforms – with 'radio' production augmented by self-scheduling through the Internet and podcasting – the future does not appear so bleak. According to the BBC's own online service, the appetite for radio current affairs programming on its Listen Again service is 'extraordinarily high' and the hits on news and current affairs issues on its website amount to millions per week – far from discouraging.

Nicola Meyrick, Head of the BBC's Home Current Affairs Department on radio, sees little to worry about with the advent of new media options:

It's an opportunity. I don't care how people listen so long as they listen to our output. For example, we have 'Listen Again' which gives us an international reach through the Internet that we never had before and the majority of e-mail reaction I now get to our programmes is from abroad (Meyrick, 2006).

The Implications of New Media Developments for BBC Radio News and Current Affairs

But Meyrick also believes that new media services are only an *alternative* to radio listening rather than a future replacement.

Some people will choose MP3 rather than radio and that number may increase over time. But one of the big strengths of Radio 4 over the MP3 player is that with the latter you've got to choose what you want. The fact is people quite often don't know or understand the schedule, so in order to choose what you want you have to know what's there, you have to make an effort, whereas R4 guides you and you may hear something and say, 'what's this?' and it turns out to be something fantastic and you would never have got it any other way, and so I think there's room for all these things and I think people have different kinds of experiences (Meyrick, 2006).

Such sentiments are reinforced by the limited research so far carried out in this area – predominantly in the US market. For example, a study by An Nguyen concludes:

The Internet will definitely become a major news medium of the future. Will it complement or alter traditional news media? The question is still open to debate ... the 'historical rule' is that no new medium eliminates older media. They survive well, and in many cases, cooperate effectively, with each other (Nguyen, 2003).

According to Meyrick, the USP (user service profile) of current affairs radio consists of a rich mix of original journalistic investigation, the structuring of complex narrative (or the refusal to be simplistic about complicated issues) and 'without being elitist', the dedication of intelligent people's time that this kind of endeavour demands. She observes that not all new media lend themselves to the long form that many of her department's documentaries take on radio. Without 'dumbing down', she says, they are already having to come to terms with a world portrayed in 'smaller chunks' (Meyrick, 2006).

It's something we've started to wrestle with but I'm personally quite resistant to it because it's not doing current affairs as we understand it. If you have to reduce it to that extent you can't get the complexity of the story across, and since our USP is depth and originality I'm not sure you can do those kind of cut-downs. But increasingly we do not, for example, regard our 8 p.m. radio slot [30 minutes] on Thursdays as the only place we can tell a [current affairs] story and it's true you can get the story across in a different way (Meyrick, 2006).

But Meyrick insists:

... there has to be somewhere people can still get the whole story and so we still have to make documentaries – there has to be somewhere to get it – maybe streaming as an MP3 download, although we know we meet a larger constituency through cut-downs, because if you stop doing the whole thing then you will stop doing the journalism that created it (Meyrick, 2006).

Helen Boaden agrees that the ability to handle stories in depth is a fundamental strength of radio. 'The great thing with radio is it's essentially an analytical media, you need narrative, you need strong stories, but you can dig into things and you have depth and analysis which is incredibly hard to deliver on television and to that extent it [radio] is closer to online' (Boaden, 2006).

However, this does not, says Boaden, preclude new means of delivery:

The key thing I think, the real challenge is ensuring that we deliver in-depth radio on technologies that people are increasingly using, because the challenge is time, always, always time. People are, it's a cliché but it's true, people are time-starved ... I genuinely think it [new media] will give radio a new lease of life. I think the convenience of it will just mean that some of the more difficult pieces of journalism that currently go on Radio 4 in the evenings, which isn't convenient for lots of people, you'll be able to hear when you want from your iPod (Boaden, 2006).

However, not everybody agrees that people are looking for technology to provide the means by which quarts of information can be put into pint-size pots of time or made portable enough to fit into the 'downtime' of busy schedules. Most people, they argue, just do not want to spend their valuable time keeping abreast of 'important' issues. In which case the question becomes a different one: is the media 'dumbing us down', or are consumers demanding only the barest minimum of attractively packaged information so that they can feel and appear informed even if they are not? Is it that people want easily digestible, 'fast-food' information, delivered to their doors by the most convenient means possible and not in the kind of detail that might help them to understand the complexities and nuances of issues that confront them – be they social, cultural, political, environmental, or scientific – as matters of real choice within a democratic society?

To preserve and fulfil its function as the guardian of public service broadcasting the BBC must retain the optimistic view which Helen Boaden is keen to ensure her News and Current Affairs teams share:

I always say to people who work for me, whether you like this or not you can't sack the audience. They can sack you but you can't sack them. And the skill is the extent to which you lead people to beyond their own choices, you excite their interest. And a kind of basic faith that often people are more curious than we sometimes assume. And actually if you only get what you already know it can get quite tedious and there'll always be a proportion of people who'll do that and there will always be a proportion of people who will want to know more (Boaden, 2006).

Linking that approach to oiling the wheels of democracy is no easy task within an electorate where voting is becoming increasingly unpopular:

> The facilitation of democracy remains at the core of what we are about but democracy isn't a simplistic thing. It's not just about people voting. Many people who are fully informed of what's going on in the world decide not to vote but they still want the information about issues. You might be a fully informed citizen, decide not to vote but spend a great deal of time working for a charity or working on a single-issue campaign. There are many ways of being a citizen ... (Boaden, 2006).

One area where it could be argued people are getting involved and expressing their 'citizenship' is Internet 'blogging' and, by extension, the provision of what is termed 'user-generated content' through portable recording devices, including the ubiquitous mobile phone, to the established media organisations. For these organisations, used to a one-way system of production and delivery of content through print, TV and radio, this may have dramatic consequences. But again Nicola Meyrick, in charge of the BBC's output of UK-based radio current affairs, remains calm:

> The idea that people feel engaged in that way rather than being passive recipients is great. I don't think it diminishes in any way what we do. Blogs are interesting and taking off massively. Even the BBC is producing its own 'blogs' – Nick Robinson [the BBC's Political Editor] is producing one. Some 'blogs' are quite good and well argued and the people writing them are quite well informed – but what we (the BBC) have that they don't is that 'blogs' are nearly all produced from second-hand sources, people who watch and read, etc., and give us their spin on an issue, but also are not bound by any obligation to get it right – or to be fair.
>
> I think because of the proliferation of media in that sense, then part of our USP is about authority – not in an elitist sense but in that you can believe what we tell you and that it has originality, because we have actually been out and talked to people and investigated it and checked it out – and I think this is going to become even more at a premium (Meyrick, 2006).

'Blogging' and the vast potential of 'user-generated' content through inexpensive hand-held devices also assaults the certainties of traditional media on another front: the question of balanced journalism. The duty to provide journalistic balance has traditionally been left to media organisations themselves, within fairly relaxed rules administered by either industry or government-appointed watchdogs.

In the future the fundamental question of what is 'balanced' will come under much greater scrutiny as the supply of information and testimony is gathered and received from a much greater variety of uncontrolled sources. The validity of the arguments put forward by media organisations in the past to defend their position of balance may well become exposed as, at best, limited by the range of their own interests, journalistic methods and sources of information. They may, for the moment at least, be the gatekeepers of information supply, but the flood that threatens may, sooner rather than later, alter the media landscape in unpredictable fashion. One consequence could be a complete reappraisal of the media's past performance as a facilitator of the democratic process and the suitability of its current structures for that role in the future.

The Director of News and Current Affairs at the BBC, Helen Boaden, appears to see the writing on the wall. 'I think it's about range of voice. I think too often we think of politics with a capital P and we don't recognise, as it were, political movements, political issues until they get to that category.'

Boaden uses the citizens' fuel protests to make her point:

> The media, and it wasn't just the BBC, and the political classes did not recognise that as an issue until the fuel protestors almost brought the country to a halt ... the kinds of people who were protesting were not the kind of people who the BBC are very good at tapping into. You might call it a 'white van' issue (Boaden, 2006).

In the pursuit of greater balance (and viewing it as one of the oldest but most effective forms of interactivity in the media) Boaden has introduced formal feedback sessions from all of the radio networks phone-in programmes. She believes this will pick up on a completely different slant from what is seen as the 'orthodox view' and cites a recent example, the Commons debate and votes on the 90 days' detention proposal for suspected terrorists.

> Although the MPs threw the measure out, most of the broadsheets supported it. Across all our 'phone-ins' people were outraged at what the MPs had done. They were far more illiberal if you want to coin it like that ... So, it's always this thing of how do you try to find the real balance ... and that's not moving away from a political agenda, those are political issues, it's just finding the voices that represent the broader spectrum (Boaden, 2006).

In addition:

> It is always about having someone in charge who challenges the orthodoxy in the room and that's why as Director of News I put a huge emphasis on getting my editors to think about what they're doing and in my departmental heads I've got good people who I genuinely don't know what their personal politics are, but they are very good at our daily editorial meetings saying, 'I don't think we are representing this view', or 'have you actually asked that hard question?' It's the range of voices that we give them. You know, there are not two views on this, there may be fifteen views and it's our responsibility to make sure those views are all presented fairly without us taking sides (Boaden, 2006).

But views are just that – opinions, a perspective on the world that may not bear scrutiny by detailed and professional journalistic investigation – the type that in radio broadcast terms is mostly confined to the BBC's current affairs output.

Boaden makes a clear distinction about the use of citizen-produced material:

> The key thing for us is where we're using it as fact we've done the checking and where we're using it as user-generated material we flag it, so people don't confuse fact with non-fact, verified information with non-verified information.

You become the accreditors and the ringmasters. But you know the interesting thing is that we've moved beyond the 'either or' culture; video did not kill the radio star actually, it's not that one will replace the other, but it's actually 'let it all happen' which of course in terms of resource is a massive challenge (Boaden, 2006).

Conclusion

The result of all of this for radio journalism is not likely to be its imminent demise, in other words. Rather it suggests a future in which radio takes a new place as one among several speech, audio-visual and online news and current affairs platforms trying desperately to find ways to keep up with the ever-increasing flow of information from user-generated and other sources. This is particularly the case given Boaden's emphasis on seeking out and listening to a much more representative range of views within society. There simply is not the time in terms of broadcast slots to handle everything that is likely to become available. New technologies, in providing a wider range of platforms for the dissemination of news and current affairs, and in the case of the Internet, for a much greater level of detail, provide part of the answer in opening up additional outlets. However, as McNair asks: 'How, in an intensely competitive environment, [will we be able] to finance the vast quantities of journalistic output now produced across print, broadcast and online media, both public and commercially funded, at local, national and international level, given the finite capacity of the audience to absorb and pay for it?' (McNair, 2003).

In the public sector where the responsibility for facilitating the democratic process weighs heaviest, Helen Boaden has a similar concern:

> I think that is a challenge for us and initially we will just actually make more available, more of what we are *already* collecting … we've probably spent thousands of pounds on really good journalism, it goes out once. We're just now, at last, getting it also on other outlets [in broadcasting] but that should be on the Web. Now, if you just take that idea, what also should be on the Web on broadband would probably be the unedited interviews because there's an audience that can want that. But can the BBC sustain multi-platform? Can they actually authentically gather news across such a broad spectrum? (Boaden, 2006)

Put another way, the BBC may not itself be capable of providing, through the licence fee, the diversity of content required for genuinely democratic discourse and action that new technology and its usage is making possible. Hard choices may have to be made about how and where it is done. The challenge for radio is to remain at the centre of that decision making.

It is important to remember also the sobering fact, pointed to earlier, that no matter how much high-quality output is provided, many of the potential news audience may choose simply not to access it.

So, with regard to the book's second core question, as the main public service provider the BBC would seem to be making significant efforts to enhance both the breadth and depth of its radio news and current affairs coverage through its embracing (but careful) use and evaluation of the user inputs that new technology has made possible. The picture in the commercial radio sector, however, has been one of significant decline in hard news coverage and most particularly in current affairs; and there is a real danger that many of those listeners who do not also visit the BBC's main news programmes will be left without any radio news coverage of substance or value. With regard to the third question, the BBC, through Boaden's policy of widening the range of voices listened to in news production, is trying to remove the previous bias towards 'traditional politics with a big P' and incorporate also political issues that previously have been less visible in news coverage. This can be seen as an attempt to better deliver the corporation's obligation towards wide and impartial coverage of news issues and events. The first question is being addressed in so far as the BBC is struggling with how to reinvigorate and expand the audience for its current affairs coverage by producing versions suitable for MP3 players, and so on, without losing the essential quality and depth of, for example, substantial documentaries. While it is, of course, possible to cover a far wider range of aspects of these questions, these are the ones that seemed most useful to examine in the limited space available.

A final observation seems worth making. It is perhaps most useful to think of radio not just as a platform but as a tradition within which particular types and qualities of speech news journalism have been produced. Even where the platforms for delivery are changing, the evidence to date suggests that the tradition seems likely to continue.

References

Barnard, P. (1998), 'No news is not necessarily good news', *The Times*, 16 May, London.

Boaden, H. (2006), interview with the author, 4 January 2006.

Campbell, G. (2000), 'Well-informed citizens increasingly rare in information age', *The Los Angeles Times*, 17 July.

DTI/DCMS (Department of Trade and Industry/Department for Culture, Media and Sport) (2000), *A New Future For Communications*, White Paper published December 2000 (London: HMSO).

Hanson, K. (2003), 'First Law of Technology explains current internet radio skepticism', Radio and Internet Newsletter. Available at <http://www.kurthanson. com/archive/news/012703/index.asp>.

ITC (Independent Television Commission) (1997), *Independent Television Commission Survey 1997* (London: ITC).

ITC (Independent Television Commission) (2001) *Independent Television Commission Survey 2001*; ICM Poll for Ofcom (London: ITC).

McNair, B. (2003), 'What a difference a decade makes', *British Journalism Review* 14 (1), 42–8.

Meyrick, N. (2006), interview with the author, 27 January 2006, London.

Nguyen, A. (2003), 'The current status and potential development of online news consumption: a structural approach', online at *First Monday* 8 (9).

Ofcom (2005), *Viewers and Voters: Attitudes to Television Coverage of the 2005 General Election*, research study conducted by ICM Research on behalf of Ofcom (London: Ofcom).

Richards, E. (2004), speaking at the Westminster Hall Debate, London.

Shenk, D. (1997), *Data Smog: Surviving the Information Glut* (San Francisco: Harper).

Chapter 8

Online Journalism

François Nel, Mike Ward and Alan Rawlinson

Introduction

This chapter has a problematic issue to confront, in so far as the relationships involved
– between the providers, audiences, perceived responsibilities and possible modes
of use of online journalism as a still very young and unprecedented phenomenon
– are undergoing rapid and often unpredictable change. For this reason, it is not easy
to fit it within the overall structure of the book's three core questions. In so far as
they can be presently examined, issues relating to these questions have already been
discussed in the Internet section of Chapter 2. While additional relevant issues will
be raised here, the main emphasis will be on trying to discern some of the potential
ways in which the online environment might impact on journalism in the foreseeable
future and to identify the implications for democracy wherever possible.

A traditional tenet of journalism has been the role of the journalist as the prime
mediator or gatekeeper – the provider of the information and analysis required
by the public to function effectively in an advanced democracy. This perspective
has informed the identification of issues seen as key to the future health of both
journalism and the public sphere, such as the range and depth of news coverage and
the balance between 'hard' and 'soft' news. However, any study of online journalism
must deal with an additional fundamental, which undermines this portrayal of the
journalist; because, within the online medium, the public is not just a recipient of
mediated information. It can also choose, compare and publish its own.

From the beginning, it was clear that the one-way, producer-driven methods of
media such as newspapers and broadcasting need not apply to online. The consumers
of online news could choose what, when and how they accessed their content because
of online's operating platform. In addition, audiences could more easily compare
different versions of stories or verify the facts directly online from the journalistic
sources. Increasingly the watchdogs were being watched. 'Audiences are ever more
demanding,' noted BBC executive Pat Loughrey (2005: 1). 'Deference is dead.'
And, as the technology has become more user-friendly, more and more consumers
have become providers, publishing their own content – first on bulletin boards and
email discussion groups and latterly through the rapid growth of weblogs and mobile
applications.

This growth in activity has, in part, been fuelled by a rapid increase in the
number of people going online in the UK. Findings from the Pew Research Center

(2006) indicate that computer use in the UK has increased by 17 per cent between 2002 and 2005, the largest growth of any country within the survey.[1] In addition, research in 2005 from Nielsen/NetRatings suggested that a significant number of those going online were visiting 'online member communities'. The survey indicated up to half the UK Internet population were viewing almost 1.8 billion web pages on member community sites in any given month. The most-visited site in that survey was Friends Reunited – the online community for those seeking long-lost friends and acquaintances. On face value, this may seem to have little to do with journalism. But Rupert Murdoch's acquisition in 2005 of MySpace.com, the popular social-networking site, for $580 million, suggests a different story. Murdoch (2005) has accused the mainstream news industry of being 'remarkably, unaccountably complacent' in its response to the digital revolution. He is clear about the challenge: '… to deliver … news in ways consumers want to receive it … we have to free our minds of our prejudices and predispositions, and start thinking like our newest consumers.' Murdoch believes these consumers want news on demand, news that speaks to them personally, and 'they want to be able to use the information in a larger community – to talk about, to debate, to question, and even to meet the people who think about the world in similar or different ways'. Hence, it is argued, his acquisition of MySpace.com and, later, ITV's purchase of Friends Reunited for £120 million.

The public's power to choose, compare and publish its own information, and the rapid formation of self-sustaining online communities, has put strains on the traditional 'gatekeeper' perception of the journalist's role. As Bowman and Willis (2003) observe: 'A democratized media challenges the notion of the institutional press as the exclusive, privileged, trusted, informed intermediary of the news.'

Some feel these strains have already become tectonic shifts. Orville Schell, Dean of the University of California at Berkeley's journalism school, believes: 'The Roman Empire that was mass media is breaking up, and we are entering an almost-feudal period where there will be many more centers of power and influence. It's a kind of disaggregation of the molecular structure of the media' (cited in Bianco et al., 2005).

All this poses a central question: what is the impact of these changes on the relationship between the professional journalist and the public? In the new 'media ecology', as Dan Gillmor (2006) puts it, where people are seeking a conversation rather than a lecture from journalists, and citizens will increasingly seek alternative sources of information, how will the journalists fashion a new relationship with the public that ensures their continuing relevance and value within the public sphere? This appears to be fundamental to any consideration of the future of journalism in the advanced democracies.

---

1   Women have accounted for much of the UK's increase in computer users. In 2002 just over half (55 per cent) of British women utilised computer technology; now three-quarters say they do, only two percentage points fewer than men.

In this chapter, this relationship – the multi-directional interface between online journalist and the public – will be defined and then examined, using a relationship model. The aim is to articulate areas where the dynamics and controls in the relationships are changing, revealing the challenges facing the journalist in the future.

Online Journalism and Journalism Online

At this point, it is worth stating that the study of online journalism in the context of this book is not only an opportunity to reflect upon online as a distinctive form of journalism. It also provides the chance to consider online as a harbinger of developments in other media.

More than a decade since the inception of online journalism, the technologies have become more widely diffused. Digital is now a common platform for all media (Kawamoto, 2003). As we write, national and regional newspapers and news magazines are publishing video and audio news, regional television is publishing text, and phone companies are piloting TV programmes on mobile handsets. Technology consultancy Strategy Analytics predicts this project alone will engage up to 50 million users by 2009, generating an estimated £3.5 billion in revenue (BBC News Online, 2006). *The Guardian*'s chief executive Carolyn McCall believes that, in ten years' time, *The Guardian* will still be delivering quality journalism, but through audio-visual media, the Internet 'and any other media' (Nicholson, 2006: 9).

While there is now general recognition of the opportunity that these new technologies can bring, there has also been much anxiety about the fragmentation of audiences and increased competition. Publishing mogul Felix Dennis recently confessed to 'worrying about the Internet day and f***ing night' (Robinson, 2006: 11).

Journalists, too, are contemplating the implications of new technologies, not only for their work and skills, but also for their professional identity and their role in society. As Hall (2001: 3) notes, ' … many traditional journalistic values such as objectivity, impartiality, accountability, balance, fairness and trustworthiness have, for old media, become ciphers …' in need of renewal in the light of this new medium. This renewal process is proving painful for many journalists because it challenges traditional roles, based around the one-way nature of mass communication to heterogeneous audiences.

Despite, or perhaps because of, this, the significance of online media has moved up the agendas of both news executives and journalists as they consider the future of their occupation.

The UK Online News Sector

News distribution online by the UK's big hitters began in 1994 with the launch of The Electronic Telegraph, which was joined by online *Guardian* and *Observer* editions later that year. Other media followed quickly. By 2001, for example, about 85 per cent of local newspapers had websites (Bromley, 2001: 6) and by 2006 Internet users could listen live to more than 350 UK radio stations and content from all the traditional television channels.

While online audiences continued to grow steadily, many traditional news audience sizes shrunk. For example, the Guardian Unlimited grew from just over 9.5 million registered page impressions (a file or a combination of files sent to a valid user as a result of that user's request to a server) in June 1999 to nearly 29.5 million in August 2001 (Bromley, 2001) and 131 million page impressions and more than 12,250,000 users by September 2005. The circulation of the printed newspaper was just 380,693 in December 2005.

However, all such figures are dwarfed by BBC News Online, ranked in February 2006 the world's tenth most popular English language website (<alexa.com>, 2006). Page impressions topped 1.1 billion in September 2003, with 32.7 million users (ABC Electronic, 2006). This figure includes all users, but traffic on the BBC News website still stands taller than the rest, with 49.9 million page impressions from 4.9 million unique users recorded in one day on 6 May 2005, the day after the General Election (ABC Electronic, 2006).

While most mainstream media continue to expand their online news offerings, there is yet to be a widely accepted revenue model to support these efforts. The prize is great: the global Internet population is set to hit 1.21 billion in 2006, up from 1.07 billion in 2005, according to Computer Industry Almanac (*The Economist*, 2006). With the exception of the publicly funded BBC, this has led to many online news operations running on a shoestring. There is not space within this limited study to explore the complex field of online publishing business models, which includes funded media (for example, the BBC), advertising-supported services (such as The Guardian Online) and partial or full subscription services (such as FT.com). *The Guardian*'s chief executive Carolyn McCall has said that she scares the wits out of her advertising sales teams with the threat of what she calls 'the alligator jaws' of declining classified sales and circulation threats from the multitude of competitive offers (Nicholson, 2006). 'There is such a large institutional cost around print that, if you let it happen, even those making good profits will soon go into the double-digit loss,' she said (*ibid.*). Organisations like the National Health Service, once among *The Guardian*'s biggest advertisers, have become its competitors through starting their own job advertisement sites. However, McCall and most other news executives realise that content drives site traffic, and traffic volume will remain a key starting point to any viable business model.

Contrast this scenario with the individual blogger or the small independent online media activist group, less preoccupied by the bottom line and often more attuned to the communication potential of the Web and Internet. Increasingly, their individual contributions are combining to form a mosaic of storytelling and information sharing. These individual activities, and their collective effect, have been given various labels, often carelessly, which now need to be clarified.

Citizen Publishing – Some Definitions

Citizen publishing, citizen media, citizen journalism – commentators frequently interchange these descriptions, with confusing results. The use of 'citizen journalism', in particular, has provoked frequent semantic tussles about whether journalism is a practice or a profession and who deserves to be called a journalist (Outing, 2005; Bell, 2006). According to Bowman and Willis (2003):

> Citizen journalism, also known as 'participatory journalism', is the act of citizens playing an active role in the process of collecting, reporting, analyzing and disseminating news and information ... The intent of this participation is to provide independent, reliable, accurate, wide-ranging and relevant information that a democracy requires.

Citizen publishing – and its level of integration with mainstream journalism – can be put into four categories, starting with the most integrated:

1. *Increased interactivity between professional and citizen* – news and information provided by the public as part of the mainstream offering. A landmark example is the contributions by citizens caught up in the London bombings in July 2005 who reported the news through photographs and video captured on their mobile phones. These contributions were integrated into the BBC news bulletins and published online, and were followed up through weblogs, such as the 'Survivor's diary' by 'Rachel from north London', which ran on BBC News Online from 7 to 14 July (Rachel, 2005).
2. *Complementary citizen publishing* – news and information provided by the public to complement the mainstream offering; plus discussion, reflection and comment on what is published. The Guardian Online is developing a greater range of blogs and messageboards, increasing the public's capacity to post their own material on the site. It is seen as risky by some, because of the potential legal difficulties, but Simon Waldman (2006) is clear about the potential benefits: 'As we embark on this new era of content, we embark on a new era of risk. And the further we move to new models of engagement, so the element of risk increases: but so does the reward, not simply in terms of direct metrics – audience, revenue, etc. – but also in terms of the long-term relevance and vitality of your brand and publishing operation.'
3. *Professionally enabled/facilitated citizen publishing* – news and information provided by the public, but with the help of mainstream providers. The Carlisle *News and Star*, for example, hosts blogs by citizens in its online news operation. The two dozen or so regular contributors in 2006 included a Cumbrian 'in exile' in New Orleans, a Los Angeles native who followed her husband to Carlisle, and Chris Whiteside 'who gives Conservative perspective on big issues both nationally and locally in West Cumbria' (<http://www.newsandstar.co.uk/opinion/blogs.aspx>). Another approach has come from the BBC, throwing open some of its online news archive to the public, encouraging people to 'download the clips, watch them, and use them

to create something unique. This is a pilot and we want to understand your creative needs. We'd like to see your productions and showcase some of the most interesting ones we receive.'

4. *Competing citizen publishers* – news and information provided by the public as an alternative to the mainstream offering. While there are citizen journalism experiments in online broadcast journalism, such as FelixstoweTV (<http://www.felixstowetv.co.uk/>), the highest profile manifestation of this has been the large scale and rapid growth of blogging.

The first weblogs[2] were identified from 1993. Six years later there were still only 23 (Blood, 2000). In the seven years since 1999, one industry report shows that the number of weblogs has doubled every 5.5 months to 27.8 million in February 2006 (Siffry, 2006: 1), as the technology has become more accessible. As Gillmor (2004) notes, when publishing online was made easier, it led to a rapid transformation from a 'read only' to a 'read/write' web, the original intention of its inventor, Tim Berners-Lee. 'We could all write, not just read, in ways never before possible. For the first time in history, at least in the developed world, anyone with a computer and an Internet connection could own a press. Just about anyone could make the news' (Gillmor, 2004).

Some online journalists value the bloggers' freedom but seek to maintain traditional journalistic values, especially accuracy. Paul Bass, the founder of <newhavenindependent.org>, a news website he runs from his home in Connecticut in the US, combines his own reporting with that of other writers, some of whom would describe themselves as citizen journalists:

> I still think there's a role for the professional journalist. We don't want to tell people what to think, but we do have the skills and the time, if we get paid for it, to go out and find information, and to analyse, and to launch a discussion. We want the public to take that discussion in new ways, we want them also to use the site to post their own information and to steer it, but we still think there's a role for a filter (Bass, 2006).

This perspective, and others like it from online journalists, informs one dimension of the working relationship between the journalist and the public, defining what the journalist regards as valuable online information and analysis. But it does not fully incorporate the other view, the public perception of what is of value. However, this second element cannot be ignored when considering the dynamics of the relationship between journalist and public. For that reason, when examining the future relationship between journalists and their public, we must consider the broad

---

2   Jorn Barger first coined the term weblog (Barger, 1997): 'A weblog (sometimes called a blog or a newspage or a filter) is a webpage where a weblogger (sometimes called a blogger, or a pre-surfer) "logs" all the other webpages she finds interesting.' It is a personal selection (and not restricted to women), often accompanied by a dose of the blogger's opinion. However, links to the source material bring transparency to the presentation and the debate that might ensue, since blogging software facilitates response from readers.

spectrum of information, news, opinion and analysis placed in the public domain by citizens *and which other citizens value.*

This broad offering – let us call it citizen publishing – will contain elements that some will call citizen journalism, be it the taking of news pictures or the publishing of authoritative specialist blogs. These and other examples are all points on the citizen publishing spectrum.

Journalism – a Definition

Before examining the relationship further, we must define what we mean by journalism. There are various perspectives from which to choose, but for the purposes of this study we will consider journalism as an ideology rather than other options offered in the literature, such as 'journalism as a profession, an industry, a literary genre, a culture or a complex social system' (Deuze, 2005: 444).

An ideological approach is pertinent to this analysis because it recognises the prime importance of the journalist's own perception of their role and responsibilities; for example, their duty to provide an 'objective' public service. This self-image – and any perceived challenge to it, such as by competing citizen publishers – is key to understanding the journalists' relationship with their public, which is the central point at issue.

Deuze (*ibid.*) notes that the key elements of this ideology have been described by researchers (Golding and Elliott, 1979; Merritt, 1995; Kovach and Rosenthiel, 2001) as:

- public service (journalists as watchdogs, news hounds, and so on)
- objectivity (impartiality, neutrality, fairness and, therefore, credibility)
- autonomy (freedom, independence); immediacy (sense of actuality, speed inherent in the concept of 'news')
- ethics (responsibility, validity, legitimacy).

Hallin (1992) points out that these ideal-typical categories solidified in a period of 'high modernism' in journalism (roughly between the 1960s and 1990s). However, it was the advent of the printing press almost six centuries ago which signalled the start of the diminishing role of the oral storyteller and the increasing dominance of a 'broadcast' model of communication between news publishers and their publics:

> The broadcast model emphasizes one (or few) to many communication flow, with little feedback between source and receiver (or journalist and audience) and a relatively anonymous, heterogeneous audiences. The intent of this communication is a combination of persuasion and information (Pavlik, 2001: 234).

However, over the past two decades researchers have highlighted the value of organisations not only speaking to key publics, but also listening and responding. The result of effectively managing these relationships around common interests and shared goals, over time, is considered to be mutual understanding and benefit for all – the interacting organisations and publics alike (Ledingham, 2003: 190). By contrast, asymmetrical relationship strategies that rely, principally, on one-way communication activities – and which emphasise either an organisation's or a public's benefit – are thought not to be effective in the long run.

Given the public's increasing desire to choose, compare and publish news and information, journalism (in general) and online journalism (in particular) could benefit from greater understanding of, and by, its publics: audiences, yes, but also advertisers, sources, owners, investors, regulators, social and political pressure groups (McQuail, 1987), all of whom are demanding a greater say in newsroom activities.

Defining the Relationship Between Online Journalists and Citizen Publishing

The need to rethink the relationship between journalism and audiences has been widely noted in professional circles and scholarly literature (Fulton, 1996; Singer, 1997; Pavlik, 2001; Nel, 2003; Deuze, 2005). But, to date, there have been few attempts to systematically examine this relationship through the lens of existing organisation public relationship theory (Ferguson, 1984; Grunig and Hunt, 1984; Hon and Grunig, 1999; Ledingham and Bruning, 1998; et al.). That is the aim of this chapter.

The consensus view at present (Hon and Brunner, 2001; Hon and Grunig, 1999; Huang, 2001; Kim, 2001; Jo et al., 2004) is that relationships between an organisation and its public comprise a number of dimensions, also identified as characteristics or outcomes of relationships: exchange relationships, communal relationships; control mutuality; trust; commitment; satisfaction. This provides a helpful framework to analyse the current relationship between online journalism and its public, particularly at that critical interface of citizen publishing.

Let us now explore how the key tenets of successful relationships have been put under stress or changed by citizen publishing activities. As will be seen, changes will be noticeable within both the journalism industry and the profession and practice of journalism.

Control Mutuality

'Control mutuality refers to the power relations between parties in a relationship. More precisely, it is seen as the degree to which the parties are satisfied with the amount of control they have over the relationship' (Hon and Grunig, 1999).

In 1995 (at a time when online journalism was in its infancy), Michael Schudson invited people to imagine a world in which everyone can deliver information directly to anyone through a computer, a world in which everyone can be his or her own journalist (Deuze, 2005). It is a scenario that, as Deuze (2005) notes, illustrates what professional experience and the literature sees as Internet technologies' most significant impact: its challenge of a fundamental 'truth' of journalism – that 'the professional journalist is the one who determines what publics see, hear and read about the world' (Fulton, 1996; Singer, 1997, cited in Deuze, 2005: 451).

Some have gone further, suggesting professional journalism institutions, as we now know them, will be marginalised or even disappear. Perhaps the best illustration of this dystopian view is proffered by Sloan and Thompson (2004) in their mini-film, *EPIC 2014*, its title being an acronym for 'evolving personal information construct'. The film narration begins:

> In the year 2014 people have access to a breadth and depth of information unimaginable in an earlier age. Everyone contributes in some way. Everyone participates to create a living, breathing mediascape. However, the Press, as you know it, has ceased to exist. The Fourth Estate's fortunes have waned. Twentieth-century news organizations are an afterthought, a lonely remnant of a not-too-distant past.

Others, including Schudson, are more optimistic, at least as far as the roles of journalism and journalists are concerned. He suggests that, in a world awash with information, people would soon become desperate to discern the reliability and validity of the information and, before long, they would be begging for help. What is more, Schudson says, they would prefer the help from a source that was at least relatively knowledgeable, relatively non-partisan and, therefore, relatively trustworthy. 'In short, if it did not exist, journalism would pretty quickly be invented' (Schudson, 1995, cited in Singer, 1997).[3]

The current reality is that neither of these extremes exists. As the audience for mainstream media continues to fragment and diminish, while the take-up of broadband, blogs and mobile applications increases, a fluid middle ground is evolving, populated by professional journalism but also by competing or complementary citizen publishing. Unless the citizen activity is directly enhancing the journalist's offering (for example, by offering news pictures from their mobile phones), all citizen publishing is competing for time and attention, altering the control mutuality balance. Citizen publishers could see this as an overdue correction towards more balanced control mutuality, where the journalists lose their long-held dominant control. However, such a development may create dissonance in the mind of the journalist; but that should not be confused with an unhealthy state of affairs for the citizen or the public sphere. Indeed, relationship theory would suggest the opposite; that this more balanced state is good for the journalist–citizen relationship.

---

3   This perspective is supported by Waldman (Rosen, 2005) who feels that coverage of the tsunami disaster 'has shown both the greatest strengths of citizens' journalism, and its greatest weakness'. The strengths lie in the volume and vividness of the personal accounts, through blogs, text messages and pictures – a revolution in supply. 'The great weakness, though, is the lack of shape, structure and ultimately meaning that all this amounts to. It is one thing to read hundreds of people's stories. It is another to try and work out what the story actually is.' Waldman argues that the journalist's skill, reducing, prioritising and shaping information, aids understanding and adds meaning.

Research suggests that although some imbalance is natural, positive stable relationships are characterised by each party having some control over the other, with each satisfied with the degree of control it has (Hon and Grunig, 1999; Grunig, 2002). That would imply that the most successful journalism–public relationships will be those in which audiences have a greater involvement in the choice of stories that are reported (setting the news agenda), how they are told (framing) and who gets to tell them (citizens or professional journalists).

Exchange Relationships

'The basis for an exchange relationship is the mutual expectation that one party provides benefits for another simply because the other has done so in the past' (Hon and Grunig, 1999).

The purchase of a media product (for example, a newspaper) is the simplest expression of an exchange relationship. The public buys the paper, so the news organisation produces another. The benefits to both groups are mutually dependent. As mentioned, the absence of a viable revenue model for online news challenges this relationship, as does the availability of competing sources of information. The symbiotic two-way relationship is endangered.

There are optimists. As noted earlier, Rupert Murdoch has made the Web a priority, announcing plans to spend up to US$2 billion (about £1.15 billion) on acquisitions. ITV launched a pilot broadband TV service, <www.itvlocal.tv>, which offers local news, weather, local films, an entertainment guide, community video and classified advertising. Internet giant Yahoo! News commissioned multimedia journalist Kevin Sites to cover the world's war zones in 2006 for a year-long special feature, 'Kevin Sites in the Hotzone' (<hotzone.yahoo.com>).

What they are looking for in exchange remains largely unchanged: audience attention and deep-pocketed advertisers eager to reach them. Global advertising expenditure across major media – newspapers, magazines, television, radio, cinema, posters and the Internet – was expected to rise by 6.5 per cent to about £298 billion (US$ 416 billion) in 2006. 'Advertisers are expected to divert more and more of their budgets to the Internet, which will capture 4.4 per cent of the global ad[vertisement] spend by 2007' (Economist, 2006: 102). These are reasons, indeed, for practitioners of online journalism to be bullish.

Communal Relationships

'The provision of benefits in these relationships is based on concern about the welfare of the other partner – not the expectation of receiving benefits in return' (Hon and Grunig, 1999).

This concept presents particular challenges for the online news sector, particularly the national providers. Concerns about the welfare of such providers will be shallow-rooted among the public because the relationship is both functional – providing immediate, accurate information and entertainment – and immature, as such services are comparatively new.

Local online provision provides greater opportunities for communal relationships. As will be seen, many local newspapers that go online have an existing emotional tie with the public that can be developed. Online newspapers such as the Carlisle *News and Star* (cited above) are encouraging complementary citizen publishing as a bridgehead into the local online communities. The aim of such news organisations is to ensure they continue to *matter* to their communities. But will this be more difficult where there are rising numbers of competing citizen publishers? It will be interesting to see if there is a limit to the public capacity to care about its information sources.

Trust

'This defines the level of confidence that both parties have in each other' (Hon and Grunig, 1999). The three dimensions of trust are listed below.

Competence: the belief that an organisation has the ability to do what it says it will do Much of twentieth-century journalism was based on the premise that journalists needed 'to know a little about a lot'. Entrusted by citizens to be their window on the world, many journalists needed to turn their hand to any editorial area, be it news, foreign affairs, politics, economics, social issues, arts and culture, or other fields such as sport. Such versatility was applauded and seen as a mark of a journalist's professionalism. It also became an increasing necessity as the number of correspondents and specialists was reduced.

Increasingly this professional requirement for journalists to spread their knowledge base thinly compares unfavourably with the range of information offered by the many citizen publishers who have a specific subject expertise or community knowledge (geographic or interest-based) that the journalist cannot match. As Gillmor states: 'Journalists cannot hope to reflect the world as well as the world itself' (2006). In time this is likely to erode trust based on the 'know everything' notion of a journalist's competence.

Dependability: the belief that an organisation will do what it says it will do Online journalists are not immune to the negative impact of high-profile failures in judgement or ethical practice among journalists. One of the fundamental challenges for the ideologues within journalism is to square the high ideals of professional practice with perceived current low public esteem for journalists.

Integrity: the belief that an organisation is fair and just Deuze (2005) notes that considerations of objectivity and ethics are central elements of the ideology of journalism. These relate closely to the notion of integrity, a central element of trust.

To validate their claims of integrity, and so keep the public trust, journalists have constructed professional codes of ethics and pursued objectivity. But this broad offering of trust by the public has pre-empted the practice of transparency by the journalist. Professional journalists have neither disclosed their sources nor their methods as they have exercised their responsibility as trusted information providers to the public sphere.

Citizen publishers such as bloggers also value integrity; but they establish it from the opposite premise. Unencumbered by the requirements of the professional ideology, they tend to be transparent about their allegiances and perspective; and they urge their readers to seek other viewpoints.

As the public's choice of information sources grows, the validity of this transparency-based model for establishing integrity is likely to increase, at the expense of the existing trust model that the professional seeks to work within. Trust is a critical element in relationships. Most scholars consider this dimension instrumental in an effective and mutually beneficial relationship. Journalists in the future may need to demonstrate increasing transparency; for example, through linking to source documents or to transcripts of their interviews, if they are to maintain the public's trust (Comerford, 2006).

Commitment

Researchers have identified several aspects of commitment – the extent to which both parties believe and feel that the relationship is worth spending energy on to maintain and promote. Meyer and Allen (1984, in Grunig and Huang, 2000: 46) noted continuance commitment (which means that commitment continues along a certain line of action) and affective commitment (which is an emotional orientation). The relationship between continuance and affective commitment lies at the heart of much of the current industry debate about the development of online news among mainstream UK providers.

Established news organisations have developed both levels of commitment through audience consumption of their 'traditional' products. Continuance has come through the regular commitment by individuals to consume the news offered by such groups, often requiring a commitment to pay before accessing the news (for example, the cover price of a newspaper). This habit has, in turn, generated an affective commitment. Such consumer loyalty has been created by the tightly targeted news content but also additional values, such as brand recognition at the national level and community identity at the local level.

The challenge facing the mainstream news providers when operating online is that consumers can continue to exercise their continuance commitment without any financial benefit to the provider, because there is an expectation among the consumers that online content comes free of charge. The costs of providing such content remains, however.

In addition, the browsing technology and therefore the mentality of the online user ensures that the continuance commitment is significantly more fragile online. This increases the importance of the affective commitment – the consumer's emotional link, their loyalty.

Acquiring a better understanding of the extent and nature of this affective commitment will become increasingly important for mainstream providers, as they seek viable revenue models for online news. Boundaries are already being tested with national sites requiring users to register and pay for certain online content. As we have seen, mainstream providers of local news host blogs to encourage a migration of their established (though shrinking) 'loyal' reader base to the online product. The aim is to create communities of users with an affective online commitment and then find ways of monetising those communities. Economics drive such considerations, but they equally reflect the changing dynamic of the relationship between the journalist and the citizen.

Satisfaction

This could be defined as the extent to which both parties feel favourably about each other; a satisfying relationship occurs when each party believes the other is engaging in positive steps to maintain the relationship. In a satisfying relationship, 'the distribution of rewards is equitable, and the relational rewards outweigh costs' (Stafford and Canary, 1991, cited in Grunig and Huang, 2000: 45). It is also suggested that satisfaction is 'critical to the short- and long-term economic well-being of an organisation' (Ledingham and Bruning, 2000: 92).

Erosion of trust and decreasing commitment can in turn lead to a diminishing decrease in mutual satisfaction. Among citizens, this has been manifested through a lack of interest in online news when the quality of what is offered has been undermined by a lack of commitment on the part of the news organisation, no matter how large the latter is. On the Web, attention builds reputation, not the reverse. Attention, and then satisfaction, is in large part generated by an evident commitment to effective content.

Perhaps a more interesting phenomenon is the impact of decreasing satisfaction levels on the professional journalist. Deuze (2005) argues that a notion of public service is central to the ideology of journalism. This sense of mission, of being the public's watchdog, is a strong part of the journalist's rationale. Most journalists draw on this regularly, particularly each month when they read their payslip, because they certainly are not doing it for the money. The journalist's sense of satisfaction is partly due to the belief that the public both rely on, and are grateful to, journalists for the watchdog role they perform. Messages to the contrary, be they falling readerships or increasing competitor citizen publishing, can be another source of dissonance and angst for the journalist. This can place a further strain on their relationship with the public. It may explain the growing antipathy among journalists towards those who appear to be turning their backs on mainstream news outputs, such as the young citizens who turn to alternative online sources of information.

Conclusions

Utilisation of this relationship model has identified stress points in the critical relationship between journalists and their public, brought into sharp focus by the rise of citizen publishing. The model has highlighted issues of competence, trust and transparency and a redressing of the control mutuality balance. It also indicates some steps journalists can take if they wish to preserve their relevance and value to the public.

The onus to adapt lies with the journalist, not the public. Ulrik Haagerup, the editorial director at Nordjyske Medier in Denmark, considered to be one of the world's most converged media companies, says journalists should remind themselves that they are storytellers (Haagerup, 2005). And storytellers have always travelled with their audiences. Such a change is central to normative considerations of the role of journalism within the public sphere in advanced democracies, which Costera Meijer (2001: 13) summarises as 'informing citizens in a way that enables them to act as citizens', particularly when those changes include, as we have noted, 'a challenge to the power that professionals have had in defining what "real journalism" is' (Reese, 2001).

If, as this book argues, making 'serious news' more accessible to citizens remains an essential aim, professional journalists will need to understand their place and function in the media 'ecology' (Gillmor, 2006) that includes multiple sources of information that are seen, by some of the citizenry, to be more credible than those provided by the professionals.

The professional online journalist typically embraces emerging technologies that provide avenues for greater dialogue with their public and allow others to collaborate in the generation of news content, resulting in mutually rewarding relationships. This is turn provides increased likelihood that the content will resonate more strongly with their audiences. Such an approach transcends considerations of merely improving style and presentation when considering how to reinvigorate news journalism to attract a wider audience.

As previously mentioned, there are examples already of online journalists encouraging public contributions to issue-driven news output. BBC News Online head Pete Clifton is asking the public to contribute their reports:

> We'll either go out and help them or we might just give them some guidance on the phone, it could be different for different circumstances, but essentially the next step that we want to try is seeing if people would like to do that, and for us to give some of our resources over to them to help them (Clifton, 2005).

Journalists will need to create further ways to interact, collaborate and share. They will need constantly to reappraise their relationship with the public to develop a better understanding of how to keep it viable and effective. Public support and engagement can no longer be assumed. Like all good relationships, in the future it will have to be worked at. Henceforth, when negotiating, journalists, for the first time since the invention of the printing press, will be reminded of the golden rule of conversation: listen at least as much as you speak.

In the opening address of the 2005 Annual Conference of the Society of Editors, the UK chairman of News International, Les Hinton, said:

> We need to understand and interact with our readers' lives, needs and concerns as never before. That connection is critical in maintaining loyalty.
>
> So much has yet to be discovered about where this technology will lead. Edison tried over a thousand filaments before he patented a successful electric light bulb, but at least he knew what his end-users wanted: light. The inventors of the telephone thought people would use it to play music. We are still finding out what people want from their new media opportunities. So are they (Hinton, 2005: 1).

But we do know this: the new and burgeoning supplies of news and information services point to the fact that journalism, far from becoming irrelevant, is diversifying in ways that can invigorate the public sphere. Hartley describes journalism as 'the sense-making practice of modernity', the very foundation of democratic policies and the primary wiring of popular culture (cited in Hargreaves, 2005: 14). The increased engagement with audiences through networked digital technologies is not a diminution of its role, but an extension of its reach, another unfolding layer in what Hargreaves calls 'the story of journalism's role as the oxygen of democracy' (*ibid.*).

References

ABC Electronic (2006), 'ABCE Database'. Available at <http://www.abce.org.uk/cgi-bin/gen5?runprog=abce/abce&noc=y> (accessed 8 March 2006).

alexa.com (2006), 'Top English language sites'. Available at <http://www.alexa.com/site/ds/top_500> (accessed 15 February 2006).

Barger, J. (2006), 'The robot wisdom weblog'. Available at <www.robotwisdom.com/log1997m12.html> (accessed 15 February 2006).

Bass, P. (2006), interview by Alan Rawlinson, 25 January.

BBC News Online (2006), 'Brits show appetite for mobile TV'. Available at <http://news.bbc.co.uk/1/hi/technology/4620792.stm> (accessed 14 February 2006).

Bell, E. (2006), 'It would be folly for a newspaper to ignore the rise of the blog', *The Guardian*, 18 February. Available at <http://www.guardian.co.uk/Columnists/Column/0,,1712592,00.html> (accessed 10 February 2006).

Bianco, A., Gard, L. and Rossant, J. (2005), 'The future of *The New York Times*', *Business Week*, 17 January. Available at <http://www.businessweek.com/magazine/content/05_03/b3916001_mz001.htm> (accessed 15 February 2006).

Blood, R. (2000), 'Weblogs: a history and perspective'. Available at <http://www.rebeccablood.net/essays/weblog_history.html> (accessed 15 February 2006).

Blood, R. (2002), 'The weblog handbook: practical advice on creating and maintaining your blog'. Available at <http://www.rebeccablood.net/handbook/excerpts/weblog_ethics.html> (accessed 15 February 2006).

Bowman, S. and Willis, C. (2003), 'We media: how audiences are shaping the future of news and information'. Available at <http://www.hypergene.net/wemedia/weblog.php> (accessed 15 February 2006).

Bromley, M. (2001), 'The British media landscape' [Online]. Available at <http://www.ejc.nl/jr/emland/uk.html> (accessed 15 February 2006).

Bruning, S.D. and Galloway, T. (2003), 'Expanding the organization–public relationship scale: exploring the role that structural and personal commitment play in organization–public relationships', *Public Relations Review* 29 (3): 309–19.

Clifton, P. (2005), interview by Alan Rawlinson, 13 December.

Comerford, M. (2006), interview by Alan Rawlinson, 1 February.

Costera Meijer, I. (2001), 'The public quality of popular journalism: developing a normative framework', *Journalism Studies* 2 (2): 189–205.

DCMS (Department for Culture, Media and Sport) (2004), 'Report of the independent review of BBC Online'. Available at <http://www.culture.gov.uk/global/publications/archive_2004/BBC_Online_Review.htm> (accessed 15 February 2006).

Deuze, M. (2005), 'What is journalism?', *Journalism* 6 (4), 442–64.

Economist, The (2006), 'The world in figures: industries', in *The World in 2006* (20th edition of annual publication) (London: Economist).

Ferguson, M.A. (1984), 'Building theory in public relations: interorganizational relationships as a public relations paradigm', paper presented to the Public Relations Division, Association for Education in Journalism and Mass Communication Annual Convention, Gainsville FL; August.

Fulton, K. (1996), 'A tour of our uncertain future', *Columbia Journalism Review* March/April. Available at <http://www.cjr.org/html/96-03-04-tour.html> (accessed 2 February 2006).

Gillmor, D. (2004), *We The Media: Grassroots Journalism by the People, for the People* (Sebastopol CA: O'Reilly).

Gillmor, D. (2006), participation in Journalism Leaders Forum, University of Central Lancashire, Preston, 31 January 2006.

Golding, P. and Elliott, P. (1979), *Making the News* (London: Longman).

Grunig, J.E. (2002), *Qualitative Methods for Assessing Relationships between Organizations and Publics* (Gainsville FL: Institute for Public Relations).

Grunig, J.E. and Huang, Y.H. (2000), 'From Organizational Effectiveness to Relationship Indicators: Antecedents of relationships, public relations strategies, and relationship outcomes', in Ledingham, J.A. and Bruning, S.D. (eds).

Grunig, J.E. and Hunt, T. (1984), *Managing Public Relations* (Orlando FL: Harcourt, Brace).

Haagerup, U. (2005), presentation, Newsplex on Tour, 13 June, London.

Hall, J. (2001), *Online Journalism* (London: Pluto).

Hallin, D.C. (1992), 'Sound bite news: TV coverage of elections 1968–1988', *Journal of Communication* 42 (2), 5–24.

Hargreaves, I. (2005), *Journalism: A Very Short Introduction* (Oxford: Oxford University Press).

Hinton, L. (2005), lecture at the 2005 Annual Conference of the Society of Editors, Cumbria, 16–17 October. Available at <http://www.societyofeditors.co.uk/speeches/conference_speeches_oct16_700pm.html> (accessed 12 February 2006).

Hon, L. and Brunner, B. (2001), 'Measuring public relationships among students and administrators at the University of Florida', *Journal of Communication Management* 6 (3), 227–38.

Hon, L.C. and Grunig, J.E. (1999), 'Guidelines for measuring relationships in public relations', published by the Institute for Public Relations. Available at <http://www.instituteforpr.org/relationships.phtml?article_id=1999_guide_measure_relationships> (accessed 12 February 2006).

Huang, Y.H. (2001), 'OPRA: a cross-cultural, multiple-item scale for measuring organization-public relationships', *Journal of Public Relations Research* 13 (1), 61–90.

Jo, S., Childers Hon, L. and Brunner, B. (2004), 'Organisation-public relationships: measurement validation in a university setting', *Journal of Communication Management* 9 (1), 14–27.

Kawamoto, K. (ed.) (2003), *Digital Journalism* (Lanham MD: Rowman and Littlefield).

Kim, Y. (2001), 'Searching for the organisation-public relationship: a valid and reliable instrument', *J&MC Quarterly* 78 (4), 799–815.

Kiss, J. (2006), 'NUJ's witness code slated by industry pundits'. Available at <http://www.journalism.co.uk/news/story1699.shtml> (accessed 22 February 2006).

Kovach, B. and Rosenthiel, T. (2001), *The Elements of Journalism: What Newspeople Should Know and the Public Should Expect* (New York: Crown).

Ledingham, J.A. (2003), 'Explicating relationship management as a general theory of public relations', *Journal of Public Relations Research* 15 (2), 181–98.

Ledingham, J.A. and Bruning, S.D. (1998), 'Relationship management in public relations: dimensions of an organization–public relationship', *Public Relations Review* 24 (1), 55–65.

Ledingham, J.A. and Bruning, S.D. (eds) (2000), *Public Relations as Relationship Management: A Relational Approach to the Study and Practice of Public Relations* (Mahwah NJ: Lawrence Erlbaum).

Loughrey, P. (2005), 'Read it, watch it, hear it, surf it', speech at the 2005 Annual Conference of the Society of Editors, Cumbria, 16–17 October. Available at <http://www.bbc.co.uk/pressoffice/speeches/stories/loughrey_editors.shtml>.

McQuail, D. (1987), *Mass Communication Theory*, 2nd ed. (London: Sage).

Maiskii, I. (1921), 'Sovremennaia Mongoliia', in Stephens, M. (1991), *A History of News* (Fort Worth TX: Harcourt Brace).

Merritt, D. (1995), 'Public journalism – defining a democratic art', *Media Studies Journal* 9 (3), 125–32.

Murdoch, R. (2005), speech to the American Society of Newspaper Editors, 13 April. Available at <www.newscorp.com/news/news_247.html> (accessed 15 February 2006).

National Statistics (2002), 'Autumn 2002: Social Trends 34'. Available at <http://www.statistics.gov.uk/StatBase/ssdataset.asp?vlnk=7206> (accessed 22 February 2006).

Nel, F. (2003), 'Power: who has it, who should get it?', *Rhodes University Journalism Review* 22 (Summer), 14–16.

Nel, F. (2005), *Writing for the Media in Southern Africa* (Cape Town: Oxford).

Nicholson, D. (2006), 'Newspapers need to get a handle on the Internet threat', *The Independent Media Weekly*, 27 February, 9.

Nielsen/Net Ratings (2005), 'A community uprising'. Available at <http://www.netratings.com/pr/pr_060206_uk.pdf> (accessed 26 February 2005).

Outing, S. (2005), 'Eleven layers of citizen journalism', Poynter Online. Available at <http://www.poynter.org/content/content_view.asp?id=83126> (accessed 22 February 2006).

Pavlik, J. (2001), *Journalism and New Media* (New York: Columbia University Press).

Pew Research Center (2006), Pew Global Attitudes Project, February.

Press Gazette (2006), 20 January, 7.

Rachel [No surname] (2005), 'Coming together as a city', BBC Online. Available at <http://news.bbc.co.uk/1/hi/uk/4670099.stm> (accessed 22 February 2006).

Reese, S. (2001), 'Understanding the global journalist: a hierarchy-of-influences approach', *Journalism Studies* 2 (2): 173–87.

Robinson, J. (2006), 'Wizard of Oz and his maxims for success', *The Observer*, Business and Media section, 12 February, 11.

Rosen, J. (2005), 'Bloggers v. journalists is over. PressThink'. Available at <http://journalism.nyu.edu/pubzone/weblogs/pressthink/> (accessed 23 February 2006).

Siffry, D. (2006), 'State of the blogosphere, February 2006; Part 2: Beyond Search', *Technorati Weblog,* 14 February 2006. Available at <http://technorati.com/weblog/2006/02/83.html> (accessed 6 March 2006).

Singer, J.B. (1997), 'Still guarding the gate? The newspaper journalist's role in an on-line world', *Convergence* 3 (1), 72–89.

Sloan, R. and Thompson, M. (2004), *EPIC 2014*. Available at <http://www.robinsloan.com/epic/>.

Stephens, M. (1997), *A History of News* (Fort Worth TX: Harcourt Brace).

Waldman, S. (2006), 'Comment is free', <SimondWaldman.net> (accessed 12 February 2006).

Ward, M. (2002), *Journalism Online* (Oxford: Focal).

YouGov (2005), Available at <http://www.yougov.com/archives/pdf/OMI050101003_1.pdf> (accessed 27 February 2006).

Chapter 9

UK Television News

Robert Beers and Paul Egglestone

Introduction

This chapter starts from the assumption that television news programmes should have an important place in society, contributing to what Chambers and Costain define as deliberative democracy, 'a healthy public sphere where citizens can exchange ideas, acquire knowledge and information, confront public problems, exercise public accountability, discuss policy options, challenge the powerful without fear of reprisals, and defend principles' (Chambers and Costain, 2000: 11). However, the sheer weight of the economic and technological forces now bearing down upon television news journalism raises serious questions as to whether it can still make the contribution that those most concerned with the requirements for a healthy democracy believe that it should. Increasingly, it seems, it is necessary to ask: to what extent is the balance, range and depth of coverage of news issues within UK television adequate for the purpose of ensuring the electorate is adequately informed? This question, which derives directly from the book's core questions, will underpin much of the discussion that follows.

The Growth of the Competitive News Battleground of 'Multichannel UK'

Figures published by the Office of Communications (Ofcom) confirm that television is the primary source of domestic news for 73 per cent of the UK population. Just 23 per cent read any newspaper or listen to radio news. In addition almost 60 per cent of the population own two or more television sets (Ofcom 2004a: Appendix). Despite this proliferation of television ownership, viewing figures for terrestrial television are plummeting. In 1995 BBC1 commanded 32 per cent of audience share. In December 2005 it had dropped to 22.7 per cent. The figures are even worse for ITV, which is down from 37 per cent to a little over 20 per cent in the same period. Meanwhile, although in 1995 satellite and cable had captured less than 10 per cent of the available audience, Sky now has over eight million subscribers (BBC Online, 2005a) and 16.5 million homes now have digital television (BBC Online, 2005b), of which a significant number use satellite or cable access routes.

There are over 200 channels on Sky's digital platform. Other operators, such as the cable companies, will soon rival Sky. The BBC and ITV are both considerably behind in the race for digital, particularly after ITV's disastrous failure to set up its own digital platform.

February 1989 brought national running TV news to the UK. Rupert Murdoch, who had transformed Fleet Street earlier in the decade, now took on television with Sky News. Seemingly understaffed and underfunded, Sky quickly developed credibility with solid news coverage, especially on breaking stories. Its audience share in the UK is, like that of most news channels, quite small, reaching 0.5 per cent of the British viewers in October 2005 (BARB, 2006). In recent years Sky has entered the global market as well, with an international feed that is available in Europe, Africa and the Middle East, for example, plus dedicated sister stations in Italy, Ireland and Australia. Sky's early acceptance and professionalism contributed to the BBC finally launching News 24 in 1997.

The BBC's large financial commitment to continuous news on both a domestic and an international channel complies with the BBC's view that scheduled news programmes, their bread and butter for decades, are giving way to an environment of news on demand, whether on TV, the Internet or interactively. The former Director of BBC News, Richard Sambrook, laid out the new corporate mantra: 'People expect to be able to get the news they want, whenever and however they want it' (Heard, 2004).

With this in mind it is important to look closely at BBC News 24's experience with around-the-clock TV news. BBC senior managers believed that the right approach to running TV news could draw in significant numbers of the younger audience who were not watching it. So they launched BBC News 24 with jacketless and jargon-free youthful presenters broadcasting direct from the newsroom epicentre. Two years later, without any significant increase in younger viewers, the BBC News 24 presentation changed to the traditional, uniform look and feel of news bulletins on the corporation's main domestic channels.

The channel's start-up had been less than impressive. 'For the first few months the main concern seems to have been not so much about the quality of programming, but more about simply staying on the air' (Lambert, 2002).

Designed around an all-digital system, the technical side included three different computer systems and a variety of new working practices. The results, according to one BBC insider, were 'a daily implosion on the air'. With BBC News 24 often looking amateurish, established BBC correspondents avoided appearing on the channel and executives winced when it was mentioned (Lambert, 2002). Confusion reined in the first few years as many attempts to fix the problems created a permanent state of disorganisation.

The operation today is on a par in terms of reportage and production with the rest of the output of BBC TV News. Star reporters and major newsmakers appear regularly. *The Independent Review of BBC News 24* by the Department of Culture, Media and Sport (DCMS) in 2002 states that its performance is now 'satisfactory in all areas, and better than that in some' (Lambert, 2002). However, the review does find fault with the channel's regional coverage, a strong component in its original proposal. In its request for the channel's government approval the BBC had said: 'The strong regional coverage will be on the basis of "opting in" rather than opting out, featuring regular visits to the BBC's regional newsrooms across the UK for live reports and comment' (Lambert, 2002). The DCMS report notes that attempts to build regular regional slots in the hourly news cycles were unsuccessful.

A third domestic continuous news competitor – the ITV News Channel – began in 2000. Conceived as a headline service, it then adopted the strap line 'Breaking News for Britain'. ITV's continuous news was certainly journalistically sound, yet its ratings were poor. Simon Shaps, ITV's director of television, said:

> The question we have asked ourselves is: what does news look like in five or ten years' time? The answer is that it looks very different from the traditional 24-hour rolling news format that we are used to now. Increasingly, viewers will want news on demand via a variety of different platforms and we are investing in the technology and expertise to deliver that (DTG News, 2005).

ITV shut down the operation at the end of 2005.

Running news ratings are, not surprisingly, dependent on the news itself and major stories see sharp increases in the number of viewers while, during periods of 'non-breaking news', the audience is much smaller and transitory. Viewers check in for a few minutes to take the world's pulse. The three American all-news channels have adopted 'appointment viewing' – programmes with an established presenter and a format tailored to his or her style – to try to establish tune-in habits with viewers. Larry King's interview show on CNN and *The O'Reilly Factor* on Fox News are successful examples of this approach. Sky News, Fox's sister channel, moved in this direction when it spent £18 million for an October 2005 relaunch with a new broadcast facility, a fresh schedule and several new presenters. Sky's broadcast day is now divided into programmes with news rather than just news programming.

While Sky continues, even after its high-priced makeover, to trail BBC in the total number of viewers, it does have an audience the BBC envies. The BBC's head of television news, Peter Horrocks, has admitted that Sky News is where 'key opinion formers' go first for breaking news. London's Metropolitan Police Chief Sir Ian Blair is a case in point. Referring to 7 July 2005, when bombs ripped through the city's underground, Sir Ian said: 'We switched on Sky as everyone does to try to get some idea of what's going on' (Robinson, 2005).

The DCMS review made the same point, much to Sky News' publicity department's delight: 'It is a fair bet that anyone who walks around a newspaper office where televisions are turned on the whole time will find them tuned to Sky News rather than BBC News 24. The same applies to government offices' (Lambert, 2002).

Market & Opinion Research International (MORI) of London has researched views of opinion leaders on continuous news channels, including politicians, academics, senior business people, and journalists, among others. While four in five ranked BBC News 24 as 'good' and praised its comprehensive news coverage and analysis, nevertheless, where opinion formers regularly kept a channel on in an office all the time, they said it was usually Sky. MORI found this especially true within the media and it 'may be linked to the perception that Sky News is more effective in covering breaking news than News 24' (Lambert, 2002).

While those who help shape British opinion are certainly prized viewers, BBC News 24 increasingly does have the mass audience it needs the most. This trend has intensified in 2005: a BBC ratings report stated: 'In July, 15 million people watched News 24 (excluding audiences who saw the channel's simulcasts on BBC One) while 13 million people viewed Sky News; and each week our lead over Sky News has increased – currently 5 million for us compared with 4.6 million for Sky' (BBC Online, 2005c).

While success in the UK generally is certainly its first concern, the BBC increasingly has an eye on the world's richest English-language market. BBC America, a largely entertainment channel, is increasing in popularity in the US and now is available in 40 million homes. It carries several daily bulletins of international news from BBC World, a channel not widely available in America. With a sense among many journalists in the US and elsewhere that American television news has seriously 'dumbed down' in recent years, the BBC is seizing the opportunity to forge its own special relationship with the country's viewers. Its World Service, available on some FM stations and on satellite radio, has doubled its American audience between 2003 and 2005 (Harding, 2005) and BBC TV news is shown at the dinner hour on a number of public broadcasting system stations.

While the BBC may be finding popularity in some sectors of American society, within others it is not. Mark Byford, when he was Director of the World Service, said in a speech to a global business media conference that broadcasters must recognise that perspectives can be radically different between countries and cultures. 'What sounds impartial to one listener in London may appear blatant bias to another listener in Cairo' (Byford, 2003).

This observation is equally relevant with regard to some in Washington DC. *The Weekly Standard*, a conservative Washington-based magazine funded by Rupert Murdoch, attacked BBC News on several occasions over the fighting in Iraq. A story with an Oxford dateline maintained that the BBC was, throughout the war, 'consistently and correctly accused of anti-war bias'. The nickname Baghdad Broadcasting Company was revived from complaints about the BBC's Gulf War coverage. It concluded: 'it just might be the BBC's desire to prevent the death of Saddam's regime that results in the mighty Corporation's own downfall' (Chafetz, 2003).

From Global Expansion to Domestic Crisis: The BBC and the Hutton Report

While few outside the American Republican right or the British neo-Thatcherite right would take Murdoch's long history of complaints against the BBC particularly seriously, the quality of its journalism came in for much more troubling questioning from other directions over its reporting of the Iraq War. In 2004, the same year that the British Broadcasting Corporation marked 50 years of television news, it was accused of 'defective' editorial management processes following the Hutton Enquiry. On 28 January 2004 Lord Hutton issued his scathing report in which he found that three BBC radio news stories accusing the British government of exaggerating Iraq's weapons of mass destruction capabilities were 'unfounded'. The findings were devastating to management and demoralising to the BBC's 2,000 news employees. Immediately the Chairman and the Director General of the BBC resigned. The reporter who broke the story left the Corporation a few weeks later.

The findings of faulty editorial management, while highly controversial in themselves, nonetheless profoundly impacted on journalism at the Corporation. The BBC News head at the time of the Hutton investigation, Richard Sambrook, said that in the wake of the report the BBC had to demonstrate it had become more transparent: 'Taking the lid off the news machine and allowing people to peek inside, together with a culture of quickly admitting and correcting error is now as essential to maintaining public confidence as the journalism itself' (Sambrook, 2004).

Even as he called to take the mask off the process, Sambrook also declared the process healthy: 'Does it follow that BBC journalism, as reflected in the Hutton Report, is defective and in need of radical reform? Not at all. I believe the issues identified in Hutton were singular and do not reflect a larger malaise.' Sambrook argues that if there had been more deep-seated problems then, with 'more than 100 hours of news on radio and television a day we would have encountered more extensive and more frequent problems by now' (Sambrook, 2004).

Still, Mark Thompson, the new Director General of the Corporation, called the Hutton debacle the 'biggest crisis for BBC journalism in 80 years' – a crisis that started nearly at the same time as the BBC was building its massive case for renewing its charter.

The House of Lords Select Committee on the BBC Charter Review issued its first report in October 2005 and, despite Hutton, found a 'vast majority of those who had testified desirous of a strong BBC with support from all its competitors and from political leadership across party lines' (House of Lords Select Committee on the BBC Charter Review, 2005).

It did cite a study commissioned by the Department of Culture, Media and Sport (DCMS) and carried out by qualitative research specialists Cragg Ross Dowson; this reported 'a marked, but not universal perception' of the BBC dumbing down its programming. Also, the committee report cited another government survey which found that 39 per cent of the British population thought the BBC had a high level of bias in its reporting. The Lords report notes that, while 'some people do criticise the BBC for having its own agenda, it is fair to say the nature of the perceived agenda tends to vary to suit the complainant's viewpoint'. And a 2005 MORI survey for DCMS showed that 77 per cent of the UK public believe the BBC to be independent and impartial and 80 per cent trust the BBC (House of Lords Select Committee on the BBC Charter Review, 2005). The Corporation may have been shaken and stirred by the Hutton Report, but the Select Committee provided convincing confirmation that its domestic reputation had recovered after the episode.

Deregulation and Increasing Pressures for Privatisation

Despite a vote of public confidence and the security that the subsequent confirmation of the continuation of the licence fee provided, the BBC was still not entirely safe from critics and predators. The long-running demands for systematic deregulation, made by lobby groups favouring a move to increased privatisation of broadcasting services, continued.

The Corporation was by now familiar with such pressures. Going back nearly 40 years, for example, under a Labour government in 1970, the '76 Group', a pressure group comprising programme makers and intellectuals, had called for a full review of the structure and financing of UK broadcasters. In 1977 the lobbyists were disappointed with the Annan Report. Despite a remit to examine ITV's profits in relation to the quality of its services, the recommendations in the report did not address the more radical questions about the relationship between the BBC and ITV. It did go as far as making a rather ambiguous commitment to 'preserve British broadcasting as a public service' (Annan Committee, 1977), but its more tangible legacy was to pave the way for a fourth national terrestrial television channel.

The Hunt Report (1982) focused on cable expansion and broadcasting policy, but in 1986 Peacock shifted the ideological ground, introducing customer satisfaction as the primary measure of quality public service broadcasting. Prime Minister Margaret Thatcher charged Peacock with the job of examining an alternative to the licence fee as a method of funding the BBC. Her motives are well documented. By the mid-1980s Thatcher's relationship with the BBC had deteriorated beyond any sensible reconciliation. She had been unhappy with the way the BBC reported on 'British troops' in the 1982 Falklands War (as opposed to '*our* troops'), being particularly annoyed by a live phone-in programme, where she received difficult questions from the public (Curran and Seaton, 1997). She also disliked the BBC's coverage of events in Northern Ireland in the early 1980s when, in order to meet its existing charter commitments, the BBC was committed to impartiality and objectivity, which in turn required coverage to be given to Sinn Fein. According to the Tory government, not all have the right to a voice – in order to have a voice, one would have to change to earn the right (Curran and Seaton, 1997). The Peacock Enquiry offered Thatcher the opportunity to explore the 'unique way' the BBC was funded. She favoured the Murdoch model of privatised news and it was Rupert Murdoch who called for the government to scrap the licence fee as a means of funding the BBC and replace it with advertising revenue. To Thatcher's chagrin, Peacock did not go that far, defending instead the quality and status of the BBC and dismissing the idea of moving to funding via advertising on the grounds of a consequent potential deterioration in quality.

However, while the BBC might have survived the Peacock Enquiry, the pressures from those demanding greater deregulation of UK broadcasting increasingly paid off. The 1990 Broadcasting Act, for example, set down a policy signalling the move towards increased competition in the provision of television services. The 1996 Broadcasting Act facilitated concentration of media ownership (see also <http://www.

mediachannel.org/ownership/>). Further relaxation of regulation on cross-ownership was proposed in the 2002 Communications Bill, which spawned the super-regulator Ofcom and paved the way for the merger of the two big ITV companies, Carlton and Granada, and the creation, in all but name, of a single ITV.

Now in place, Ofcom has set about its task of determining the legislative framework for future broadcasting:

> We value trustworthy and independent news programmes which increase our knowledge of the world, and content which reflects the different parts of the UK and informs our cultural identity. Although commercial broadcasters will provide some of this content, intervention is needed to ensure that there is sufficient range, volume and quality of programming made in the UK and for UK audiences (Ofcom, 2005).

But in a multichannel, digital world, the position of news on mainstream channels, the future of the regular news bulletin and the commitment to resourcing news-gathering operations when market factors determine their viability, are all questionable. Clive Jones, Chief Executive of ITV's recently formed Independent News Group (hereafter referred to as ING) claims, 'if it's left to the market, we're all f****d' (Jones, 2005).

In its recent review of public sector broadcasting (PSB), Ofcom concluded that there are 'two key rationales for PSB: to correct market failure and to realise social value' (Ofcom, 2004b) However, considerable confusion arises from the fact that, while the review states that PSB could be justified by serving a 'non-market' provision, it contains little in the way of any definition of 'non-market'. There is a danger also that a debate conducted so clearly within a 'market' context automatically disenfranchises any commodity for which there is no apparent use or exchange value.

But just to make life even more difficult for the BBC, should its proposals ever be implemented, the review states that: 'It [PSB] must also justify itself by its audience size and share; PSB should be on channels with high reach and impact.' But to receive public funds, 'it must be clear that the market would not deliver similar output, of the same quality, on the same scale' (Ofcom, 2004b).

Sarikakis confirms the general direction of contemporary legislation: 'The public service broadcasting system and the BBC, in particular, are facing a continuing threat, where the system is destined to be deemed "obsolete" under the neo-liberal market-driven ethos of British politics' (Sarikakis, 2004: 113). Some of the worrying implications of this ethos for television news reporting are discussed below.

Back to the Commercial Sector: The Real Effect of Deregulated Market Pressures

Moving away from mainstream BBC television channels, BBC1 and BBC2, over on Channel 3, Independent Television News is already feeling the heat of the market. 'The culture of ITN has changed from one dominated by journalists, where it considered itself a centre of journalistic excellence run by journalists for journalists, to one dominated by commercial calculations, or perhaps more fairly, one that is more businesslike' (Harrison, 2005: 132).

Within the broader discussions on the role of PSB, spanning all genres and covering commercial franchise operations and the BBC's remit, the debate on quality within genres is often secondary to the battle for survival. News, as a genre, has been criticised for 'dumbing down' – 'dumbing down' in its selection of stories, over-simplifying within individual news items, and across the schedule in its limited range of programming dealing with difficult subject matter in an intelligent and non-patronising way. Research produced by the Communications and Media Research Institute of the University of Westminster shows that, in 2003, ITV did not feature a single international programme under the (ITC) categories of politics, development, human rights or environment – all genres deemed to be 'difficult' and in areas traditionally regarded as 'hard news'. Even in less difficult genres the same issues are apparent. Recently BBC4 marked the 30th anniversary of the serious arts programme *Arena*, now replaced by *The Culture Show*, a provider of trite, anodyne anti-intellectual arts coverage scheduled to coincide nicely with *Front Row* on Radio 4. And what of serious documentary programmes like *Everyman*, *Credo*, *Heart of the Matter* and, of course, *Panorama*? *Panorama* is still on air, although it is in a new graveyard slot and has had a serious makeover. *Everyman* makes an occasional outing on BBC2, but has no regular programme slot and there are now less than a dozen *Everyman*s a year.

Within television news, traditional journalism appears to be losing ground to soft news. Clive Jones, Chief Executive of ING, refutes this and is conveniently curious about the definition of 'hard news', or traditional news journalism. He believes any definition needs 'broadening' to include 'celebrating the region you live in' and offers an anecdote of his early career in television 20 years ago. 'Regional news made you feel like you lived in Baghdad. Rapes, murders and violence.' He does not accept that his new definition of news, which includes 'celebrating the region you live in', has anything to do with 'dumbing down'. 'Stories are now better, writing's better, questions are harder, camerawork better ...' (Jones, 2005).

In the regional newsroom at Granada TV in Manchester, Richard Frediani acknowledges the changes in television news:

> The type of stories we'd cover has changed. Our audience has changed too. There's more consumer issues for instance. Is it right to do consumer news? As a news editor I need to ask – what affects more people? In that sense it's about news values – but news values that are better tuned into the audience. People have redefined news so there has been a change in the news agenda (Frediani, 2006).

To a not particularly critical ear these assorted comments may well sound like attempts to so blur the distinction between hard news and soft news that unthinking minds in time forget that such a critical divide ever existed.

This poses an interesting question about the legacy ITV's journalism is trading on – a question highlighted in *The Story of ITV: The People's Channel* (Bragg,

2005a). Producer Melvyn Bragg documented the evolution of ITV in a weekly genre-by-genre celebration of creative talent in the respective regions making up the ITV network. Programme 5, his final offering, covered news, current affairs and documentaries, recalling an era when ITV 'supported inquisitive, awkward programmes that challenged establishments worldwide, and placed investigative journalism and documentaries squarely on ITV' (Bragg, 2005b). A legacy of 'hard-nosed' programmes, like *This Week* and *World in Action*, have long vanished as a result of commercial pressures and have been followed by *Dimbleby* and *Tonight with Trevor McDonald*. The implication of the network's current spin is that ITV are still committed to investigative journalism and documentary making. The schedules offer a different reality. Celebrated radical documentary film-maker John Pilger 'made 21 programmes for ITV in six years in the early and mid-1970s. In the last six years, ITV has shown six Pilger documentaries' (Herman, 2005).

While *Dimbleby* is no *This Week* and *Tonight with Trevor McDonald* is clearly not a substitute in form or content for *World in Action*, the political, social and economic landscape of the UK has also changed. It is not what it was 20 years ago. The multichannel digital world of broadcasting, where viewers vote with their remotes, is equally different. Important as the subject matter of Pilger's latest works may be, does the form of factual documentary need an overhaul in order to win back audiences? At a time when Michael Moore, Errol Morriss and Morgan Spurlock can attract millions to cinemas worldwide – by making a few concessions to the medium in which they work – should television news and factual programming sit up and take notice?

Clive Jones thinks ING already does: 'Changing demographics as the news moves around the schedule have affected the way a story is presented. Figures show there are more ABC1s at 10.30 p.m. than at 5.45 p.m., so the news is more "upmarket"' (Jones, 2005). He offers the following story treatment example. In July 2003, Microsoft banned Internet chat rooms. This story, as covered in the ITN 5.45 p.m. bulletin, is family-based. It includes issues like the threat of 'grooming', paedophilia, and so on. The same story at 10.45 p.m. has a 'business' treatment – that is, Microsoft quit chat rooms to avoid the predicted stream of expensive legal actions against them. This retargeting of a story is editorial policy across ING. Frediani at Granada endorses Jones' view: 'We know a bit more about our audience than we did and this affects the way stories are done. Reporters need to think more about who's watching at various stages in the day and stories need tailoring to fit different demographics' (Frediani, 2006).

Undoubtedly, this is intelligent programming for news, but it still fails to explain two trends in ITV's current approach to television news and documentaries. First, why has such 'tuned-in' thinking failed to find a way of reinventing the hard news-related investigative documentaries of the style, class and impact of *This Week* and *World in Action* for the new millennium? Second, why does a commercial sector with such a long tradition of quality news journalism find it necessary to fudge so cynically and unconvincingly the distinction between hard and soft news, both in its justification of its current approach and in its output? It is the very fact that such questions need to be posed that demonstrates starkly both the height from which ITV as a public service broadcaster has fallen and the real, seriously damaging and democratically disabling impact that excessive deregulation and the unleashing of market forces can have. Governments and their regulatory authorities have not yet lost all the Crown Jewels of commercial television news and current affairs, but few remain.

However, as Chapter 4 demonstrated, market forces are not the only pressures at work on quality news and current affairs programming. Together with technological factors they form but one half of the 'ec-tech' squeeze. It is to the second part of this equation that we now turn.

Technological Factors and Television News Quality

The impact of technology on the production and dissemination of news cannot be understated. Despite Clive Jones's insistence that 'it's not just about the technology', ITV are spending £40 million connecting every commercial regional newsroom around the UK by the end of 2006. He claims also that 'desktop editing will be the norm at ITV within three years' (Jones, 2005). He states that video journalists will be the core of the newsroom and a new grade of 'creative technicians' will perform the traditional 'craft' roles. Jones is non-committal when pushed on defining the new grade, suggesting that there will be room for camera operators, craft editors and creative technicians. The future of ING news is 'undoubtedly interactive. The red button click will offer breadth and depth beyond the current constraints of a time-based news report. Personal video recorders (PVRs) will also enable people to select the news, even the items they want.' And of course there are plans to offer news content for mobile phones and PDAs (personal digital assistants), though here the politics of public service broadcasting need to play out before an essentially commercial operation will invest. ITV believes that the BBC's current approach to providing free content to new media platforms such as mobile phones undermines competition and plurality in those markets.

Jones is realistic about the effects of new technology on journalism: 'Technology provides the opportunity to take feeds from agencies worldwide. Journalists will do much more editing – more "reportage" rather than "journalism"' (Jones, 2005). Those most concerned with the quality of news journalism would worry about the cost-cutting, corner-cutting implications of such a statement – the fact that, yet again, news organisations are putting more distance between themselves and the events that they are supposed to be 'reporting' on. The most radical criticism is that this kind of thinking transforms journalists from being 'on the spot', authentic news reporters to being just second-hand 'news assemblers', the production-line operatives who piece together products made and thought out elsewhere. By extension, such a devaluation of the role of journalists destroys also the credibility of the organisations who employ them as first-rank news organisations.

These dangers are acknowledged in the public sector, where Pat Loughrey, Head of BBC Nations and Regions, warns his 2,000-strong team of journalists against 'air-conditioned journalism', a by-product of too much reliance on technology. In his end-of-year performance assessment for 2005, Loughrey demanded that journalists 'must work harder to find and tell stories that will be memorable' and dismissed stories created without leaving the office:

> One of the sadnesses of the technological revolution in journalism is that one can get by with so-called reporting that is based entirely on the PC. It would be tragic if we let new technology facilitate a sterility of journalism where the number of stories diminishes because we haven't the energy or the enterprise to broaden the base (*Broadcast*, 2005d).

Does this reliance on technology really reflect a set of exhausted and unimaginative BBC journalists? Or does it show staff developing a new modus operandi – working practices better suited to a news environment perpetually delivering content for more outputs with 20 per cent fewer people to do the jobs? If BBC Director General Thompson gets his way, Loughrey will lose 735 staff in Nations and Regions. News will be 'leaner and fitter', with 420 jobs to go and a further 424 in BBC Factual and Learning. Something has to give when so much meat is cut from a bone that is already short of fat. 'You cannot make the same high standard programmes with 20 per cent fewer staff,' says Jeremy Dear, General Secretary of the NUJ (*Broadcast*, 2005d). And in the face of 2,050 job losses in content and output divisions across the BBC, Loughrey's cry for journalists to get out more, work harder and faster and improve quality will sound hollow to many.

Thompson believes the cuts are essential. The need to release money from the licence fee to invest in a digital future is his primary justification for them. In a speech at the Edinburgh TV Festival in August 2005 he said:

> On demand is the core of the digital debate and may even change what we mean by 'broadcasting'. The BBC must be at the forefront of developments ... I believe that a broadly based, multimedia, licence-fee-funded BBC with a brand that everyone knows, along with great, relevant content that everyone can use and which demonstrably creates public value, will actually make more sense than it does today (*Broadcast*, 2005b).

Along with just about every other broadcaster, the BBC is playing digital catch-up. Companies like Yahoo, whose asset value already outstrips the entire television industry in the UK, are looking for partners to use their platform and portals to disseminate content. Broadcasters are acutely aware of the need for strategic partnerships. Whilst they may not guarantee a long-term future, they do keep the 'Yahoos' out of content creation for now.

And then, of course, there is the question of broadband. 2006 will be the watershed year for broadband across Europe. It is already in 23 per cent of homes in the UK. Broadband TV – formally known as Internet Protocol TV – will make TV more web-like, with a choice of millions of programmes to download. The application, using peer-to-peer technology, enables viewers and listeners to download TV and radio programmes they may have missed up to seven days after broadcast. But it also represents a new paradigm for the broadcaster: it is a shift from the old 'push' media (where viewers watched what broadcasters dictated they watch, when they said they could watch it) to 'pull' media (where the viewer decides what to watch and when to watch it). The personal video recorder will enable audiences to time-shift more readily. The challenge for any television channel, regardless of genre, will be winning and retaining audiences in the 500-channel 'digital supermarket'.

This does, of course, create a particular problem for news programming. Where people choose not to watch programmes in sequence, then (as was pointed out in Chapter 4) news will cease to be something that they encounter automatically if watching mainstream television programmes throughout an evening; it will become instead an experience that they have only if they choose to. It is too early to tell precisely what impact this will have on news viewing figures and, as John Drury's chapter on the future of radio points out, the extent to which viewers maintain their loyalty to news programming will be determined not just by technological factors, but also by cultural influences and personal preferences. But whatever happens, the new possibilities that broadband opens up increase the uncertainties for news programme makers and the danger of uncertainty often is that investment is withheld, diluted as a result of being fired in too many directions in an attempt to at least partially cover all options, or cut back. Mark Thompson's bright new digital future may see the ending of yet more journalists' futures and the raising of even more questions about both the future of news journalism and the democracy within which it remains a vital organ of interpretation and communication.

From Citizen Kane to Citizen Journalism?

While everyone connected with the television news media is talking about the possible new opportunities and threats that the gathering pace of technological innovation might bring, one thing that is becoming clear from the discussion so far is that nobody is quite sure what the real implications of this process are, or whether many of the possible new uses of media technology may turn out to be a disappointment in practice. Even Rupert Murdoch has been hedging his bets with regard to some of the trickier questions of what to invest in a situation where many of the mass public's preferences with regard to the usage of new media platforms remain so uncertain. Keeping this uncertainty in mind, it would be useful to focus on two of the key emerging new developments – local television and citizen journalism – and to look at what some of their possible consequences might be.

ITV, for example, are dabbling with local TV, delivered via broadband in Brighton and Hove. Their experiments with 'local' television are shamelessly commercial, in line with the broader corporate strategy. If local content can generate a revenue stream by persuading local dentists and solicitors to advertise, then local TV delivered via broadband will be rolled out in all 16 ITV regions.

Lindsey Charlton, managing director of Meridian and project director for ITV Local, calls ITV local television 'Citizen TV', defining it as an electronic local newspaper where the user decides what they will watch. Charlton says:

> Yes, I'll push boundaries. New technology that enables members of the public to upload their own videos will doubtless push the boundaries. But ITV has a fifty-year history as a responsible broadcaster. Taste and decency will still apply. The public will have the right to upload their content – but we retain the right to publish (Charlton, 2006).

MY TV (launched on the pilot service on 11 January 2006) offers citizens the chance to create their own TV channel. Will anyone be watching? Charlton says: 'It always comes down to content. If the content is good – and if it's what the audience want – they'll watch. And broadband is a hungry beast. We always need more content. But not if it's rubbish' (Charlton, 2006).

ITV are not alone in their foray into broadband. The BBC have local TV pilots in the West Midlands. The service builds on the existing local radio infrastructure and is available on the Internet and digital satellite. The Corporation hopes to provide a new local news service for approximately 60 areas across the UK. A press spokesperson for the BBC said: 'The service will embrace the latest broadcasting technology to create and distribute genuinely relevant local news and information.' The pilot service provides around ten minutes per hour of original material for Birmingham, the Black Country, Coventry and Warwickshire, Hereford and Worcester, Shropshire and Staffordshire.

So what is on local TV? So far, ITV's content spans 'what's-on' guides, classified advertisements and repeats of existing regional programmes. The BBC's Midlands local news channel's top story on 27 December 2005 was: 'A camera in the Bullring [a large shopping centre] has been named one of the world's 25 most interesting webcams. It ranks alongside cameras at the Eiffel Tower and the pyramids.' Cynics might have serious doubts about the kind of news values at work in such instances.

What local TV does provide is a clear opportunity to try to engage people in the latest TV executives' obsession – participatory or citizen journalism. Loughrey at the BBC is evangelical: 'we must make more space for, and nurture, citizen journalism and user-generated content across our output' (*Broadcast*, 2005d). At ITV, Jones also places the public in the frame: 'Everyone's a potential journalist. The first photos of Boscastle [a village in Cornwall severely flooded on 16 August 2004] were from mobile phones – as was the first video footage' (Jones, 2005). On the day of the London bombings in July 2005 the BBC received over 1,000 pictures from members of the public. But despite the apparent opening up of many of these channels to the public, Jones is adamant there will still be a need for traditional journalism skills, defining journalism as 'good storytelling and explaining difficult issues in a clear way' (Jones, 2005).

In academia the subject of participatory journalism is not a new one. Brian McNair at Stirling University writes: 'The public in a democracy should have the opportunity not just to read about, or to watch or listen to the development of public debates as spectators, but to participate directly in them' (McNair, 2000: 105). In the same vein, Lewis et al. wonder whether the traditional formulaic process of news production creates disengaged citizens, asking: 'In a climate of declining political participation, does the way journalists report the world encourage or discourage citizens to engage with politics and public life?' (Lewis et al., 2004: 153).

In short, is the audience television journalists profess to serve disenfranchised by the mechanics of production and excluded by the social elite who control the conventions of the tradition and make the decisions about what makes news and how its participants are presented on TV? Tim Gardam, former Director of Programmes at Channel 4, is certainly in favour of increased audience participation and suggests that it might be a means of re-engaging an uninterested audience in news and current affairs:

> The future of television in a multichannel world is going to be to identify those viewers who see themselves as your members. The use of text messaging votes and other means of being a participant in material onscreen is being exploited aggressively by entertainment. What news and current affairs hasn't done is to extrapolate that into the idea of membership as a citizen. Videophones will make a big difference in this type of programming (Hargreaves and Thomas, 2002).

Technologically, these new possibilities could be facilitated by some of the experiments being conducted currently by the major television players. The BBC, for example, is piloting iPM (integrated media player), a device that makes the TV set perform a lot more like a computer than a television in terms of audience interactivity. It also includes a personal video recorder (PVR), recognising viewers' increasing desire for 'on-demand' programming. In September 2005 BBC1, BBC2 and News 24 started a 16-channel trial of mobile TV using DVB-H (digital video broadcasting hand-held) transmissions.

This provokes a series of pertinent questions. First, despite the assurances of programme makers, there must be a real doubt as to whether or not increased audience participation will help or hinder the impartiality of television news. Just as there are serious doubts as to whether the growth of blogging has added to the voices involved in democratic discussion, or instead mainly given a public platform to a rather small, non-representative proportion of electorates at the expense of the majority, who prefer not to put themselves in the spotlight (or who simply cannot afford the technology to do so), there must be serious questions as to just how representative local TV 'citizen voices' might be, whether they be expressed via videophones, text messages, or whatever. Those who have had the curious experience of watching existing programmes displaying text messages may feel that they have a right to be decidedly unoptimistic. There is, in addition, the fear, expressed by McChesney (2000) and others, that the growth of 'citizen journalism' may simply be used as a cost-cutting device that pushes more expensive traditional journalism out of the picture on the news platforms on which it is used. But there is also the question of whether the *majority* of the public actually *wants* it. There is plenty of speculation about what audiences want. *FACT* is the BBC's audience research bulletin. Its

September 2005 edition challenged several assumptions about audiences' apparent desire to embrace technical innovations, watching and interacting with programming on new platforms. *FACT*'s report concluded that: the top 200 programmes during 2005 contained no multichannel programmes; a third of the population do not receive multichannel television; and approximately nine million UK citizens have neither the Internet nor digital TV at home (*FACT*, 2005)

In the light of findings like these, quite what is driving the obsession with new technology is unclear.

Conclusion

The recent history of UK television news and current affairs broadcasting has been one shaped significantly by deregulation and the unleashing of market forces. This has seen increasing conglomeration, the move to multichannel television and increasing accusations of 'dumbing down', most particularly with regard to ITV news. This gradual unleashing of almost unbridled economic forces, which indirectly impact on the options facing even the publicly funded BBC, has combined with a startling rate of technological development to pitch television news operations into a future of unparalleled unpredictability. Finding viewers for news is harder than ever before in an age of audience fragmentation and growth of technologies that enable the public to by-pass news entirely in their daily television watching habits. It is one of the main factors that has been propelling news organisations more in the populist direction of ill-thought-out 'citizen journalism' and the fudging of the distinction between hard and soft news. With regard to the former, there is undoubtedly an argument to be made for revising news values in order that they become more reflective of the 'real world' outside the newsrooms within which they are shaped; and for giving the electorate a genuine feeling that they can influence the political decision making that so often seems to assume that, outside of periodic elections, voters should leave things to 'the experts' and the people they have elected. But it is entirely another question to ask whether it is worth risking the undermining of the reputation of serious journalism and journalists by giving an increasing role to the 'citizen journalism' of those who are elected only by themselves to partake of it and whose professional or representative credentials generally are non-existent. A rational appraisal of the situation might suggest that news organisations are looking for lower-cost options at a time when traditional news operations are becoming more expensive to run (due to declining audiences) and that populist options, within which the real issues can be fudged, are made attractive by this. What is being avoided is the much more difficult issue which is the real key to a genuine, high-quality informational role for news in a democracy; namely, how can hard news be made more attractive to its potential audience without compromising its value though trite populism? This is a question that seems to have become less popular with television executives of late. Unless it is answered effectively and quickly, democracy has a poor future.

References

Annan Committee (1977), *Report of the Committee on the Future of Broadcasting* (Cmnd 6753) (London: HMSO).

BARB (Broadcasters' Audience Research Board) (2006), *Monthly Multi-Channel Summary* (BARB Report), January. Available at <http://www.barb.co.uk/about. cfm?flag=about>.

BBC Online (2005a), 'Eight million subscribers for Sky', 19 December.

BBC Online (2005b), ' "Nearly two thirds" watch digital', 9 December.

BBC Online (2005c), ratings report. Available at <http://news.bbc.co.uk/newswatch/ ifs/low/newsid_4740000/newsid_4748000/4748011.stm>.

Bragg, M. (2005a), *The Story of ITV: The People's Channel*, broadcast on ITV1, 26 June to 24 July.

Bragg, M. (2005b), Programme 5, 'Window on the World', in *The Story of ITV: The People's Channel*, broadcast on ITV1, 24 July.

Broadcast (2005a), 'Unions reject BBC offer', *Broadcast*, 1 June; published by EMAP Media, London.

Broadcast (2005b), 'Mark Thompson Edinburgh speech', *Broadcast*, 30 August.

Broadcast (2005c), 'Compulsory redundancies are inevitable', *Broadcast*, 16 November.

Broadcast (2005d), 'Loughrey warns against lazy reporting', *Broadcast*, 16 December.

Byford, M. (2003), 'Connecting with a world audience', speech given to the AIB Global Media Business Conference, 29 April 2003. Available at <http://www.bbc. co.uk/pressoffice/speeches/stories/byford_world_audience.shtml>

Chafetz, J. (2003), 'The disgrace of the BBC', *The Weekly Standard* 8 (47); published Washington DC.

Chambers, S. and Costain, A. (eds) (2000), *Deliberation, Democracy and the Media* (Boulder CO: Rowman and Littlefield).

Charlton, L. (2006), interview with the Managing Director, Meridian and Project Director, ITV Local, by Paul Egglestone, January.

Curran, J. and Seaton, J. (1997), *Power Without Responsibility: The Press and Broadcasting in Britain* (London: Routledge).

DTG News (2005), 'ITV shuts news channel one month early', The Digital TV Group Ltd. Available at <http://www.dtg.org.uk/news/news.php?class=sectors& subclass=&id=1370>.

Eldridge, J., Kitzinger, J. and Williams, K. (1997), *The Mass Media and Power in Modern Britain* (Oxford: Oxford University Press).

FACT (2005), inhouse publication of the BBC, produced by the BBC Audience Research Unit, September.

Frediani, R. (2006), interview with the News Editor, Granada Television, Manchester, by Paul Egglestone, January.

Frost, C. (2000), *Media Ethics and Self-Regulation* (London: Longman).

Harding, P. (2005), interview with the Director of English Networks and News BBC World Service by Robert Beers, October.

Hargreaves, I. and Thomas, J. (2002), *New News, Old News* (London: ITC/BSC).

Harrison, J. (2005), in Johnson, C. and Turnock, R. (eds), *ITV Cultures: Independent Television Over Fifty Years* (Maidenhead: McGraw-Hill).

Heard, C. (2004), 'Fifty years of TV News, Entertainment News'. Available at <http://news.bbc.co.uk/2/hi/entertainment/3829605.stm>.

Herman, D. (2005), untitled article, 'Smallscreen' column, *Prospect* 112, July.

House of Lords Select Committee on the BBC Charter Review (2005), 'First Report, 2005, Chapter 2: The Importance of the BBC', House of Lords Publications on the Internet. Available at <http://www.publications.parliament.uk/pa/ld200506/ldselect/ldbbc/50/5002.htm>.

Jones, C. (2005), interview with the Chief Executive, Independent News Group, by Paul Egglestone, January.

Lambert, R. (2002), 'Independent review of BBC News 24', Department of Culture, Media and Sport. Available at <http://www.culture.gov.uk/global/publications/archive_2002/review_bbcnews24.htm>.

Lewis, J., Whal-Jorgenson, K. and Inthorn, S. (2004), 'Images of citizenship on television news: constructing a passive public', *Journalism Studies* 5(2), 153–64.

McChesney, R. (2000), *Rich Media, Poor Democracy: Communication Politics in Dubious Times* (New York: New Press).

McNair, B. (2000), *Journalism and Democracy: An Evaluation of the Political Public Sphere* (London: Routledge).

Nichols, J. and McChesney, R. (2000), *It's the Media, Stupid* (New York: Seven Stories Press).

Ofcom (Office of Communications) (2004a), 'The communications market 2004 overview'. Available at <http://www.ofcom.org.uk/research/cm/overview/#content>.

Ofcom (Office of Communications) (2004b), 'Is television special?' Report available at <http://www.ofcom.org.uk/consult/condocs/psb/psb/summary/157377.pdf>.

Ofcom (Office of Communications) (2005), 'Review of public sector broadcasting: Phase 3 – Competition for quality'. Available at
<http://www.ofcom.org.uk/media/news/2005/02/nr_20050208#content>.

Puttnam, D. (2003), 'News – you want it quick or you want it good?', *British Journalism Review* 14(2), 50–57.

Robinson, J. (2005), 'BBC News admits "opinion-formers" prefer Sky', *The Observer*. Available at <http://media.guardian.co.uk/bbc/story/0,,1647394,00.html>.

Sambrook, R. (2004), 'Tragedy in the fog of war', *British Journalism Review* 15 (3), 3–7.

Sarikakis, K. (2004), *British Media in a Global Era* (London: Arnold).

Chapter 10

The Changing Face of Sports Journalism and its Relationship with Hard News

Guy Hodgson

Introduction

The purposes of this chapter are, first, to assess the extent to which sports journalism increasingly has become an essential underpinning economically of traditional hard news journalism within the UK, while (where relevant) drawing some international parallels. Not only is it still a valuable inducement to readers to buy print news, but it has migrated from its once-traditional home at the rear of newspapers – for example, into their business, celebrity and lifestyle and political sections. An assessment of the implications for hard news journalism of this phenomenon will be made at the end of the chapter – to what extent is it a means of drawing people in to reading hard news, where it shares a page with sports-related news, for example?

Curiously and paradoxically, one of the things that will be shown is that, while sport has been a lifeline for some parts of the media that have been traditional hard news providers, the changes that have affected it in recent years have seriously undermined others, particularly the regional press within the UK.

Second, in the context of all of this, an assessment will be made of the some of the key qualitative changes that have occurred within the business of sports reporting itself. This is a form of journalism that has an often unrecognised importance in its own right, in so far as it is focuses on an area of human activity that, globally, is central to many people's lives. It has its own conventions, rules and obligations to its audience and to the people whose feats it reports. How, therefore, does it remain true to principles of good-quality journalism in the face of fierce commercial pressures to deliver a style of coverage that will keep the news organisation of which it is a part in sound financial health or, at the very least, still in business?

In short, this chapter is concerned with how a specific genre of journalism can cope with the responsibility of both supporting financially the struggling area of hard news journalism, while remaining true both to its principles as a legitimate form of journalism in its own right and to its audience. The perspective, in line with that of the book as a whole, is on both the *present* and the *future*.

In order to address these questions adequately it is necessary first to begin with a *historical* analysis of the evolution of sports journalism. The constraints of the book project mean that it is only possible to look at the UK perspective in detail here, but much (although not all, particularly in the case of Italy) of what is said can be translated into an international context.

The Evolution of Sports Journalism in the UK and the Emergence of Television Dominance

The analysis commences with what is often seen as the 'golden age' of newspaper sports journalism. It was an era when the principal source of sports news was the print medium and when football, indeed most winter sport, was played predominantly at 3 p.m. on a Saturday, There were midweek fixtures but they were restricted, almost without exception, to Tuesdays and Wednesdays. Managers were friends with journalists and editors, telephone numbers were swapped with alacrity, and footballers, rather than shun the reporters, would seek them out, knowing that the much wealthier members of the Fourth Estate would always be ready to buy a drink in return for stories.

Now sport has become a world where quotes are embellished as newspaper reporters crave something different from what is being delivered into homes via 24-hour television, radio and online; where television has gone from servant to master; where leading footballers earn more in a week than a Fleet Street reporter can earn in a year.

It is also a world where sport events start at the behest of television producers rather than the convenience of the paying customer, where a reporter could cover a football match every day of the week and where top sports performers treat the media as irritants at best. At worst, the relationship has fallen to such depths that Sir Alex Ferguson, Manchester United's most successful manager in history, refuses to speak to reporters after matches. Instead they have to hover round television sets, tape recorders and pens ready, to record what is broadcast on the club's own television channel, MUTV. Inevitably the questions are unchallenging.

There are dozens of reporters there, too. In the 1960s the press rooms would be inhabited by representatives of the nationals, regionals and weeklies, all newspapers and relatively few in number, while now they are brimming with journalists providing reports for television, radio, websites, chatlines and, on the horizon, mobile phones. Lord's, Wimbledon, Twickenham have been forced to expand their media facilities; at Anfield, the home of Britain's most successful football club, the press box and room creak and threaten to burst under the pressure until Liverpool build a new home.

The number of sports reporters has expanded, but so have the number of pages. 'Unlike hard news,' Roy Greenslade wrote in *The Guardian* in August 2005, 'where the impact of TV and the internet appears to have eroded sales, sport tends to boost readership' (Greenslade, 2005).

There was a time when the sports desk on a newspaper was regarded with amusement, and even condescension, by other sections. The 'toy department' was a frequent put-down. Editors would show an interest when Wimbledon and an Ashes cricket series was imminent, but otherwise their attention rarely strayed on to the sports pages. That changed with the advent of satellite television. When Rupert Murdoch launched Sky in 1991 he needed hooks to entice the public to pay for his channels and the one that dragged in most was live football. It was the Premiership that levered subscriptions out of pockets and when an entire station could thrive on the back of football, even newspaper executives could see that sport was important.

Now sport has a worth as a commodity, not only in financial terms, but in enticing viewers, listeners or readers into areas they would otherwise ignore. There have been arguments that this is an example of 'dumbing down', where sport and celebrity gossip have grown at the expense of harder news, but Steven Barnett has argued that there is no concrete evidence of such displacement in the UK. 'We need to consider the real possibility that the massive expansion in airtime in broadcasting and pagination in the local and national press is obscuring the continued availability of "serious" material' (Barnett quoted in Seaton, 1998: 76).

Between 1984 and 1994 almost every national newspaper in the UK increased the number of its pages by at least 50 per cent, the *Sunday Express* and *Mail on Sunday* tripling in size. On television, Sky provided the first 24-hour rolling news programme in February 1989 and the BBC followed suit in March 2000. 'All these pages and channels need to be filled,' Barnett wrote, 'but not necessarily at the expense of material that was previously available' (Barnett quoted in Seaton, 1998: 77). Sport, as this chapter will later reveal, filled much of the void.

The biggest indicator that sport had moved from being a glorious irrelevance to a vehicle for more serious matters was when both the *Daily Mail* and *The Sun* used the 2002 World Cup to promote their Euroscepticism. On 1 June, under the headline 'England expects, Becks', the *Daily Mail*'s text (below) referred to comments made by the England football manager:

> In one of the most extraordinary calls to arms since Nelson told his men what England expected of them, he invoked the nation's indomitable fighting spirit with a rousing pre-match speech ...
>
> He added: 'How would Europe and the rest of the world have been today if England had not been so good?
>
> 'You have won two world wars, even if the Americans helped you in the last one, and you have suffered a lot and taken a big responsibility' (*Daily Mail*, 1 June 2002, 2).

The manager in question, Sven Goran Eriksson, is a Swede and is unlikely to have sufficient grasp of British history to quote Lord Nelson, but if he did he would surely not have contrived the link between the wars against Napoleon and Hitler. Peter Anderson wrote that the covert message within the 'finest hour' mythology was that Britain does not need Europe as much as Europe needs it and that only the US is an essential close partner:

> It contains also the implication that the political systems and ability to defend themselves of Britain's continental partners are not able to stand up to real challenges, hence the need

for Britain to jealously guard its sovereignty from the continentals and to place its trust predominantly in the USA as far as security matters are concerned (Anderson, 2002: 2).

The Sun, he also noted, showed that this covert device is used across all the Eurosceptic tabloids by employing the same technique on page 2 of its issue the following day with regard to its coverage of the England team during the World Cup (*The Sun*, 2 June 2002: 2).

Both pieces appeared outside the normal sports pages and add credence to the argument that sport is being used for political purposes by those papers most inclined towards propagandising. It also underlines the value that editors now place on sport to deliver a message, particularly when the pieces in the *Daily Mail* and *The Sun* are seen in the context of more detailed and more obvious virulently 'anti-Brussels' pieces that both papers had been running during that year.

While sport's role in the media has become more important, the media have also changed sport, to an extent that there have been more changes in the last 15 years than in the previous 100. Vic Wakeling, the head of Sky Sport, told *The Guardian* in 2004:

> When we started, rugby union was an amateur sport, rugby league a winter sport, cricket was always played in daytime, now it's played under floodlights. However television might change over the next five, ten years, people will want to watch more live sport. The interest is huge. We know that the BARB [Broadcasters' Audience Research Board] figures are nowhere near the true figure. People watch in pubs, in market squares. We add on 50 per cent for big matches (Brown, 2004).

The television figures for sport are enormous. The highest ever British audience was for the marriage of Prince Charles and Diana Spencer but numbers two, three and four are football matches; the largest domestic viewing figure after midnight (and the overall record for BBC2) is 18.5 million for the Dennis Taylor–Steve Davis world snooker final in 1985; the number watching Liverpool defeat Milan in the Champions League final in May 2005 peaked at around 20 million. Compare that to the viewing figures for Britain's most popular soap in December 2005, *Coronation Street* at 11.9 million (BARB, 2005), and the fact that *Big Brother* has been Britain's socio-viewing phenomenon of the new millennium on the back of 6.7 million (Manchester Online, 2005), and the figures are given a true perspective.

Indeed, sport could claim to have assumed a social significance in that the broadcast of its showpiece events is the one occasion when a large proportion of Britons come together to do the same thing at the same time. When there were only two channels on British television there was a strong possibility that two strangers meeting in a bar had watched *Steptoe and Son* the previous evening and could talk about the programme. With 102 channels the mathematical probability of even that limited shared experience is reduced to minimal levels. Yet 17.1 million people watched England play Brazil in the quarter-finals of the 2002 football World Cup at 7.30 a.m. on a workday morning. It was a common meeting point.

BSkyB and cable companies introduced multiple channel television to British homes and along with the technical innovations that brought, they also revolutionised the coverage of sport. People may argue that the golden age of television was the 1960s and 1970s in terms of comedy and drama, but no one would make the claim for televised sport. Forty years ago, the only domestic club football match shown live was the FA Cup Final and the keen supporter's opportunity to see First Division fare was confined to highlights packages on *Match Of The Day* on the BBC on a Saturday night and ITV's regional football package on a Sunday afternoon. The Olympics, England's cricket Test matches and Wimbledon were shown live on the BBC but transmissions ended, often at crucial moments, when important news broke or the station had to switch to another sport to honour contractual obligations. For the rest, there was the much cherished but, in retrospect, painfully limited, *Grandstand* (BBC) and *World Of Sport* (ITV) on a Saturday afternoon. The coverage was formulaic, but it had to be because the director had only three or four heavy and static cameras to work with, and slow-motion replays were dependent on a machine known as 'the disc' which could record only around 40 seconds of action and had no storage capacity.

Radio, too, used to confine itself to very big events and Saturday afternoons so that, even in the 1980s, before every top domestic football match was covered, it was not unusual for supporters to show their allegiance by staring at a teletext screen, praying the number of goals by their team would increase at the next flick of the screen.

In 2005 Sky, alone, had three channels dedicated to sport, a sports news channel, and a pay-per-view channel. There was an average of 100 outside broadcasts a month, each manned by around 60 people, and in September 2004 Sky Sport broadcast its 3,000th live Premiership match. Each football game was covered by ten cameras and was supplemented by such innovations as instant highlights of a game in progress, the player-cam, the fanzone commentary, the clean feed without commentary and, for the Ryder Cup, the option of the American commentary. The cost for 2004/5 for Sky Sport alone was more than £720 million which, to put it in perspective, was £430 million more than the BBC spent (Brown, 2004).

It was money, gambling huge sums of it, which won the sports franchises. Premiership football was bought by Sky for £304 million for five years in May 1992, dwarfing the bids from ITV and the BBC. The Ryder Cup and England's overseas cricket Tests followed soon afterwards. In 1996 the first live domestic pay-per-view event was broadcast, attracting 660,000 customers for the Frank Bruno versus Mike Tyson boxing match. Rugby league and rugby union also form big parts of the Sky portfolio, but as the money increased so did the dependency and sports could face ruin if Sky suddenly pulled out as ITV Digital did in 2002, owing football £178.5 million, forcing several lower division clubs into administration.

Television knows it has the power and is flexing it. The Premiership will receive £1.7 billion from Sky and Setanta for three years from 2007/8, but many of the live matches will be shown at times the Football Association would never have agreed to when they had the financial whip in their hands, 12.30 p.m. and 5.15 p.m. on

Saturdays. This means that people cannot travel to support their favoured team if they also wish to catch the start and finish of the televised matches.

When Manchester United supporters successfully protested against Murdoch's plans to buy the club in 1998, one of their arguments was that Sky would switch the team's playing times to the early hours of the morning to accommodate a potentially huge television audience in the Far East. It seemed fanciful at the time, a resort to the direst of outcomes to embellish their case, but now it would not be a total surprise if Old Trafford, Stamford Bridge, Anfield, and so on, were throwing open their doors at 4 a.m. When Ricky Hatton won the world light welterweight title against Kostya Tszyu in June 2005, the fight, staged before a 22,000 crowd at the Manchester Evening News Arena, began at 2 a.m. on a Sunday. The inconvenience to the local supporters paying upwards of £40 a ticket was nothing to the fact that the fight needed to be shown at prime time in the US. The future of sports journalism is unclear but it is certain that Saturday 3 p.m. will play a lesser part.

The Changing Nature of the Audience for Sport and Sports Journalism

Surprisingly, the attendance figures at football matches have withstood the barrage of inconvenient kick-offs and blanket television coverage, but there has been a marked change in the audience. In the 1960s and 1970s the football ground was the province of the young, white, predominantly working-class male. However, the Heysel and Hillsborough disasters in 1985 and 1989 ensured the arrival of all-seater stadia; and hugely escalating wages for the performers have driven up prices so that tickets for 'working-men's ballet' cost as much, and even more, than Sadler's Wells. The working-class teenager has been replaced by the middle-aged and middle-class of both sexes and all races (although black and Asian people are still massively under-represented in football crowds). The atmosphere has changed from the cockpit to the theatre and prompted Roy Keane, then Manchester United's captain, to brand quieter supporters as the 'prawn-sandwich-eating brigade'.

Now the raucous atmosphere has moved from the stands to the pubs, where people gather to watch sport (often via Sky channels) in a manner that was unheard of 20 years ago. It has become part of the British way – pints and the Premiership – to an extent that people flocked to watch the 2006 World Cup in the local even though many of the matches were played in the afternoon and were available on terrestrial TV.

Vic Wakeling, Murdoch's head of Sky Sport, who was encouraged by the Athens Games to broaden Sky's sports coverage, defined the company's approach:

> Can we make that [sport] attractive to the viewers …? A lot of it is about personalities. Right from the outset we demanded our directors get closer with their shots. Before Sky came long, close might have been from the knees up. Now we're tight on them, right in the guy's face … you see the sweat dripping. It's about making people who don't support those teams care about who wins or loses. You're not going to watch an event if you don't care (Brown, 2004).

The immediate future for televised sports journalism will be technical as picture quality is enhanced to the high-definition, sharp standards already seen in the US. On this aspect, Wakeling commented:

> It will make it that bit better, especially for the pub market. I don't know anyone who can map out the long-term future of sports coverage. If they do they are probably bullshitting. Ten years ago very few people had heard of digital, DVDs, games, the Internet. You couldn't have envisaged what we are doing now (Brown, 2004).

The Significance of the Changes in the Nature of Sport and Sports Journalism for Local and Regional Newspapers

The move away from Saturday afternoon sports fixtures to suit the needs of television companies has already had implications for newspapers, which relied on reports on the local team as a selling point. *The Sporting Pink*, the *Manchester Evening News*'s Saturday night paper, switched to Sunday publication as Manchester United, City and Bolton Wanderers played on Saturday afternoons on fewer occasions, and is now no longer published. Newcastle's Saturday evening sports paper ceased publication in December 2005 and Birmingham's *Sports Argus* closed in May 2006.

The circulation of regional Sundays has also dropped and in March 2005 Birmingham's *Sunday Mercury* reported figures down 12.7 per cent year-on-year to 75,049. A spokesman for the *Mercury*'s publishers, the Birmingham Post and Mail, said: 'The poor performance of local football teams and ever-changing fixtures from Saturday to Sunday, or even Monday, has had a significant impact on sales' (*UK Press Gazette*, 2005).

Peter Montellier, editor of Newcastle's *The Sunday Sun*, whose circulation dropped 7.3 per cent over the same period, concurred:

> The whole nature of Sundays has changed radically over the last ten years. Most pubs are open to midnight now and the shops are open all day. Sundays are another entertainment day and people aren't buying papers as much. Regional Sunday newspapers compete with the nationals, which are giving away more free CDs on their cover. On top of this there is voracious and aggressive new competition from the weekly magazine market with *Nuts*, *Zoo* and *Grazia*.
>
> The main driver, though, is the migration of Premiership football from Saturdays (*UK Press Gazette*, 2005).

For those who wish to see hard news continue to be presented on as many platforms as possible, television sports reporting and its economic muscle has hit the regional newspaper market's ability to 'stay in the game'. It has undermined the financial support which print sports journalism used to help provide for the news journalism of this sector.

The Impact of the Changing Nature of Sport and Sports Journalism on National Newspapers

If television, radio (which has expanded its sports coverage on the coat-tails of TV) and local and regional newspapers have changed, so have the English national newspapers. They have been transformed in two fundamental ways in the last 35 years; they are bigger and their news values have altered, particularly the popular tabloids. The first is down to advancing technology that has reduced production costs; the second is due to a revolution in the way we receive our news.

Newspaper circulations are falling as 24-hour radio and all-day television, the Internet and even mobile phones have become the first port of call for news. Newspapers have had to change. The broadsheets (in character if not size) are, in the words of *The Independent*'s editor Simon Kelner, moving in the direction of becoming 'viewspapers', adding informed comment to the greater detail newsprint can add to stories seen on *ITV News* the night before. The tabloids do not neglect the big stories but, outside rare and obvious exceptions like the Iraq War, hard news is becoming an increasingly rare commodity in them as the emphasis becomes celebrity- and television-focused. Their view is that there is no point merely regurgitating quotes that have been seen repeatedly on television, so attention to politicians and 'real' stories has dwindled and the tabloids have a different world of news inhabited by soap stars, nobodies projected by an appearance on reality television, and sports personalities.

The latter have a particular currency because they are 'real'. Soap stars are famous for acting as someone else, and the bulk of the stories in tabloid newspapers concern their characters rather than themselves; the *Big Brother* contestants are disposable chaff, here one month, forgotten the next, but top footballers, boxers, cricketers, and so on, have a longevity. England footballer Wayne Rooney was making headlines when he was 16; if he is not worn out by the constant attention and intrusions into his private life, and does not have his determination dulled by his massive earnings, and also escapes injury, he could still be playing at 36. The public sees Rooney at work, on the football field, for 90 minutes every week, shares in his highs and lows, and recoils or revels in his occasionally loutish language. He and his image are part of the British public's lives. The attraction for editors, be they in television, radio, the World Wide Web or newspapers, is obvious.

Sport has always been an important ingredient of television news – the action pictures bring relief from talking heads and reports on key sporting events have traditionally been a valuable hook to persuade viewers to sit through the hard news items that generally are placed before the sports attraction. This is particularly the case at weekends. But it is in newspapers that the increasing interest in sport is best reflected. The difference, the way sport has moved from the back pages so that it inhabits every section of a newspaper, can be seen by a trip to the news-stand. On 26 May 2005, every English national newspaper front page had some reference to Liverpool's win in the Champions League final. That was to be expected, it had been an extraordinary triumph of lurching fortune, and it had been watched live on terrestrial television by a significant proportion of the British population. For quality newspapers it is an example also of the way in which they are now prepared to use sport as a hook on the front page to persuade people to buy and maybe even read a product that consists substantially of hard news.

Two weeks earlier a football financial story had made it to the front pages – Manchester United's takeover by Malcolm Glazer. *The Times*, still billed as the paper of the establishment, even led on the £790 million purchase. United, as a business, ranks as 'small fry' compared to the turnover of Britain's leading companies, yet FTSE-listed water and electricity companies, with a greater bearing on British lives, have been sold to foreign owners while barely making a ripple outside the financial pages. Clearly, this could be seen as an example of a sports-related issue being used as a hook in hard news products.

A comparison between today's newspapers and those of the 1960s and 1970s emphasises the grip that sport, but particularly football, has taken. An examination of the back page of *The Daily Mirror* of Monday 22 June 1970 would suggest the previous day had been quiet. Sport could not even fill the page and a non-sport news story was tucked on to the left-hand side. It was not even a particularly compelling report, but merely a forward-looking piece to the first meeting of Edward Heath's newly-elected Cabinet.

Except it was not a quiet sports day, it was a momentous day. When asked to nominate the greatest football team in history, repeated surveys point to that of Brazil in 1970. That team embodied Pele's enduring description 'the beautiful game' and, the previous evening, the players had achieved their destiny by beating Italy to win the World Cup. Yet it was not the lead story in *The Daily Mirror* the following day, there was merely a two-column × 11 cm picture of Pele holding the trophy and an 8 cm report. The main story, justifiably in domestic terms, was Tony Jacklin winning the US Open Golf Championship at Hazeltine, Minneapolis. He was the first Briton in 50 years to win the trophy which American golfers covet most, and a measure of his achievement is that no European has emulated the feat since. The back page devoted 32 column centimetres to the story and one three-column × 15.5 cm picture. It was on page 23 that Brazil had their show, with a 41 cm report by Ken Jones in Mexico City and a 4 cm sidebar of quotes, 'England gave us our toughest game'.

On page 22 there were also events that would have merited the back page on lesser days. England were in the midst of a cricket Test against the Rest Of The World but, with no play on the Sunday, the report was confined to 18 cm, and no scorecard. Wimbledon fortnight also began that afternoon, an occasion which has spawned special supplements in many subsequent years. Then it was allowed a box seven columns wide × 13 cm deep that incorporated Peter Wilson's preview and picture byline, a small two-column picture of Rod Laver and the order of play for Centre Court and Court One.

Add to that the fact that a page of racing and sport, on a big day, had been cramped into just under four tabloid pages, making up about 16 per cent of the 24-page newspaper. Significantly, sport was virtually isolated in its ghetto at the back of the paper, straying on to the front page only with two short stories on Jacklin and

Brazil (26.5 cm) and on page 5 with a picture story on new tennis fashions to tie in with the start of Wimbledon.

Move on exactly 35 years to *The Daily Mirror* of 22 June 2005 (average circulation 1.7 million), and the proportions were approximately the same. The sports section took up 11 of the 64 tabloid pages, again comprising around 16 per cent of the total paper. It was elsewhere in the *Mirror* where the difference lay.

The front page was virtually totally devoted to sport. The top half had a picture of David Beckham, the England football captain, dressed only in swimming trunks with the accompanying headline 'Becks on Legs'. The lower half of the page was the lead story 'My Sex Pest FA Boss', an allegation at an employment tribunal by a former secretary, Faria Alam, about the Football Association's executive director, David Davies. The only non-sport elements on the page were a teaser for 'Your Life Beach Babe Survival Guide' and a statement under the masthead 'Make Poverty History'. Only 92 words of copy accompanied the Alam story on page 1, but a double-page spread comprising four reports, more than a thousand words, four photographs and five headline elements filled pages 4 and 5.

Wimbledon's coverage comprised five pages in the sports section at the back of the paper, but just in case readers did not have the patience to get that far, page 9 was devoted entirely to Britain's last hopes, Tim Henman and Andrew Murray. On page 11 Sue Carroll's lead comment piece endorsed Alam's right 'to kick FA where it hurts', pages 12 and 13 contained photographs of the Beckhams on holiday, and on page 13 the lead story was about an alleged rape involving Arsenal's Robin Van Persie. Add the sport section and 18 pages were devoted to or related to sport and, as 10 of the *Mirror*'s 64 pages were wholly filled with adverts, three were devoted to television listings and two to puzzles, cartoons and horoscopes, it comprised 46 per cent of the pagination. In terms of column inches, it made up more than 50 per cent of the editorial.

France, Spain and Italy have daily newspapers devoted entirely to sport – *L'Equipe*, *El Mundo Deportivo* and *La Gazzetta dello Sport* respectively – a phenomenon alien to Britain. *The Sportsman*, a daily paper aimed at people interested in gambling on sports events, was launched in the spring of 2006 but went out of business six months later, a victim, partly, of the current emphasis on sport in the existing national daily newspapers.

A Changed Agenda in Sports Reporting

As can be seen from all of the above, the quantity of sports coverage has spread and it is being used increasingly as a hook in serious hard news print products, but there has been a qualitative change too. 'Sports journalism now is more emphatic and dramatic than it was in the past,' said Paul Hayward, chief sports writer at the *Daily Mail*. 'It's about comment, analysis and reflection' (Greenslade, 2005). Until the advent of television, blow-by-blow accounts of sporting events were the norm because the vast majority of the audience had not seen them. Now, with highlights packages and sports news channels, most goals, tries, wickets, controversial incidents, and so on, have been viewed even before newspapers have been 'put to bed'. The reporter is under obligation to provide something different, and comment and quotes are the staple commodities.

The problem with quotes, however, lies in the culture. Sportsmen, often not particularly articulate, find at an early age that a careless remark can be magnified into something it was never meant to be, as newspapers strive for the sensational. Hence they become circumspect, their quotes blander and reporters have to contrive artifices to get a story.

Reporters often have to put quotes into English as the interviewee struggles with his or her language or goes off on an incomplete train of thought. The late Bob Paisley, the winner of three European Cups with Liverpool and arguably the greatest British football manager of all time, would habitually refer to 'doings' when he could not recall a player's name – as in 'the midfield was strong and doings did well on the left wing' – and reporters had to fill in appropriately. Sir Bobby Robson, another hugely respected figure in football, frequently forgot or got his players' names wrong and the journalist made the correction.

That is legitimate reporting, but less healthy practices have become more commonplace in the last 30 years. Often faced by a stream of blandness from a sports figure or politician, the tabloids have built stories by using anodyne quotes made spicier by the language around them. This is fine when you know the rules. It is only when someone who does not know these rules is exposed to this treatment that the practice is revealed in its full tawdriness.

The Overall Implications of Current Trends in Sport and Sports Journalism for Television, Radio, the Internet and Newspapers

The circulation battle mentioned above has meant that one sport dominates the sports sections of UK newspapers, television and radio – football. And just as the coverage has polarised, so has the money within the sport. Television and radio have provided that money, both directly and by providing the platform for clubs to market their brand, and their grip on all sport will get firmer. Start times are already dictated by the needs of the armchair supporter, but that supporter may not come from London, Edinburgh or Cardiff; the temptation will be to bring in the biggest audience, be it from Tokyo, Tehran or Tallahassee.

There are also other pressures. In November 2005 the European Commission ruled that English football will henceforth be divided into six packages with no broadcaster able to win more than five. This encouraged Setanta, the Irish pay-TV operator, to break Sky's monopoly in the last round of bidding, but although the money will be increased from 2007/8 there is no guarantee this trend will continue. Soon clubs are likely to be allowed to negotiate separate deals so that Arsenal, for example, will sell rights to their home matches to Sky, meaning that more money will be drawn naturally to the clubs who command the biggest audiences. This scenario gained more credibility when Malcolm Glazer bought Manchester United in 2005, plunging himself and the club into debt. Glazer's business plan was based on the premise that United's brand, while already vast, had potential for considerable growth in global terms, but he needs individual control of television rights to access markets in the US and the Far East. Manchester United versus Liverpool, brought to you by MUTV (Manchester United Television), is round the next corner, or should that be block?

The implications for sports journalism are considerable. The number of jobs in television will increase as clubs set up their own television networks and have to fill the time between matches with interviews, previews, reviews, and so on. In turn, some of these pictures will appear on websites, which are also booming as clubs have realised the potential of the Internet, have established official sites and largely reduced the unofficial sector to chat forums. Players, too, now produce their own websites, but clubs, aware of the potential for business or conflict, are increasingly bringing those inhouse. At the same time, as more sports coverage is brought 'inhouse' it becomes increasingly difficult to distinguish between the resulting 'journalism' and public relations.

Radio sport, too, has had a renaissance in recent years and Radio 5 Live and Talk Sport have employed journalists in an unprecedented way. Every Premiership match has a BBC reporter present and in the 2005/6 season most weekends had 5 Live commentaries. Talk Sport, meanwhile, had exclusive rights to England's foreign cricket Test matches.

With an increase in sports information being relayed by reporters to the websites and mobile phones used frequently by the technology-savvy young, the outlook for sports journalism overall would be promising, but for newspapers. Round-the-clock news, falling numbers of commuters on public transport in many parts of the country and an increasing reluctance by the young to pay for news has caused the circulation of all papers to dwindle, but evening newspapers, which struggle to bring lunch scores at cricket matches for people who can see the close-of-play details on Ceefax or the Internet, have suffered most. London had three evening newspapers in 1951 (ABC in Butler and Sloman, 1975: 389) with a combined circulation of 3.8 million; now it has one which sells 348,000.

Sales of regional Sundays have been hit, as we have seen, by the moving of football games from Saturday, but national newspapers, while incorporating more sport within their covers, are also in decline. Sports journalism will remain one of the means by which that decline is at least slowed, helping to protect the hard news coverage of those newspapers that believe it is important, but it cannot arrest it. The nationals will become niche products, costing much more.

The outlook would be depressing but for the Internet, which appears likely to save the printed word by 'taking up the slack' as newspapers continue to decline into a future of smaller readerships. Newspapers have Web versions of their editions and the trend is towards getting people to subscribe to them. Journalists, too, are increasingly aware that their bylines are as likely to appear on a www. site as under a masthead. Henry Winter, football correspondent of *The Daily Telegraph*, said:

Twenty years ago I studied a photo-journalism course because I was convinced the economics of newspapers would mean reporters would go to an event, write a piece, and take a camera along as well. It didn't happen, the jobs of a journalist and a photographer are very specialised, but the Internet is different. With the newspaper market shrinking, I expect I will be doing as much writing for the Internet as for print.

The momentum appears to be moving away from newspapers, just as the money from football is being drawn from smaller clubs to an elite. Already there is a gap between the Premiership and the rest and the next likely move will be a further gap created by a European League. The Champions League is one step in that direction and the recurring question in boardrooms is: why should Chelsea/Arsenal/Manchester United/Liverpool play the relative paupers of Reading or Portsmouth when they could be meeting Juventus or Real Madrid?

The question then would be: could hard-pressed newspapers and radio stations afford to send, feed and provide hotels for reporters to visit foreign stadia every week, or employ expensive freelance football journalists in 20 football capitals? Would it not be simpler if an agreement could be reached with the clubs so that reporters could watch the away matches at home press rooms, with a special television feed afterwards for interviews with managers and players? These, of course, would be conducted by the club's own reporters. That way the newspapers would have something different, the club would have control of the questions and would also carry the unsaid, but nevertheless potential, threat that these privileges could be removed if the reporting becomes over-critical. Perfect control. The danger for newspapers, of course, is that they are intimidated into producing bland coverage with reduced reader interest which, in losing sales, further reduces the financial base on which hard news provision depends.

Conclusion: The Implications of the Changing Face of Sports Journalism for Hard News Providers

The preceding discussion has highlighted a number of trends relating to the agenda set down in the introduction, some of them pointing to expanding prospects for specific branches of sports journalism, while others are indicative of managed decline. It has also identified changes in sports reporting as 24-hour news and increasingly fierce commercial pressures have had their effect. The purpose in this final overview, however, is to consider the key implications of what has been discussed for hard news journalism, the core concern of this book.

First, it has been pointed out how Rupert Murdoch's BSkyB demonstrated powerfully the role that sport and sports reporting can play in attracting an audience and thereby helping significantly to underpin the products of media companies. From a hard news point of view, all of this paved the way for the success of Sky News in revolutionising television news through its 24-hour format and becoming a quality news provider to rival some of the BBC's output. Equally, however, sport has retained its traditional role for the pre-Murdoch broadcasters (the BBC, ITV, Channel

4) as one of the hooks used to persuade people to tune into hard news programmes in anticipation of their reporting of the highlights of key football matches, athletic events or whatever, most particularly at weekends. In its various manifestations on television, sport, particularly its 24-hour coverage on both hard news and dedicated sports news channels, has been one of the main factors in making the medium the dominant provider of news and entertainment in the UK.

As has been shown also, however, the ability of television companies to change radically the times at which sport is played has, in conjunction with frequent live coverage of matches and events and 24-hour commentary and news, made serious inroads into newspapers' markets at local, regional and national levels. While the massive increase in the number of pages and column inches devoted to sport indicates that newspaper proprietors believe that it is a crucial ingredient in their attempts to manage decline and, in some cases, at least partially reverse it, there can be no denying the fact that they simply cannot compete with television for immediacy or excitement in their coverage. They can use sport to lead people on to pages where hard news also is covered, as increasingly has become the case in the quality press, but, as has been pointed out earlier, the popular tabloids have radically cut their hard news coverage in recent years, leaving readers little to be led to.

So while sport continues to be seen as a key reason why many continue to buy hard news print copy, it can only cushion some of the impact of television and other factors mentioned earlier, not eradicate it.

Equally, it should be remembered that sport has not benefited all television companies equally. Rupert Murdoch's vast resources and his preparedness to gamble millions has meant that he has been able to reduce significantly the access of his rivals to the coverage of major sporting events. This is one of many factors that has contributed to the troubles of one of the two original UK television channels, ITV. It could be argued that the consequent need to boost audiences in other areas to retain advertising revenue is one of the factors that has fed into the damaging 'mobility' of the main ITV news within the schedules in recent years, together with what many critics see as a decline in its quality.

The future looks likely to be one in which, while television retains its dominant position as a sports journalism provider, and national and regional newspapers continue to decline, new technologies expand their share of the market. Some newspaper editors and journalists see as much of an opportunity as a problem in all of this, in so far as they can develop parallel and complementary sports and hard news operations via the Internet, mobile phones and the as-yet-undreamt-of technologies that may follow tomorrow. It is imperative that they should be successful in this if the coverage of hard news is to be financed adequately in the future. One of the most crucial things that this chapter has shown is that sports journalism is now a key part of the 'bottom line' upon which hard news journalism depends. The sports desk is no longer the 'toy department'.

References

ABC (Audit Bureau of Circulations), reprinted in Butler, D. and Sloman, A. (1975), *British Political Facts 1900–1975* (London: Macmillan).

Anderson, P. (2002), 'Patriots or scoundrels? London's Eurosceptic tabloid dailies and the nationalist question', unpublished research paper.

BARB (Broadcasters' Audience Research Board) (2005), rating report for 11 December 2005. Available at <http://www.barb.co.uk/viewingsummary/weekreports.cfm?report=weeklyterrestrial&RequestTimeout=500> (accessed 4 January 2006).

Barnett, S. (1998), 'Dumbing Down or Reaching Out: Is it Tabloidisation Wot Done It?', in Seaton, J. (ed.) (1998), *Politics and the Media: Harlots and Prerogatives at the Turn of the Millennium* (London: Blackwell).

Brown, M. (2004), 'The player', *The Guardian*, 'Media Guardian' section, 6 September. Available at <http://www.media.guardian.co.uk/mediaguardian/story/0,,1297786,00.html> (accessed 1 April 2005).

Greenslade, R. (2005), 'The transfer season opens', *The Guardian*, 'Media Guardian' section, 1 August, 6–7.

Manchester Online (2005), 15 December. Available at <http://www.manchesteronline.co.uk/men/news/s/191/191697_space_cadets_viewing_figures_nosedive.html> (accessed 4 January 2006).

UK Press Gazette (2005), 3 March.

Part 3
Comparative Perspectives from
Other Large Advanced Democracies

Chapter 11

Journalism in Japan

Yoshikazu Yada

Introduction

Journalism in Japan has undergone substantial change during the two decades from the mid-1980s to 2005. The most conspicuous result is the manner in which hard news, of political and social events and issues, is increasingly presented in a simplified and trivialised manner, drawing on entertainment formats pioneered in popular TV shows. At the same time, audiences and sources of news have been fragmented, mainly through technological innovations that have seen the Internet advance into the news arena.

Allied to this has been the continued pursuit by television journalists of interesting, rather than important, stories: this tendency has thus been accelerated across all media. A major contributory factor for the universal nature of such changes is the traditionally homogeneous character of Japanese journalism brought about by the 'press club system'. Therefore, in television, newspapers and other media, hard news in such areas as politics, diplomacy, economy and finance all tend to be presented in a superficial manner, which denies the possibilities of deeper discussions of important and complex issues. Since World War II, Japan has accomplished a historically unique economic reconstruction and is now the second largest economic power in the world. In the area of journalism, however, Japan does not function sufficiently well to implement its mission of providing people with a range of news and information which will enable them to think about, and understand, their society and history in an effective manner.

This chapter starts by addressing the problem of turning hard news into soft news through a culture of *waido-sho* (TV shows that gained popularity through sensationalism, scandal and gossip) and then considers issues around the fragmentation of information in the Internet era. The present status of newspapers, which are losing subscribers in the face of a growing atmosphere of distrust, are discussed and linked to issues surrounding the 'press club system'. The conclusions address key themes in changes in the media environment and the future of Japanese journalism.

From Hard to Soft News

National newspapers and broadcasting in Japan are vast in scale and cover the whole country. The circulations of nationwide newspapers, according to Japan ABC, show that the largest is the 10.07 million of the *Yomiuri Shimbun*, followed by the *Asahi Shimbun*'s 8.27 million and the *Mainichi Shimbun*'s four million. The *Nihon Keizai Shimbun*, which is a business newspaper, has a circulation of 3.02 million. Total newspaper circulation, including large and small regional newspapers, was 53 million in 2004. National newspapers, like *Yomiuri* and *Asahi*, account for 50 per cent of this, followed by a 40 per cent share for local and regional papers, and some 10 per cent by sports newspapers. The main newspapers in Japan publish both morning and evening editions; that is, they issue newspapers twice a day. Gross circulation goes up to 70 million when evening editions are added. The household diffusion rate of newspapers in Japan is the second highest globally, with about 90 per cent of the adult population reading newspapers. The size of the industry, its importance in Japanese society and the scale of newspaper sales is clear when compared with the total 55 million sales figure for newspapers in the US, which has a population more than twice that of Japan.

The situation of television is similar to newspapers. There are five big commercial broadcasting stations based in Tokyo – Nippon Television Network, Tokyo Broadcasting System (TBS), Fuji Television Network, Asahi National Broadcasting (TV Asahi), and Television Tokyo Channel 12 (TV Tokyo). They have 127 affiliated TV stations in other cities and regions and through these their programmes are seen nationwide. In a similar manner the public broadcaster NHK covers the whole country through its networks. It is a mechanism whereby programmes from Tokyo penetrate into every corner of the nation.

These key commercial stations have close capital and personnel relations with national newspapers like the *Yomiuri* and the *Asahi*. For example, according to the *Kaisha Shikiho* or *Company Stock Guidebook* (2006), the largest single shareholder in the Nippon Television Network is *Yomiuri Shimbun* group Honsha, with 14.8 per cent of the stock. In the same manner, the largest shareholder in TV Asahi is *Asahi Shimbun* with a share of 33.8 per cent. Furthermore, both the chairman and the managing director were formerly executive directors of *Asahi Shimbun*. Although TV firms and newspapers have been tied closely in Japan, laws and regulations restrict the way this can be done through the principle of non-concentration. However, these do not prevent key stations in Tokyo having affiliated stations in other local areas. It also allows newspaper companies to have close links with TV stations, both in stock and human relations, reflecting a historical situation in which newspaper companies led the establishment of the nationwide broadcasting system after World War II.

In this situation, today, the *waido-sho* have played a key role in turning hard news into soft news. The *waido-sho* cover all kinds of news and information, such as murders, accidents, disasters, scandals, gossip and sport. At the same time, hard news on political and economic issues is reported in a similar manner. Such an approach to mixing up hard and soft news results in little distinction being made between the two. Programmes of similar style are broadcast from morning to night, not only on weekdays but also at weekends, when they achieve audiences in the top 20 per cent of the ratings (Video Research, 2005).

They became popular in the mid-1980s against a background of people wanting to watch more news programmes (see NHK, 2005). And it brought profit to TV stations. In these programmes a well-known newscaster plays the main role, several reporters convey news, and several commentators express their views on the issues. They are not normal news programmes but rather entertainment shows and thus producers have to be highly conscious of audience ratings. This makes the line between news and entertainment unclear. This trend is identified by Croteau and Hoynes (2006) who argue that 'changes in media structure and practices have had a significant impact on media content. The quest for profits often leads to media that are homogenized and trivial, and the boundaries between commerce and information are rapidly disappearing.'

Journalist Toshio Hara (1997), who is a former Kyodo News Service supervising editor, commented: 'Placing the first priority on audience ratings in making programmes exacerbates this tendency. It is a crime that *waido-sho* operate under a rule of "interested in everything" without a sincere consideration of human rights. In fact, they along with viewers enjoy the unhappiness or misery of others.' In addition to the above, he pointed out that the three principles of *waido-sho*, namely putting emphasis on immediacy, moving images and emotion, are damaging trust in television.

Reimei Okamura (2003), a professor at Daito-Bunka University, stated: 'Sophisticated and good-quality programmes of culture and non-fiction by commercial broadcast companies disappear during peak viewing hours. Those that remain are broadcast late at night to only small audiences.' He added: 'Entertainment programmes which are similar in tone are made one after another by all the TV stations. The same popular entertainers appear as members of these kinds of programmes, which have no difference in theme. This situation is common to all commercial stations.' And he concluded: 'Not even in the United States, where competition among commercial broadcasters is fierce, is there found the extreme situation of establishing priorities dedicated to a sense of amusement and audience ratings.'

Soichiro Tahara (2005), a journalist with a television background, pointed out that 'variety programmes are at the core of the focus on amusement for commercial terrestrial broadcasters and a lot of people feel disgust with those kinds of programmes, saying they are too vulgar.'

In programmes in which influential politicians appear to discuss important issues, there is often insufficient time provided. Statements tend to be fragmented and make little sense. Moreover, the same story is often repeated by different TV stations. As a result, rather than focusing on content, people are only left with an impression of a particular person having appeared on a programme and having spoken about an issue. It is thus difficult in such circumstances to have serious policy discussions. Moreover, newspapers often pick up stories from *waido-sho* and publish them.

Hideo Ohtake (2003), a professor at Kyoto University, commented:

In the USA, good-looking politicians become popular through TV. At the same time, newspapers [this refers to quality papers] dampen this popularity with incisive comments and explanations. Although the influence is limited to readers of these quality papers, it impacts on opinion leaders' thinking, which has an indirect influence on the public. In Japan, however, newspapers tend to further burnish the popularity of people who have become popular on TV. One reason for this is the close business linkages newspapers have with TV stations. The result is that newspapers are restrained in their criticisms of TV. This can, therefore, lead to situations where upsurges of popularity for particular politicians or political fever take Japan, including opinion leaders, by storm.

Atsushi Kusano, a professor at Keio University who serves as chief director of the NPO Institute for Media Research, pointed out in policy recommendations made public in December 2005 that: 'TV media which pursue ease of understanding tend to simplify complicated problems.' Citing the example of debate over Yasukuni Shrine visits by the prime minister, he commented that: 'Many programmes from beginning to end do nothing more than focus on a dualistic approach relating to support or opposition [to the visits]' (Kusano, 2005).

After the inception of the Koizumi administration in 2001, the tendency of politicians, regardless of whether they are from ruling or opposition parties, to appear on television frequently has become more widespread, compared with what happened in the 1980s. They appear even on variety shows and quiz shows. That is because the politicians found that they could not avoid competing with the Koizumi administration, which has adopted a strong PR strategy using such elements as television, a homepage and an email magazine to enhance its exposure.

This trend alters relationships between politics and media. Akira Fujitake (2002), a professor at Gakushuin University, said: 'Television has changed the style of reporting of politics, including in newspapers, and opened a new phase in politics. Change of reporting style of politics has made changes to politics itself. Then, in a chain of interactions, change in politics changes reporting.'

The general election on 11 September 2005 reflected the relationship between such television coverage and politics. Prime Minister Junichiro Koizumi conducted an electoral campaign which focused on the single issue of support for, or opposition to, the privatisation of postal services, which was easy to understand. He was successful, with the ruling Liberal Democratic Party achieving a historic result and securing 291 seats. According to the *Asahi Shimbun*, people who watched television often voted for the ruling party (*Asahi Shimbun*, 2005).

In the variety shows, well-known newscasters make their personal feelings clear and express their own opinions frankly. Through the TV camera, they urge viewers to become angrier in response to major accidents or injustices. This kind of attitude can be regarded as a deviation from the self-discipline of journalism. It has to be noted that there is a possibility of this attitude coming to the surface in delicate political matters and discussions even though, at present, such behaviour only relates to accidents and the like.

Fragmentation of News

Today, many people, especially in younger age groups, obtain news through the Internet. Against a background of the rapid spread of personal computers and mobile phones, the manner in which new technologies are changing journalism is a major issue.

At the end of 2004, according to the White Paper on information and communication in Japan (Ministry of Internal Affairs and Communications of Japan, 2005), 79.48 million people in Japan used the Internet, which represented 62.3 per cent of the population. In 1999, five years earlier, the Internet-using population was 27.06 million, which was 21.4 per cent of the population. The 2004 figures are thus about three times those of 1999. The Internet utilisation rate among younger generations is high, with 92.3 per cent of those in their twenties and 90.5 per cent of those in their thirties being Internet users.

There has been a striking increase in expenditure on Internet advertising. According to Dentsu (2005), the largest advertising agency in Japan, this increased by 54.8 per cent in 2005 from the level of the previous year. This compares with a decrease of 0.1 per cent in television advertising, which accounts for a substantial portion of total advertising, and newspaper advertising expenditure also decreased by 1.7 per cent. As for the actual amount of money expended, 280.8 billion yen (US$ 2.4 billion) was spent on Internet advertising during 2005, while that for radio was 177.8 billion yen (US$ 1.5 billion). It was the second year running that advertising expenditure for the Internet had surpassed that spent on a conventional medium.

A special feature of Japan is that the number of users of cellular phones and other hand-held devices is increasing rapidly. The number in 2004 was 58.25 million compared with 25.04 million in 2001. As most of these devices provide Web access, increasing numbers of the population can link to the Internet when away from homes and offices.

The White Paper (Ministry of Internal Affairs and Communications of Japan, 2005) explained that the Internet is used for gathering information in a wide range of sectors and that it has become an indispensable medium for daily life. When people were surveyed about the media they used to obtain information, it was shown that they used the Internet to gather news, in addition to using it to obtain information on items such as travel, shopping, hobbies and amusement.

With a sense of misgiving, Keiichi Katsura, a media studies authority and a professor at Tokyo Information University, says as follows in Aoki and Yukawa (2003):

> The opportunities for absorbing information are becoming divided into segments, with each consumer seeking to obtain only the particular information he or she is interested in. The culture of younger people's use of mobile phones is perhaps leading that change. They are not interested in other people, and mobile phones are becoming the best medium for them to use in obtaining information for themselves and their close friends.

The changing relationship between information and people cannot be stopped in the Internet generation. The relationship between news and people is also changing. It can be said that a certain kind of independent and individual way of accessing and picking out news has developed among the people who focus on areas such as work, everyday life, hobbies and study. The age of television and newspapers, where they unilaterally provided people with information, has begun to change.

Professor Yasuaki Narita (2004) of Rikkyo University explained the phenomenon as follows: 'The attitude now is to use information independently as the need arises.' In addition, he described the method of access to news in the Internet age thus: 'Based on what is effective for oneself, assessments are made about importance and people themselves decide the implications of news.' He concluded that: 'It is clear that the image of the role that news or journalism should play will need to be fundamentally modified.'

According to the White Paper, in response to a survey about how they obtained news, with multiple responses being permitted, the largest number, 84.0 per cent, indicated television, followed by 67.4 per cent for the Internet and 62.2 per cent for newspapers. The use of the Internet thus already exceeds that of newspapers in sourcing news (see Ministry of Internal Affairs and Communications of Japan, 2005). The decline of newspapers is clear from the times people allocate to individual media. In 2004, the time spent on reading newspapers was 31 minutes while, on the other hand, 37 minutes was devoted to the Internet. Of course, more time was spent watching television; at three hours and 31 minutes this greatly exceeded the time spent on other media (see Ministry of Internal Affairs and Communications of Japan, 2005).

This fragmentation can be seen to have an impact on where people source news and also on the type of news they receive. Much of the material on Internet news sites contains a bare minimum of information with a headline. They do not thoroughly convey the background to news or the influence news has on society. This trend is even clearer in accessing news from mobile phones. That is probably adequate in such areas as checking stock prices, exchange rates, soccer results, information on the arrest of a murderer and the next day's weather forecast. However, the news available through Internet sites on issues such as tax reform, debate in the Diet (the Japanese parliament) concerning the budget and the central bank's monetary policies, all of which have a serious and direct impact on the daily lives of people, is insufficient for deep consideration of the themes. Furthermore, this might strengthen a characteristic of journalism in Japan previously described, namely a simple dichotomy between whether an issue is a good or bad one and whether or not it should be supported. A full picture of issues cannot be obtained through news on Internet sites.

The news placed on Internet sites by newspaper companies is limited and in an abbreviated form of the original published article. Usually, moreover, articles such as long commentaries are not seen online.

On the other hand, the White Paper judged from the survey that the setting up of blogs had become widespread by 2004. Fully 84.9 per cent of blogs focus on personal life diaries, hobbies and sports. Social news, politics, economy and business featured in only 2.7 per cent. While blogs are having an impact on conventional mass media in the US, and writers of blogs attend White House press conferences, the situation of blogs in Japan is that, because of their immaturity compared with the US, they cannot yet handle hard news.

The Decline of Newspapers

Until around 2000, the total circulation of newspapers had continued to increase. However, according to a survey by the Japan Newspaper Publishers and Editors Association, circulation began to decrease from a peak of 53.77 million in 1997 to 53.02 million in 2004. There do not appear to be any factors which will lead to a renewed increase in circulation. The number of homes reading newspapers is also decreasing. Japan's huge circulation numbers have been supported by a delivery system which covers the entire country. There is no country that has as comprehensive a delivery network as Japan. About 94 per cent of newspaper circulation in Japan relies on this delivery system which has maintained its importance.

However, Keiichi Katsura is cited in Aoki and Yukawa (2003) as saying:

> I think it is unusual across the world for most of a country's citizens to read quality and tasteful newspapers. Therefore, it would not be strange if quality newspapers with huge circulations which are full of general information that all the family can read were to erode away. In fact, that change might already be rapidly occurring.

Such a trend can be seen most clearly in the younger generation. According to a survey in 2003 by the Japan Newspaper Publishers and Editors Association of people aged 18 to 35 living in and around Tokyo, fully 38 per cent of single people did not read newspapers. Another investigation by the same association revealed distrust of newspapers. It showed that the ratio of those who thought that current newspapers could be trusted decreased from 55.2 per cent in 2001 to 48.1 per cent in 2005. Furthermore, those who thought that newspapers reported the events factually decreased during the same period from 53.7 to 46.4 per cent.

As for the total time devoted to reading newspapers, that reduced from 25.8 minutes in 2001 to 23.9 minutes in 2005. Moreover, the time spent on reading by those in their twenties and thirties was less than 20 minutes in 2005, with the former spending 11.7 minutes and the latter 15.1 minutes reading newspapers.

The percentage of people who read newspapers every day decreased from 80.8 per cent in 1999 to 74.6 per cent in 2005. It is striking that, among younger generations, a lifestyle which does not involve a newspaper is becoming more common. Among people in their twenties and thirties, 50.9 per cent and 61.6 per cent respectively read a newspaper every day. This contrasts strongly with people in their fifties, of whom 80 per cent or more read newspapers.

Rising Media Distrust

During the past two decades, newspapers and television in Japan have occasionally published false reports or been involved in scandals. This has gradually reduced the level of trust in the media. Currently, only about 50 per cent of people think that reports by mass media are largely accurate (see NHK, 2005: Figure 4).

Katsufumi Amano (2004), a professor at Nihon University, points out that there were a series of false reports in 1989 which media experts term '*Heisei no sandai gohou*' (three major false reports of the Heisei era). They were the '*sango jiken*' by the *Asahi Shimbun*, the '*Glico-Morinaga goho jiken*' by the *Mainichi Shimbun*, and the 'hiding place of a serial killer' by the *Yomiuri Shimbun*. Fumiyasu Goto (1996), a former professor at Ferris University, has referred to these false reports. He says the '*sango jiken*' (coral case) was the fabrication of a picture of damaged ocean coral by a photographer. The president of the newspaper group resigned after the cameraman admitted his actions. '*Glico-Morinaga goho jiken*' was a false report by a journalist who misunderstood police information and wrongly reported the arrest of a suspect in a kidnapping case. The case of 'hiding place of a serial killer' was similar, involving reporters of *Yomiuri* writing a story based on subjective impressions of police sources. In both instances the reporters were responding to strong pressure to provide scoops.

In succeeding years, there were also false reports and illegal quotations in major newspapers from time to time. In 2005, the *Asahi* released a false story about the lower house election based on a fabricated report made by young reporters. It became the focus of strong criticism.

In the TV sector, the halting of programmes because of criticism and pressure relating to staged (as opposed to genuine) performances called '*yarase*' in factual programmes is far from unusual. At NHK, staged performances were identified in 1993. Other issues involving NHK have included illegal accounting by a special correspondent which came to light in 2004/5, a suspicion that NHK re-edited a programme under pressure from ruling party politicians, and the arrest of a reporter for serial arson in 2005. In addition, Nippon Television Network Corporation's practice of distorting audience ratings by paying money to viewers was detected in 2003.

In addition to such scandals there have been concerns over media abuses since the mid-1980s. The problem of harm being caused by reports has come to the fore in relation to the naming of suspects arrested in criminal investigations. There are also concerns about the media scramble to cover major accidents involving many victims, where insufficient consideration is given to human rights and individual privacy.

Yoshio Tokuyama (2003) of the *Asahi Shimbun* commented that:

A pattern of perversion has been established, where the mass media, which had been recognised as an ally defending people from those in authority, have turned into entities which are hostile to citizens. Moreover, the media, which should be keeping watch on those in authority, have rather come instead to be allies of those in authority.

In democracies, the media are in a position to keep watch over the power of government. However, the situation is reversed in Japan, with the mass media attracting suspicious eyes and harsh criticism.

It is natural for there to be sensation-seeking tabloids in any country and it is normal for the media to focus to some extent on scandals. However, in Japan today, all of the mass media, including television, newspapers and magazines, are acting in the same manner, with negative impacts on readers' and viewers' trust in the media. If this situation continues, it will lead to further distrust in all the media. If that happens, it will become very difficult to correctly convey hard news and there is a possibility that the foundation for democratic discussion will be destroyed.

A famous columnist for the *Nihon Keizai Shimbun*, Yasuhiro Tase (1994), stated that: 'We cannot allow distrust of journalism to spread. In a society where journalism does not retain some soundness, there is a danger of corruption of power and a certain kind of fascism emerging.' Kiyofuku Chuma (2003), a former executive director of the *Asahi Shimbun* with oversight of the newspaper's editorial function, expresses a sense of crisis, saying: 'There is a possibility that the foundations of newspapers will collapse from their core if correct measures are not taken.'

As a result of the situation, the Act for Protection of Computer Processed Personal Data, which is regarded by administrative organs as curbing the media, was easily passed in 2003.

The Challenge from Online Corporations

In 2005, major moves aimed at operational integration with media firms were made by two IT companies, Livedoor and Rakuten. Livedoor, which at the time had total market value of about 1 trillion yen (US$ 8.6 billion), suddenly acquired 35 per cent of the stock of the parent company of Fuji Television Network and sought a capital tie-up with the Fuji Sankei group in February. In its approach, Livedoor declared that conventional media would be overcome by the Internet. Rakuten, an online retail specialist with a total market value of over 1 trillion yen (US$ 8.6 billion), proposed an operational integration with TBS by establishing a joint holding firm in October 2005. In making its proposal, Rakuten bought 15.46 per cent of TBS stock, which it subsequently raised to over 19 per cent. The two companies entered into an adversarial relationship.

Ultimately, the ambitions of the two companies were thwarted after they encountered strong opposition from both inside and outside the broadcasting industry. In addition, President Takafumi Horie of Livedoor was arrested in January 2006 on suspicion of having violated securities laws in order to inflate the company's stock price and total market value.

Although mergers and acquisitions in the media sector in Japan have not, as yet, occurred frequently, both events clearly demonstrate that media companies need to pay closer attention than they have to date to their relationships with the market and to influences on journalism.

Behind these movements, the fusion of broadcasting and telecommunication is progressing rapidly. Broadband and digital television are certainly spreading throughout the country and it can be said that conditions are in place for integration of the two. According to the 2005 Internet report of the International Telecommunications Union (ITU), broadband communication charges in Japan are the lowest in the world. In such a situation, the spread of broadband seems to be accelerating. The impact on journalism of this trend deserves to be carefully monitored.

The Press Club System and Homogeneous Journalism

From the mid-1980s, one thing has remained unchanged – the press club system. The press club system operates as a kind of cartel for news and information based on close relationships between news gatherers – major newspaper companies and TV stations – and news providers, such as government and big companies. Membership benefits the major players in society in handling useful news and information exclusively. They enjoy a superiority that other small players cannot. A key of this system is that membership of clubs is allocated to companies, not to journalists, meaning that no individual journalist can play a big role in this system or access key news sources. The foreign press also receives cold treatment.

There are said be a total of 800 to 1,000 press clubs throughout the country but no accurate figure exists. According to Hayashi Toshitaka, a professor at Waseda University, the origin of today's press club was the *Gikai-deiri kishadan*, a group of journalists from each newspaper company in Tokyo that came into existence when the Imperial Diet was convened in 1890. It developed into a journalist organisation for nationwide newspapers and it became a 'joint newspaper club'. It was the forerunner of the present association of journalists of the Diet. From about 1900, clubs were set up in major public organisations such as government offices, the Bank of Japan and the courts of justice. At the end of the Meiji era, the system was assumed to have spread to all the main government offices in Japan.

The press club system thus has a history of nearly 120 years, including a period of censorship by the government prior to World War II. After the war, for the first time, Japan secured freedom of the press through article 21 of the Constitution. However, the structures of media corporations in Japan have been organised in a way which is compatible with the press club system, which can be said to be Japan's information network. They exist in central government, local government, police stations and political parties. In the private sector press clubs are established in major businesses such as power companies and large banks. Journalists use the clubs as the base for their coverage. There is usually a room where journalists who belong to a press club receive information every day and conduct interviews.

From the standpoint of news providers it is simple and convenient to provide information through press releases to clubs rather than to each medium individually. Manipulation of information is also easy. From the standpoint of the media, there is an advantage in having press conferences as a group and being able to obtain more detailed information through requesting it through the press club.

However, the closed-style operation of press clubs is intermittently criticised, including by international bodies such as the EU delegation in Japan, the media of foreign countries and also by domestic magazine journalists and freelance writers, who are not members of the clubs.

Furthermore, under the press club system, it is quite easy for an individual journalist or medium to be affected subliminally by a Japanese group mentality, which can result in homogeneous coverage of an issue. Kazuyoshi Hanada (2005), a former editor in chief of *Shukan Bunshun*, a Japanese weekly magazine, noted that: 'The news-gathering power of large newspapers has declined. That is because they rely 80–90 per cent on press releases.' This is the essence of the press club problem, namely that the media find it easy to depend on sources of news provided by announcements by government bodies, major institutions and leading companies.

Takashi Tachibana (1984), a famous journalist with experience in the US, pointed out: 'From the perspective of newspaper personnel in the United States, it is natural that the news in each newspaper is quite different. It is, on the other hand, rather strange when, as in Japan, the same news appears in all newspapers.'

Karel van Wolferen, who is regarded as an expert analyst of Japan, explained that the press club structure performs a self-censorship function (1989: 96). He also pointed out that 'the major source of the power of the Japanese press is its monolithic nature'. He added:

> Lead articles in the days following important events tend to be non-committal, vague and ambivalent, and are generally indistinguishable from each other. Most of what these papers print is a predictable product of desk editors, compiled from 'feeds' supplied by a number of reporters and influenced by extraneous political factors. The result is almost never challenged, again with the exception of the routine controversies. All Japanese read approximately the same things every day and have their opinions formed by what is in effect a single source (van Wolferen, 1989).

Shigeki Matsui (2005), a professor at Osaka University, says that:

> It is not a bad thing that the government has a system to provide information to the mass media. If the public obtain necessary information through the system, it should be promoted. The problem is that the information is only provided to a limited number of the media, which carries the risk of the government manipulating and controlling information. The press club system ought, therefore, to be abolished.

Moreover, the press club system, under which the media tend to be under pressure to handle efficiently all the releases which they receive, weakens journalistic activity. Toshio Hara (1997) said that:

> Journalism in Japan is sometimes criticised for its lack of desire from an objective perspective to set agendas for solutions to various social problems. I believe that this stems from the habits of what is a mere façade of objective reporting. It can be said

that 'release journalism' in the press clubs plays a major role in making reporters and journalists passive.

Kiyofuku Chuma (2003) said that: 'Both sides of an issue are described together, and nothing is added. The commentary is also well balanced. It is left to the viewer or reader to decide what stance to take.'

However, there are differences of opinion among scholars and specialists about 'passive' reporting and whether such balanced neutrality simply presents audiences with stark choices between extremes of 'right or wrong'. Complex and difficult issues, such as a visit by government ministers to Yasukuni Shrine, where war criminals from World War II are deified, was a case in point, as is the reporting of revisions to the Constitution, pension problems, restructuring of national finances and interest rate policies. It is very difficult for readers and viewers to rationally make accurate judgements on issues when they are presented in terms of pros and cons, or differing options are simply outlined side by side. It cannot be said that journalism in Japan today offers a sufficient diversity of hard news and comment.

Yasuharu Dando (2005), who is one of the pioneers of Internet columns, commented: '[Journalism in Japan] has pursued homogeneous reporting based on commercialism. That is now out of date. Without more active work on the part of journalists, a key function of journalism, namely that of uncovering facts, has tended to be lost.'

Conclusions

Where is journalism in Japan, characterised as it is by homogeneousness, likely to head in the initial years of the twenty-first century as utilisation of the Internet becomes more comprehensive and integration of broadcasting and platforms proceeds? Some trends are clear, including the manner in which hard news is increasingly turned into soft news and treated as 'entertainment' and news sources become more fragmented. These tendencies are reinforced by the historical press club system and some movements towards deregulation.

Moreover, there are many fundamental questions being asked of journalism in today's society where the Internet is making ever-increasing inroads and other technologies which impact on traditional lifestyles are developing rapidly. Many believe that online platforms will result in rapid and radical change in news media structures and delivery. Tetsuo Jinbou (2005), a video news network representative, commented: 'Existing conventional media such as broadcasting and newspapers will become part of the Internet sooner or later. The reason for that is that the Internet is clearly superior to them in terms of its efficiency in transmitting information.' Others are concerned about the challenges journalism faces from rapid cultural and social changes. Keishi Saeki (1997), a professor at Kyoto University, commented: 'In a sense, it is arrogant in today's complicated world to think that journalism can report neutrally and scientifically present well-balanced propositions.'

Heightened dissatisfaction in Japan with conventional media has brought growing expectations for radically new journalism on the Internet. For example, Tooru Maekawa and Kiyoshi Nakano (2003) pointed out:

> As at April 2003, there were as many as 63 million cellular phones that could connect with the Internet in Japan. If people have a cellular phone, they are able to access the Internet from anywhere, and information can be provided to and from anywhere in the world through email or via individual websites and electronic bulletin boards. It is as if there are 63 million journalists deployed throughout Japan.

Such a comment is perhaps excessive in terms of its expectations of net journalism. Kouichi Edagawa (2001), a non-fiction writer, said: 'I think that the Internet is a medium only for those persons who have a strong reliance on their own judgement capabilities.' In fact, sound journalism is indispensable for us to live in a democracy. This way of thinking is summarised by David T.Z. Mindich, Associate Professor at Saint Michael's College:

> Despite that it frequently displeases heads of state, we need good journalism. We need it because it gives us information about whether we should support our country's war plan. We need it because, as in the case of Watergate, it's important to know when our leaders are corrupt. And most of all, we need it because without it, there is no reliable information of any kind. And without reliable information, we have no democracy (Mindich, 2005).

Then what can we do? It is not realistic in discussing journalism in Japan to ignore the current way in which the mass media operate through a structure based upon the press club system. Other historical factors have also influenced working practices. For example, all the police stations and local governments across the country are always covered by specific reporters from each large newspaper and TV station. Tetsuya Shibayama (1997), a part-time lecturer at Kyoto University, commented: 'The process of producing news differs greatly according to country and region, with the whole concept of news reflecting the culture of each country. Japanese journalism, which has a most efficient system for gathering news, is a product of Japanese culture.'

Although the future is not clear and debate is also murky, we Japanese have to reconstruct sound journalism based on culture and historical backgrounds. We must not forget the responsibility the pre-war media had for paving the way toward and promoting World War II. Professor Teruo Ariyama (2005) has pointed out that newspapers in Japan had never thought about the relationship between newspapers and democracy during the post-war era. He added: 'Not questioning oneself adequately leads to a lack of scepticism, with the media being in a situation of following others blindly. People feel comfortable when they find that they are the same as their neighbors but the media is insufficiently questioning and critical.'

The issues confronted by journalism in Japan are weighty.

References

Amano, K. et al. (2004), *Shin Gendai Masukomiron no Pointo* (Tokyo: Gakubunsha), 49.

Aoki, N. and Yukawa, T. (2003), *Nett ha Shinbun wo Korosunoka* (Tokyo: NTT Shuppan), 93.

Ariyama, T. (2005), *Shimbun Kenkyu* 644, May, 63.

Asahi Shimbun, (2005), 'Report', 26 October.

Chuma, K. (2003), *Shimbun wa Ikinokoreruka* (Tokyo: Iwanami Shoten), 58, 163.

Cook, P.S., Gomery, D. and Lichty, L.W. (eds) (1992), *The Future of News* (Washington DC: The Woodrow Wilson Center Press).

Croteau, D. and Hoynes, W. (2006), *The Business of Media* (Thousand Oaks CA: Pine Forge Press), 189.

Dando, Y. (2005), *Sekai*, January, 132.

Dentsu (2005), available at <http://www.dentsu.co.jp/>.

Edagawa K. et al. (2001), *9 gatu 11 nichi Media ga Tamesareta hi* (Tokyo: Transuato).

Fujita, H. (1991), *America no Journalism* (Tokyo: Iwanami Shoten).

Fujitake, A. (2002), *Waido sho seiji ha nihon wo sukueruka* (Tokyo: KK Besutoserazu), 183.

Fujitake, A. (ed.) (2005), *Zusetsu Nihon no Mass Media* (Tokyo: Japan Broadcast Publishing).

Goto, F. (1996), *Gohou* (Tokyo: Iwanami Shoten), 52, 58, 158.

Hanada, K. (2005), *Nihon kouhou gakkai Info* 17, 12.

Hara, T. (1997), *Journalism no Shisou* (Tokyo: Iwanami Shoten), 30, 45, 160.

Hargreaves, I. (2003), *Journalism: A Very Short Introduction* (New York: Oxford University Press).

Hashimoto, Y. and Yoshii, H. (eds) (2005), *Network Shakai* (Kyoto: Minerva Publishing).

Hongou, Y. (2000), *Shimbun ga Abunai* (Tokyo: Bungeishungu).

Ichikawa, M. (2003), *Hyogen no Jiyu no Houri* (Tokyo: Nippon Hyoron Sha).

Ishizuka, M. (2004), 'Japan's Mass Media', in *About Japan Series 1* (Tokyo: Foreign Press Center, Japan).

Jinbou, T. (2005), *Asahi Shimbun*, 5 March.

Kaisha Shikiho (2006) (*Company Stock Guidebook*) (Tokyo: Toyo Keizai Shinposha).

Kusano, A. (2005), *Seisaku Teigen Yoriyoki Terebi Houdou no tameni* (Tokyo: NPO [non-profit organisation] Media Kensho Kikou).

McLuhan, M. (1967), *Understanding Media*. Japanese edition translated by Y. Kurihara and N. Koumoto (1987), *Mediaron* (Tokyo: Misuzu Shobo).

Maekawa, T. and Nakano, K. (2003), *Cyber Journalism Ron* (Tokyo: Tokyo Denki University Press), 223–4.

Matsuda, H. (2005), *NHK Towareru Koukyo Hoso* (Tokyo: Iwanami Shoten).

Matsui, S. (1994), *Mass Media Hou Nyumon* (Tokyo: Nippon Hyoron Sha).

Matsui, S. (2005), *Mass Media no Hyogen no Jiyu* (Tokyo: Nippon Hyoron Sha), 249.

Mindich, D.T.Z. (2004), *Tuned Out: Why Americans Under 40 Don't Follow the News* (Oxford: Oxford University Press), 95.

Ministry of Internal Affairs and Communications of Japan (2005), *Information and Communications in Japan* (the 2005 White Paper).

Narita Y. (2004), *Asahi Inquiry and Research* 173, October, 15, 18.

NHK (2005), *The NHK Monthly Report on Broadcast Research*, August. Available at <http://www.nhk.or.jp/bunken/>.

Noguchi, Y. (1995), *1940 nen Taisei* (Tokyo: Toyo Keizai).

Ohtake, H. (2003), *Nihongata Popyurizumu* (Tokyo: Chuo Kouron Shinsha).

Okamura, R. (2003), *Terebi no 21 seiki* (Tokyo: Iwanami Shoten), 136, 138.

Saeki, K. (1997), *Gendai Minshushugi no Byouri* (Tokyo: Japan Broadcast Publishing), 144.

Shibayama, T. (1997), *Nihongata Media System no Houkai* (Tokyo: Kashiwa Shobo), 216.

Shibayama, T. (ed.) (2004), *Nihon no Journalism towa Nanika* (Kyoto: Minerva Publishing).

Shimoyama, S. (1995), *America Journalism* (Tokyo: Maruzen Library), 146, 149.

Tachibana, T. (1984), *America Journalism Houkoku* (Tokyo: Iwanami Shoten).

Tahara, S. (2005), *Asahi Shimbun*, 18 March.

Tamura, N., Hayashi, T. and Ooi, S. (eds) (2004), *Gendai Journalism wo Manabu Hito no Tameni* (Kyoto: Sekai Bunka Publishing).

Tase, Y. (1994), *Seiji Journalism no Tsumi to Batsu* (Tokyo: Shinchosha), 201.

Tase, Y. (1998), *Journalist no Sahou* (Tokyo: Nihon Keizai Shimbun).

Tokuyama, Y. (2003), *Houdou Kiki* (Tokyo: Shueisha), 68.

Utagawa, R. (2005), *Shimbun ga Nakunaru hi* (Tokyo: Soshisha Publishing).

van Wolferen, K. (1989), *The Enigma of Japanese Power* (New York: Vintage Books).

Video Research (2005), 'Audience rating survey of Kanto area including Tokyo'. Available at <http://www.videor.co.jp/>.

Yamada, K. (2004), *Hou to Journalism* (Tokyo: Gakuyo Shobo).

Chapter 12

Journalism in Germany

Knut Hickethier

Introduction

Journalism in Germany after 1945 is characterised by two main forms of media organisation: on the one hand is the private commercial form of the press in the diverse manifestations of the daily press, ranging from the magazine to specialist and human interest publications, and on the other hand is the public structure of broadcasting, which was completed only in 1984 through the admittance of private programme producers. Despite this difference, standards and quality barometers were established in journalistic practices which became effective across the board and which formed a self-perception of obligation to national democracy, to the establishment of an active public and to the aim of providing comprehensive information.

In the years following the end of World War II and the suppression of the Nazi regime by the Allied forces, press, broadcasting and film were reorganised in the Western Zones (later to become the Federal Republic of Germany). All existing publishing companies had to stop the production of their newspapers and the Allies gave licences for new newspapers to individuals who had not been connected politically with the Nazi regime. Consequently, numerous regional and several national newspapers came into being; among these are some that are still among the leading national quality press, such as *Süddeutsche Zeitung*, *Frankfurter Allgemeine*, *Frankfurter Rundschau*, *Die Welt*, *Die Zeit* and *Der Spiegel*. These were inextricably linked with the Allied concept of re-education aimed at the democratisation of German society, and they assumed important functions in the creation of a critical and educated populace.

In broadcasting (at first radio and, from 1952, television) there was also fundamental change. The existing national broadcasting organisations were taken over by the occupying forces and where they were still intact (such as in Hamburg) began to broadcast once more. German employees were recruited from those people who were shown to have no contrary political leanings or from the group of returning refugees. The Allies organised broadcasting along decentralised lines mirroring the 'public institution' style of the BBC. Broadcasting was designed to be neither state-run nor commercially oriented but to establish autonomous and independent institutions which were to provide independent information, education and instruction as well as entertainment.

In the emerging GDR (German Democratic Republic) the media, after an initial phase, were controlled directly by the state. The journalistic practice which grew out of this can largely be dismissed as far as further considerations on the future of journalism are concerned. The journalistic self-awareness which developed in the GDR, that of being party-political agitators and propagandists on Leninist lines, disappeared without a trace when the GDR came to an end in 1989.

With the founding of the Federal Republic the media system established by the Allies acquired stability, both through the passing of press and broadcasting laws in the respective Federal states and as a result of emerging German jurisdiction in the higher courts.

In addition, the public status of broadcasting was established in 1961 through a judgement handed down by the Federal Constitutional Court and the way was paved for cable and satellite television. At the same time an enormous expansion in broadcasting took place with the extensive growth of radio (additionally on medium wave through UKW) and television (from 1963 with a second channel, ZDF, and from 1965 with a third channel, ARD). The written press was also characterised by an unprecedented process of expansion. Whereas the number of daily newspapers grew from 150 in 1949 (after the ending of the licensed period) to 500 at the beginning of the 1950s, so in the preceding years a concerted distinctive movement developed from which several media groups emerged, such as the Axel Springer publishing house, the Bauer publishing house and Gruner & Jahr. As part of the formation of these media concerns, programme listings magazines (such as Springer's *Hör Zu*) took on a certain importance as they could be produced cheaply from information provided at no cost by the broadcasting organisations and could be sold en masse.

Along with daily and weekly newspapers in the 1950s there emerged a multitude of specialist periodicals, illustrated popular magazines and weekly entertainment magazines (the so-called 'rainbow press'). Since the 1960s especially there has emerged a target-readership differentiation in the magazine market, with publications for women, young people, parenting, gardening, cooking, motoring and sport.

Through the development of the media, aided by the reconstruction of the German economy and growing social well-being, journalism found an increasingly improved sphere of activity. The number of full-time journalists increased rapidly from 20,000 in 1981 (Koszyk and Pruys, 1981: 96). In 1989 this number had already grown to about 31,000 (Noelle-Neumann et al., 1989: 52) and at the last survey of journalists in 1993 this figure was 53,000 (Bentele et al., 2006: 118). In addition, countless people were employed on a part-time basis in journalism and the media. The number of private individuals alone working in broadcasting in 1973 was given as about 100,000 (Drews-Bernstein, 1973: 186). As evidenced by these figures, the number of journalists has increased rapidly in recent years and with this the number of freelance workers has also significantly increased. The number of women involved in this profession has also similarly increased although they are still largely under-represented in senior positions in media companies.

Journalism as a profession is not determined by any compulsory practical training and numerous efforts to establish journalist training have changed little in the last few decades. Even today, a freely available high-school education followed by a professional training period (*Voluntariat*) of 1.5 to 2 years is sufficient to train an individual in the core aspects of a journalistic qualification (Blöbaum, 1994).

Journalists are organised mainly into two associations, and out of all employee groups they represent one of the highest levels of membership. The most important associations are the German Association of Journalists (DJV) which was founded in 1949 and today has around 40,000 members, and the German Union of Journalists (DJU) which was founded in 1951 as a journalist worker association in the Printing and Paper Union and today has around 21,000 members.

The social and economic situation of journalists has improved continuously since the 1960s, as journalist associations have been able to negotiate increasing wage claims and also because social acceptance of the journalistic profession has increasingly improved. For this reason high levels of job satisfaction became the rule, even into the 1990s, and this is demonstrated by the rather low levels of attrition.

Journalism in Different Media

Although the media are very varied in the manner in which they engage with the public and organise social communication, the self-perception of journalists with regard to the media is fundamentally not too dissimilar. Compared to other professional groups who are involved with the media, such as technicians, directors, camera operatives, dramatists, writers of fictional programmes, actors, continuity announcers, and so on, who also sometimes work as journalists (in the same way as journalists sometimes work as directors, camera operatives or broadcasters), a relatively homogenous image of the journalist has been established across all media. Journalistic research in the last few decades (by writers such as Hömberg, Blöbaum, Weischenberg and Pörksen) has also contributed to this to some extent.

The Journalist's Job

In the broadest sense journalism work involves the collation, checking, adaptation and production of information and is mainly embedded within media institutions working in editorial offices (broadcasting and press). Journalists also work in news agencies or in businesses, associations or state institutions, and increasingly the opportunity of working in the sphere of business communication is opening up to them. They can be employed either within or as an additional resource in these institutions, independently or as a so-called freelancer, although there are still differences in the types of fixed and freelance work carried out.

The journalist job profile has historically had a bad image. As 'hacks', journalists were often involved in excessive fault-finding or carping. At the same time, Germany has brought to the fore renowned, thoughtful and exceptional journalists such as Heinrich Heine, Ludwig Börne, journalist and political commentator Theodor Fontane, Karl Kraus (with the Viennese magazine *Die Fackel*), Kurt Tucholsky,

Theodor Wolff, Egon Erwin Kisch and Carl von Ossietzky. Journalism, social critique and a decidedly democratic world view are inextricably linked with each of them.

The self-perception of the journalist profession is nowadays more closely linked with everyday media work but also with a role which has been assigned from within society: the journalist is the creator of a sense of public knowledge, the broadcaster of news and the generator of public opinion. Great significance is thus attached to journalism for the functioning of a democratic society, even if in public debates this repeatedly leads to heated disagreements about the influence of journalists, their work and ways in which they can be controlled. The fact that scandals often occur concerning the boundaries of reporting is evidence of the functioning of open debate and indeed the aim of open debate is to bring together society's interests. In addition an open debate often requires secret or previously withheld information to be revealed.

For this reason, journalists working in editorial offices or media institutions within German society enjoy *special rights for the collation of information* (this is why there exists a duty of providing information for journalists by the authorities and why press passes sometimes give privileged access to the scene of an incident) and *informant protection* (the right to silence on the identity of sources).

On the other hand the *Federal press laws* (along with the broadcasting laws) oblige journalists to check the veracity of information before publication. Press journalism has created the German Press Council, to control and manage complaints. This has formulated journalistic principles (press code of honour) which describe the rules and conduct of journalistic work practice and, in the case of a serious breach, sanctions (mainly of a moral nature) can be imposed (cf. Bentele et al., 2006: 118). In the same way, public broadcasting institutions and internal broadcasting committees are established and in commercial broadcast media the Federal media institutions act as a supervisory body for managing complaints and sanctions.

Since the 1970s *editorial committees* have been formed in several press organisations, mainly public broadcasting concerns, which attempt to reinforce and defend journalistic independence against management direction. As a result of the strong economic pressure being brought to bear on the media in recent years their importance is, however, on the decline.

Alongside the established media there has always existed since the 1960s an *alternative journalism* which has sought to create counter public opinion and alternative cultures. Its development had as its high point the founding of a daily newspaper *tageszeitung* (*taz*) in 1979, which has headed the German press market ever since. The founding of alternative broadcast programmes in 1984/5 was made possible by the public channels on cable networks which saw themselves as a kind of independent popular radio and television in which the journalistic work consisted of supporting suburban groups, popular initiatives, and so on, in the formulation of their concerns and protests. Their contribution to public debate has remained rather limited.

Many of these alternative media, particularly the new journalistic forms and writing styles developed by *taz*, have nevertheless entered into general journalism in the last two decades with both a modernising and enriching effect. Conversely *taz*, in its quest for a larger readership following the collapse of the alternative culture movement, has brought its approach more closely in line with that of the general principles of journalistic practice.

Media-specific Journalistic Differences

Between the different media there are small discernible distinctions in the type of journalistic work carried out. One of these lies in the *different level of media topicality*, as the most topical forms of media, radio and television must react relatively quickly to incoming reports from news agencies and check them. In television there is also the need to acquire pictures to accompany the events and to prepare these accordingly. Radio and television are also time-constrained media which are dictated to by the chronological *limits of presentation* and by the large range of information to be communicated. Correspondingly, daily newspapers can allow more space for individual items which can be reported on more extensively, and also present more reports overall. As a result of the need to secure the day's latest news, there is also increased pressure to react quickly to new reports, to check their content and, more importantly, their accuracy. Weekly newspapers such as *Die Zeit*, magazines such as *Der Spiegel* or popular magazines such as *Stern* are more removed in time from daily events and as such have more opportunity to research the facts thoroughly and to highlight and present the background of the events in more detail.

In recent years online journalism, as a rapid information medium, must now be added to the list. News can be broadcast worldwide very quickly by online media. On the one hand this medium carries independent pieces of information from individuals, political groups and interest groups. In political conflict zones reports from the warring parties, which would otherwise be difficult to access, are broadcast along with reports from independent NGOs who are generally not under the obligation or control of governments. On the other hand media concerns have established their own Internet portals through which they can offer information platforms in addition to their press and broadcast activities. Through these they can offer further, sometimes very detailed, information, documents, pictures and sound along with commercial product marketing, and so on.

There are clear recognisable *structural differences in the information available to the public*. On the one hand there are existing media which offer information with a very strong journalistic flavour. They sort and assess incoming information and put together a *well-prepared, clear and concise journalistic output* to which media users can quickly become accustomed and which is characterised by a pre-defined self-perception created through the media and editorial offices. On the other hand there are broad and *differentiated offerings* of very varied information which goes unchecked in regard to the accuracy of its content and the influence of other interests. The general user cannot access this information easily as to do so requires some knowledge of Internet structures. These include chat rooms, mailing lists, blogs and other forms of Web-based interactivity.

There are also numerous contributions from very specific interest communities who have established their own information platforms (communities) in many areas of individual and social life such as health, hobbies, political interest groups, belief groups, consumer groups and the environment. Through these they can relate their respective specific interests with one another.

Fragmentation of the Public Versus Information Flow

Discussion consequently often ensues regarding the *fragmentation of the public* which occurs through new media and which is said to be damaging to the democratic cohesion of society as it can lead to disintegration. This hypothesis must now be considered, as citizens generally use not just one but a variety of different media in which the information gained in one medium can be compared and checked against that appearing in other media. Media therefore do not simply deliver information in one or the other way but build places where information is available on the topics which interest the media user.

The hypothesis of the fragmentation of public opinion is also connected with the hypothesis of *information overload* which is especially directed at the broadcast media. There exists a fear of *excess* of information made possible by the numerous channels. In Germany there are 22–30 free-to-air TV channels, both public and commercial, which can be accessed, along with approximately 20–30 radio stations in a given regional reception area and 220 satellite TV channels, and so on. The continued growth in media consumption (German citizens from the age of three spent on average 8.5 hours per day in media consumption in 2005) has also given rise to the fear of a complete media overload and, simultaneously, the destruction of society and the individual.

The actual practice of communication does, however, look different. On television people mainly watch five to six main channels (ARD, ZDF, RTL, SAT.1, ProSieben and Dritte Progamme) with the other offerings seen by relatively few people. News programmes are broadcast on all the main channels.

The impression of *information overload* is mainly as a result of the acceleration of the amount of audio-visual media which has seemingly led to an increased demand. This must, however, be seen in context, since for all the entertainment channels, such as MTV, whose programmes are produced very quickly, there will also always be slowly and carefully produced programmes which enable a different perception.

As every individual can post information on the Web and at the same time acquire information freely and independently from existing media outlets, there did exist the fear that journalistic activity could be rendered superfluous. However, this has not proven to be the case. The setting-up of search engines such as Google, one of the major systems for channelling and ordering the mass of information, shows why there is a strong need for pre-sorting and selection. Therefore, the demand has grown for information which is checked, weighted and cleaned of the *information garbage* in general circulation. Media users want to participate through the media in important societal events and to devote their time to following their own information interests. Journalistic spheres of activity have, as a result of online media, been somewhat broadened.

Target Groups, Environment and Media Markets

Media-specific differences in journalism are eclipsed by the various forms of reporting which are directed by a specific understanding as to what the public likes to read, hear or see. This then explains how the range of representation forms differs between extensive and serious news in, say, *Frankfurter Allgemeine Zeitung* and the broad, simple tabloid offerings in *Bild* which is geared to a readership oriented towards sensationalism. There are also noticeably clear differences between the news programmes on public and private channels, although the differences in this case are perhaps less clearly marked. Educational and income-related variables in *journalistic target groups* are also discernible in the make-up of the users.

Moreover, within the various offerings there is a difference between a somewhat older readership and radio/TV audiences more oriented towards public channels, and a younger public which is more attracted to private entertainment channels. All these observations on trends should, however, be viewed with caution as the public's user preferences are not strictly dictated by one environment alone and can change increasingly according to situations and other specific reasons.

The concept of specific target groups determined by factors such as income, education and age has now disappeared. Instead, more recent research has resulted in the view that habits are determined through *differing cultural milieus* characterised by pleasure of experience, the need for harmony, conservatism or progressiveness, and so on (Schulze, 1992). This more recent orientation is also related to the fact that different publics, which have been culturally formed as a result of media offerings, not only have a different view of the world and therefore a different information need, but also differ in their *preferences for using media.*

For a reader who commutes to work in a factory or a large organisation, an in-depth full-page article on the political entanglements in Afghanistan is less important than one on suspected corruption in their town's cleaning service. Many readers and viewers prefer to be entertained rather than informed, not least because they believe that they have no real influence over political affairs. For this reason they are content with a few sentences about a political event. The increase in television viewing in recent years (the average television consumption by Germans over the age of three rose from 2 hours 15 minutes a day in 1985 to 3 hours 45 minutes in 2005) is linked to the growing preference for entertainment and that television serves to occupy the free time of numerous people, particularly the approximately 10–12 per cent of the population who are unemployed. Interest in journalistic reporting is therefore not low; rather there is a clear basic interest of broad sections of the population who wish to be informed about political or economic events in an entertaining manner. This also results in more entertainment-oriented journalism spreading from fringes of society toward the mainstream.

Interest in comprehensive journalistic reporting, in a revealing, investigative form of journalism which brings to light the processes taking place behind the everyday news, has not disappeared, however. Rather it is concentrated on the education and information elites already in existence who rely on the latest information to maintain their advantage over other groups.

Nonetheless, the market in which the media fight each other for audiences has become more disputed because media usage has only slowly expanded, or even stagnated, in relation to the marked increase in media outlets, and consequently there has been an increase in the intensity of the struggle for a slice of the market.

The offerings in the German media market are mainly pitched at a national level but nevertheless do overlap in isolated cases to include the other German-speaking countries. The make-up of the spoken media is a determining factor here. Access to other offerings is clearly available (in the press market of international newspapers, in the broadcast market of non-German channels) but this has become marginalised and is generally used by national information elites for special-interest topics and by special-interest groups. Consequently, all initiatives to create a European public sphere have to date proved unsuccessful because they could not overcome language barriers.

The *influence of international media organisations* is also considerable and this necessitates constant adaptation in order to be successful in terms of not only linguistic adjustment but also of a clear cultural alignment with the habits and preferences of a German public.

Media in Germany represented, and still represent, an expanding market, especially since the middle of the 1980s. This market is shaped by the Bertelsmann Group, the Springer publishing house, the WAZ group and other media groups who are also Europe-wide and fully active in the area of special-interest publications (for example, women's and fashion magazines) and numerous products appearing in many languages.

In recent years foreign businesses have started to make inroads into the German market – the American Haim Saban purchased the SAT.1-ProSieben Group and the British entrepreneur David Montgomery acquired, with Mecom and VSS, the newspapers *Berliner Zeitung*, *Berliner Kurier*, *Tip* and *Hamburger Morgenpost*, although to date little change has been noticed in contents. The difference from the previous business structures lies in the fact that for the first time investors unfamiliar with the domain are entering in large numbers into the media industry whereas previously business owners only entered into the market to fulfil their journalistic ambitions.

It is certainly not yet possible to speak in terms of an internationalisation of the German media landscape. Nevertheless, opposition has been expressed in journalistic circles, for example to the takeover of the Berliner Zeitungsgruppe by Montgomery.

Journalism's Contribution to the Democratic Process

Despite any differences which exist as a result of the variety of media and its forms, centralised regulations relating to the public and journalism are maintained. This is now discussed in terms of the public responsibility of the media and journalism.

Public Responsibility

'The press fulfils a public duty, by producing and disseminating news from matters of public interest, by expressing a point of view, through criticism or by any contribution to the creation of opinion.' This wording comes from article 3.2 of the Saxony press laws of 1992 and corresponds with the jurisdiction of the supreme authority of the Federal Constitutional Court. Through the help of the press (and at the same time from broadcast media) the public should be able to get hold of the information they need on matters of general importance to allow them to rationally form their own opinion (*information function*). On the other hand, the media inform the political class and the government about opinions within society, what the subjects think about their government (*liaison function*). From the point of view of the media users, the media are also seen as instruments of critique and control of the political class (*critique and control function*).

From this normative perspective there emerge three *constitutional commitments of the state* which also impact on the work of journalists:

1. So that the critique and control function acting against public (state) power is not endangered, the state is not allowed to directly influence the shape of the content and must do everything in its control to ensure that state organs have no major influence on the shaping of their content.
2. As the process of creating public opinion must be secured within a pluralistic society, the state must do everything within its control to ensure that the different groups in society are represented equally in the media and that different points of view can be represented equally. The state must also see to it that all media reflect the variety within society.
3. The state must also see to it that the rights of others are not violated as a result of *press freedom*. In the case of a conflict between the private interests of individuals and the interests of society, the state must ensure that the necessary balance is achieved (cf. Bentele et al., 2006: 202).

As a result of this understanding all state intervention in the processes relating to content has significantly reduced in the last few decades. The claim that there is regular intervention in media organisations, particularly when economic interests come to the fore and threaten to endanger the requirement for journalistic and economic variety in the media, has however remained undisputed. The argument over the purchase of the television channel SAT.1-ProSieben by Springer and its banning by the supervisory committee has its origin in precisely this understanding of variety which does not lead to such consequences in other countries like France.

The Concept of Journalistic Quality

The understanding that the media and journalism have a public responsibility has set in motion a *debate on quality within journalism.* There are clear differences here between the presentation of quality in the non-journalistic output of the media (for example, of entertainment and fiction) and journalism. As the media have become conglomerates with multifunctional and multitextual offerings with different usage patterns, so the debates on quality have increased. We will consider here only the journalistic presentation of quality.

As far as quality in journalism is concerned, the following criteria (only summarised here) are given: relevance, topicality, variety, balance, objectivity, accuracy, transparency, intelligibility, originality and legitimacy. The concept of quality linked to these criteria is used on different levels and can be related to an individual contribution, to several contributions to a topic, to a programme, an edition or the entire programme (Blöbaum, 1994). Since public communication is always concerned with the mediation between different people and interests, the concept of quality is itself disputed and applicable in many ways. It is not a major topic of public debate. It is only brought into play when flagrant violations occur of one or several regulations of this normatively understood concept of quality.

The most important point connected to the others is the aspect of the *reduction in complexity.* It is the task of the media to mediate the political and societal processes, now becoming more and more complex, to the population and to 'clarify' their importance so that the media users at least obtain a better understanding of events. This signifies reduction which nevertheless should not lead to simplification. As the media by definition are mediators, and journalists working within them have the task of organising the processes of mediation, they must find the forms with which this complexity can be reduced, explained and made clearer. Only when that succeeds can the media become authorities, which can link different specialist debates back to society's perception of itself, and make them useful to the processes of debate within society. Only when this can at least be safeguarded as a target view and initially realised can the informing of the people, necessary for the continuation of democracy, be guaranteed.

The Principles of Separation

The three principles of separation, established over a period of time, have proved themselves more practical in determining journalistic quality. As a consequence, journalistic contributions must be set apart from the factually worthless information contained in the following:

- advertising or related forms such as public relations;
- literary text forms, particularly fictional and entertaining texts;
- dedicated expression of opinion.

The separation of factual information from *advertising* is the oldest of these and through the process of professionalisation of journalism in the eighteenth century developed into the separation of *artistic forms* in the nineteenth century. The separation of *opinion* dates from an earlier period and has its origins in English-speaking journalism. These serve to help media users adopt a more straightforward process for checking and assessing information and can be seen as barriers within journalism which should ensure certain standards.

It is not coincidental that even in recent years these principles of separation have been consistently violated and that this rupture has led to public debates. The upholding of these principles of separation is increasingly becoming a yardstick for assessing whether the media are to be trusted and also for the credibility of the information imparted through the media.

The relationship between society and journalism and the state, between the media public and the champions of this public opinion (that is, the journalists) has, despite the varied political, juristic and scientific protection, caused heated debates in recent years. Talk of a crisis is now to be heard regularly.

Is There Currently a Crisis in German Journalism?

Since the turn of the millennium, above all since the economic breakthrough of the 'New Economy' and the economic recession in place in Germany since 2000, the media have been put under increasing economic pressure. The cause of this has been the downturn in advertising as a result of the economic recession and the resultant fall in revenue in commercial media, ranging from press houses to privately run broadcasting companies. The press sector has also noticed a gradual long-term downturn in sales. Broadcast media appear to have reached the limits of their expansion in their previous forms.

Change in Societal Scope

The recent dominance of economic factors has had a massive impact not only on publishing houses but also on privately run television companies, as is the case at SAT.1-ProSieben. This represents only a part of the financial stringencies seen in all aspects of life in society, from universities and other educational establishments to social services and areas such as the commercial management of prisons, as seen in the Federal region of Hessen. These processes are not new in the Western world, certainly not in the English-speaking world, but in Germany with its 'pure capitalism' and strong social-democratic leaning (social market economy) this was new and led to much condemnation at a political level.

Apart from the global conditions which exacerbated this development, there were other home-made problems in the Federal Republic of Germany created as a result of the financial crisis of public budgets and the economically problematic integration with the GDR, whose desperate economy became a hospital case for the FRG and drained an unknown amount of the public wealth. Cuts in public spending also led to much condemnation at the political level.

The fact that financial constraints also hit the media hard, where it was not just a topic to be covered but actually affected their own situation, meant that there was the possibility that media financed by advertising could have gone bankrupt at the beginning of the new millennium as a result of the economic crisis.

Economising in Media Production

In addition to this, newspaper firms and broadcasting companies in the 1990s had invested a lot of money in online ventures and so-called cross-media activity (a combination of print production and television programmes, and so on) and had put little money to one side in order to overcome crisis situations, which were always prone to occur and which had become noticeable after 2001. There had also been increasing competition between the national newspapers from as early as the 1990s, which had led to the situation where chief editors and owners spent their time headhunting prominent star journalists from one another. By the mid-1990s the 'main players' (Thomas Middelhoff and the Haffa brothers, according to Rudolf Augstein, Axel Springer and Gerd Buccerius) determined the course of the media industry (Pörksen, 2005: 11).

Following the economic crisis Bernhard Pörksen (2005) noted that 'the businessmen (Bernd Kundrun, Haim Saban)' were in control and they quote the chief editor of a specialist magazine: 'Almost all publishing houses are management-driven businesses, where irrationality has no place' (*ibid.*). This 'irrationality' is meant to signify an insistence on journalistic quality, on clear research, on original formulations and the development of journalist forms which are appropriate to the needs of society and the mood of the time.

The consequence of this was that in journalistic circles financial hard times were confronted with the *aim of reducing costs*. Whole editorial offices were integrated (for example, the editorial offices of the national newspaper *Die Welt* and the local newspaper *Berliner Morgenpost* were merged). In other press firms, cutbacks were carried out (for example, *Die Zeit* did away with its own media editorial office) but, above all, countless freelance staff were no longer able to work in their usual field.

As a consequence there was a *threat to quality journalism* as serious and investigative journalism costs money for research, careful preparation and presentation. Many freelance employees were forced to suffer as a result of the cutbacks, as described by the media journalist Peter Heinlein:

[On the one hand] fewer commissions were agreed because the budgets were dramatically reduced. As a result there were many attempts to resolve these problems internally. On the other hand the number of freelance workers increased and they would offer to work at vastly reduced prices in order to keep their names in print (Heinlein in Pörksen, 2005: 101).

The separation between 'clean' journalism and the influence of economic and other interests began to be eroded. On the one hand the distance between editorial information and advertising or PR-driven information was weakened. This breaking down of the limits, noted by Bernhard Pörksen and the journalism academic Walter Hömberg (1999), has pointed out that this has led to a situation where nowadays, under increasing time pressure, journalistic contributions must be compiled and a newspaper or programme filled, and this in turns leads the stronger journalists – often against their will –to fall back on pre-formulated text material from PR agencies. A domain has been established where a quasi-journalistic text and image production source contributes to the media and this is becoming increasingly extensive. According to information from the DPRG (Deutschen Public Relations Gesellschaft e.V.) – the association for PR companies – there are between 30,000 and 50,000 people working in this field. Journalists are sought here because they have the know-how required to smoothly feed interest-driven information into the media.

Uncritically used PR material is not only to be found in numerous reports – we hear often about events carried out especially for the purpose of media reporting – but there were also numerous scandals in 2005 about illegal product placement (even in programmes from public broadcast companies). The public debate has, however, led to new codes of honour being agreed and an increased level of vigilance sought.

On the other hand there have been numerous examples of the *crossing of the boundaries between literary and journalistic forms* which was seen as a very positive development by challenging paralysis of traditional journalistic forms. These marginal forms are often described as 'New Journalism' and are frequently well established in the field of soap operas (see Bleicher and Pörksen, 2004). As long as they were identified openly, they were largely unproblematic, but this was not always the case as, for example, when Tom Kummer carried out interviews which, although thought out in great detail, never occurred, or when the film-maker Nicolas Born produced news films about spectacular events so deceitfully that they were broadcast as news by the television companies.

The blending of opinion and factual information has also increased in recent years, although there have been fewer scandals reported about it. The public has, in the meantime, become accustomed to hearing and reading opinions, as often news programmes carry reports about the opinion of this or that politician, union representative or businessman regarding the facts of a situation. For this reason they are welcomed in the media as they save journalists from having to check complex content themselves.

This can also be seen in the argument formulated by the journalism researcher Siegfried Weischenberg:

> In any case journalists are pioneers who are changing the world of work: phenomena such as outsourcing, self-employed and instable working conditions and the tremendous

acceleration of business through information technology. The disappearance of entire professions such as the typesetter was experienced in this area much earlier than in other areas. To this extent it is an early warning system for the world of work (Weischenberg in Pörksen, 2005: 281).

The Influence of Digitalisation

The reaction to the economic downturn in the media, carried out with the emphasis on reducing costs, was (and still is) driven by the use of new technologies. The digitalisation of the media – as much in print as in broadcast on the level of production and sales – has led to radical changes such as the ending of whole types of work, the reduction in many journalistic control procedures and the shift of numerous production processes onto journalists, amongst many others.

Coupled with this, however, new job roles within journalism have grown up in the online and multimedia areas. Online editors process the output from many media organisations on to their homepages and 'links' sections. Designers devise user interfaces for online and offline offerings such as CDs. Multimedia authors prepare their contributions from scratch for different media; *information brokers* use offline and online media to research information on specialist subjects. The job fields expand, new profiles develop repeatedly in this already open domain of work and become part of the overall journalistic sphere of work.

Based on the results of a survey of journalists in 1993, the following was presented as a profile for a journalist:

> The typical German journalist is male, married, has completed a high-school education, is 37 years old, has worked for ten years as an editor for the same newspaper (eight and a half of these on a fixed contract): he works in one of the so-called classical departments, earns a net income of just 3900 DM per month (approximately 2450 Euros) and is involved with a trade union (*Sage & Schreibe*, 1995).

This profile has now largely lost its relevance. Freelance work is now dominant, as opposed to having a fixed contract; entry into the profession takes much longer; many high-school certificate holders lurch from work placement to work placement and nowadays many more women work as journalists. 'Flexibility' is becoming the watchword even in journalism, according to the prognosis of the cultural sociologist Richard Sennett (2005).

Politics and Journalistic Blends

There was also a change that occurred in the understanding of the roles of public politics and this change was created by the media. On the one hand, politics started to align itself more markedly with the media and to adapt to the media presentation norms and the requirement for telegenic presentation. This led to an increased entertainment slant within politics; prominent politicians appeared in entertainment programmes in order to gain viewers' support. On the other hand, politicians reacted in a hasty and ill-considered way when faced with the all-too-eager media spotlight. The political academic Thomas Meyer (2001) spoke of the development of a 'mediacracy' and the media academic Andreas Dörner described 'society's experience of politics' as 'politainment' (Dörner, 2001).

Whilst the staged production of politics was driven and supported by the media, some media companies decided on a firm policy of influencing political life. Determined reporting was thus undertaken against environmental politics and the social and employment policies of the Red/Green coalition of the Federal government. The Berlin editorial office of *Der Spiegel* took on a definite leaning towards neoliberalism by which it measured the government's performance. Some newspapers carry out targeted campaign journalism. Media are '… increasingly becoming political activists in their own right' (Schwan, 2005: 7).

The effect of economics-driven media can also be seen here. The President of the Europa University Viadrina in Frankfurt an der Oder described this process as follows:

> Media have to win their viewers and readers on a short-term basis and need news every day. Consistency becomes unimportant and scandal becomes a success criterion. Problematic trends thus emerge out of this, for example in the reporting on political reforms. Firstly the reforms are supported abstractly, then the real side-effects are criticised, technical conversion defects are bemoaned and before they come into being their failure has already been announced (Schwan, 2005: 7).

Future Prospects

What are the future prospects for journalism? As far as the numerous new forces are concerned, which range from digitalisation and economic imperatives to entertainment journalism, researcher Bernhard Pörksen has spoken of an *Entgrenzung* and has outlined these on four levels for the future. (By *Entgrenzung*, Pörksen means that media and journalism on an international level are subject to increased economic pressures and this threatens to break down traditional boundaries.) On a macro level of society this is couched in terms of an increase in press activity, the increasing power of the thinking behind audience and circulation, strict control of finances and the integration of media into a global entertainment industry. On the level of individual organisations there are fears of an *Entgrenzung* between the editorial office and the marketing department, and an increasing outside influence on reporting by PR and advertising agencies. On the micro level of direct interaction the results showed that journalistic core activities (researching, writing, editing, and so on) are being superseded by other activities and the journalist's perception of an event is more directed by economic considerations. On the level of texts it is noticeable that 'forms are becoming more flexible'. 'Hybrid forms which stem from primary, informative commentary and, above all, entertaining elements are increasing' (Pörksen, 2006: 76).

The head of the Henri-Nannen school, which trains journalists, has spoken of the need for a 'useful journalism' which is geared towards the interests of its readers and viewers (Fasel, 2005). It remains to be seen how this will be achieved by economically orientated media owners.

As a reaction to the penetration of PR information into journalism and in the context of scandals about product placement and other dishonest media influences, there have been many protests and an ongoing debate about the quality of journalism. An initiative involving many journalists was formed in early 2006 (<www. netzwerkrecherche.de>) and this has agreed a new ten-point code of conduct which speaks out much more strongly than the press code of honour against all forms of PR influence and refuses to grant journalist status to PR representatives.

Overall, the future prospects give no grounds for pessimism since 'it is not quality journalism which is in crisis but its economic basis' (Weischenberg in Pörksen, 2005: 282). New forms are being created as a result of journalism's reaction to these challenges – others are gaining in acceptance and are holding their ground. However, there exists a need for serious journalism that tackles public issues and the readiness of many journalists to provide it.

References

Bentele, G. et al. (2006), *Lexikon Kommunikations- und Medienwissenschaft* (Wiesbaden: VS Verlag).

Bleicher, J.K. and Pörksen, B. (eds) (2004), *Grenzgänger. Formen des New Journalism* (Wiesbaden: VS Verlag).

Blöbaum, B. (1994), *Journalismus als soziales System: Geschichte, Ausdifferenzierung und Verselbständigung* (Opladen: Westdeutscher Verlag).

Dörner, A. (2001), *Politainment. Politik in der medialen Erlebnisgesellschaft* (Frankfurt/M.: Suhrkamp).

Drews-Bernstein, C. (1973), 'Freie Mitarbeit bei Hörfunk und Fernsehen: die Arbeitnehmerähnlichen Unternehmer?', in Schmidt, H. (ed.) *Solidarität gegen Abhängigkeit. Mediengewerkschaft* (Neuwied: Luchterhand), 185–196.

Fasel, C. (2005), 'Zeitgeistmagazine haben keine Zukunft', *Tagesspiegel*, 22 October, 27.

Hickethier, K. (1998), *Geschichte des deutschen Fernsehens* (Stuttgart/Weimar: Metzler Verlag).

Hömberg, W. (1999), 'Journalismus und Journalistenausbildung in den vergangenen drei Jahrzehnten', in Belz, C., Haller, M. and Sellheim, A. (eds), *Berufsbilder im Journalismus. Von den alten zu den neuen Medien* (Konstanz: UVK), 17–30.

Koszyk, K. and Pruys, K.H. (1981), *Handbuch der Massenkommunikation* (München: DTV Verlag).

Meyer, T. (2001), *Mediokratie. Die Kolonisierung der Politik durch die Medien* (Frankfurt/M.: Suhrkamp).

Noelle-Neumann, E. et al. (eds) (1989), *Fischer Lexikon Publizistik Massenkommunikation* (Frankfurt/M.: Fischer).

Pörksen, B. (ed.) (2005), *Trendbuch Journalismus* (Köln: Halem Verlag).

Porksen, B. (2006), *Die Beobachtung des Beobachters. Eine Erkenntnistheorie der Journalistik* (Konstanz: UVK).

Sage & Schreibe (1995), special issue, June.

Scholl, A. and Weischenberg, S. (1998), *Journalismus in der Gesellschaft. Theorie, Methodologie und Empirie* (Opladen/Wiesbaden: Westdeutscher Verlag).

Schulze, G. (1992), *Die Erlebnisgesellschaft. Kultursoziologie der Gegenwart* (Frankfurt/M. and New York: Campus Verlag).

Schwan, G. (2005), 'Das aufgeklärte Publikum muss sich wehren', in *Frankfurter Rundschau*, 5 September, 7.

Sennett, R. (2005), *Die Kultur des neuen Kapitalismus* (Berlin: Berlin Verlag).

Chapter 13

Journalism in the United States of America

Heinz Brandenburg

Introduction

Contemplating the uniquely deregulated state of the US media market, the Harvard scholar Helen Shaw recently suggested that the US 'provides an international case history of the impact of the commoditisation of news' and 'now serves as a media laboratory to observe the challenge to democracy and information from ownership concentration' (Shaw, 2003: 2).

Among the advanced democracies, the US media landscape is clearly unique. Notwithstanding the emergence of a fringe element of public radio and broadcasting in recent decades (Rowland, 2002), it lacks a powerful public service provider which could put a restraint on the treatment of news as a commodity. However, neither the public, nor journalists or academics in the US would consider their domestic media landscape as necessarily deficient, or outright insufficient for a modern democracy.

Indeed, since the 1980s, when debates about deregulation and the abolition of public broadcasting monopolies began in Western Europe, the US 'media laboratory' has served as a normative model for neoliberal modernisers who promote a purely market-based system of information provision. A prototypical example of this argument can be found in Noam (1987), who proposed a public choice model of distributive broadcast policy. His objective was to predict programme diversity as a probability function of institutional structures, assuming a normal distribution of viewer preferences across a continuum ranging from 'low culture' to 'high culture'. He argued that the need for 'independent public-broadcast authorities, program regulation, and protectionist entry restrictions ... in order to assure quality programs declines as television program distribution ... enters the realm of regular economic-exchange transactions and leaves that of political allocation'. Computer-simulating the outcomes of different broadcast policies, from public service-oriented regulation to unregulated free markets, he concluded that those elite constituencies who care for high quality programming

> ... can be served by the market, where their economic strength generates consumption options which previously needed to be provided through the political system. Hence, the importance of politics in broadcast issues declines, because the redistributive role of the medium is less important than before (Noam, 1987: 164).

Noam essentially rephrases, in formal terms, the promise of the 'marketplace of ideas'. The virtually unrestrained commodification of news in the absence of a public service ideal is understood to be not just unproblematic, but indeed superior to what Noam defines as 'redistributive broadcast policy'.

The US 'media laboratory' provides us indeed with a fascinating test case that allows us to measure how much of its inherent promise the 'marketplace of ideas' is capable of delivering. To this end, this chapter proceeds in three steps. The first part describes key features of the US media landscape: its market structure, news treatment, its dominant paradigm of professional journalism, and the appropriation of 'freedom of the press' as a corporate right. The second part evaluates the impact of these structural properties of the media market on the content and nature of its commodity: the 'softness' of the news product, its range and depth, and the accessibility of balanced presentations of news to the average citizen, using among other sources survey data that allows us to gauge public opinion about the state of the US media and news quality. The third and final part discusses proposed remedies for alleged shortcomings of the US media system. These include re-evaluations of required news standards and the propagation of public or civic journalism.

What will not be found in this chapter is any detailed discussion of the role of the Internet in the US news media. This is not due to any ignoring of its specific functions and importance. Rather it would seem inappropriate to reiterate the data that has been presented already in Chapter 2 relating to the conclusions of the Pew Research Center, Van Dijk, and so on. What can be noted here simply is that the data discussed in the earlier chapter illustrates that, despite its enormous potential, the Internet, *in the way it is actually being used*, provides only limited compensation for the weaknesses in the traditional US news media that will be identified during the course of the analysis here.

The Marketplace of Ideas

When debating the current state of newsmaking in the US, it is important to note that the US Constitution was the first, and remains one of the few, to explicitly mention not just *freedom of speech* but with it *freedom of the press* as one of the quintessential features of democratic governance. The First Amendment states that 'Congress shall make no law ... abridging the freedom of speech, or of the press'. Some of the key controversies about media policy making revolve around interpretations of what the Founding Fathers intended by inserting 'freedom of the press' in the Constitution. The normative position is that freedom of the press is not an end in itself but a means to an end, the end being equal access to information and government accountability: 'Freedom of the press is a specific historical form and an extension of the individual's freedoms of thought and expression' (Splichal, 2002: 17).

According to Martin (2001: 168), the Founding Fathers 'defended the right to press liberty not for individual expression in our current, increasingly self-indulgent sense but rather so that the community might hear and judge the merit of others' views'. And the liberal critic of deregulation, Robert W. McChesney (2004) points to a frequent omission in one of Thomas Jefferson's most ubiquitous aphorisms: '[Were] it left to me to decide whether we should have a government without newspapers, or newspapers without government, I should not hesitate a moment to prefer the latter' (letter to Edward Carrington, 16 January 1787, quoted in McChesney, 2004: 29). McChesney suggests that while 'Jefferson's letter to Carrington is sometimes taken as arguing that the government should let private interests rule the press' (2004: 29), such an interpretation can only be sustained if one omits the immediately following passage, which states: '... but I should mean that every man should receive those papers, and be capable of reading them'.

The full reading of Jefferson's statement suggests that he considered a functioning, universally accessible system of information provision and public debate a more necessary condition for democratic governance than an elected government itself, and ultimately even a sufficient one. Such normative views on press freedom are also reflected in initiatives undertaken by the Founding Fathers to subsidise the press: 'Public policy from the outset of the American Republic focused explicitly on getting the news to a wide readership, and chose to support news outlets by taking on costs of delivery, and, through printers' exchanges, of production' (Cook, 1998: 44).

However, already early in the twentieth century, media corporations began to dispute the conditional nature of press freedom, instead using it as a legalistic tool to evade public regulation. In her history of press business practices and federal regulation thereof between 1880 and 1920, Lawson (1993) describes how the American Newspaper Publishers Association (ANPA), founded in 1887, went to the Supreme Court in 1912 to challenge the Newspaper Publicity Act of the same year, which required explicit listings of owners and editors as well as separation of advertising from news content in order for newspapers to qualify for postal subsidies. Although the Supreme Court ultimately rejected this legal challenge, the case remains nonetheless notable, since it was the first time in US legal history that First Amendment rights were brought to bear against such government regulation. This illustrates a tendency described by Splichal (2002: 9–10), which is to 'give preference to the concept of press freedom as a corporate right over the individual freedom to publish'.

Ever since this first appropriation of the concept by a press association to justify the business demands of media operations, freedom of the press has become increasingly disassociated from its intended constitutional purpose, namely to provide the public with equal access to information and diversity of political debate. If 'news is a business' (Papper, 2005) and 'like all other business, newspapers, radio stations, and television stations are out to make money' (Applegate, 1996: 17f.), then the constitutional principle of freedom of the press opens itself for reinterpretation – from being understood as a means to an end to becoming an end itself, namely the absence (or minimisation) of market regulation. While reinterpreting the constitutional principle, proponents of deregulation do not, however, renounce the validity of normative principles like the 'public interest'. For example, the former chairman of the Federal Communications Commission (FCC), Michael Powell, who resigned in 2005, has on the one hand repeatedly stated that business logic should drive the process of media regulation: 'Government policy needs to follow the rule of capital and investment, not always the other way around.' But he has also tended to evoke normative justifications for treating freedom of the press as a corporate right: 'The public interest works with letting the market work its magic. [...] This abundance means more programming, more choice and more control in the hands of citizens' (quoted in McChesney, 2004: 260).

Uses of the *marketplace of ideas* metaphor are just as ambivalent as interpretations of the constitutional principle of freedom of the press. According to Napoli (1999), we can distinguish between interpretations from democratic and economic theory perspectives. Democratic theory interpretations, which can be traced back to John Milton and John Stuart Mill, 'typically have been associated with calls for ... regulation', while economic theory interpretations 'typically have been associated with arguments against government regulation of the communications industry' (*ibid.*: 151f.). Using content analysis of FCC decisions from the mid-1960s to the late 1990s, Napoli shows how the activities of the FCC moved from arguing the case for regulation during the 1970s to increasingly championing the case for deregulation since the Reagan administration (*ibid.*: 161f.). This has been accompanied by increasing dominance of the economic uses of the marketplace of ideas metaphor, which eventually during the 1990s became the almost unchallenged line of argumentation within the FCC (*ibid.*: 163). Deregulation has become the prerogative of FCC activity over the past 30 years, and democratic uses of the marketplace of ideas metaphor have taken on the function of occasionally evoked corollaries to the predominant economic justification.

> [T]he degree to which the Commission's use of the metaphor has acknowledged both the marketplace of ideas' political and economic effects contrasts sharply with a growing body of research suggesting that the FCC's analytical resources and energies are devoted almost exclusively to the effects of its decisions in the economic realm (Napoli, 1999: 165).

There is an inherent problem, if not an outright contradiction, in the argument that economic freedom of the press (that is, deregulation) is also in the public interest. The traditional pro-business public interest argument states that competition results in diversity, and indeed that the market will outperform any redistributive media policy in covering the democratic need for information provision (Noam, 1987: 183). However, deregulation since the 1980s has predominantly been aimed at enabling media mergers, like the ones between AOL and Time Warner, or CBS and Viacom in recent years, and allowing more concentrated media ownership within local markets. The obvious outcome of deregulation is a trend towards oligopolistic market structures. And since classic economic supply and demand functions no longer operate in oligopolistic markets, formal models of information provision, like that of Noam (1987), which assume perfect markets and deduce predictions about increased product diversity, fail to apply. Then FCC chairman Michael Powell did acknowledge this tendency during the debates about a further relaxation of market concentration rules in 2003. He even tried to argue that market concentration not only avoids being detrimental to information provision, but also may have beneficial consequences for citizens: 'Monopoly is not illegal by itself in the United States. People tend to forget this. There is something healthy about letting innovators try to capture markets' (quoted in McChesney, 2004: 260).

The US media market is indeed highly concentrated, in terms of both horizontal and vertical integration. Horizontal integration refers to the acquisition of competing brands in order to increase the share within one particular market. Vertical integration denotes the merging between different media, or the owning of not just the media product but also the production facilities. The result is the emergence of competitors like Viacom, News Corporation, Disney, Time Warner or General Electric who are becoming major players in different media sectors. A *New York Times* article in 2003 pointed out that the above-mentioned five largest media corporations 'were each major players in more than seven [...] media sectors – encompassing film, radio, TV, cable, music, theme parks, and publishing' (McChesney, 2004: 182).

The US media sector is a good example of how quickly, and seemingly unavoidably, profitable markets become characterised by concentration. Once the newspaper business became seriously profitable in the first few decades of the twentieth century, the average number of daily newspapers per local market shrank dramatically. Emery and Emery (1996: 293) found that whereas before 1920 only around 40 per cent of daily newspapers in the US had no competitor in their market, this number had risen to around 80 per cent by 1930. Hence, in addition to the oligopolistic structure of national markets, the US media system is also characterised by monopolies in many local markets. This is also the case in local television and radio markets. In the latter, Clear Channel increased its market share from ownership of around 500 local stations in early 1999 to 1,200 across 185 local markets by mid-2000, which amounts to twice as many stations as the nearest three competitors together and a presence in exactly as many markets as the nearest three competitors combined (PEJ, 2005: Radio/Ownership). In general, market concentration has dramatically increased since the Telecommunication Act of 1996, which allowed for widespread deregulation. Waterman (2000) reports that the combined annual revenues of the six largest media corporations, which had risen only modestly from $8 billion to $23 billion between 1977 and 1997, suddenly leapt dramatically in the next year to $85 billion (see also Williams, 2002: 455f.).

This process of market concentration and conglomeration has tangible consequences for newsmaking: it necessitates the prevalence of professional journalism and the objectivity norm, and furthers the commodification of news.

Professional Journalism

A, if not the, defining characteristic of American journalism is its commitment to objectivity in reporting, which 'still today distinguishes US journalism from the dominant model of continental European journalism' (Schudson, 2001: 149). This is not to say that European reporters are not observing the basic attributes of journalistic objectivity, like accuracy, fairness and truthfulness. The difference is that, according to Donsbach (1995) and Schudson (2001), in US journalistic culture, objectivity amounts to a moral code, which demands the strict separation of news from editorial opinion and avoidance of political bias in reporting. From a normative point of view, professional journalism embodies the democratic version of the marketplace of ideas notion, where newspapers offer accessible information in unadulterated form, on the basis of which rational individuals can engage in public deliberation (Applegate, 1996: 32; Miraldi, 1990: 140f.).

The American Society of Newspaper Editors adopted in their founding convention in 1923 a journalistic Code of Ethics, which declared: 'News reports should be free from opinion or bias of any kind' (quoted in Schudson, 2001: 162).

At the same time, journalism was becoming a serious profession, taught at academic journalism schools. Schudson also points out that from the 1930s onwards, 'publishers could use the objectivity norm as a weapon against unionisation in the newsroom (how could a reporter be "objective" if he joined the Newspaper Guild?)' (2001: 163).

The objectivity norm becomes instrumental, and a justificatory necessity, in news markets that are bereft of competition. If there is only one provider of news, as is the case in the vast majority of local newspaper markets in the US, this provider has to subscribe to the norm of objectivity and professionalism, since partisan tendencies cannot be balanced out in the absence of diversity. In turn, the dominance of professional journalism in US news markets may explain why newsmakers do not appear to rate diversity as an important value in the public sphere. Indeed, we find that, in debates about media convergence, media practitioners tend to take the view that the merging of different news operations (press, cable, online, and so on) in joint media centres is entirely beneficial, since it allows making optimal use of scarce resources (Bradley, 2003; Thelen, 2003). Also, diversity is not required since news is no longer considered contentious or political in nature. In the world of professional journalism and media conglomerates, news has become redefined as 'journalism-based products', reducing the citizen to the status of 'news consumer' (Bradley, 2003: 519).

The News Market and its Product Qualities

Once news is defined as a sellable commodity, the essence of professional journalism – the objectivity norm – becomes an inescapable characteristic of news, irrespective of whether its emergence reflects normative concerns of journalists or not. Rather than functioning as an appraisal of the democratic function of journalism, objectivity (fairness and balance) has become a trademark. And, as a trademark, it is bereft of substance and opens itself to re-definition, as most notoriously illustrated by Fox News and its claim to provide 'fair and balanced' news coverage. Fox News, as well as predominantly conservative talk radio (Barker, 2002), uses partisan slant as a sales strategy. It should, however, be pointed out that Fox News not just 'parodies the idea of impartiality by branding itself "fair and balanced news"' (Shaw, 2003: 15), it effectively positions itself in the news market by implying that its tendency to give space to conservative viewpoints serves (a) as a counter-balance to the allegedly pervasive liberal bias in the mainstream media[1] and (b) to make it representative of (alleged) majority viewpoints amongst the non-intellectual, and not necessarily liberal, American public. In that sense, Fox News goes beyond parodying the notion of impartiality. It either defines itself as the remedy to the US media's traditionally tilted and hence not impartial presentation of reality, which would mean that its right-wing slant creates overall fairness and balance. Or else, and this is perhaps the more likely (and indeed more worrying) proposition, Fox News redefines fairness and balance as a question of being fair to one's audience rather than to the subject matter of reporting.

'Trademark' objectivity is, however, not only problematic because it is conducive to redefinitions. In the mainstream media (that is, network television and the article sections of broadsheet newspapers), the commitment to professional standards generates shortcomings of a different nature. Most notably, professional journalism takes news out of context. The commodity character of news has a significant role to play in this process. Whereas from a normative point of view, an individual news story has a functional value, in that it contributes to a citizen's breadth and depth of information and hence his or her willingness and ability to form opinions and to participate, from a business perspective as well as from the viewpoint of professional journalistic ambition, the news story itself, and its narrative value, are of primary interest. Both the sellable qualities of a news story, and the extent to which a journalist can gain peer recognition from it, depend on the properties of the story itself, not on how it fits into the larger picture of political, social or economic structures and developments. Miraldi (1990) and Entman (1993) have both emphasised how 'episodic framing' dominates news production, at the expense of thematic frames. Story-driven news production also tends to emphasise conflict, because of its dramatic qualities and its amenability to balanced, two-sided coverage.

In the realm of political news, the joint effect of episodic framing and emphasis on conflict, in combination with the commitment to objectivity, is to depoliticise matters of potentially great public concern. Glasser (1992: 176) has argued that objective reporting 'is against independent thinking; it emasculates the intellect by

---

1   The alleged 'liberal media bias', which has produced little if any systematic evidence in support of the general hypothesis (see D'Alessio and Allen, 2000 for an overview), is a widespread claim and finds constant repetition in the US media. Conducting a Lexis-Nexis search, Niven (2002) found over 600 news items referring to political bias. Of those, 81 per cent were arguing the case of a liberal bias, while only 5 per cent debated the possibility of an overall conservative or pro-Republican bias. This treatment of a not very well substantiated hypothesis in the US media has effects on the public, as polls conducted by the Pew Research Center for the People and the Press (PEJ, 2005: Network TV/Public Attitudes) and repeated Gallup polls since 2001 have found (Gallup News Service, 23 September 2004).

treating it as a disinterested spectator'. Questions of healthcare reform or defence spending receive treatment by the US media largely not with regard to the subject matter under debate, but predominantly with regard to how majorities form on these issues, what the strategies of the protagonists are, and so on. On the one hand, this presents politics as an arena where public concerns are played for partisan advantage, which, according to some scholars, triggers or at least reinforces public cynicism about politics and politicians (Capella and Jamieson, 1997). On the other hand, it undermines the civic usefulness of the news product, because it emphasises story value over information value. This argument is also corroborated by Slattery et al. (2001) who provide empirical evidence for the presence of 'embedded sensationalism'; this means that while coverage of government and policy matters still dominates television news, they found increasing human-interest elements in how these institutions and issues are brought to public attention. Embedded sensationalism (that is, 'a visual portrayal or detailed verbal description of a topic that, taken alone, would be coded as sensationalism and/or human interest' (*ibid.*: 294)) was present in only 10.7 per cent of government stories in 1968, but in 29.7 per cent of such stories in 1996 (*ibid.*: 297, Table 2).

Economic necessities, despite or sometimes even in conjunction with professional attitudes, can generate two additional forms of bias or distortion: covert propaganda and synergy bias.

Covert Propaganda

Bagdikian (2000), Cunningham (2003) and McChesney (2004) all point to the tendency among professional journalists to try and remove suspicions about story selection bias by turning to official sources. Necessarily, this reduces the subjects of public debate to those selected by political elites. Sourcing of stories becomes paramount, since it is not the integrity of the journalist but the nature of the source that lends credibility to news content. This aspect of professional journalism is congenially supplanted by the drive for economical ways of undertaking news production. As McManus (1994) and Curtin (1999) have argued, the most economic means of engaging in story selection and story production is that of passive discovery, which is accomplished through the use of information subsidies (in other words, press releases). Although the vast majority of journalists would claim that they refrain from using press releases, empirical studies like that of Curtin (1999) show that, inadvertently or in indirect fashion, journalists quite regularly rely on source material to generate and structure their reports.

Successive US governments, and none more so than the Bush administration, have become increasingly adept at exploiting this reliance on prefabricated source material. In early October 2005, the Government Accountability Office found that the government 'repeatedly violated federal law by trying to sway public opinion using "covert propaganda" at taxpayer expense' (*St. Petersburg Times*, Florida, 12 October 2005). Quoted violations included the use of 'video news releases' (that is, prefabricated news stories which generally fail to indicate the government as source); employment of an advertising agency to monitor the amount of positive and negative news coverage; and funding of positive coverage through payments from government departments to journalists like Armstrong Williams. In response, the US Senate Committee on Commerce, Science and Transportation unanimously voted in favour of a 'Prepackaged News Story Announcement Act', which 'requires that all prepackaged, government-produced news stories – which are designed to be indistinguishable from those created by independent news organisations – include disclaimers notifying the audience that the government produced or funded the news segment' (*States News Service*, 20 October 2005; see also *US Fed News*, 20 October 2005). Previously, the government had repeatedly claimed that, as long as news stories are factual, there should be no requirement to notify about the originator (*The New York Times*, 1 October 2005).

The website <prwatch.org> regularly monitors the practice of video news release (VNR) usage, and reported in its quarterly journal in summer 2004 that VNRs were typically being sent in two versions, a fully edited version for immediate broadcasting, and an unedited version that allowed customisation by the broadcasters. Certainly, the professional credo of American journalists will, in many instances, encourage them to avoid using prefabricated press releases or VNR without some substantial form of editing. But their general reliance on official sourcing opens the door for this type of propaganda strategy. With increasing economic pressures, especially on less well-resourced local media, the practice of broadcasting this material unedited becomes more frequent.

Synergy Bias

The influence of media owners on the editorial line or the content of news products remains a potential source of bias, notwithstanding the nominal insistence on a church–state type of division between business interests and newsgathering rationale and practice. Ownership-induced political bias, epitomised by Rupert Murdoch, who has frequently been accused of interfering in editorial decision making (McChesney, 2004: 24, 115), constitutes a relatively obvious and straightforward challenge to the objectivity norm. A different form of bias derives from economic interests, in particular within growing and increasingly diversified media conglomerates. All of the major networks in the US, as well as cable channels, radio stations and newspapers, are by now not just part of large, horizontally and vertically integrated media corporations, but indeed are elements of vast corporations, within which news production is but a marginal subdivision. Corporations like Disney, Viacom, Bertelsmann or Time Warner have business interests, for the pursuit of which the ownership of a news division can be quite instrumental. Anecdotal evidence points to the deliberate use of news media to covertly advertise products of their parent company. For example, 'the May 20, 1996 cover of *Time* featured a movie still of Time-Warner's *Twister* for a science story on tornadoes, coinciding with the movie's release' (Williams, 2002: 457). In similar vein, Disney used its network ownership of ABC to celebrate its own 25th anniversary during morning news programmes (*The New York Times*, 27 March 2000).

This phenomenon is understood as 'synergy', which is a business concept implying that cooperation of different parts of a company can maximise productivity and hence profit margins. Williams (2002: 456) argues that 'synergy is often the point of many conglomerate mergers where the strengths of one company or division complement the other'. The value of news divisions for conglomerates is their potential to generate exposure and credibility that cannot be achieved through advertising, and, most importantly, some control over the inclusion/exclusion of policy matters with serious implications for business in/from the news agenda. Williams (2002) investigates the placement of promotional items in newscasts, while arguing that the second form of synergy bias, 'the omission of items' (*ibid.*: 456), is notoriously difficult to investigate.

However, a prime example of synergy bias in the form of omission is at least partly traceable, namely the media handling of the FCC's intended rule changes in 2003, which proposed to Congress lifting the ban on cross-ownership, permitting corporations to purchase two to three TV stations in markets, depending on size, and allowing increased market coverage to over 40 per cent of the American public (see documentation on <www.journalism.org> or in McChesney, 2004: 285). Naturally,

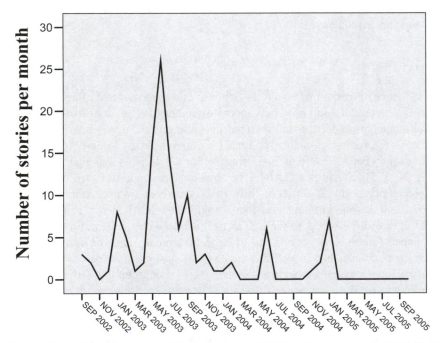

Figure 13. 1 Combined monthly coverage of FCC rule changes in *USA Today*, *The New York Times* and *The Washington Post*

the largest media conglomerates in the US were also the key lobbyists for the FCC rule changes. Undoubtedly, this generates a conflict of interests for their news divisions. Public opinion in the US tends to be suspicious about media concentration, but at the same time few Americans are aware of the exact corporate structure of their media landscape. Hence, the key strategy of lobbyists, as well as of FCC chairman Michael Powell, who was strongly in favour of further deregulation, was to keep a low profile. And so did the news media. A Lexis-Nexis search for varying search terms including 'FCC', 'deregulation' and 'Powell' in three of the largest and most reputable US daily newspapers, *USA Today*, *The New York Times*, and *The Washington Post*, reveals that a total of 135 stories appeared in those three papers over a three-year period between September 2002 (when the biennial review of FCC rules was announced for the coming year) and September 2005. That amounts to an average of just over one story per newspaper per month, quite evenly distributed across the three papers. *The New York Times* ran a total of 56 stories, with *USA Today* only producing 37 articles in the sample period. We cannot read too much into these totals, other than that they appear low; but this might simply be explained by the argument that this is a highly bureaucratic issue that does not generate much audience appeal. The data become somewhat more interesting once we look at the distribution of stories over time during those three years (see Figure 13.1). The curve has one clear peak with 25 stories, which occurred in June 2003, when the rule changes were officially announced. There are smaller peaks, for example in January 2003, when the dissenting Democrats on the FCC board called town hall meetings to debate the proposals; in September 2003, when Congress first rejected financial resources for implementation of the rule changes; in June 2004 when Congress eventually repealed the rule changes; and again in January 2005 when the Supreme Court rejected an appeal against the Congressional ruling. In between, we find little coverage if any.

This is quite notable, given the amount of public interest and engagement. Between June and September 2003, the FCC and members of Congress received over three million emails, almost invariably voicing opposition to the proposals. The town hall meetings also ran the entire period between January and June 2003, while Congress was debating the issues repeatedly between September 2003 and January 2004 (again, see documentation on <www.journalism.org> or see McChesney, 2004: 252–97).

For once, this illustrates the reliance of media on official sources and authority-induced media events. Only when political or legal decisions were actually taken did the media report. But furthermore, it reveals the lacklustre way in which the American news media approached an issue that they preferred not to talk about, because of the vested interests of their parent corporations.

Trust in Journalism and Satisfaction with News Content

Americans no longer appear to regard the objectivity norm of professional journalism to be in operation. Decreasing levels of trust in almost all types of media accompany this. Interestingly, among cable and network TV, Fox News is the only channel that has seen an increase in public trust between 2002 and 2004 (PEJ, 2005: Network TV/Public Attitudes). ABC News, CBS News, NBC News, CNN and MSNBC have seen a steady erosion of public trust since 2000. An enduring downward trend can be witnessed for the traditional news operators – newspapers, local television and network TV. Since the mid-1980s, the percentage of the population that voiced trust in local or national television journalism has decreased by 10 per cent – from 32 per cent in 1985 to 22 per cent in 2004 (PEJ, 2005: Local TV/Public Attitudes). Perceived 'believability' of newspaper reporting has seen the most dramatic erosion. In 1985, 80 per cent of survey respondents said that they believed all or most of what they read in their daily newspaper. This number dropped to 50 per cent in 2004 (PEJ, 2005: Newspapers/Public Attitudes).

Not only are American citizens becoming less satisfied with the services they receive from their news media than they have been in earlier periods, but there is also mounting evidence that they are not being well supplied with information, resulting in low levels of political knowledge. This has always been a pervasive problem of American politics, already noted in the earliest election studies (Berelson et al., 1954). Most recent evidence shows that, whether with regard to the Iraq war (Kull, 2003) or the US presidential election in 2004 (Pew Research Center for the People and the Press, 2004: 6; PEJ, 2005: Local TV/Public Attitudes), in particular those who rely on Fox News or on local television as their principal source of news tend to lack knowledge or to have the most frequent misperceptions. Regular PBS (public service broadcasting) viewers are most knowledgeable and are dramatically less likely to have political misperceptions (Kull, 2003: 13), but they form a tiny minority of the American public.

Effects of Competition and Concentration on News Content

When we are finding little public satisfaction with, and insufficient information gains from, consuming products that the news market provides, this raises some doubts about theoretical (Noam, 1987) or political arguments that 'abundance means more programming, more choice and more control in the hands of citizens' (former FCC chairman Powell, quoted in Rosen, 2000).

Noam's (1987) argument that free market competition will increase diversity, and provide at least as much high-quality programming as a public monopoly, can, and has been repeatedly, put to the test. Deregulation tends to lead to market concentration and hence reduces diversity. And there is indeed little evidence to suggest that market concentration, for example in local TV markets, has led to an improvement in news quality. The Project for Excellence in Journalism's (PEJ) 'Annual report on American journalism' on <www.journalism.org> reports that 'growing ownership consolidation' has actually led to 'an expanding workload, often without expanding resources'. As a result, 'the use of so-called feed material' has increased. In general, their assessment of the current state of local television, one of the most highly concentrated US media markets, is bleak:

> Against this background, many newsrooms gradually converged on a style that might be called the 'hook and hold' approach. The approach, which is reinforced by the tendency of local TV news personnel to shuffle from market to market for career reasons, has led to a style of news that is predictable from one market to the next and even from one station to the next, and may defy even the desire of station managers and news executives to change. It has also caused some viewers to give up on local TV news altogether. [...]

> The 'hook and hold' approach is a mindset about what viewers want that imparts a surprisingly static, formulaic structure to most local newscasts. The approach begins with a natural desire to hook viewers at the start. [...] The result is that the stories that lead newscasts turn out to be in a notably narrow range of topics, mostly incident-based [...] made up of crime accidents, fires and disasters (PEJ, 2005: Local TV/Content Analysis).

A further element of concern to the researchers of the PEJ was the disappearance of the reporter in local news. They found that 'a reporter's appearance in a story is a predictor of quality', in so far as when reporters are presenting stories onscreen, they are likely to present various points of view about the subject matter, hence providing a 'connection between packages and the depth of reporting' (*ibid.*).

One of the core findings of the PEJ report was that 'the trajectory increasingly is towards those [models of journalism] that are faster, looser and cheaper' (PEJ, 2005: Overview). For the most part, 'faster, looser and cheaper' do not sit easily alongside quality in terms of news production values. Many of these trends in local television can be linked to the increased reliance of local broadcasters on outside consultants. The use of consultants and their market research has led to homogenisation of the news product and its presentation, prompting some local TV journalists to complain that consultants 'are almost telling news organisations what kind of news people want to hear' (Aucoin and Jurkowitz, 1999).

Network television and newspaper journalism still prove to be more substantive, better and more transparently and diversely sourced than cable, radio or local TV news. This is very interesting, since we find a substantially inverse relationship between journalistic quality and believability. The public considers print media (including *The New York Times*, *The Wall Street Journal* and *Time*) to be less believable than any cable TV channel, or indeed local TV. Local TV news is rated believable by 59 per cent of respondents, only trailing NBC News, *60 Minutes*, and CNN in terms of believability (PEJ, 2005: Newspapers/Public Attitudes). Hence, perceived believability generally does not reflect news quality, as measured by the PEJ.

Two Problem-solving Strategies

Rethinking Whether Sinking News Quality Poses a Problem

Patterson is one of the many US media scholars to worry about the rise of soft news, fearing that a decrease in depth and quality of coverage may lead to a further weakening of a democracy which is already scoring low in terms of participation and trust in public institutions (Patterson, 2000). While acknowledging that 'public affairs reporting in the United States has never been impressively sophisticated, and it has now gotten noticeably less so', Zaller (2003) argues that, 'the full news standard makes unrealistically heavy demands on many citizens' (*ibid.*: 110). The 'full news standard' is a concept that assumes a requirement of high levels of information, especially in the face of political dealignment. The more independent a voter becomes, the more evaluative his or her decision should be. High levels of information should hence allow independent and rational decision making. However, as Zaller points out, high levels of political information are strongly correlated with partisanship. And since floating voters are traditionally less informed, 'raising the bar on news quality is likely to result in a situation in which swing voters acquire even less information than they now do' (*ibid.*: 116f.). Accordingly, Zaller proposes a functioning model of modern American democracy in which citizens rely on the media to act as 'burglar alarms'. This means that the job of journalists is to bring urgent problems to the attention of citizens, while not bothering and boring the voter with too large a range of policy questions. Citizens become selectively informed, and therefore spend most of their media-consumption time prioritising between the stories competing for their attention.

> The standard of news coverage I advocate can now be expressed as follows: journalists should routinely seek to cover non-emergency but important issues by means of coverage that is intensely focused, dramatic and entertaining and that affords the parties and responsible interest groups, especially political parties, ample opportunity for expression of opposing views. Reporters may use simulated drama to engage public attention when the real thing is absent.
>
> The name for the standard is the Burglar Alarm standard. As with a real burglar alarm, the idea is to call attention to matters requiring urgent attention, and to do so in excited and noisy tones (Zaller, 2003: 122).

By this token, the distinction between soft and hard news becomes blurred, since the soft news standard largely relates to the presentation of news (human interest), and not necessarily to the subject matter. Even serious policy questions of healthcare or foreign affairs can be brought to the attention of citizens in the attractive packaging of soft news. This is also an argument repeatedly put forward by Baum (2002, 2003, 2004) and Prior (2003), who claim that entertainment-seeking audiences can incidentally be exposed to high-profile political issues, foreign and domestic.

Graber (2003) supports the 'burglar alarm' model, also pointing out that extraordinary events, like the 2000 election recount, 9/11 or the Iraq war, lead to increased public interest in political matters, and also that 'media coverage of the complex aspects' of such crucial and extraordinary events tends to become 'far more detailed and analytical than during less critical times' (*ibid.*: 148).

Going Public (or Civic)

Such re-evaluation of information standards is a recent trend in communication research. The majority of American scholars, media critics and journalists themselves tend to hold on to the assertion that public knowledge is woeful, that it is so woeful because it is badly served by the mass media, and that this insufficient information provision is a result of the commodification of news. Some, like McChesney (2004) and Rowland (2002), propose that public broadcasting could help alleviate the problem by providing more solid information and also by challenging the standards of journalism in commercial media, if only it were funded as well as the BBC in Britain or public service in general in Western Europe.

In the absence of Congressional willingness and the fact that public support for expanding public broadcasting is low and unlikely to grow, a recent tendency in US debates has been to question the professional model of journalism. One of the problems with professional journalism is clearly the deliberate detachment from subject matters as well as from audiences. Proponents of *public (or civic) journalism* propagate a rethink, which should start by 'seeing people as citizens rather than spectators, readers, viewers, listeners, or an undifferentiated mass' (Rosen, 2000: 680). The role of a public journalist is then to identify 'issues of public concern through direct inquiry with citizens', which turn the journalist and, indeed, the news organisation into 'a kind of switching device' by framing the news 'in a way that invites people into civic activity and political conversation' (*ibid.*). Talking from a normative perspective that aims to redefine the role of journalism in traditional democratic terms, Rosen advocates an experimental approach, in which the journalist tries to go beyond the usual newsgathering routines, to write an engaging, civic-minded and constructive report that 'starts with the citizen' (*ibid.*: 681). The aim is to derive the electoral agenda from public concerns rather than the public relations efforts of the media. Rosen refers to this as experimentation 'with a citizen agenda' (*ibid.*: 682).

A problem with public journalism is, according to Glasser (2000), that it undermines its normative intent by remaining theoretically underdeveloped. It is primarily propagated by practitioners – journalists and editors – and implemented as common practice in newsrooms without journalists being properly introduced to the meaning, practices, goals and standards of public journalism. The majority of US broadcast and print journalists and editors emerge from journalism schools where they are trained according to the standards of professional journalism. Public journalism sometimes appears as a conversion movement.

Even more critical, according to Glasser, is the tendency to substitute 'the community's judgement, however defined, for the judgement of journalists' (2000: 684). In that sense, public journalism is similar to calls for direct democracy, which are also based on the empirically unsupported claim that public judgement is 'good judgement' and thereby generally preferable to professional, political or journalistic judgement.

Conclusions

It cannot be denied that professional journalism in the US is in a deep crisis. Fox News has been successful, not just in attracting viewers but also in challenging the traditional norm that journalistic objectivity consists of fair and balanced treatment of news subjects. Fox News has generated demand for fair and balanced treatment of audience opinions, beliefs and values instead. As can be seen from polls reported earlier (PEJ, 2005), tendentious reporting on Fox News, as well as commercialised, homogenised, human-interest-driven local news reporting, score equal or higher in terms of believability with the general public than do the traditional vestiges of professional journalism, network television and the broadsheets.

Commodification of news has succeeded in undermining the essential normative purpose of journalism, namely to provide the public with information. News content tends to be no longer publicly judged in terms of its informational value, but in terms of its potential to satisfy consumption patterns. Professional journalism in its current form is rather part of the problem than part of any solution. Neither public cynicism nor withdrawal from informational content can be counteracted by producing 'higher-quality journalism-based products'. In the light of the absence of a strong public service element in US journalism, and, as was pointed out earlier, the failure of the Internet to provide adequate compensation for the myriad failings of US news journalism, it must remain doubtful how large elements of the public may rediscover the usefulness of being informed. And since we can expect little commercial interest in the de-commodification of news and journalism, the marketplace of ideas may be rather incapable of self-regulating this problem.

References

Applegate, E. (1996), *Print and Broadcast Journalism, A Critical Examination* (Westport CT and London: Praeger).

Aucoin, D. and Jurkowitz, M. (1999), 'Outside consultants play a key role in shaping broadcasts', *Boston Globe*. Available at <http://www.personal.kent.edu/~glhanson/readings/tv%20news/bglobe.htm>.

Bagdikian, B.H. (2000), *The Media Monopoly*, 6th edition (Boston MA: Beacon Press).

Barker, D.C. (2002), *Rushed to Judgment. Talk Radio, Persuasion, and American Political Behavior* (New York: Columbia University Press).

Baum, M.A. (2002), 'Sex, lies, and war: how soft news brings foreign policy to the inattentive public', *American Political Science Review* 96 (1), 91–109.

Baum, M.A. (2003), 'Soft news and political knowledge: evidence of absence or absence of evidence?', *Political Communication* (20), 173 90.

Baum, M.A. (2004), 'Circling the wagons: soft news and isolationism in American public opinion', *International Studies Quarterly* (48), 313–38.

Berelson, B., Lazarsfeld, P.O. and McPhee, W.N. (1954), *Voting* (Chicago IL: University of Chicago Press).

Bradley, D. (2003), 'Convergence: a survival strategy for local media', *Journalism Studies* 4 (4), 518–21.

Capella, J.N. and Jamieson, K.H. (1997), *Spiral of Cynicism: The Press and the Public Good* (New York: Oxford University Press).

Cook, T.E. (1998), *Governing with the News: The News Media as a Political Institution* (Chicago IL: University of Chicago Press).

Cunningham, B. (2003), 'Rethinking objectivity', *Columbia Journalism Review* (4). Available at <http://www.cjr.org/issues/2003/4/objective-cunningham.asp>.

Curtin, P. (1999), 'Reevaluating public relations information subsidies: market-driven journalism and agenda-building theory and practice', *Journal of Public Relations Research* 11 (1), 53–90.

D'Alessio, D. and Allen, M. (2000), 'Media bias in presidential elections: a meta-analysis', *Journal of Communication* 50 (4), 133–56.

Donsbach, W. (1995), 'Lapdogs, watchdogs and junkyard dogs', *Media Studies Journal* 9 (Fall), 17–30.

Emery, M. and Emery, E. (1996), *The Press and America: An Interpretive History of the Mass Media* (Boston MA: Allyn & Bacon).

Entman, R.M. (1993), 'Framing: towards clarification of a fractured paradigm', *Journal of Communication* 43 (4), 51–8.

Glasser, T.L. (1992), 'Objectivity and News Bias', in Cohen, E.D. (ed.), *Philosophical Issues in Journalism* (New York: Oxford University Press).

Glasser, T.L. (2000), 'The politics of public journalism', *Journalism Studies* 1 (4), 683–6.

Graber, D.A. (2003), 'The rocky road to new paradigms: modernizing news and citizenship standards', *Political Communication* (20), 145–8.

Kull, S. (2003), 'Misperceptions, the media and the Iraq war', Program on International Policy Attitudes (PIPA), Knowledge Networks Poll: The American Public on International Issues. Available at <http://www.pipa.org/OnlineReports/ Iraq/IraqMedia_Oct03/IraqMedia_Oct03_rpt.pdf>.

Lawson, L. (1993), *Truth in Publishing: Federal Regulation of the Press's Business Practices, 1880–1920* (Carbondale IL: Southern Illinois University Press).

McChesney, R.W. (2004), *The Problem of the Media. U.S. Communication Politics in the 21st Century* (New York: Monthly Review Press).

McManus, J. (1994), *Market-Driven Journalism: Let the Citizen Beware?* (Thousand Oaks CA: Sage).

Martin, R.W.T. (2001), *The Free and Open Press: The Founding of American Democratic Press Liberty, 1640–1800* (New York: New York University Press).

Miraldi, R. (1990), *Muckraking and Objectivity: Journalism's Colliding Traditions*

(Westport CT: Greenwood Press).

Napoli, P.M. (1999), 'The marketplace of ideas metaphor in communications regulation', *Journal of Communication* 49 (4), 151–69.

Niven, D. (2002), *Tilt? The Search for Media Bias* (Westport CT: Greenwood Press).

Noam, E.M. (1987), 'A public and private-choice model of broadcasting', *Public Choice* 55, 163–87.

Papper, R.A. (2005), 'The TV news consumer', in Project of Excellence in Journalism (PEJ), 'The state of the news media: an annual report on American journalism'. Available at <http://www.stateofthemedia.org/2005/printable_localtv_guest. asp>.

Patterson, T.E. (2000), *How Soft News and Critical Journalism are Shrinking the News Audience and Weakening Democracy* (Cambridge MA: Shorenstein Center for Press, Politics and Public Policy, Kennedy School of Government, Harvard University).

PEJ (Project of Excellence in Journalism) (2005), 'The state of the news media. An annual report on American journalism'. Available at <http://www.stateofthemedia. org/2005/>.

Pew Research Center for the People and the Press (2004), 'Perceptions of partisan bias seen as growing – especially by Democrats. Cable and Internet loom large in fragmented political news universe', Pew Research Center. Available at <http:// www.people-press.org>.

Prior, M. (2003), 'Any good news in soft news? The impact of soft news preference on political knowledge', *Political Communication* (20), 149–71.

Rosen, J. (2000), 'Questions and answers about public journalism', *Journalism Studies* 1 (4), 679–83.

Rowland, W.D. (2002), 'Public Broadcasting in the United States', in Schement, J.R. (editor-in-chief), *Encyclopedia of Communication and Information* (New York: Macmillan Reference).

Schudson, M. (2001), 'The objectivity norm in American journalism', *Journalism* 2 (2), 149–70.

Shaw, H. (2003), *The Age of McMedia. The Challenge to Information and Democracy*, manuscript, Harvard University. Available at <http://www.wcfia.harvard.edu/ fellows/papers/2002-03/shaw.pdf>.

Slattery, K., Doremus, M. and Marcus, L. (2001), 'Shifts in public affairs reporting on the network evening news: a move toward the sensational', *Journal of Broadcasting & Electronic Media* 45 (2), 290–302.

Splichal, S. (2002), 'The principle of publicity, public use of reason and social control', *Media, Culture & Society* 24 (1), 5–26.

Thelen, G. (2003), 'For convergence', *Journalism Studies* 4 (4), 513–5.

Waterman, D. (2000), 'CBS-Viacom and the effects of media mergers: an economic perspective', *Federal Communications Law Journal* 52, 531–50.

Williams, D. (2002), 'Synergy bias: conglomerates and promotion in the news',

Journal of Broadcasting & Electronic Media 46 (3), 453–72.

Zaller, J. (1999), *A Theory of Media Politics: How the Interests of Politicians, Journalists and Citizens Shape the News*, manuscript (Chicago IL: University of Chicago Press).

Zaller, J. (2003), 'A new standard of news quality: burglar alarms for the monitorial citizen', *Political Communication* 20 (2), 109–30.

Chapter 14

Journalism in Italy

Paolo Mancini

The Origins

Explaining the Italian system of mass communication to international audiences is no easy task. This is because of several anomalies which make Italy significantly different from many other countries, and because the mass media system reflects these anomalies and it is organised in a totally original and very different way from other countries. Nor is it easy to answer a question which has often been put to me by my foreign colleagues: how has former Prime Minister and media entrepreneur Silvio Berlusconi managed to become such an important figure in Italian history? How did his networks emerge? What kind of relationship did he have with the world of politics? Has television been important in determining his success?

Questions about Berlusconi can help us to understand these relationships. I do not believe that Berlusconi represents an episode in the history of Italian society or, particularly, in the history of mass communication. Rather, his entrepreneurial and political story have to be placed within that of the traditional relationship between politics and mass media of which Berlusconi represents just one episode. Equally, the economic dimension of his television enterprises can be explained in the light of a production and distribution structure which he found to be already established and working. In other words, the revolution of commercial television represented principally by Berlusconi has, in many respects, joined the traditional elements of Italy's mass communication system which were already established. These elements have progressively changed as they have adapted to new needs.

The key to interpreting this ambiguous relationship between traditions and change, between persistence and innovation, is very simple: in Italy, mass communication, and particularly journalism, did not emerge, nor develop independently from other social systems. Above all it has never distanced itself from the political or economic systems. Its dependence on other systems is closely linked to the economic structure of media industries in Italy and with the traditions of the specific professional model which is widely used by those who work within the mass media industry. It results in certain distinctive features: the spread of 'impure'[1] publishing which makes journalistic and media logic subject to the interests of their owners; strong roots in

---

1   The term 'impure' is used in publishing when newspapers belong to owners whose main financial interests are outside the field of publishing.

the party press which, even though they have almost completely disappeared today, have left their mark on practice and on professional models which are still prevalent and marked by what the English-speaking world calls advocacy journalism. It means a style of journalism which assumes a point of view, makes it its own and acts on it accordingly, by allowing interpretation, comment and the reporting of facts to overlap, and by confirming and renewing the old tradition of literary gazettes. This represents a typical and enduring feature of the professional Italian model. Finally, another element which characterises Italian journalism is the financial involvement of the state. When the 'welfare state' was introduced, it became heavily involved in the media market, as owner, financer and regulator. In the following pages I will try to explain this characteristic.

In fact it is precisely in the situation already mentioned that the Berlusconi phenomenon emerged and developed, by his use to his own advantage of a professional approach, that of advocacy journalism, which many others had used, exploiting the already well-established practice of allowing functions to overlap. Similarly Berlusconi, and his networks, have grown up within the tradition of a consumer culture which has already seen, and subsequently strengthened, the predominance of television in the face of a very low circulation of print press, and also of a very elitist standing of daily newspapers which, following commercialisation in the 1980s, were forced to adopt some of the discursive strategies used by television. This exacerbated both self-referencing gossip and sensationalism. The roots of the failure of Italian news journalism to distance itself from the political and corporate establishments date back to the same period as the emergence of the press. As one of Italy's leading historians, Alberto Asor Rosa, noted, Italian journalism has two main roots, one literary and the other political (Asor Rosa, 1981).

Descent from literary origins is common to journalism in many countries. Jean Chalaby wrote a very interesting essay on this subject, in which he claims that journalism as we know it today is an 'Anglo-American invention'. By examining French journalism, Chalaby underlined the substantial difference from the Anglo-American model, highlighting the length of time that French journalism has overlapped with and identified with literature, to the extent that it considered itself a secondary product of literature, a far more prestigious profession. In the experience of the French, at least, better journalism was the one which had more links with literature and art (Chalaby, 1996). This type of journalism tends more towards comment and evaluation, interpretation and judgement, and care over a 'literary' style and writing 'beautifully' than it does towards simplicity and a dry recounting of facts which constitute the basic quality of journalism in the modern sense of the word. Moreover, in France, a longer, tougher political struggle (the ongoing battle between modernity and conservatism, symbolised by the severity and length of the French Revolution and its successive events) has accentuated the unavoidably controversial and interventionist character of journalism, further removing it from care, attention to detail, accuracy of what is reported and from the Anglo-American model and the ideal of objectivity and neutrality which characterises today's dominant model of journalism. The ongoing political conflict often leads to, and aids, the phenomenon of corrupt journalism which delays the emergence and development of a true print press market and therefore of the professional practices which today make up the framework of modern journalism.

In many ways the professional model which is developing in Italian journalism is following the same stages and models as the French (it was not by chance that the Napoleonic invasion was to give a great boost to Italian journalism), emerging in an essentially literary field, taking on its discursive practices. It would not be imprudent to claim that the effects of this trend are still being felt today: if Italian and foreign journalism share this literary and political origin, then in Italy this origin, although perhaps historically distant, has continued to influence the dominant professional model for a long time, through a series of different historical and cultural events.

Obviously it cannot be denied, particularly when a real market in mass communication began to emerge after 1980, that literary origins have progressively lost their importance, although their effect can still be felt today in the style of writing, in the essentially elitist nature of the professional model, and in the choice of news, and so on.

In fact, the political origins which remained strong for many years have become no less important. The whole history of the Italian Risorgimento of the nineteenth century was achieved through newspapers as well as battlefields; *Il Risorgimento* became the newspaper of Cavour and Balbo;[2] *L'Italia del Popolo* was Mazzini's new newspaper, *La Gazzetta del Popolo* the newspaper of Giovan Battista Bottero (Castronovo and Tranfaglia, 1979). The men who were to bring about a united Italy, who were motivated by a social conscience, were first and foremost journalists, and journalism was an instrument for organising their battles and for recruiting new energy. In many countries, journalism has gone through this experience, and at some point has distanced itself from it. This separation of journalism from politics in Italy was to come only later, if indeed it was to come at all.

In fact, after the years of the Risorgimento, the experience of the party and advocacy press continued and developed with party newspapers. While the more informative newspapers emerged, *Il Corriere della Sera*, *La Stampa*, *Il Secolo* and *La Nazione*, the emerging socialist and Catholic mass parties set up organs of their own. *L'Avanti* appeared in 1896 while the Catholic world was surrounded by a plethora of smaller, and primarily local, newspapers. But it was the period after World War I, when political conflict became more extreme, that would bring about an even more marked politicisation of Italian journalism. In the face of increasingly heated conflict between the socialist world and fascism, which was just emerging, it was necessary to take sides. Mussolini himself, who started off as a journalist, is perhaps the most obvious example of the overlapping between journalism and politics (Murialdi, 1986; Farinelli et al., 1997).

---

2   Camillo Benso di Cavour (1810–61) was Prime Minster of the Kingdom of Savoy, and created diplomatic and military politics which in 1860 were to influence the unification of Italy. Cesare Balbo (1789–1853) was another important figure in the Risorgimento, as were Mazzini and Botero.

The years of his dictatorship and, in 1925, the end of all freedom, were to impose 'by edict' the even more political (or dictatorial) shift within the Italian press. The function of the press was now essentially one of providing support to the regime (Cannistraro, 1975). Mussolini's press releases, papers containing information for publication which the government sent to newspapers, began a practice of directives and suggestions which was to remain unaltered until after the end of the dictatorship.

However, it was with the resistance and the period immediately after World War II that the foundations of today's political parallelism were laid. The fight against fascism actually forced newspapers to assume a role in spreading the ideas of freedom and in preparing the fight against dictatorship. On the one hand the Allied forces that landed in Italy tried to introduce the ideas on freedom and neutrality of the press which are so deeply rooted in Anglo-Saxon countries. On the other hand this attempt clashed with the organisational needs of the resistance and the liberation. The newly founded parties and groups which were responsible for them, and which formed a part of them, needed real means of communication to be able to defend their ideas and rally their supporters. The action of the PWB (Psychological Warfare Branch)[3] was aimed both at providing troops in action with propagandist support and at fighting any possible return of fascist ideas: adopting the principles of freedom of the press formed part of this objective, which was pursued firstly by allowing those newspapers connected with anti-fascist groups to reopen. Yet this premise hid the contradiction which would characterise the return of freedom in this field. On the one hand a Press Plan for Italy was actually adopted, one of whose objectives was the introduction of 'honesty and neutrality'; on the other, the newspapers to which the Allies granted publishing rights were those connected to groups and parties involved in fighting for liberation or, at any rate, those very close to individual proprietors who acted as anti-fascist press watchdogs.[4] Behind the PWB's choices, and particularly behind the adoption of the Press Plan for Italy, is a model for democracy based on a two-party system with an abstract neutral media. This was not actually the kind which was becoming established in Italy: here the groups which were behind setting up the resistance multiplied, and the lengthy military and political combat required the involvement of all possible means of fighting, which included daily newspapers (Pizarroso Quintero, 1989).

In other words, the return of democracy to Italy was not possible without the support of individuals or groups connected with anti-fascism and, obviously, it meant that their means of communication had to be primarily means of intervention

---

3   The PWB (Psychological Warfare Branch) was an organisation originally formed in 1942 by the British and the Americans to manage means of communication in countries which had been occupied.

4   In 1944 the single commission for the creation of a register of journalists was entrusted with the task of removing journalists who had connections with fascism.

and political debate.[5] Also the men who freed Italy – Parri, Nenni, Carlo Levi and Pertini – were first and foremost journalists. The old tradition of party journalism was rekindled and strengthened by the fight for liberation: on 26 April 1945 *L'Italia Libera* appeared in Milan, followed, within days, by *L'Unità* (the Communist Party daily), *L'Avanti* (the Socialist Party daily), *Il Popolo* (the Christian Democrats' paper) and then by others. Murialdi, one of the main historians of Italian journalism, gives some very interesting statistics which demonstrate the importance of newspapers associated with resistance groups. In 1945 the paper used for dailies in Milan 'was shared out according to the following criteria: 50 per cent to the seven party newspapers, 20 per cent to the *Corriere d'Informazione* and the remaining 30 per cent divided between the *Lombardo* and the political weekly newspapers' (Murialdi, 1995: 39). The whole mass media system began to emerge, firstly with the resistance and then with the liberation, as an arena in which the various media could debate and communicate the point of view of whichever group they belonged to.

Thus, literary supremacy became political supremacy, which could be expressed in two ways: one taking into account true party publishing, and the other the party spirit or political parallelism of newspapers that claimed to be independent. We have already seen how, with liberation, various party organs emerged, re-emerged and developed. To these may be added the Social Democrat's *L'Umanità*, the Liberal Party's *L'Opinione*, the Social Movement's *Il Secolo* and so on.[6] These newspapers continued until the mid-1990s; that is, until the end of the so-called First Republic. Only the first three, and particularly *L'Unità*, had a reasonably significant circulation, but together they contributed towards establishing and consolidating a professional model which would see the work of journalists as secondary to the demands of party propaganda and socialisation. Very often these newspapers were used as a way into the profession for young or not-so-young practitioners who then joined other newspapers. Party newspapers were, however, part of a cultural environment, part of a network of personal relationships linked to the political parties, and constituted a living framework for communication and mobilisation. Activists often contributed for free to party press circulation and in organising party newspapers festivals, among which the 'Unità festival' was the most important.[7]

Beyond party press, some authors spoke about parallelism to refer to the close relationship which exists between journalism and politics, either in structure or in

---

5   An example of this occurred at the Naples daily *Il Risorgimento*, the first newspaper, in 1943, to express publicly anti-fascist ideas: 'it was partly a product of the Allies, aimed at bringing about discussions with the Italians, and partly of the Committee for National Liberation, which made the military government realise that a new newspaper was necessary' (quoted in Murialdi, 1995).

6   Other newspapers, like *Paese Sera* with the PCI (Italian Communist Party), had a minor role in supporting the political parties.

7   Of those party newspapers which still survive today, *L'Unità* was sold to a private group, albeit with strong ties to the DS (Democratic Left), the successor to the former PCI (Italian Communist Party).

content, which often goes as far as their overlapping or blending into one. Grossi and Mazzoleni wrote:

> What is meant by political parallelism is a specific way in which mass media operates at various levels (organisational, economic, professional, thematic and ideological). This way involves substantial support – more or less explicit, and more or less pronounced – of the institutional political class, though beginning with a varying level of professional autonomy (Grossi and Mazzoleni, 1984: 139).

Others have used the metaphor of 'Scarfoglism'[8] to connote an interventionist journalist, ready to take sides, like a French king's musketeer, for the causes he believes in (Murialdi, 1986). Yet others have, very successfully, used the metaphor of 'a journalist cut in half' to emphasise how a professional working in the field of information is only half his own master, with the other half belonging to the economic and political groups with which he is associated (Pansa, 1977). Giovanni Bechelloni, a sociologist, was for many years a close observer and fierce critic of the close relationship between political systems and systems of mass media. He highlighted many times how Italian journalists always show that they need an enemy to fight, and giving up interventionist journalism is therefore not at all easy and, from an objective point of view, involves taking a 'tortuous path'.

Political parallelism reached its peak in public television when the rationale of *lottizzazione* (sharing out) started, after the period of undisputed domination by the Christian Democrats in the 1970s, remaining essentially unaltered to this day. What is meant by political *lottizzazione* is the sharing out of positions of responsibility in any organisation, in this case in a media organisation, based on a criterion of political affiliation. In its golden age (from the mid-1970s until the beginning of the 1990s) the sharing of the public service broadcasting body RAI allocated responsibility for its leading news programme, TG1, to the Christian Democrats, TG2 to the main ally of the Christian Democrats, the Socialist Party, and so responsibility for the news programme with the smallest audience, TG3, to the main opposition party, the Communist Party. Thus, amidst controversy and opposition, the three news programmes took it upon themselves to favour the point of view of the political forces with whom they were associated. Similar division affected the management of non-journalistic programming and even radio. After 1994, even with a change of the political actors, the *lottizzazione* continued to grant TG1 to the government coalition, while TG2 and TG3 were divided between other allies of the government and the opposition.

These customs, as we will shortly see, are also connected with structural aspects such as the absence of 'pure' publishing and state intervention, which both contributed to maintaining (almost intact) a model of journalism, the reasons for

---

8   Edoardo Scarfoglio was an Italian journalist active during the late nineteenth century and was particularly well known for the determination with which he fought political battles through *Il Mattino*, the Naples newspaper which he edited and which, shortly afterwards, was to become the most important daily in the south of Italy.

which are historical. However, even this model could not be seen as unequivocal or standard. Firstly there are newspapers which are more specifically informative (*Il Corriere della Sera*, *La Stampa*) while others, such as *La Repubblica* or, nowadays, *Il Foglio*[9] definitely seem to prefer comment and interpretation. In most cases, even in local newspapers, the role of providing information prevails; however, other elements do still appear. Similarly in television there are channels with a clear political connotation – Berlusconi's Mediaset's Rete 4 or RAI's RAI3 – and others where it is far less obvious, for example, RAI1 and Canale 5. The latter two, as they represent television news programmes with the biggest audiences on RAI and Mediaset respectively, clearly avoid assuming a real stance, thereby respecting the true nature of television news programmes aimed at as big an audience as possible.

Moreover, there is no doubt that the print press in Italy has been the vehicle for initiating innovative experiments in the field of information, particularly through its ability to develop different professional models and help them emerge; these often provide alternatives to traditional models. There have been, and still are, attempts at experimenting in television too, in particular RAI3's experiments around the end of the 1980s (Guglielmi and Balassone, 1995), which have still only been partly successful in breaking the prevalent practice of *lottizzazione* and consequently in following established models.

The Consequences

Within the field of the print press there are two main consequences of the professional traditions outlined so far: the low circulation of daily newspapers and impure publishing, which have already been mentioned. These two elements continuously overlap and still characterise Italian journalism today. In their turn they are linked, as we will later see, to the great importance of television.

In the rankings of numbers of readers, Italy figures among the lowest in Europe (only the Greeks and Portuguese read less). This statistic will later be put into context in terms of certain customs which relate to cultural use. Firstly, it is necessary to take into account a particular press system which has not been discussed so far: unlike many other countries, there is no variation in Italy within the field of daily newspapers. There is no such thing as so-called elite or broadsheet dailies on the one hand, and popular or tabloid papers on the other, as can be found in Germany, France and the UK. The extent to which newspapers vary is tending to become progressively less marked throughout the world, with the move towards greater use of the tabloid format. Even the most important elite dailies are increasingly tending to resemble the tabloids in content and size (an example being the transformation of

---

9   *Il Foglio* is a daily newspaper founded at the end of the 1990s by Giuliano Ferrara, a journalist heavily involved in politics, first with the Italian Communist Party and in more recent years with Forza Italia. He is also involved in television, is greatly admired and is much discussed for his controversial verve.

the London *Times* since it was purchased by Rupert Murdoch). However, it is still the popular press which has the largest circulation (Dahlgren and Sparks, 1992).

In Italy, however, all newspapers, local and national, have a twofold character: both popular and elite at the same time. In spite of this, the elite dimension certainly remains prevalent. It is the so-called tradition of the 'omnibus' newspaper, taken from the name of the Longanesi newspaper which, around 1930, standardised the character which combined the qualities of glossy magazines and political newspapers and subsequently encouraged cultivated newspapers to use this popular format (Mancini, 2000). According to many people, both *La Repubblica* and *Il Corriere della Sera* – particularly the latter under the management of Paolo Mieli in the 1990s – would maintain this nature of a 'treacle' newspaper, meaning one with no clear boundary between being a cultivated or a popular newspaper, always in search of a scoop.[10] As we will discuss later, the consequences of the commercialisation which began in the 1980s would seem to emphasise even further the integration of the traditional elite and/or political stance with the demands of sensationalism.

In Italy the place of the popular daily newspapers has been taken instead by weeklies, the most notable being *Gente* and *Oggi*[11] which have not only achieved good sales but have also taken away storylines and a potential role from daily newspapers. On the subject of Italian journalism's typical elite nature, we could not omit making reference to an essay called 'Fifteen hundred readers', written by the journalist, Enzo Forcella. The essay, which originally appeared in 1959 in *Tempo Presente*, has recently been republished as 'Problemi dell'informazione'. It provides a picture of Italian journalism which captures in a succinct and illuminating way some of the problems of Italian journalism of the time; problems which, to some extent, can still be found today. Forcella wrote:

> A political journalist, in our country, can count on about fifteen hundred readers: ministers and all their undersecretaries, some Members of Parliament, party leaders, trade unionists, high prelates and some industrialists who want to appear informed. The rest do not count, even if the newspapers sell thirty thousand copies. Firstly, there is no evidence that general readers read the front pages of newspapers, and in any case their influence is minimal. The whole system is organised according to the relationship between the journalist and that group of privileged readers (Forcella, 1959: 451).

Later, Forcella continued by introducing the subject to which we will return.

> Naturally, writing is only for one's own pleasure if there is no paying public. The relationship between the fifteen hundred readers and the political journalist is very close, in a sense it could be said to go as far as identifying with him: every morning they have breakfast with him (if they are in the habit of reading the newspaper while they have

---

10   This can be seen in the interesting debate described in 1994 in *Reset* (no. 12, December 1994).

11   *Oggi* and *Gente* deal mainly with everyday topics and gossip in the world of cinema, show business and the aristocracy. They are aimed at women.

their coffee), often they invite him to lunch and share their thoughts with him, through colleagues or friends (Forcella, 1959: 452).

In conclusion, Forcella reinforces what has been said so far, even if his view is limited to the field of political journalism: there are few readers associated with a group of self-referencing newspapers which standardise jargon (Marletti, 1985). But Forcella also claims, from the viewpoint of someone working in the industry, that Italian journalism is made up more of comment and interpretation than of facts. It is worth quoting his words:

> When I began as a journalist I thought that journalism was above all about information, fact, news ... I realised slowly, too slowly in fact, that I was very wrong. For a political journalist, facts alone never speak. They say either too much or too little. When they say too much, they must be spoken softly, when they say too little they must be supplemented to convey their message. But achieving clarity in this job is a difficult skill (Forcella, 1959: 454).

A few years later, Sandro Viola, another important name in Italian journalism, corroborated the close relationship between politics and journalists:

> For years and years, in fact, Italian journalists have believed that they were playing the politician, and have enjoyed the thrill of doing so. The comings and goings in the *Transatlantico di Montecitorio*[12] arm in arm with leaders and deputy leaders, the pleasure of debating with them the thousand and one nuances that cropped up from 'non-political asides', had made them true protagonists of the system. They (journalists) were not only critical witnesses, but also important players in the scene being played, to the extent that their political jargon ended up becoming almost the exact copy of the political discourse itself, which by this time was heading towards failure.[13]

The spread of what in Italy is defined as impure publishing has been the main consequence of the elitist nature of Italian journalism. To make good the losses which had progressively accumulated (largely as a result of low circulations) since the beginning of the twentieth century, almost all Italian newspapers not belonging to political parties have been bought by large financial groups (banks, iron and steel or textile companies, and so on) who have used them to achieve and maintain approval for their own interests. This process began around 1920 when large iron and steel groups and banks took over Italian daily newspapers which, by this time, were in serious financial difficulty. A typical recent example of this is the case of *Il Giorno*, a daily newspaper founded in 1956 by Enrico Mattei, CEO of one of the main groups of public industries in Italy, ENI (the Italian oil group). The newspaper was to help achieve approval of the interests, needs and even regulations of the state-controlled

---

12 The *Transatlantico* is the name of the long corridor inside the Palazzo di Montecitorio, the Chamber of Deputies where politicians and journalists usually meet.

13 S. Viola, 'The pens of the regime', in *La Repubblica*, 23 May 1993.

industries. Piero Ottone, former editor of *Il Corriere della Sera*, witnessed the birth of *Il Giorno* and stated:

> The real aim or primary function of a newspaper was to control the polemic against daily newspapers which were supported either by private industry or by legitimate receipts from sales and advertising, that were in favour of the Confederation of Italian Industry and private industry, and which were continuously at war with the involvement of the state as represented by ENI (Ottone, 1996: 178).[14]

Even today a significant number of Italian daily newspapers are owned by groups whose main financial interests are outside publishing. For instance, *La Stampa* belongs to Fiat; *La Repubblica* to CIR, a finance company; most of the shares of *Il Corriere della Sera* belong to a bank; *Il Messaggero* and *Il Mattino* belong to a building contractor.

At the same time the economic difficulties of the press have led to the state adopting economic subsidy policies, even of political daily papers; these subsidies have strengthened the traditional partisan character of most of the Italian press, as has also happened in many other Western democracies (Hallin and Mancini, 2004). There have been, and still are, economic subsidies in favour of newspapers, particularly those of political, cultural and religious groups.

As a result of this overlapping with other social systems, no typical pattern of behaviour or common press practice have been adopted and broadly accepted. Historically, as is the case in other countries, the professional autonomy of Italian journalists has always been rather weak; advancing their career has depended less on respecting rules and procedure or on success with the public (as far as this matters) than on their relationships with their own political or financial patron. Instances of journalists becoming politicians or vice versa are still very common. Adequate self-regulation processes have not been developed (self-regulation being essential for a profession to be recognised) and until a few years ago, no training processes had been introduced to improve and standardise professional behaviour. This has further highlighted the frailty of the profession's identity, and has defined the need for external intervention into self-regulation, in order to eliminate the shortcomings of the profession. On many occasions Parliament, the Constitutional Court and other levels of the judicial system have intervened in order to define and impose professional standards. This seems to be the enduring picture even today in spite of a strong formal institutionalisation by which, to be a journalist in Italy (almost the only case in the world), it is necessary to be registered with the Association of Journalists (*Ordine dei Giornalisti*) and pass a professional examination. It involves membership of a professional organisation which has no consistent or broadly accepted equivalent elsewhere.

---

14 By 'daily newspapers supported by private industry' Ottone is referring to *Il Corriere della Sera*, then the property of a textile group, and *La Stampa*, by that time owned by Fiat, and so on.

The Dominance of Television

A further consequence of the elitist nature of the Italian press is the great importance assumed by television and in particular TV news. More so than in other countries, in Italy television is the main source of information for viewers and the main agenda setter. Print media very often deal with issues according to how much they have been analysed on television, and how much has been said about them in TV news programmes. Since the 1980s this role has been increasing still further. With the commercial deluge, as Jay Blumler (1992) defined it, which got under way in the 1980s, the whole mass communication system in Italy has been revolutionised: there has been exponential growth both in the consumption and production of communication; new television stations, new radio stations and new newspapers have appeared; the number of viewers and readers has increased; and advertising agencies and research institutes have emerged. But above all, there has been a change in the nature of mass communication, which has increasingly organised itself around television, particularly commercial television. From television being a system that revolved exclusively around its role as a public service, and from print media revolving around economic subsidies and impure publishing, the media have become a less partial system, by reason of commercial competition. As elsewhere in Europe, the role of public service radio and television has been radically reduced whereas that of commercial television has grown. In addition to these changes, Berlusconi has appeared on the scene, first as an entrepreneur and then as a politician, and this has changed the whole of Italian society.

It could be said that 'officially' the story of commercial television in Italy began with the ruling of the Constitutional Court of 1976.[15] The ruling was confined to declaring invalid articles 1, 2 and 45 of the reform of RAI in 1975; these articles provided for a public monopoly, whether at a national or local level. In reality, the ruling stated that there should be a public monopoly, namely of RAI, across the whole country, whilst allowing private television channels to broadcast in restricted local areas. So Parliament faced the need to legislate on the matter in a different way. However, the Italian Parliament was unable to produce a reform law for the whole television system which would deal with the issues raised by the Constitutional Court. Only in 1990, with the so-called Mammi law, named after its main sponsor,[16] was a new regulatory structure achieved, but meanwhile 14 years had passed, during which time television had grown and developed with no legislative guidelines. Many of the problems which affect Italian democracy today (see the issue of conflict of interests regarding Berlusconi) were born with this legislative vacuum. It is in fact during this period that the new structure of the Italian mass communication system emerged and became established. But it developed in an uncontrolled way, as Nelson Traquina observed about the situation in Portugal (1995). Throughout this 14-year

---

15 The Constitutional Court checks the constitutionality of laws and other government acts. Moreover, it represents the final step in the Italian jurisdictional process.

16 Every law in Italy has a sponsor who expounds and promotes it.

period there was no law on television broadcasting, there was no allocation of frequencies: it was a question of 'first come, first served' and, above all, there were no clear regulations about what 'interconnection' means, in terms of how, and if, two stations which operate in different parts of the country, may be connected.

It could be said that the story begins with Berlusconi's construction venture: whereas throughout Italy radio stations and private television channels spring up and often fail within the space of a few months, Berlusconi decided to provide a new housing development which he was constructing (Milano 2) with closed-circuit television which would serve the blocks of flats. Very quickly, and just in the wake of what was happening elsewhere in Italy, this first nucleus became a station on the air, Telemilano. In 1980 it changed its name to Canale 5, which still exists, and secured the services of the well-known television character Mike Bongiorno. In the same year Canale 5 won the broadcasting rights for football's Mundialito, representing another important stage in the fight which had only just begun with the other private channels. It was the beginning of the 'Berlusconian' affair which was to have a determining effect on the transformation of the whole of Italian society.[17]

The resourcefulness of Pubitalia, the advertising agency associated with Berlusconi's networks,[18] is a fundamental element of his swashbuckling strategy; he combines qualities of great entrepreneurialism with the right amount of political connections, while behaving in the very Italian tradition of fostering close links between the political and mass communication systems. There were many stages in the success of his Fininvest Group (which later became Mediaset), some of which are to do with its regulatory structure (therefore implying that political support was necessary to resolve problems) and others are more immediately connected with strategies for competing for market dominance. But Berlusconi introduced something very original into the traditional closeness between media and politics. For the first time this closeness was, at least initially, used solely for profit in his media organisation and not to support ideas, position or political or economic strategies.

And so we are entering a period of a mixed television system which is witnessing competition between two main television groups, RAI on the one hand and Mediaset on the other, who between them share a large part, around 90 per cent, of advertising resources. Next to these two giants there are a multitude of local networks with few resources and low-quality programmes, reflecting the limited resources at their disposal. And so a new way of operating television has emerged which is completely different from that which existed during the public monopoly of RAI. Even television journalism is dramatically affected by it.

---

17   Various books, for the most part vehemently critical, relate the Berlusconian affair: G. Ruggeri (1994), *Gli affari del Presidente* (Kaos Edizioni); C. Fracassi and M. Gambino (1994), *Berlusconi – Una biografia non autorizzata* (Avvenimenti); G. Fiori (1995), *Il Venditore* (Milano: Garzanti).

18   In Italy advertising space is sold to 'concessionary' advertisers, organisations which just have franchises on television space and can sell it to advertisers.

Obviously programming of public television coverage is also affected by the new competitive situation. Far more time is allocated to entertainment, while in the field of news there have been changes in its conversational style, which are based increasingly on dramatising and personalising events. There have also been changes in the rationale for selecting news which, even if it hinges largely on political events, as was the case up to the time of the commercial deluge, now increasingly tends to favour the facts of everyday life. In other words, the old political rationale which controlled the programming of public television has partly declined, even though it is still in operation: it has progressively become more of a show in order to respond to the demands of competition between channels. This has resulted in many television programmes which provide in-depth analysis of issues, such as *Porta a porta*, *Ballarò* and *Matrix*, which combine two characteristics – showbusiness and party spirit – in other words, providing a strong political content while turning television news into a show. The hosts of these shows, just like news anchormen, have progressively assumed a greater profile, aimed at winning over viewers, which was unknown in the years when the logic of public radio and television coverage applied.

Print media have undergone a very similar process of change. In order to respond to the need to compete with other newspapers, traditional partisanship has given way to a more discursive and even highly dramatic style, with high-sounding headlines where conflicts are accentuated and the pursuit of the scoop is constant. On the one hand this change has certainly modernised the press, although its circulation has not increased significantly, but without rules, it has also resulted in a 'rampant' kind of journalism, ready for action, and a desperate search for news which is often not supported by adequate checks.

In this way, in both the written press and television, the traditional characteristics of Italian journalism – partisanship, carelessness, little checking of sources – have merged with the new needs dictated by market logic and been applied to forms which are professionally and traditionally weak.

Conclusions

The Italian press has always been highly political. But the nature of this has traditionally been in its close association with political parties and the political establishment. The only major variation to this trend was the development of an 'impure' press, owned by industrial conglomerates and used to exert political power for their commercial advantage. This political parallelism reinforced, rather than challenged, the cosy relationship between the press and powerful elites.

Such a situation is remarkable, in that it potentially creates a democratic vacuum for citizens who find themselves largely unrepresented and absent from the public sphere. Effectively, the press was speaking for political parties, not for voters. Such tendencies were reinforced by the manner in which RAI was traditionally captured for purposes close to party propaganda in the 'carve-up' of its channels.

The mould was broken by Berslusconi who, initially at least, used his entrepreneurial skills to create TV channels that pursued, for competitive advantage, the popular rather than the political. The immediate impact was on RAI but soon the whole news media was forced to consider the commercial logic of expending swathes of words on speaking to a mere 'fifteen hundred'.

Whilst in many countries the populist and often sensationalist nature of such commodified news agendas are seen as threatening to ideas about citizenship, they have, in the unusual history and circumstances of Italy, at least partially, reconnected journalism to the public, albeit treated largely as consumers. The impact and effectiveness of such 'marketplace democracy' – and Berlusconi's role in it – is uncertain and debated. However, it marks a significant phase in the evolution of the Italian news media and their interpretation of political roles.

References

Asor Rosa, A. (1981), 'Il giornalista: appunti sulla fisiologia di un mestiere difficile', in *Storia d'Italia* (Turin: Einaudi).

Bechelloni, G. (1992), *Il mestiere di giornalista* (Naples: Liguori).

Blumler, J. (1992), *Television and the Public Interest* (London: Sage).

Cannistraro, P.V. (1975), *La fabbrica del consenso* (Bari: Laterza).

Castronovo, V. and Tranfaglia, N. (1979), *La stampa italiana nel risorgimento* (Bari: Laterza).

Chalaby, J.K. (1996), 'Journalism as an Anglo-American invention', *European Journal of Communication* 11 (3), 303–26.

Dahlgren, P. and Sparks, C. (1992), *Journalism and Popular Culture* (London: Sage).

Farinelli, G., Paccgnini, E., Santambrogio, G. and Villa, A. I. (1997), *Storia del giornalismo italiano* (Turin: Utet).

Forcella, E. (1959), 'Millecinquecento lettori', *Tempo presente* 6.

Grossi, G. and Mazzoleni, G. (1984), 'Per un'interpretazione del rapporto tra Parlamento e sistema informativo: analisi ed indicazione di ricerca', in Camera dei Deputati (ed.), *Informazione e Parlamento* (Rome: Camera dei Deputati).

Guglielmi, A. and Balassone, S. (1995), *Senza rete* (Milan: Rizzoli).

Hallin, D. and Mancini, P. (2004), *Comparing Media Systems* (Cambridge: Cambridge University Press).

Mancini, P. (2000), *Il sistema fragile* (Rome: Carocci).

Marletti, C. (1985), *Prima e dopo* (Turin: Eri).

Murialdi, P. (1986), *Storia del giornalismo italiano* (Turin: Gutenberg).

Murialdi, P. (1995), *La stampa italiana dalla liberazione alla crisi di fine seculo* (Bari: Laterza).

Ottone, P. (1996), *Preghiera o bordello* (Milan: Longanesi).

Pansa, G. (1977), *Comprati e venduti* (Milan: Garzanti).

Pizarroso Quintero, A. (1989), *Stampa, radio e propaganda* (Milan: Angeli).

Traquina, N. (1995), 'Portuguese television: the politics of savage deregulation', *Media, Culture and Society* 2, 223–38.

Chapter 15

Journalism in France

Raymond Kuhn

The term 'journalism' first entered the French language in 1778. Yet for the next 100 years or so the notion of the 'journalist' was rivalled by that of the 'publicist', with writers and politicians continuing to act as major sources of copy for newspapers and periodicals (Ferenczi, 2005: 3). This had an impact on the form and style of French journalism during the second half of the nineteenth century, since the 'importance conferred upon the literary form kept the telegraphic style of Anglo-American news reports away from French newspapers' (Chalaby, 1996: 311). In emphasising the historical differences in the status and evolution of French journalism from its Anglo-American counterparts during the nineteenth and early twentieth centuries, Chalaby also argues that Anglo-American newspapers contained 'more news and information than any contemporary French papers' and had 'better organized news-gathering services' (Chalaby, 1996: 305). It was not until the industrialisation of newspaper production towards the end of the 1800s that journalism in France became a recognised source of regular employment with its own rules and professional codes of practice. Yet thanks to its literary and political origins, even after its professionalisation French journalism long continued to be characterised by a fondness for ideas, personal opinions and commentary over 'facts' and for editorialising rather than investigation (Ferenczi, 2005: 5).

If not necessarily in crisis, journalism in France at the start of the twenty-first century certainly faces a series of mutually overlapping challenges. New information outlets such as free newspapers, rolling news channels and the Internet compete with long-established mainstream media for audiences and revenue; commercial pressures are in the eyes of some critics leading to a 'dumbing down' of news coverage; novel areas of journalistic specialism jostle alongside traditional fields for resources and news space; political journalists stand accused of enjoying too close a relationship with politicians; among audiences, the young in particular have to a large extent switched off from traditional forms of news consumption; and on the production side the upper echelons of the journalistic profession remain dominated by white, middle-class, middle-aged males.

This chapter is organised in four sections. The first provides a broad overview of key features of the media landscape and the journalistic profession in contemporary France; the second considers the issue of the marketisation of the journalistic production process; the third section examines the contribution of journalists to a healthy public sphere; while the final section concentrates on selected current developments and future trends in French journalism.

The Contemporary Media Landscape

Formative Influences

The development of the French media landscape since 1945 has been influenced by a range of technological, political, economic and socio-cultural factors. In this section the contribution of these different variables will be distinguished for the purposes of analysis, although it must be remembered that in the real world they usually combine with each other in complex multifaceted processes of interaction. It is, therefore, frequently difficult, and quite often impossible, to make a simple causal link between a specific change in media structures and functioning on the one hand and any single formative variable regarded in isolation on the other.

Since the media are technologically dependent industries, it is evident that technological advances will have made a significant contribution to the evolution of the media landscape. In the press sector, the development of new printing technology in the 1970s and 1980s allowed for a French equivalent of Murdoch's 'Wapping revolution' in Britain. Print workers found themselves surplus to requirements and the power of print unions severely weakened as journalists increasingly took on the function of managing the formatting of their own text. In the broadcasting sector the introduction of FM in the 1970s allowed for a significant expansion in the supply of radio services, while the development of new distribution technologies such as cable and direct-to-home satellite in the 1980s and the transition from analogue to digital platforms over the past decade have led to a huge growth in the supply of television content. The Internet is not just an additional source of information for users, but has given rise to new types of journalistic content and to new modes of interaction between user and content supplier. More recently, the growing convergence embracing telephony, television and broadband has meant that consumers may now access media content via an array of household and portable devices.

Yet notwithstanding the impact of technology, one should be wary of embracing a simple technological determinism in an explanation of change in the French media landscape. Political intervention through executive control of the policy-making process has frequently been crucial in the organisation and regulation of the media. For example, the events of World War II led to an important break with the pre-war media system, with the reconstitution of both press and broadcasting sectors at the Liberation heavily influenced by the statist ideals of the Resistance movement. Newspapers accused of collaboration with the Nazi occupiers were closed down and their assets redistributed to owners untainted by collaboration, while many new titles also came into existence. In the broadcasting sector, dominated until the end of the 1950s by radio, the Liberation government established a state monopoly which was defended by politicians of different political persuasions for virtually the next

40 years, most notably during de Gaulle's presidency in the 1960s (Chalaby, 2002). Governmental intervention has been central on the supply side in broadcasting; for example, in directing certain initiatives such as the state-led cable and satellite projects of the late 1970s and 1980s. Market entry by commercial interests into broadcasting was allowed only after the Socialist government of President François Mitterrand abolished the state monopoly in 1982, while the right-wing government of Prime Minister Jacques Chirac went even further in making the politically motivated choice to privatise the leading public sector channel TF1 in 1987. It could be argued, therefore, that while technology may frequently offer policy stakeholders opportunities for change, political elites often have to provide the necessary will for reform.

Economic factors have also played an important role in influencing the French media's development. The huge fallback in the number of different newspaper titles published since the post-war high point of 1946 is at least in part a result of competition in a saturated market. In the broadcasting sector the state monopoly largely protected public sector television and (to a much lesser extent) radio from commercial competition. However, with the expansion and economic liberalisation of the broadcasting sector since the 1980s, advertising revenue has played a greater role in broadcast funding, with even public service television heavily dependent on advertising as a revenue stream. Advertising and subscription have become crucial for success and even survival in what have become highly competitive markets. Two examples illustrate this point. First, a national commercial television channel, La Cinq, went into liquidation in 1992 because of its inability to secure an audience of sufficient size or the desired socio-economic composition to attract advertisers. Second, in 2006 plans were announced to merge the two principal digital satellite platforms, CanalSatellite and TPS, in the face of growing competition from the digital terrestrial platform established less than a year previously. To put it bluntly, most media outlets in France are businesses run for profit, with management focused on the financial bottom line.

Finally, changes in French society and cultural practices have also played a role in influencing media structures and behaviour. Powerful new groups of media consumers (including women, ethnic minorities, the gay community and the young) have emerged as target markets. Their tastes and interests are catered for by a range of niche media in print, broadcasting and online sectors, including celebrity magazines, minority interest radio stations, themed television channels and a host of dedicated websites. In contrast, mass audience media such as traditional newspapers and generalist television channels are in decline, even if the process is at a relatively early stage in the case of television.

Principal Media Sectors

Journalism in contemporary France operates within a highly developed and differentiated media landscape, which ranges from local newspapers with minuscule circulations to the global reach of new information and communication technologies.

French citizens can now access information from an unprecedently wide range of outlets, organised in three broad media sectors: print, broadcasting and online.

The print sector includes around 4,000 publications which can be differentiated in terms of geographic reach (local/regional/national), periodicity (daily/weekly/ monthly/quarterly), content (general information/specialist interest/vocational and technical) and target audience (mass/niche). The newspaper sector is currently very weak, with low sales figures by the standards of several major Western European democracies. At the start of the twenty-first century only 149 daily newspapers were sold in France for every 1,000 inhabitants, compared with 299 in Germany and 321 in the UK. The newspaper sector notably lacks a daily title with a large nationwide circulation – no French daily sells anywhere near a million copies – with the result that there is no equivalent of the popular agenda-setting influence or mobilising impact of the British tabloids. For instance, in the face of competition from *Le Parisien-Aujourd'hui* in the 'popular' segment of the market, *France-Soir* has seen its circulation plummet from over a million in the 1950s to around 50,000 in 2005, with the result that even its very survival has been thrown into question.

The leading national newspapers (including *Le Monde*, *Le Figaro* and *Libération*) are rich sources of political information for their readerships, none more so than *Le Monde*, which regards itself as a broad-ranging newspaper of intellectual ideas on economic, social, cultural and political issues. Indeed, despite their comparatively low circulations, the national daily titles can be regarded as central players in the French press, since they act as agenda setters for other media such as national radio and television. They are also influential media with political elites. *Le Monde* in particular has acquired the reputation of exerting independent, but also unaccountable, power through its capacity to support or undermine particular politicians and policy options (Péan and Cohen, 2003). Some national titles have very specific journalistic content, including *Les Echos* (finance and business) and *L'Equipe* (sport). Both these niche titles have bucked the general trend of falling circulations among daily national newspapers.

Yet it remains the case that with the main national titles selling predominantly in the Paris area, three out of four French citizens never read a daily national paper. In circulation terms the newspaper sector is dominated by regional titles, such as *Ouest-France* in Brittany, which frequently benefit from a quasi-monopoly status in their particular geographical market. In recent years paid-for titles, both national and regional, have faced increasing competition from free newspapers such as those published by the *Métro* and *20 Minutes* chains and distributed in Paris and other urban centres. In contrast to most newspapers, a wide range of magazines enjoy buoyant sales figures. Women's magazines and television listing publications are only two of the many genres which enjoy high circulations in this section of the print media. Weekly news magazines, such as *L'Express*, *Le Nouvel Observateur* and *Le Point*, provide high-quality analytical journalism for their socially upmarket, politically knowledgeable readerships, while the popularity of celebrity magazines testifies to an apparently insatiable consumer appetite for insider gossip about the stars of showbusiness, sport and the media.

The supply of radio services has grown enormously since the abolition of the state monopoly. Major players in contemporary French radio include national broadcasters such as France Inter (public service) and Europe 1 and RTL (commercial). Along with some local, community and rolling news stations, these provide political information in the form of news, commentary, political interviews and audience phone-in slots. However, with their continuous diet of music many popular stations show little or no interest in news or politics. Moreover, there is no French equivalent of the high-profile radio talk-show hosts in the US with their vituperative, populist approach to political debate.

The television sector has changed beyond recognition from the highly restricted provision of the state monopoly (Kuhn, 1995: 109–64). At the end of 2005 the majority of viewers continued to receive only a maximum of seven channels via free-to-air analogue distribution: two advertising-funded commercial channels, TF1 and M6 (both generalist); four public service channels, France 2 (generalist), France 3 (regional), France 5 (generalist/family-oriented) and Arte (cultural); and the pay-TV channel, Canal+. However, the introduction of digital terrestrial services earlier that year was poised to open up multichannel television to those viewers across the country who had so far not chosen to subscribe to digital services from satellite or cable platforms.

In terms of national and international political information, the most important medium is national television, notably the news programmes of TF1 and France 2. The TF1 evening news is regularly watched by an audience of around ten million, while its competitor on France 2 attracts about six million viewers. Moreover, the advent of multichannel television has increased the range of political information outlets available to audiences, including rolling news channels such as i-télé and LCI. In contrast, during the past decade there has been a marked reduction in the amount of political programming shown on generalist channels, especially the commercial variants, because this type of product is not considered to be sufficiently popular to attract large audiences (Neveu, 2005). News sells and is an important 'brand' for some television channels; but current affairs and political debate programmes are now largely confined to those channels for whom such programming is part of their public service remit.

Finally, there is the burgeoning online sector. In terms of supply, most mainstream media outlets, such as TF1 and *Libération*, have a dedicated website with information provision and a range of interactive services. Alternative minority media have also established a Web presence to maximise their audience reach. After a comparatively slow start, domestic take-up of the Internet is now well implanted in France. Yet the medium has still not become a major provider of political information for the mass electorate. In part this may be because the Web is still largely a 'pull' technology where consumers actively have to search out information – in contrast to television which is a 'push' technology. Yet as information provision becomes more sophisticated in being tailored to the interests of the individual consumer and as the younger generation, more accustomed to Internet usage, moves into mature adulthood, it is likely that the impact of the Internet as an information source for French citizens will increase substantially.

Media Regulation and Partisanship

All French media are subject to general legislation, for example regarding the protection of national security, which limits their freedom to publish: the right to free expression is no more absolute for the media than for an individual citizen. In addition, there are two broad areas of media-specific regulation dealing with structures and behaviour respectively. One set of rules is designed to inhibit concentration of ownership, both within and across media sectors. The second set of regulatory provisions, particularly applicable in the broadcasting sector, is targeted at aspects of media content.

By the standards of some other member states of the European Union the level of cross-media ownership concentration in France is not especially high. In particular, there is no equivalent of Murdoch's hold in the UK over a large slice of television distribution and national newspaper circulation or of Berlusconi's domination of the media in Italy. Most of the main national newspaper groups – with the exception of Lagardère Media – have no major stake in national television or radio, although some regional newspapers have an ownership share in local radio and/or television. The current regulatory regime on ownership, based on audience share and reach, is quite liberal in terms of the imposed thresholds, both within and across media sectors. Moreover, while some foreign groups such as Bertelsman have entered French media markets, in general the latter are dominated by domestic companies such as Bouygues and Dassault-Socpresse. In part this is because of regulatory limits on the freedom of non-EU nationals to hold a direct ownership stake in particular media sectors, which has effectively kept the big US global giants at arms' length. Such restrictions have traditionally been defended by elites across the political spectrum on both cultural and economic grounds (Kidd and Reynolds, 2000).

In terms of content regulation the main distinction to be drawn is between broadcasting (highly regulated, especially the public service outlets) on the one hand and the press (minimally regulated) and the Internet (largely self-regulated by service providers and users) on the other. State regulation of broadcast content, which is both proscriptive and prescriptive, can be explained historically with reference to the medium's legal status as a state monopoly, the scarcity in frequency spectrum and the assumed power of television to influence audience attitudes and behaviour. With regard to political information and news content on radio and television, norms of balance and impartiality have long been enshrined in regulatory provisions as well as being part of broadcast journalists' code of professional practice.

The current regulatory authority for broadcasting is the Higher Broadcasting Council (Conseil Supérieur de l'Audiovisuel or CSA). The CSA has acquired a reputation for functional independence since its foundation in 1989, despite the fact that its members are appointed by leading political office-holders including the President of the Republic. The CSA has responsibility for the allocation of radio and television licences, key managerial appointments in the public sector and the verification of broadcasters' compliance with content regulations. The regulatory authority also monitors the allocation of time to different political actors (the President, the government and political parties) outside of election periods and to presidential and parliamentary candidates during election campaigns.

In contrast, there is no regulatory authority monitoring the activities of the French press, not even a self-regulatory body along the lines of the UK Press Complaints Commission. Newspapers have traditionally been free to editorialise and campaign in favour of a particular political stance and there is no regulatory requirement for individual newspaper titles to strive for internal political balance. There is a strong tradition in France of committed political journalism (Ferenczi, 2005: 23) with French journalists 'having the habit of interpreting and reprocessing the information according to the political doctrine that the newspaper defended' (Chalaby, 1996: 305). For much of the twentieth century the range of ideological values represented across the French party system helped foster a richly partisan canvas of political journalism. In the immediate post-war years several different newspapers enjoyed close and explicit links with political parties. Of these, now only the Communist daily *L'Humanité* still survives. Yet like the Communist Party itself the newspaper is a pale shadow of its former self, in terms of both circulation and influence on its readership.

Yet although free to support particular parties, French newspapers as a whole are now generally much less overt and strident in their partisanship than some of their British counterparts. Of the main national titles, *Le Monde* has tended to represent a centre-left stance, *Le Figaro* is sympathetic to the mainstream right and *Libération* is vaguely leftish and anti-establishment. However, these general value orientations do not necessarily correlate with editorial support for a particular party or candidate at elections. *Le Monde*, for example, gave support to the presidential candidacy of the right-wing Edouard Balladur in 1995. In addition, therefore, to the long-standing decoupling of newspapers from political parties, there has arguably been a decline in the importance of ideology as an integral part of a newspaper's 'mission'. This has even been described as French dailies coming closer to an 'Anglo-American' form of pluralism in terms of the expression of political views (Charon, 2005: 113). This is not just a media phenomenon, driven by the need to maximise readerships in a declining market sector. It also reflects the decline of ideological conflict in French electoral politics over the past two decades, influenced by the inter-related processes of liberalisation, Europeanisation and globalisation. In addition, regional newspapers have the reputation of being reluctant to adopt a strong partisan position on political issues for fear of alienating sections of their electorally diverse readership.

The Journalistic Profession

It is difficult to make generalisations about the status of journalists in contemporary France. Members of the profession work in different media sectors (press/radio/ television/online), for outlets with differing levels of prestige, performing different journalistic functions (reporter/correspondent/commentator/photo-journalist) and with different levels of job security and income. The highly paid celebrity journalists of the Paris television newsrooms may on the face of it have little in common with the temporary contract staff of a small-scale local weekly newspaper. Yet there are also ties which bind this variegated profession together.

One of these is the legal status of journalists. Legislation dating from 1935 provides the formal statutory framework for the journalistic profession and provides its members with certain benefits enshrined in law. The legislation defines the notion of journalist based on criteria of professional status: a journalist is not simply someone who writes in the press, but rather a person for whom this activity provides the principal means of their livelihood. In addition, the legislation introduced a 'conscience clause', whereby if a journalist believes that a significant change in the editorial line of the publication which employs them harms their honour or reputation, then the journalist may submit their resignation without incurring any financial penalties. A system of professional identity card was also introduced, delimiting access to the profession and, in the words of the principal journalists' trade union, allowing 'the control of journalism by journalists' (Martin, 1997: 229).

Another potential source of unity across functional divisions and reputational hierarchies lies in journalists' trade union representation. Many journalists belong to their own independent union, the Syndicat National des Journalistes (SNJ), which was founded in 1918 as the Syndicat des Journalistes and adopted its current title in 1928. The SNJ exists to promote the interests of journalists in their relations with media owners and managers, to provide legal advice to its members where appropriate and to influence governmental media policy. Yet although it is the most popular of the journalists' trade unions in terms of membership, the SNJ does not have a monopoly of official representation. Journalists may choose instead to be a member of the journalist branches of the general trade union confederations such as the CGT, the CFDT and FO, as well as the middle-management union confederation, the CGC. In short, trade union representation of French journalists re-introduces vertical lines of inter-union demarcation which militates against a united profession, even if on a day-to-day basis the different unions frequently collaborate on issues related to the defence of the interests of the profession.

In terms of sociological characteristics, French journalists tend to be young, have political views favouring the left, come from middle-class backgrounds and be brought up in the greater Paris region. There has been a notable feminisation of the profession since the late 1960s: women represented only 17 per cent of journalists in 1970, 25.1 per cent in 1982 and 37 per cent in 1995 (Martin, 1997: 397). As a result, there are now many more female journalists than in the past. Some women have even made it to the upper ranks of the profession: Christine Ockrent and Arlette Chabot have followed in the footsteps of Françoise Giroud and Michèle Cotta as role models for aspirant female journalists in the political realm. For the most part, however, women remain under-represented at managerial and editorial level, banging their heads against the 'glass ceiling' of male-dominated newsrooms. In addition, the level of formal educational attainment has improved significantly:

while in 1966 only 17.7 per cent of journalists were graduates, by 1990 this figure had climbed to just under 40 per cent. Conversely, the number of journalists with less than the school baccalauréat (the rough equivalent of English 'A' levels) had dropped in the same period from over 31 per cent to 20 per cent. French journalism has thus become a graduate-dominated profession, with many new recruits coming from journalism schools.

Statistically, ethnic minorities are substantially under-represented in mainstream journalism compared to their numbers in the French population as a whole and this is particularly evident in the profession's upper echelons. For instance, one of the most obvious contrasts between France and Britain is the former's relative lack of non-white news anchors on its mainstream television channels. Moreover, it is only relatively recently that this under-representation has been given greater political salience, as part of the wider debate about the 'inclusion/integration' of ethnic minorities in French society. This under-representation of ethnic minorities in mainstream journalism forms part of a broader socio-cultural and political issue, rather than one simply linked to media employment practices. Nonetheless, this does not prevent media executives and the journalistic profession addressing the problem within their own professional contexts if the will is there.

Journalism and the Market

Depending on one's perspective, journalism can be regarded as an account of 'reality', a cultural narrative or part of the process of political struggle. It is also increasingly a commercial product. Of course, this has always been the case to some degree: outside of public service outlets, journalism has invariably had to sell to survive. Yet the market pressures on journalism over the past couple of decades have increasingly focused critics' attention on the economic environment in which journalists function and journalism is produced.

There are four inter-related factors driving the process of marketisation. The first, to which we have already made reference in the preceding section, is the technologically driven expansion of the media. This has particularly affected the broadcasting and electronic sectors which now provide more opportunities for journalistic expression than ever before. Yet while expansion allows for more media outlets to enter the market, it also engenders competition for source access, audiences and advertisers.

Increased competition among media outlets is the second factor in the process of marketisation. Competition frequently (though it has to be said not inevitably) exercises a downward push on operational costs. This in turn has an impact on the working environment of journalists, on the willingness of media owners to allocate sufficient financial resources to journalistic endeavours and, ultimately, on the journalistic product itself. Moreover, cost-trimming is by no means confined to media outlets with low levels of profitability. The news division of TF1, for example, has no permanent correspondent at the EU headquarters in Brussels, nor in several European capital cities. Instead it relies on news agency copy, the input of freelancers and, in the case of major events, the contribution of a temporary correspondent sent to the location for the purpose. In contrast, *Le Monde* and the French news agency Agence France-Presse both have excellent networks of permanent foreign correspondents across the globe.

The third factor is liberalisation. This is particularly germane to the broadcasting sector. During the period of the state monopoly, the newsroom of the public service broadcasting organisation was largely immune from market pressures. Some internal competition between the news divisions of the two main national channels was introduced in 1969, though with limited financial consequences. The break-up of the unitary public service broadcasting corporation into separate companies in 1974 encouraged greater competition between the channels, which now relied heavily on advertising revenue for funding. The economic liberalisation of the broadcasting system which followed the formal abandonment of the state monopoly in 1982 did not just lead to the entry of new commercial players. It also had an impact on the existing public service channels, because the commercial companies, which of course included TF1 after its privatisation, to a large extent set the tone for the whole of the television sector through their ratings dominance. Due to the legacy of political control (see following section) the French public service broadcasting institutions have never enjoyed the legitimacy or popular support from which the BBC has benefited in Britain. Thus, economic liberalisation did not just pose a financial challenge to public service broadcasting newsrooms through the increased importance of ratings, but also a normative challenge regarding the status and function of news in a competitive market. Public service journalists have increasingly had to balance information norms with the need to attract a regular audience if *France-Télévisions* is to justify its call on the licence fee.

The final factor is the increasing sophistication of market research in corporate decision making. Ratings are not just quantitatively significant in measuring the size of the audience. Media executives and news editors also have extensive qualitative data on the sociological composition of their audiences (including age, gender, social class and income) which they can use to influence the fabrication of the news product, both in terms of the news agenda (what is covered and what is not) and the framing of news stories (from what angle a story is presented). While such market research may not determine a programme's news agenda or issue framing, since other news values will also come into play, they increasingly inform the strategic process of resource allocation within newsrooms. An example of how audience composition influences the journalistic product is shown by the difference in content between the lunchtime news broadcast of TF1 and the main evening news programme on the same channel, with the former geared to a more provincial, rural and elderly audience. Some of the market research data on readership age profiles must be worrying for newspaper executives and editors. For instance, 44 per cent of the readership of *Le Figaro* is over 60 years old, while less than a quarter of the readership of *L'Humanité* is under 35 (Charon, 2005: 108).

Political Journalism and the Public Sphere

If the news media are to contribute to a healthy and effective public sphere in civil society, then journalists should assist (and certainly do nothing to obstruct) the performance of certain key functions. The most important of these include the provision of accurate information to citizens and the holding of political elites to account for their public actions. Moreover, in the performance of these functions, journalists should behave in a socially responsible and professionally ethical manner, maintaining their independence from politicians and vested interests alike. How does recent French journalism match up to these normative criteria?

There is no doubt that historically French journalism has often failed to meet these standards. French media outlets have frequently enjoyed close links with politicians, with political journalists facing accusations of a collusive and deferential relationship with governing elites. In the years before the outbreak of World War II, for instance, many newspaper journalists received financial 'gifts' from government ministries to write stories supportive of official policy, while during the de Gaulle presidency the output of state television news was closely controlled via Ministry of Information diktat and the appointment of politically sympathetic news editors (Bourdon, 1990).

Official censorship and overt interference in journalistic output by politicians are now much less common. French politicians, like their counterparts in other advanced democracies, have become more professional in their political communication activities and now seek to shape their relationships with the media through the use of public relations techniques rather than explicit forms of political control (Kuhn, 2005). Politicians are more likely to seek to manage the news agenda and the framing of issues through the exertion of pressure and influence at what they deem to be the appropriate level of the media chain of command: proprietor, chief executive, news editor or political reporter/correspondent. To help them in this, several politicians enjoy a close social relationship with journalists and vice versa. While some of this may appear 'normal' and even inevitable, the danger of such inter relationships is that journalists may come to rely on the off-the-record 'spin' from their official sources and run the risk of being 'captured' by them (Carton, 2003).

In this interdependent relationship between politician and journalist, the professional cultural norms of the journalistic milieu are important. Deference on the part of journalists to politicians may well be on the wane in France. However, it still remains more of a feature of the French political communication system than in Anglo-American democracies where a journalistic tradition of adversarial contestation, critical watchdog and 'Fourth Estate' thinking is more firmly implanted. For instance, French television interviews between leading politicians and broadcast journalists often seem tame compared to the cut-and-thrust of their equivalents in Britain, with the French President in particular accorded sacerdotal treatment by interviewers who are usually reluctant to push home their interrogative advantage.

In addition, certain aspects of a politician's life are generally regarded as out of bounds to journalistic investigation in France, notably matters related to sexual behaviour and orientation. The existence of President Mitterrand's illegitimate daughter, Mazarine, was revealed to the French public by *Paris Match* only in 1994, by which time she was nearly 20 and Mitterrand had been the elected head of state for over 13 years (Chemin and Catalano, 2005). While a reluctance to infringe on the private lives of politicians may be considered by some to be an admirable journalistic trait, in this case it should be remembered that Mazarine and her mother were being lodged at the taxpayers' expense and that public money was also being spent on Mazarine's protection by state officials. These were clearly subjects of legitimate public interest.

Some journalists certainly knew of Mazarine's existence prior to 1994, but did not go public with the information, either through fear of political reprisals or from a mistaken sense of respect for presidential privacy. Their reluctance to 'spill the beans' may also have been influenced by the existence of strong privacy legislation in France, notably the law of 17 July 1970 which also covers matters such as the publication of photographs without the consent of the interested party. Those who consider that their privacy has been breached by media intrusion can take the offending party to court and, if found guilty, the media source can be fined and compelled to pay damages and publish a retraction. In practice this means that mainstream media outlets are wary of running foul of the law and tend to err on the side of caution.

Journalistic deference to politicians in contemporary France should not, however, be overstated. For instance, over the past 20 years or so, journalism and sections of the judiciary have been objective allies in the process of exposing instances of corruption in local and national politics. Journalists from different media outlets, including the iconoclastic weekly paper *Le Canard Enchaîné*, *L'Express* and *Le Monde*, played a prominent role in the coverage of a series of financial scandals involving leading Socialist and Gaullist politicians from the 1980s onwards. Revelations of the illegal siphoning off of money for party coffers or personal gain rocked the French political establishment and led to the introduction of new legislation on party funding. President Chirac himself was not spared, with stories about cash payment for family holidays splashed in magazines and newspapers. During the recent premiership of Jean-Pierre Raffarin, the term of office of the Minister of Finance, Hervé Gaymard, was brought to a premature conclusion by media revelations of the amount of public money which was being used to subsidise the use by his family of a huge apartment in an upmarket district of Paris. Unable to counter the media allegations against him, the minister was forced to resign. While in the French context this was a successful example of 'attack journalism', in general French journalism lacks the tabloid news values of much of the press in the UK. Gaymard was pilloried, but the tone of coverage was more restrained than that which often accompanies the 'feeding frenzy' media calls for a ministerial resignation in the UK.

Another facet of journalists' contribution to a healthy public sphere concerns the exercise of media power through the capacity to inform citizens about issues and policies. This is not simply a question about the quantity of information made available in the public domain; it is also about its quality. Journalists have a social responsibility to seek to ensure that the mediated information they provide the public is accurate, proportionate and appropriately contextualised. Not all French journalism meets these standards by any means. A notable case in point is the role played by key media outlets, notably the main national television channels, in their news coverage of the issue of *insécurité* in the run-up to the first round of the 2002 presidential election.

The television news agenda in the 2002 campaign was very narrow, focusing largely on the issue of law and order, the pre-eminence of which was bolstered by a steady news diet of crime stories, especially on TF1, in the early months of the year. The focus of television news on law and order items was not driven by politically partisan factors, but by media-centred variables. Incidents of crime and personal violence made good stories because they were events-driven, conformed to news values of human interest, drama and sensationalism, attracted audiences in a competitive market and, in the case of TF1, supported the brand image of 'the people's television' which the channel wished to portray. Yet by frequently framing the story in terms of a societal breakdown of law and order, the media played an important priming role in establishing the issue as a criterion by which voters judged candidates. In so doing, television news almost certainly gave a boost to Le Pen's campaign and facilitated his passage to the run-off ballot. Conversely, the virtually unanimous anti-Le Pen journalistic coverage prior to the second round of voting showed the media articulating and reflecting the widespread concern among French voters regarding Le Pen's views and values.

Current Developments and Future Trends

Contemporary French journalism is beset by a variety of challenges which are driving changes in work practices, journalistic cultures and journalists' relations with both sources and audiences. Two general points are worth noting about this changing journalistic environment in France. The first is that many, if not all, of these changes are to be found to some degree in other advanced democratic societies: France is neither unique nor exceptional, even if the possibility of national specificity should not be ruled out, nor its importance underestimated. Second, while in this section the main changes are treated separately for analytic purposes, in the real world they are frequently interlinked.

The first set of changes are related to *technological shift*. The most important and most obvious technological advance in recent years has been the advent and routinisation of the Internet as a means of information distribution and usage. The rise of the Internet has impacted on French journalism in six ways:

1. The World Wide Web has opened up to journalists a cornucopia of information which can be easily accessed from their desks in the newsroom. Journalistic production has thus benefited from the 'googleisation' of information supply.
2. Mainstream media outlets have transferred some of their output on to the Net

in a bid to attract and retain audiences, maintain their commercial profile and publicise their brand. In so doing the product may have to be tweaked to satisfy the exigencies of the new medium. For instance, the Web version of *Le Monde* – *LeMonde.fr* – is not just a replica of the hard-copy newspaper. Instead it is a multi-tiered information resource which provides more background to running stories, links to other relevant websites and opportunities to users to engage in interactive exchange.

3.   Professional journalists now publish directly on the Net, with different content and sometimes in a different style from their output in traditional mainstream media. Journalists' blogs are a notable example of innovation in this respect.

4.   The Internet has allowed a whole array of other social and political actors to publish blogs. In providing alternative viewpoints to Internet users these blogs may either contribute to the de-professionalisation of journalism ('we are all journalists now') or enhance the legitimacy of professional journalists because of the latter's publicly recognised accredited status.

5.   The Internet is contributing to changes in patterns of audience usage, especially among the young, who increasingly look to the Internet as their primary source of information about the world.

6.   The Internet, along with satellite technology, has speeded up the process whereby information enters the public domain: many events are now reported in 'real time' which enhances their actuality but may detract from their broader contextualisation.

The second change in contemporary French journalism relates to the *market entry of new information providers in mainstream media*. In the print sector, the main newcomers are free newspapers. These do not just offer competition for readers and advertisers to their established paid-for rivals. They also provide a specific type of newspaper product – 'news lite' – for their predominantly urban readerships: short articles, little or no columnist or investigative journalism and a non-partisan approach to politics. In the broadcasting sector, the principal entrant in recent years has been rolling news channels, catering directly for news junkies in the audience, but also acting as a complement to the traditional news programmes of the parent channel, as in the case of LCI and TF1.

The third change embraces *formats and content*. Newspaper re-launches with new formats have become commonplace. The latest format of *Le Monde*, introduced in 2005 to provide a cleaner look to the layout and to make photographs an integral part of journalistic content, makes the newspaper resemble in stylistic terms a French version of *The Guardian*. This has led to charges from some readers that the newspaper is 'dumbing down' its coverage, while the newspaper management prefer to talk about essential modernisation. Conversely, mainstream television news programming in France retains a traditional quality in comparison to its British equivalent: the news anchor – there is usually only one – remains seated and reporters in the field provide packaged items rather than engaging in two-way interchanges with the news anchor in the studio.

With regard to journalistic content, new or previously under-exploited areas of specialism such as the environment, the arts, social change and lifestyle issues (health, personal finances and leisure) jostle alongside the more traditional fields of politics and crime for editorial resources and audience attention. The politics of the EU is also an expanding specialism and, in contrast to much British political journalism on this topic, in France it tends to be treated as a political field in its own right rather than simply part of domestic political debate (Baisnée, 2002). Some types of journalistic coverage, such as straight parliamentary reporting in newspapers, have been abandoned. In national political coverage there is arguably less coverage of ideas and more of personalities, strategies and process. In part this is due to the reduction in ideological conflict at elite level (see the first section) and in part to the greater attention paid by the contemporary generation of French politicians to image management and self-promotion via the media.

The final change can be seen in *audience behaviour*. The expanded media landscape allows audiences to escape from the mass straitjacket imposed by the previous scarcity of supply. The era of the mass audience is not yet fully over, but it is surely coming to an end as more niche media outlets target specific sections of society. Faced with unprecedented choice among media outlets, audiences roam and graze for news and information. Audiences are also becoming more active consumers, not just in exercising choice among media products, but also in seeking out information relevant to their lives and engaging in greater interactivity with content providers. Digital and Web-based technologies will further encourage these trends in media usage by audiences in the future.

There is no single overarching explanatory variable for these myriad changes. New technology clearly creates new opportunities for journalists and audiences alike, helping to establish new patterns of media production, distribution and consumption. However, some of the above changes, for instance in newspaper formats and fields of journalistic coverage, have nothing to do with technological shift. Rather they are driven by processes of social and political change, generational turnover (both in society and the journalistic profession) and commercial responses to new demands from media audiences.

References

Baisnée, O. (2002), 'Can political journalism exist at the EU level?', in Kuhn, R. and Neveu, E. (eds), *Political Journalism: New Challenges, New Practices* (London: Routledge).

Bourdon, J. (1990), *Histoire de la télévision sous de Gaulle* (Paris: Anthropos/INA).

Carton, D. (2003), *'Bien entendu ... c'est off'* (Paris: Albin Michel).

Chalaby, J. (1996), 'Journalism as an Anglo-American invention', *European Journal of Communication*, 11 (3), 303–26.

Chalaby, J. (2002), *The de Gaulle Presidency and the Media* (Basingstoke: Palgrave Macmillan).

Charon, J.-M. (2005), *La presse quotidienne* (Paris: La Découverte).

Chemin, A. and Catalano, G. (2005), *Une famille au secret* (Paris: Stock).

Ferenczi, T. (2005), *Le Journalisme* (Paris: PUF).

Kidd, W. and Reynolds, S. (eds) (2000), *Contemporary French Cultural Studies* (London: Arnold).

Kuhn, R. (1995), *The Media in France* (London: Routledge).

Kuhn, R. (2005), 'Where's the spin? The executive and news management in France', *Modern & Contemporary France* 13 (3), 307–22.

Martin, M. (1997), *Médias et Journalistes de la République* (Paris: Editions Odile Jacob).

Neveu, E. (2005), 'Politicians without politics, a polity without citizens: the politics of the chat show in contemporary France', *Modern & Contemporary France* 13 (3), 323–35.

Péan, P. and Cohen, P. (2003), *La face cachée du Monde* (Paris: Mille et Une Nuits).

Conclusions

Peter J. Anderson

Introduction

The opening four chapters were written without the benefit of seeing all of the country studies that make up the bulk of this project. It is, however, noteworthy that the majority of those studies back up the tentative conclusions about the state of the news media within the advanced democracies that were offered in Part 1. It is in the light of this observation that we need not repeat in detail the carefully qualified conclusions of those early chapters, but instead refer the reader back to them where necessary. In an age where technology facilitates the global transmission of more words than previously could be imagined, there would seem to be a virtue in brevity.

The view that readers hold of the current shape of journalism within the societies studied within this book will be conditioned by their ideological perspective concerning the role of news media within contemporary democracies. For example, those who take the view that news is just one more product within a market economy will not be concerned if it is suggested here that some key news producers are not meeting the needs of a properly functioning democracy (but are making adequate profits). Equally, those who argue that the needs of democracy are met as long as there is at least one major news producer committed to comprehensive and relatively impartial coverage of news within a society will not be dismayed by what is perceived as the marked deterioration of news standards in every sector of the important (in terms of audience size) terrestrial UK broadcast news media other than the BBC and Channel 4 (although it should be noted that the BBC itself has been the subject of some well-reasoned and penetrating criticism – see, for example, Lloyd, 2004). The intention here is not to tell people what their views of the current state of news should be. Rather it is to set out the situation as it is seen through the eyes of our contributors and to portray its consequences through the lenses of sample ideological perspectives on the role of news within a democracy and to do so as objectively as is possible. Referring back to Chapter 3, those readers who wish to will be able to extend the exercise to additional perspectives. The intention then is to show how the problems that might be seen through the lenses of two of those perspectives – competitive democracy and participative democracy, both of which might be seen as sub-divisions of meaningful democracy (all defined in Chapter 3) – might be addressed.

The Three Core Questions

The three core questions that were laid down at the beginning of the book were covered to one extent or another in all of the country studies. They asked:

- To what extent is traditional hard news losing ground to soft news across the media of the advanced world and what can be done to reverse this trend if this is a serious problem?
- To what extent is the range and depth of coverage of news issues within the advanced democracies adequate for the purpose of ensuring that electorates are adequately informed about the world around them?
- To what extent is it possible to access balanced presentations of the news within the various advanced democracies within this study?

Each of these will now be addressed in turn in relation to the findings of our contributors.

Question 1: Hard News Versus Soft News

The overall picture very clearly is one of a continuing slide towards soft news, although to varying extents within different countries and on different news platforms. The most worrying instance of this undoubtedly is in the US, not only because public knowledge of public affairs (outside of the informed elites) is so poor already, but because of the enormous power that its government exercises without the participation of a properly informed general public to keep an eye on it. Deregulation, pushed forward by powerful conglomerates and interest groups addressing willing ears in Washington, has forced news standards down across most of the broadcast media and facilitated the rise of Fox News as a global symbol of the deterioration of American democracy. Local TV news in particular has lost much of its hard news agenda. The fact that public service broadcasting is relatively a fringe activity in the US mediascape means that there is little within American society to counterbalance this trend. Van Dijk (2005: 118, 119), together with the latest findings published by the Pew Research Center, cited in Chapter 2, make it clear that at the moment there is no evidence to show that Americans are using the Internet regularly for alternative sources of in-depth, high-quality political news in significant numbers. What is perhaps most alarming, as Brandenburg points out in his chapter, is the fact that the softer news producers clearly are persuading their audience that their simpler view of the world is more reliable than that of some of the remaining bastions of traditional American quality journalism.

In France too, despite the fact that conglomeration has had a more moderate impact due to continuing government controls on media ownership, commercialisation has taken a noticeable toll. For example, Kuhn notes that, while news still sells and is seen as a valuable brand for specific television channels, 'current affairs and political debate programmes are now largely confined to those channels for whom such programming is part of their public service remit'. Newspapers in France, key examples of which traditionally have been repositories of quality hard news, as in the rest of our country studies, are faced with shrinking markets and also competition from free 'news-lite' papers. In line with the American findings Kuhn notes that, as yet, there is no sign of the Internet becoming a major provider of high-quality political news to compensate for this, although he does see a future in which Internet information providers will more successfully target their products, particularly at today's younger generations of Net users. On the whole, however, the French approach to news remains both harder and more deferential than, for example, is the case in some other advanced democracies.

Our Japanese contributor notes that Japanese journalism is faced with serious questions as a result of the trivialisation of the news occasioned by the blurring of the distinction between hard and soft news in the interests of audience ratings and profits following deregulation. As in the other country studies, he notes a shift of younger generations away from newspapers to the Internet, but with little use of this for the purpose of accessing political news. He argues that the increasing trivialisation of news supplied by traditional providers, combined with the lack of confidence of many citizens in making judgements for themselves about the quality of news information available from the various providers on the Internet, is resulting in the effective disenfranchisement of some voters.

For our German contributor, the move towards an entertainment-based approach to popular news provision seems to be less of a worry, given that that is the form in which, he argues, many of the population seem most interested in receiving news. He points out that comprehensive traditional journalistic reporting still remains and is consumed by the educational and information elites. Equally, in the unique context of Italy, the importance of which our contributor has been reminding non-Italians about for some time (Mancini, 1997, for example), he implies that the populist softening of news presentation that has occurred under Berlusconi's influence has been at the very least forgiven by many, bearing in mind that the competition that spawned it has reduced the hold of the political and corporate elites over the Italian news media and made the public less of a spectator in an elite-controlled news process.

In the UK, most of our authors recorded what they regarded as a damaging softening of news across various platforms. The radio chapter noted in particular the decline of commercial radio as a serious news provider in the wake of deregulation. Deregulation was seen as a problem also in the television chapter, resulting in the blurring of the boundary between soft and hard news in some of the commercial news sectors and a serious decline in the coverage of hard news on the main commercial news provider's channels. Even the BBC, the large remaining bulwark against the commercial preferences of powerful global industry figures like Rupert Murdoch, has significantly reduced its serious current affairs programming.

The national newspapers chapter noted how the fierce competition that the sector faces, both within itself and from other media platforms, has resulted increasingly in a move towards an entertainment approach in the presentation even of serious news and how this is spreading now up the market spectrum. The sports journalism chapter showed in depth how one long-established aspect of soft news has become an essential underpinning even of hard news papers and how equally it is migrating into every section of both the popular and quality press.

All of these tendencies are linked in to the 'ec-tech' squeeze outlined in Chapter 4. While technological advance has provided the new and modified platforms that have opened up the technical possibilities of competition to the traditional news providers from everything from multichannel television to the Internet, the economic pressures unleashed by deregulation have combined with such innovation to force news providers into an increasing competition for audiences and advertising. Soft news has been seen by many as one of the easiest ways of boosting audience size.

However, neither economics nor technology could have had the impact that they have had on what is supposed to be one of the key requirements for a meaningful democracy – the provision of a reliable, sufficient supply of hard news of a reasonable depth (see Chapter 3) – without the agreement of governments. Conscious government decisions to deregulate or to avoid new regulations have been one of the most crucial influences on the growth of soft news provision. How this situation might be remedied, if it is agreed that it needs to be remedied, will be proposed later in the chapter.

Question 2: The Adequacy (for Democracy) of the Range and Depth of the Surviving Hard News Provision

As Chapter 3 pointed out, whether it is concluded that particular forms of journalism foster or damage democracy is dependent upon which form of democracy is being referred to. Our discussion in that chapter pointed to the usefulness of focusing on both competitive democracy and participative democracy and it should be noted that journalism that provides an adequate range and depth of hard news provision is required for both.

When we examine news journalism as described in the national chapters, the picture we get is again varied. It is useful to start once more with the US, for the same reason as above – the huge power that is at its government's disposal to use around the world in the name of the American people who, in their capacity to elect and eject national politicians, potentially are one of the few available effective checks and balances on the use of that power.

In his chapter on the US Brandenburg noted in considerable detail how the competitive pressures following deregulation, together with the lack of any significant public broadcasting presence to act as a counterbalance to their effects, has led to a significant 'dumbing down' of the range as well as the depth of news across much of broadcast television at both a national and a local level. As yet, this is not compensated for to any adequate degree by the Internet, as noted in the previous section. The print media equally cannot do much to make up for it. Those newspapers that retain a traditional commitment to wide-ranging hard news have limited circulations. A large part of the American public is relying on news products whose commitment to wide-ranging, in-depth hard news coverage is greatly deficient when compared to an organisation like the BBC. It is perhaps for this reason that the Corporation has started to make inroads into the US market during recent years. Brandenburg notes that those people who rely most on the Murdoch-owned Fox News and local television are the worst informed on major political issues. For the US, the remaining hard news provision falls far short of the needs of the world's most powerful democracy.

As far as Germany, France and Italy are concerned, our authors are much less troubled by the implications for democracy of the quantity and quality of the remaining hard news provisions in these states. As noted above, our German contributor is unworried by the fact that many German television viewers seem to be content with relatively brief details of news events because in-depth, wide-ranging journalism reporting is still available for those who want it. Similarly, the author of the chapter on France, while noting that coverage of current affairs and political debates largely has become 'ghettoised' within those channels with a public service remit, thus reducing the range and depth of serious background and contextualising information available to the public, is comforted by the knowledge that news still remains a brand that can sell to audiences of ten million and six million respectively, and by the fact that it is, overall, 'harder' than in some other key democracies. Our Italian contributor is concerned more with the fact that Berlusconi's influence has taken news away from its position as something that was shaped predominantly by political or corporatist interests – a situation in which hard news was of little democratic value because of its bias in favour of different parts of the establishment – than with any reduction in the range and depth of its coverage. The situation in Japan, however, is painted as an altogether more worrying one.

Our Japanese contributor notes that the tendency towards fragmentation and the making of hard news into an entertainment is predominant not only in Japanese television but also in newspapers and other media. In consequence, hard news in such areas as politics, diplomacy, economics and finance tends to be simplified. Its contents tend mainly to just skim the surface of events and this makes it difficult for the Japanese public to find the information necessary for discussion of such important and complicated issues. He concludes that journalism in Japan does not function sufficiently well to implement its mission of providing people with a range of news and information that will enable them to think about their society and history in an effective manner.

Most of our UK contributors are concerned also about decreasing range and depth in the coverage of hard news issues. In the television chapter, for instance, it was noted how a study found that in 2003 ITV did not feature a single international programme fitting within the (ITC) categories of politics, development, human rights or environment. The authors noted how these were all genres deemed to be 'difficult' and occurring in areas traditionally regarded as 'hard news'. They noted also the extent to which current affairs programmes and documentaries were losing their place on ITV and to a lesser but still significant extent on the BBC's main channels.

Our radio contributor, John Drury, concluded that there is now a massive contrast between commercial and public service radio, with the former having almost entirely given up any commitment to wide-ranging, in-depth news coverage following the competitive pressures and ethos that have been unleashed by deregulation. The BBC, on the other hand, was noted to be making real efforts not only to maintain its breadth and depth of news coverage across the various platforms on which radio material can now be accessed, but also to expand them. At the level of mainstream radio, the 'citizen' element of this endeavour sounds at the moment to be more concerned with broadening the news agenda to include political issues previously given less importance by editors, but which nevertheless are important to listeners, than with the more cynical trend of 'going citizen' to cost-save. Indeed, Drury notes that the current BBC Head of News and Current Affairs wonders whether the ambitious vision that confronts the BBC, of which radio is a part, is in fact affordable.

Our national newspapers chapter noted very little coverage of hard news in any range and depth within the popular 'red tops', and declining coverage in the mid-market and even the quality end of the spectrum. This was partially occasioned by even the quality papers increasingly presenting themselves as 'magazines', within which hard news is but one key aspect, in order to better compete in the circulation battles that all are fighting. However, the author was comforted to a degree by the decision of *The Independent* and *The Guardian* to re-position themselves as commentators and analysts, looking in depth, over the course of an average month, at a wide range of serious news issues from both home and abroad.

Our local and regional newspapers chapter presented a more complex picture in which our contributor advised caution with regard to the view that news at these levels is being significantly 'dumbed down' across the board as a result of commercial pressures. She acknowledges that there are real worries in this regard but points out that hard news is still seen as having a role to play in sustaining democracy at regional and local level by some key figures within the industry. The difficulty, she emphasises, is in judging how the hard news/soft news balance will shift, given that newspapers at these levels are undergoing significant technological and organisational changes, the consequences of which are difficult to predict.

So, within three of our country studies most of the authors have serious worries about the extent to which the range and depth of hard news coverage is decreasing. In the UK the situation is less pronounced because of the continued counterbalancing presence of the BBC as a large-scale producer of high-quality hard news although, as mentioned earlier, friendly critics have pointed out that it too has some serious issues to address in its journalism (Lloyd, 2004). In Japan and the US, however, the world's two most economically powerful states, no such checks and balances exist and the relevant authors conclude that in neither state is the public accessing the information that is necessary for the functioning of a meaningful democracy.

Once again, the key factors at work in creating this situation are the 'ec-tech' squeeze and the decisions of the various governments to permit deregulation. The extent that the latter has been permitted in most cases seems to correlate with the extent that authors are worried or unworried about the range and depth of hard news coverage, except in the rather special case of Italy.

It is now necessary to address the third and final question.

Question 3: Balance in the Presentation of the News

The final question raises immediately the old debate as to whether balance should be aimed for across media sectors or within individual news producers. Our UK studies suggest that, while the BBC has been accused of bias domestically by political parties or individuals who are dissatisfied with its perceived viewpoints, or by powerful rivals such as Rupert Murdoch internationally, most of the British population still regard it as generally impartial in its coverage of the news. This does not mean that all of its news presenters are impartial or deferential. The main anchor of the flagship BBC2 programme *Newsnight*, Jeremy Paxman, for example, from time to time can be demonstrably biased on some issues, such as the EU, and vigorously interrogative in his interviewing style. However, it is with regard to the BBC's overall coverage of news – on television, radio and online – that the perception that it is relatively impartial remains. It provides a powerful counterbalance to the robust partisanship of the national print media sector and its presence is one of the reasons why the latter remains lightly (self-)regulated.

As the American chapter has shown, the US professional focus on objectivity raises different issues in so far as it is supposed to apply *across the nation's media*. Our contributor cites arguments that see this kind of universal objective approach as leaving the audience uninvolved and encouraging a focus on processes and conflicts rather than more controversial and therefore problematic in-depth analyses of issues. He mentions also the way in which Fox News has distorted the notion of impartiality, in the process undermining not only the value of news but also the perceptions of those who rely on it.

For our Italian contributor, the influence of Berlusconi has weakened the political element in news programming in favour of the need to attract mass audiences in the new competitive environment. This observation might be argued to lead to the conclusion that television, the main source of news in Italy, has to become less partial politically in order to maximise its number of viewers. In France, Kuhn shows that it is still the case that, even though the broadcasters have been freed from state control, the political classes are shown much more deference than in countries like the UK. This raises obvious problems for balanced coverage of political events and issues. On the other hand, he argues that there has been a decline in the importance of ideology as an integral part of newspapers' 'mission'. He sees this as being driven by the need to maximise readerships in a declining market sector, and the decline of ideological conflict in French electoral politics over the past two decades, which has been influenced by the inter-related processes of liberalisation, Europeanisation and globalisation. He notes also that regional newspapers have the reputation of being reluctant to take strong partisan positions on political issues in case they alienate sections of their politically diverse readership.

The German chapter shows that the essential yardstick for judging the degree to which quality journalism is present in a news product in that country is still the extent to which journalism is kept distinct from advertising or public relations, literary text forms and dedicated expressions of opinion. Our contributor demonstrates also how economic pressures in recent years have led to these 'separations' being breached repeatedly. Cutbacks in staffing and general resources have led, for example, to journalists compromising their impartiality by incorporating public relations material in their reports. Equally, cutbacks have meant there have been fewer resources available to finance the proper investigation and fact-checking of stories, which again can lead to the compromise of impartiality. In addition, a number of media companies have, through their news products, adopted strong positions on political issues in recent years and it is suggested that again media economics may be part of the explanation for this, with stances being adopted which are designed particularly to sell more newspapers.

Both inside and outside Japan, as our contributor demonstrates in detail, there are still serious concerns about the impact of the press club system on the objectivity of reporting in that country. He points out that the system makes it easy for a journalist or the organisation he or she works for to be affected subliminally by a group mentality, which can result in the homogeneous coverage of an issue. He mentions also concerns that large Japanese newspapers rely for 80–90 per cent of their news on releases within the press clubs, issued by government bodies, major institutions and large companies. He highlights also the fact that the system causes the same news reports to appear across the whole range of Japanese newspapers. Furthermore, various scandals, fictional reports and abuses of media power in recent years have started to undermine public trust in the news media and threaten further perceptions of the accuracy and impartiality of its reporting. The Internet offers little in the way of a viable alternative to the traditional media because much of its news is insubstantial in content and supplied by established news producers, while independent blogging covering news issues and people's preparedness to access it are still very much in their infancy in Japan.

The pictures that emerge from our various country studies are varied but, for the most part, demonstrate that the extent to which people can access balanced news, either within individual news products or across the range of a nation's media, varies considerably with different consequences for meaningful democracy as broadly defined in Chapter 3. Ironically, in the US, where the commitment to professional objectivity across the national media is perhaps the most long-standing, there are serious concerns that this might actually be weakening meaningful democracy, to the extent that it exists in the American political system, by reducing, for example, the in-depth coverage of news issues. While worries in France and Italy may be less visible, the German chapter suggests that there is a growing cause for concern about the balance of reporting in the national news media under the pressure from economic influences. The Japanese contributor showed there to be real problems within Japan, most particularly resulting from the long-established press club system. The UK, with the continuing, although periodically pressured position of the BBC as a large-scale provider of news that is charged with being impartial across its range of coverage, and a contrasting highly partisan, competitive newspaper press, remains the country that can perhaps claim to have 'the best of both worlds'. However, there are large swathes of the UK population, particularly among younger generations, who do not regularly access its highest-quality news programmes or newspapers, or use the Internet for significant levels of hard news accessing. One of the issues to be discussed in the next section, therefore, is how younger generations can be attracted to quality news sources. As our various chapters show, this is a problem that is common across the countries and continents that we have examined.

Finally, it should be noted that concerns about problems of balance, the range and depth of hard news coverage and the competing claims of hard and soft news will be addressed at appropriate points below.

Journalism and Democracy: Present Problems and Future Remedies

Chapter 3 showed how different perspectives on the role of journalism within liberal democracies, together with different understandings of what liberal democracy should be about, are capable of producing widely differing verdicts on the extent to which the news media currently are meeting the informational needs of the advanced democracies. It is not our intention to offer any 'one size fits all' answer to what the relationship between journalism and democracy should be. Rather, having considered in detail the various findings of the country studies, it seemed to us useful to engage in a little thinking 'outside of the box', focusing on the current problems facing democracies and the news media within them.

From the point of view of news organisations, the current major problem in many cases is one of declining or shifting audiences. Newspapers are, for the most part, losing readers across the advanced democracies, television news audiences have been fragmented as a result of multichannel and digital television technology as well as the competition from other new platforms, and mainstream online news operations, while attracting new audiences, are proving costly to operate for many. The greatest audience loss is amongst the younger generations and is hitting newspapers the hardest, as our various country studies have shown. The task for journalism, therefore, is one of finding how to reconnect with those potential news audiences that have been lost, without losing those that are still loyal, *and* remain financially viable.

This is also a problem for the governments of democracies, because lost audiences for hard news are far more difficult to address or engage. Equally, political disengagement can, if it becomes significant enough, undermine the very foundations of democracy. Our solution, because of the scale of the problems involved that have been revealed by this and other studies, understandably perhaps is to *suggest a means* by which remedies to the current ills can be found. To this end we will put forward the idea of a democratic media institute, a concept that sounds fanciful, 'academic' and even frivolous perhaps but, as will be seen, merits serious consideration. It extends far beyond the useful but relatively narrowly focused Institute that was set up at Oxford University following the success of John Lloyd's critique of what the media have been doing to politics in Britain (Lloyd, 2004).

Before our ideas are explained, however, it is necessary to examine briefly the current state of thinking on the future of journalism and how to reconnect with shrinking audiences.

Our Present State

For Rupert Murdoch, delivering a much-covered speech at Stationers' Hall in London in March 2006, the future of journalism seemed reducible to graspable certainties:

> ... great journalism will always attract readers. The words, pictures and graphics that are the stuff of journalism have to be brilliantly packaged; they must feed the mind and move the heart.
>
> And, crucially, newspapers must give readers a choice of accessing their journalism in the pages of the paper or on websites such as Times Online or – and this is important – on any platform that appeals to them, mobile phones, hand-held devices, iPods, whatever. As I have said, newspapers may become news sites. As long as news organisations create must-read, must-have content, and deliver it in the medium that suits the reader, they will endure.
>
> Great content always has been, and I think always will be, king of the media castle (Murdoch, 2006).

However, from the viewpoint of the serious end of journalism, this does not really deal with the question as to *what kinds* of 'great content' will actually attract the interest of younger generations when it is packaged as hard news, of precisely how it can be packaged to attract their attention and whether that 'packaging' will increase their knowledge and understanding of their societies in a manner that will enable them to participate meaningfully in a democracy.

While the often vaguely elaborated mantra of 'great content' currently is being chanted by Murdoch and senior BBC executives as one of the keys to salvation of news organisations, one of the things that has become apparent from the various country-based chapters within this book, particularly the detailed UK studies, is that in reality the news media currently is confused about the future. As was explained in Part 1, this is hardly surprising given the ever-increasing pace of technological change and the fierce economic pressures that have emerged in the wake of deregulation. There is much talk about the opportunities and threats presented by the new platforms for news communication, convergence and changing audience preferences, but there is probably less certainty than in any stage of modern media history as to what all of the new developments really mean. For all the currently fashionable talk about 'citizen journalism' in its various forms, for example, there is little hard evidence that any version of it will be the 'mass' future of journalism and *radically* change the nature of the profession. Ward et al. provide a useful representation of the arguments currently being espoused in its favour in their chapter on online journalism. All of the evidence of the past, for example, is that when presented with opportunities to participate *directly* in public discussion and opinion formation regarding serious political issues (never mind the 'less exciting' job of reporting the news), while the public can be provoked into vigorous debate through whatever forums are available by occasional big issues that arouse mass dissatisfaction (such as the poll tax in the UK during the Thatcher period), initial popular enthusiasm declines over time and is supplanted by other concerns. The field for the most part is left to what used to be called 'activists', the professionals and those who traditionally wrote in to the letter pages of newspapers or phoned in to broadcast programmes. As pointed out in Chapter 2, a 2006 national survey of American bloggers found that only a small proportion focus their coverage on politics, media, government or technology and an even smaller percentage of these people engage in what traditionally would have been called reporting. Indeed, for all the hype in some academic and industry quarters, the belief at senior levels of the BBC is that many of the *worthwhile* hard news and political discussion blogs currently in operation are actually being run by journalists wanting some independence from their day-time employer's views (Clifton, 2006).

More than one of our contributors concluded also that in their countries, while news blogs that are independent of traditional news providers did receive varying levels of attention in addition to that given to mainstream online news sites, *on the whole users still preferred to access the Internet mainly for other forms of information*. In line with the views of senior figures in the BBC, noted in the UK radio chapter, many people still prefer authoritative guidance and interpretation through the complexity of daily hard news events. If they do turn to the Internet it is only a minority who turn to blogs for news. Chapter 2 showed how in the US only 9 per cent of Internet users do so, for example. It was noted in the same chapter how, even during the heightened politicking of the 2005 UK General Election, only around a third of young voters – as members of the most Web-dependent of all the current generations – turned to the Internet as a whole as their primary source of political news and information, never mind blogs in particular. The same chapter noted how in the US in 2006 only 30 per cent of 18–24 year olds, once again from the most Web-conscious generation of adults, were regularly accessing the Internet for news.

'Citizen journalism' (in the specific form of public response to invitations from the BBC and others to send in digital news photographs, comments and stories for use by their news operations) can indeed increase interactivity and immediacy and, to a limited extent, turn journalism more into a 'conversation' (which, among other things, can increase transparency – via BBC weblogs, for example). However, there is no evidence that *overall* it is of sufficient or consistent enough quality to replace mainstream journalism rather than provide a generally minor add-on to it. (Even where usage of citizen contributions has been substantial, as during the 2004 Asian tsunami disaster, for many quality and coherence issues seemed to emphasise that such large-scale usage is likely to remain restricted to such massive, highly exceptional news events as far as quality news providers are concerned.) Furthermore, Simon Waldman, director of digital publishing at Guardian newspapers, has pointed out that even in the case of such an internationally popular and respected online news site as that of *The Guardian*, the newspaper's own tracking of usage has shown that most people accessing the site do so simply to read the content and not to engage in a 'conversation' (Waldman, 2006).

None of which is to *deny* that the various current and emerging news-related activities on the Internet, or other new developing platforms, may become the main news conduits of the future. The simple truth is that there is no evidence to rule that possibility out and, indeed, mainstream and alternative Internet hard news providers might well become more skilled at attracting a wider public to visit their sites. Equally, there is a lot of ill-supported supposition but as yet no solid evidence to prove that non-mainstream forms of hard news provision will, on their own, dominate future news provision.

For the media industry the consequences of this uncertainty are troubling. With shareholders looking over their shoulders in the case of commercial companies, or the need for a continued ability to justify funding via licence fees in the case of the BBC, media executives have conflicting fears of 'missing the next boat' or of getting it wrong with a risky investment in a new news technology and seeing millions of pounds, dollars or euros disappear into a black hole. That uncertainty in turn can cause companies to withhold investments in some areas of existing activity, or even cut back on them, as in the case of the BBC and its national news operations, in order to release resources for a very uncertain gamble with the future. Equally, attempts can be made to cover as many options as possible, which leave news operations denuded of resources as cash is 'scattergunned' across a range of areas of new investment which may or may not pay off.

For politicians also, there is uncertainty, as Chapter 4 illustrated, although its existence often is only recognised fully when it is too late. New technological advances are frequently supported and enabled without adequate prior thought as to their impact on the crucial news and information provision which meaningful democracy requires – despite, in several cases, the existence of official commissions, reports and investigations which should have alerted political decision makers to their potential implications. Surprise is then often expressed when unanticipated consequences emerge, such as ITV's demoting of *News at Ten* – a one-time favourite with UK politicians – as the network struggled to cope with the competition introduced by multichannel television. It is notable how the UK's Prime Minister at the time of writing has been enthusiastically supporting the rapid switchover to digital television without any apparent grasp of the downside for news communication within his democracy.

In short, from a democratic point of view, the situation regarding the news media is a mess and has been for some time. The consequences for meaningful democracy of over-enthusiastic deregulation – some of the most negative of which have been demonstrated in this book – have never been thought through properly in most of the advanced societies within the democratic club. Equally, the news media themselves have suffered from some of them and in the case of those within the field who would have preferred to protect hard news in a way that has not proved possible for their companies, the outcomes of all of the well-orchestrated pressures and lobbying of Rupert Murdoch and others have severely damaged the news operations they profess to believe in.

A Democratic Media Institute of Unparalleled Scope

There is an old argument that desperate times require desperate measures. The future of democracy is faced with a time bomb in the shape of a generation of young adults within which many have turned away from both traditional politics and the hard news media, even when the latter have extended their operations online. While the often-quoted assertion that there is little new in this and that the responsibilities of later life – of families, mortgages, and so on – tend to generate interest in both news and mainstream politics as people mature has had some foundation in the past, the scale of the switch-off seems to be far greater than before and it is combined with a future in which hard news will have a formidable and unprecedented range of competitors for people's attention. It is not uncommon to hear UK journalism lecturers complaining that many students are now entering university without even a basic understanding of the operation of their own political system and show little interest in the political content of newspapers or the various other arms of the news media. Indeed, the declining interest of the young in hard news providers has been becoming apparent for some time. Citing Shaw (1989), Dahlgren noted in the 1990s that 'the marked decline of literary culture and skills among younger generations is having a profound impact on the whole newspaper industry in the USA' (Dahlgren, 1997: 13). In July 2006 an influential US report noted that: 'The views and habits that continue to constrain the size of most news audiences are shared widely among younger people. They are much less likely than older Americans to get great enjoyment from keeping up with the news, or to get the news at regular times' (Pew Research Center for the People and the Press, 2006). If the interest of younger generations of citizens of the democracies is not re-engaged there is no guarantee that democracy as a form of governance will have a long-term future. It is as simple and alarming as that and neither politicians nor the news media have very much in the way of inspired ideas to redress the situation.

What is needed, therefore, is for both government and those sections of the news media that are still committed to the provision of hard news[1] to recognise that they have a commonality of interest in the problem, the one in the shape of declining audience revenue (in other words, a market issue), the other in the form of a direct threat to its political existence. They need to recognise also that, because the scale of

---

1   It would be naïve to assume that all major news providers would be concerned enough to seek a solution to the problem (Calabrese, 2000).

the problem now is so widespread, its solution will require a substantial investment of both time and money.

We have no wish to engage in utopianism and are well aware that what often is most logical is equally the least obtainable. Nevertheless, if only to demonstrate the scale of what is required, it can be pointed out that it would be worth setting up a high-powered institute or 'laboratory', funded jointly by governments and industry, to conduct in-depth investigation of a variety of specific areas of the problem *in a manner that no single university department or industry research unit could attempt and no past official commission/enquiry has been able to match.* Given the global nature of democracy, the global nature of much of the media industry, and the commonality of significant trends in some audience attitudes and behaviour that is emerging, it would need to be multinational in personnel and scope (although there would be little hope of Washington's support or official participation on the basis of current US government attitudes towards the regulation of the news media – indeed, it could be argued that the decline in the quality of hard news coverage in the US noted by Brandenburg and others suits those political interests that do not wish specific matters to be subjected to scrutiny). It would need to investigate *in more depth than hitherto* such key issues as the causes for the increasing switch away from conventional news media amongst younger generations of adults. For example, has this situation arisen because:

- the heavy reliance on some technologies in their education and home upbringing has reduced their ability or preparedness to read conventional print text?
- they are being influenced by an economic/technological culture in which news is something they are no longer willing to pay for?
- newspapers and other conventional media are speaking to them with the wrong voice, whether they be online or offline?
- mainstream politics has become too 'managerial' and uninspiring for them to want to read or hear about it?
- modern consumer and television culture has turned their interest more on themselves and away from the outside world?
- the significant reduction in ideological polarity since the end of the cold war has taken the interest and challenge out of political affairs?
- they are disinterested in politics and media reports about it because they feel that there is nothing that they can do to influence it?

But this would be only a small part of what would need to be a very complex and detailed investigation, far in excess of anything currently being done by research organisations in this field. It would need to include proper, multi-country comparative investigations of, for example:

- the consequences for democracy of various forms of existing and proposed deregulation (with proper protection against industry interference in the study);

- the consequences for democracy of the introduction and various forms of use of new media technologies;
- the extent to which educational systems are contributing to the scale of disinterest in politics and the hard news media;
- the extent to which both politicians and the media are contributing to cynicism about politics and the hard news which reports it;
- the extent to which an 'unofficial' Singapore/Chinese-style cultural deal has taken root amongst young people which causes them to take little interest in politics as long as they are able to access the consumer goods and lifestyle that they aspire to;
- the extent to which corporate news culture has taken the excitement and imagination out of journalism;
- the extent to which balanced news is achievable and desirable;
- the extent to which hard news can be made as interesting as soft news.

The studies would be *linked and long-term with frequent interim reports*, reflecting the fact that *generational interests and societies themselves change so rapidly nowadays that every set of conclusions would need to be updated in depth every two or three years*. Their purpose would be twofold: first, to provide the basis for better understanding at governmental level of what is needed for both meaningful democracy and maybe even the survival of democracy itself, in so far as the media is crucial to both; second, to provide the industry with a better understanding of how, in the various societies within which it operates, it could reconnect with the audiences that it has been losing. Naturally, industry funding would have to be provided in such a way that it could not compromise the political purposes of the enterprise.

Whether or not a formal body (whose remit would far exceed previous national commissions on the news media, and so on) is created to examine the issues we have raised in this chapter is a matter for national governments. The proposal above is only a suggestion and if it achieves nothing else, at least demonstrates the scale of response that is necessary to what rapidly is becoming a 'silent' problem of alarming proportions. Equally, the issues we have mentioned above are but a small part of the ground that would need to be covered, as the substantial literature on regulation, deregulation and general questions of the quality of news provision demonstrates (for example, Curran, 2002: 216–36; Calabrese, 2000: 43–62; Franklin, 1997; Hoggart, 2004: 108–39; Zelizer, 2004: 164–6; Harvey, 2004: 194–210). There is a slowly dawning realisation among some European governments of the scale of the task that confronts their educational systems if the basic interest in politics that both democracy and the news media rely on is to be sparked amongst upcoming generations of young people (BBC, 2005, for example), and this also necessarily would form part of the ground to be investigated. What, in our view, is not in doubt is the urgent need for these issues to be addressed. Readers may well have reached their own conclusions. Whatever the case, we hope that the above discussion has at least established the need for a proportional, international response to developments in news journalism which, if not controlled, risk undermining the very foundations upon which the democracies are founded.

References

BBC (no author cited) (2005), 'Move to "sell" EU to the French', BBC Online, 29 June 2005.

Calabrese, A. (2000), 'Global Debates over Media Standards', in Sparks, C. and Tulloch, J. (eds) *Tabloid Tales – Global Debates over Media Standards* (Lanham MD: Rowman and Littlefield).

Clifton, P. (2006), *Participation in Journalism Leaders' Forum*, University of Central Lancashire, Preston, 31 January.

Curran, J. (2002), *Media and Power* (London: Routledge).

Dahlgren, P. (1997), 'Introduction', in Dahlgren, P. and Sparks, C. (eds), *Communication and Citizenship: Journalism and the Public Sphere* (London: Routledge).

Franklin, B. (1997), *Newszak and News Media* (London: Arnold).

Harvey, S. (2004), 'Living with Monsters – Can Broadcasting Regulation Make a Difference?', in Calabrese, A. and Sparks, C. (eds), *Toward a Political Economy of Culture* (Lanham MD: Rowman and Littlefield).

Hoggart, R. (2004), *Mass Media in a Mass Society: Myth and Reality* (London: Continuum).

Lloyd, J. (2004), *What the Media are Doing to our Politics* (London: Constable and Robinson).

Mancini, P. (1997), 'The Public Sphere and the Use of News in a "Coalition" System of Government', in Dahlgren, P. and Sparks, C. (eds), *Communication and Citizenship: Journalism and the Public Sphere* (London: Routledge).

Murdoch, R. (2006), 'Murdoch speech at Stationers' Hall: full text', <www.timesonline.co.uk>, 13 March.

Pew Research Center for the People and the Press (2006), 'Online Papers Modestly Boost Newspaper Readership', Pew Research Center. Available at <http://www.pewresearch.org/reports/?ReportID=38>.

Van Dijk, J. (2005), *The Deepening Divide: Inequality in the Information Society* (London: Sage).

Waldman, S. (2006), *Journalism Leaders' Forum on Leading Innovation*, University of Central Lancashire, Preston, 17 October.

Zelizer, B. (2004), *Taking Journalism Seriously* (London: Sage).

Appendix

Edited Interview with Helen Boaden, Head of BBC News and Current Affairs, 4 January 2006

John Drury

This interview with the BBC's Director of News and Current Affairs, Helen Boaden, focused on the future of radio journalism, but she also reflected on a number of important broader issues for the future of journalism in the UK (particularly the BBC) and democracy. This is an edited and abridged transcript of the interview.

JD: *Are there any issues specifically peculiar to radio?*

HB: If you think of television as essentially a narrative medium and you know the power of pictures can overtake content at times, the great thing with radio is it's essentially an analytical media. You need narrative, you need strong stories but you can dig into things and you have depth and analysis which is incredibly hard to deliver on television and to that extent it's more aligned to online ... because online gives you the chance to see just the headlines, or the first two parts of a story, or to actually go into fantastic depth. Now radio doesn't give you quite the depth of online, but actually always it gives you the chance to understand more. So all that thing that we talk about at the BBC, about specialism and the need to give people more depth if they want it, in many ways Radio 4 and Radio 5 Live offers that as an opportunity. The key thing I think, the real challenge, is ensuring that we deliver in-depth radio on technologies that people are increasingly using because the challenge is time, always, always time. It's a cliché, but it's true, people are time-starved, and I'll tell you a really interesting thing that has just happened. We've just done a trial where we've put 20 radio programmes available for download on the iPod. The very first download ... was ... the Reith Lectures, the High Commission. We did the Reith Lectures because we thought it's a wonderful amalgamation of modernity and tradition and it's got no commercial value and we had an amazing response. They were quite difficult, complex lectures, but people picked up on them from across the world. We had emails from them saying, 'What are these Reith Lectures, who is this guy Reith? Where can I contact him?' ... So that did well and then we made the whole 20 available, not all news and current affairs, and if you look at the top ten iPod downloads of the last few months (not our top ten, the overall), Chris Moyles is number one from Radio 1, without the music, ... they're downloading just what he says because it's so funny. The *Today* eight o'clock interview comes in the first five but, really interestingly, if you go further down within that top 20, *File on Four* and *In Business* are massively downloaded and that is because there is an audience out there for that in-depth, high-quality journalism. [People] can't always be at a radio, or even at their computer at the times that it's on, but want to listen and will download it and listen at their convenience, so for me the great saviour ... of long-form, in-depth radio is likely to be new technologies, digital technology, and I think the same is true of television ...

JD: *So what about television?*

HB: Well, in television if you look at audiences for ... current affairs in digital homes, they fall off a cliff. The audiences for current affairs, arts programmes and religious programmes just go down dramatically in digital homes. I suspect, although I can't prove this, that it's not that people are indifferent to the subject. It's just time-starved, tired people and they've got a lot of choice and would probably choose entertainment at the end of a busy day and not something gritty and difficult like *Panorama*. I suspect also, however, that if we are clever and we make available those full-length programmes, but also edited versions of them on broadband for you to either ... watch on your computer, or eventually to download on your Sony, I suspect that that will be a way of using that material and cultivating a new audience. So the BBC is highly unlikely to ever give up on those genres, but we are going to have to be clever and I think we're thinking ahead about how we use all that material. So I'll give you an example. We did a *Panorama* about bullying... that goes out once. If we could put that on broadband and also have an edited version – of say 20 minutes – of the top five important things you need to know about bullying, you may not have watched it the first time it went out on BBC 1, but when you need that information because suddenly you've discovered your child is being bullied, you can go onto the BBC website and there's the programme.

JD: *Do you agree that news' primary function is to integrate the democratic process and to facilitate it?*

HB: Yes, I do ... in terms of the BBC one of our commitments is to ... citizenship ... you know, 'inform, educate and entertain' remains our credo. It remains at the core of what we are about and that is about the facilitation of democracy and democracy isn't a simplistic thing. It's not just about people voting. Many people who are fully informed of what's going on in the world decide not to vote, but it's the information. It's the quality of that information and it's the range of voices that we give them ... there are not two views on this, there may be 15 views and it's our responsibility to make sure those views are all presented fairly without us taking sides.

JD: *In that sense, does it mean that if you start to widen the agenda of news to, for example, creature comforts, consumerism, celebrity news, this kind of* *thing, a lot more sport, that you are actually diluting that relationship with the democratic and the service that you are providing?*

HB: No, because I think essentially people are citizens, but they are also consumers and they have many modes [of expressing themselves]. I think the challenge will be – and I think it's a challenge for politicians as well as for us – ...that if you want a national debate about something overtly political at a time when people can ... through the new technology, through digital technology, select their own agenda, how do you engage everyone in a national debate? The technology will be such that if you want you could actually get ... your own news bulletin. You can ask to be either texted or you can download all the things that interest you. So you're interested in health, you're interested in sport, you're interested in celebrity and entertainment. Those might be the only stories you chose to connect to ... I think that is worrying, but I don't think there is anything you can do about it ... it's the way humans are; if you give people choice they will choose to select out as well as to select in.

JD: *You're not worried about the consumers taking over the asylum, as it were?*

HB: Well, I don't think you can stop them. I think that's the point. I always say to people who work for me, 'Whether you like this or not you can't sack the audience. They can sack you but you can't sack them.' And the skill is the extent to which you lead people to beyond their own choices, you excite their interest – and a kind of basic faith that often people are more curious than we sometimes assume. Actually if you only get what you already know it can get quite tedious and there'll always be a proportion of people who'll do that and there will always be a proportion of people who will want to know more.

JD: *Isn't it true then that what you could do as a strategy is write off 90 per cent of the population as not being interested in these core values of news – and democracy will still survive by just generating even more interest and more curiosity with the new technologies from that ten per cent?*

HB: From the BBC there is an absolute commitment to try and offer news and current affairs that appeals to all audiences, so that's why we have a news service on One Extra. That's why we have *Newsbeat*, which remains an incredibly powerful way of getting to a younger generation that really doesn't think it's interested in politics and current affairs and then interestingly enough actually is. We know that from our phone-ins and from when we text. The BBC, particularly in radio, actually has always been brilliant at understanding what will engage an audience and ... melding what you might call a serious agenda with the less serious agenda. ... that 'inform, educate and entertain' and the entertainment bit hasn't been forgotten along the way. But to some extent none of us quite know how this world is going to pan out. ... We've made all sorts of assumptions about what audiences will find interesting, which may or may not turn out to be true. I mean we know that audiences generally, apart from what you might call a Radio 4 audience, the *Newsnight* audience, [aren't] passionately interested in party politics. But ... in the next election, where it's likely to be a real, genuine fight, then it will be interesting to see if people suddenly do become interested in party politics … you can't necessarily predict what they're going to find interesting. Every morning at my editorial meeting I always ask the guy who runs our online site what have been the most used stories on our website and sometimes it's global warming and sometimes it's pictures of the weather … and … when they found that giant squid … that doesn't surprise me, but actually what does surprise me is some of the other choices that come along. And sometimes that's as simple as we had great pictures of it. To me … the most stimulating thing is that audiences constantly challenge our assumptions about them.

JD: *What about attracting a younger audience for the future for radio? I mean when you've got the competition … iPods, online, blogging, etc?*

HB: Well, I mean I think I'd be a fool to say it's not a huge challenge. The young audience isn't even that young … 35–54 is quite a challenge for all news outputs, radio and television, and what we're doing is we're using the new technologies to offer what we already do … we're cross-trailing. We're … assuming that they will continue to be an educated audience that wants things in depth and we haven't been disappointed in that so far.

JD: *This is because people get older?*

HB: People get older … there's a whole thing that when you're quite young, most of the time you don't watch or listen to much news at all. That's not new. Well, it may be that that's becoming more serious for us, but that's always been the case. Once you get your first mortgage and what happens in the real world counts you start to adjust.

JD: *It's more about capturing the young audience when it gets older?*

HB: To a large extent. But also reinforcing the BBC brand and our news values with those younger people who do connect through things like *Newsbeat* and One Extra and on the television. The Six O'Clock News is a reasonably young audience. Five Live is important for us. Oh, the other thing is online. Online is incredibly important to us. It's very striking to me when I go down to talk to a lot of colleges and Radio Academy events how many young people say, 'Oh I've got the BBC as my home page, BBC News is my home page.' So actually they don't listen and consume that much … it may not help radio or television, but they are getting their news in a very, very useable form and that's the point. I think that coming generations won't necessarily see it as tri-media in quite the way that you and I do – it's just what's handy from here, at this point.

JD: *Do you have any quality concerns about the coverage. I mean going back to the democratic question?*

HB: It's not so much about balance … it's about range of voice. I think, and I've said this publicly, … too often we think of politics with a capital P and we don't recognise … political movements, political issues, until they get that category, so I'll give you a good example – the fuel protests of several years ago, not the one that went with a damp squib. Both the media – and it wasn't just the BBC – and the political classes did not recognise that as an issue until the fuel protestors almost brought the country to a halt and that was interesting to me because it clearly *was* a political issue … but it was also the kinds of people who were protesting were not the kind of people who the BBC are very good at tapping into. You might call it a 'white van' issue. I mean I'll give you another example. Those who wanted to get out of Europe altogether for years did not get, I think, a fair shout on the BBC because they were seen as slightly beyond the pale in some way.

JD: *Isn't that a kind of polite way of saying the BBC is too left-wing?*

HB: Well, I don't think it's left-wing … I don't think it is liberal. I think it's this thing of a sort of magic circle, which I think a lot of London papers, London-based broadsheets have as well, as what is seen as the … consensus. So, for years if you were saying 'let's get out of Europe', it was seen as … so baffling, so extraordinary that you had … made a judgement that it wasn't a voice that should really get much of an airing. We then get UKIP and we discover that 20 per cent of the population feel this and as soon as you've got a party then everyone breathes a sigh of relief because you know what to do with it and one of the things that I've started as Director of News is much more feedback from our phone-ins, because we have them on Radio 2, Radio 5 Live and Radio 1 and very often you pick up on a completely different slant from … the orthodox view. Take recently, the 90-days detention. The MPs threw it out, most of the broadsheets supported it. I tell you, across all our phone-ins people were outraged at what the MPs had done. They were far more illiberal, if you want to coin it like that. On the drink deregulation, where again the broadsheets and the tabloids had been fiercely against it, our phone-ins came down in favour of it. 'Why can't we have a good time?' So, it's always this thing of … finding the voices that represent the broader spectrum.

JD: *I must admit when I listen to something like Victoria Derbyshire [phone-in on BBC Radio 5], that's like opening the door of democracy and letting everybody in.*

HB: [I] completely agree, and now you see we get the notes from that circulated [within News and Current Affairs] … it's part of the editor's task now at the end of that show to write up what was the balance of calls and anything surprising and then that gets distributed to the editors of other programmes, so they start thinking, 'Oh that's interesting, have we actually had that voice reflected in our programme?' If you listen to Jeremy Vine it'll be the same.

JD: *Going back to the technology though. In a way phone-ins were the first forms of blogging.*

HB: Yes, they were. If you talk about interactivity, people are a bit silly about this. They think it all happened with digital technology. The phone-in was the first interactive technology.

JD: *It's probably the purest form of interactivity.*

HB: Yes, absolutely, [I] completely agree. And actually, most people, in commercial and BBC terms … are pretty skilled at the phone-in these days … I mean, really interesting about it. But it's a great barometer. It's not definitive, but it's just another way of looking at issues.

JD: *But just linking it to the Internet and so on ... the democratisation of information ..., does that ... tell you something, that if phone-ins provide that vehicle [interactivity], then the Internet as it develops, or is developing, will increasingly do so [instead] and you're happy with that?*

HB: Well, let's go to the ugly phrase 'user-generated material' ... that's emails, it's texts, it's photos, it's videos that people send to us, mostly before we start soliciting them. I mean it was fascinating on 7 July that we got so many before we asked for them and you did get this sense of people going back to their offices and telling the BBC first about what they had seen ... it was extraordinary and it was very touching ... people who were saying, 'I'm sending you this. I don't want it to appear in a tabloid newspaper' ... we had a few of those. Now user-generated material will continue to grow. A year ago I had a meeting with my team where someone said we needed to set up a sort of authentication and verification system for all this material coming in and luckily we did set it up. It's just actually a table full of journalists who know how to ring people back or check things out. There's nothing special about it. There's proper journalism. But some people, some of my colleagues at that time, thought this was a waste of time and money because this was going to take years to take off. You know within seven months it had taken off. That's going to continue to happen. The key thing for us is where we're using it as fact we've done the checking and where we're using it as user-generated material we flag it so people don't confuse fact with non-fact, verified information with non-verified information.

JD: *So in a way you become a kind of accreditor?*

HB: You become the accreditors and the ringmasters and people will want different things, so I don't think we are going to lose a great chunk of the ... 'you, the BBC, tell me what's the most important things that's happened today and I know I can believe it'. Equally I think there'll be other audiences, depending on mood and age and inclination, who will actually want to go online and go to one of our sites and see what's on there. You know the interesting thing is that we've moved beyond the 'either or' culture, video did not kill the radio star actually... look at Terry Wogan, and it's not that one will replace, but it's actually 'let it all happen', which of course, in terms of resource, is a massive challenge.

JD: *Can the BBC sustain that? Can they actually authentically gather news across such a broad spectrum?*

HB: Well, I think that is a challenge for us and initially we'll just actually make more available, more of what we are already collecting. Because don't forget, there's a lot of stuff ... if you produce a *Newsnight* film you've probably spent thousands of pounds on really good journalism – it goes out once. We're currently just now, at last, getting it also on News 24, but that should be on the Web. Now ... if you just take that idea, what also should be on the Web, on broadband, would probably be the unedited interviews ... The real trick is going to be how we authenticate all the user-generated material, because sometimes we get thousands and thousands of people sending stuff in.

JD: *But that for you could be a great resource, if you can monitor it and if you can filter it?*

HB: Yes, it will, but what you'll probably get to is a situation – and again this is all, as it were, work in progress – … where what you use that you've authenticated *you say* is authenticated and then you make no such claims for anything else you make available to the public. [In other words] you're just really clear with people. So you know, 'this thing is on here, we're not claiming it's true. We're saying this is what someone has sent us. This we have checked out and it's copper-bottomed.' And that would be true of audio material as well.

JD: *And you couldn't see that kind of information gathering swamping authentic news?*

HB: Well, … it has that [potential] but you see there's still so much news gathering that you do that probably only professionals, at least at the beginning, will be able to do. I mean … stuff from abroad, very often you need a cameraman and a reporter where situations are dangerous … what was interesting in the Bunsfield fire was that we had people who were going into quite dangerous situations – amateurs – to get us video footage for the BBC to go on our website. Well, in the end we had to say, 'do not put yourself in danger'. I don't think it will ever come to a point where it is swamping, but clearly it's going to throw up new challenges as we go into it.

JD: *Moving on, would you worry if the BBC was the only bastion of serious news and current affairs coverage?*

HB: The only survivor? … Yes, I'd really worry.

JD: *You're not just saying that because you work at the BBC?*

HB: No, no, I'm really not. I just think if you're talking about democracy it's incredibly … without sounding pretentious about it … it's incredibly important that you have a multiplicity of outlets. It's like newspapers, you need many voices, you need many stances, you need the public to have a lot of choice … the collapse of the ITN news channel – it wasn't hugely viewed, although I think it was a good channel …, I don't mean this [to be] patronising, for the resource they had, but … it's just another player not there. That's not a good situation in a democracy.

JD: *What about your rivals – Sky, for example?*

HB: Well, I admire Sky and they do a very good service and they do stick to … rock-solid core journalistic values and a lot of people who have worked at the BBC have worked at Sky and vice versa. I don't think Mr Murdoch is necessarily growing his media empire for democracy … it just happens to be a useful business.

JD: *I just wanted to ask you a little bit more about this question of intentional and unintentional bias.*

HB: I think in the end, where there is unintentional bias, that's the hardest nut to crack because, by definition, if it's unintentional people don't know they're guilty of it. So, the key thing now is you've got to have editors who are incredibly aware and very challenging of their own approach to a story as well as the approach of their journalists … I learnt a lot of it from working on *File on 4*, because the ethos there was as the story became more muddled it generally became more accurate and you got through the muddle to something clearer at the other end, but the muddle was part of you suddenly having to examine your own prejudices and I can tell you, all the good stories we did … went through that process. Now, obviously that's long-form journalism of a high quality and a great depth and not every news story has that. But it is always about having someone in charge who challenges the orthodoxy in the room and that's why, as Director of News, I put a huge emphasis on getting my editors to … think about what they are doing and in my departmental heads I've got good people … I genuinely don't know what their personal politics are, but they are very good at our daily editorial meetings at saying, 'I don't think we are representing this view' or 'have you actually asked that hard question?'

JD: *Is there an alarm that goes off in your head whenever the news becomes what you would regard as too soft, that the agenda becomes a bit woolly?*

HB: Yes, there is. There is an alarm that goes off in my head, but often it's less about the content of the story, because I think you can do an incredibly broad range of stories, it's about the way that you do them.

JD: *What about the future of television current affairs?*

HB: Television will remain incredibly important and it still gets huge audiences. The BBC won't give up on television, serious television that's aimed at giving the citizen the knowledge that they want, but you can certainly see a time when there's less and less of that material on commercial competitors, but … just because of the way they're funded and our charter obligations, apart from … a genuine commitment to it. But if you look across the piece, radio and online could well be the two sources of the most information and the most in-depth information. I think it would be foolish to write off television, but in terms of offering range and depth radio and online are very hard to beat.

JD: *Are you happy that the electorate is getting everything it needs from a service like the BBC?*

HB: Well, I don't think you can ever feel that the electorate is getting everything it needs and often it's a process of you and the electorate together discovering what they want to know. It was interesting in the last election that we did some fantastic stuff online, we did some fantastic stuff on radio and television, but we did some especially inventive stuff online which the audience loved in modest numbers until the election was over and then they came to it to find out what had happened in their constituency. We got amazing numbers coming in.

JD: *But voting figures are down. You think it's about the politics?*

HB: I don't know that it's about the politics, but what I do know is you can be a fully informed citizen and choose not to vote. Voting is only one way of judging citizenship. You might be a fully informed citizen, decide not to vote, but spend a great deal of time working for a charity, or working on a single-issue campaign. There are many ways of being a citizen and I think that's one of the challenges to all of us ..., including the political class, because party politics has determined the way we've seen citizenship for a very long time and actually I suspect citizens and consumers ... blend slightly. People are expressing their citizenship in many different ways.

JD   *And in a way you could say there's no excuse for the electorate to say it's not [informed about what's going on politically] because it's accessible, it's there?*

HB: I would never be complacent. I would never say we've got it right, we've given them everything they need. We're learning all the time. But if you want to find out about most things in this country the BBC at least would give you a fighting chance of finding out. And how you use that ... the extent to which you engage with it is down to the individual and that's the great thing about democracy – you're not forced to do it.

Index

Note: Numbers in brackets preceded by *n* refer to footnotes.